Stefan Lorenzmeier/Dorota Miler (eds.)

The New Law

Suggestions for Reforms and Improvements of Existing Legal Norms and Principles

Nomos

The Deutsche Nationalbibliothek lists this publication in the Deutsche Nationalbibliografie; detailed bibliographic data are available on the Internet at http://dnb.d-nb.de

ISBN 978-3-8487-4088-8 (Print)
978-3-8452-8397-5 (ePDF)

British Library Cataloguing-in-Publication Data
A catalogue record for this book is available from the British Library.

ISBN 978-3-8487-4088-8 (Print)
978-3-8452-8397-5 (ePDF)

Library of Congress Cataloging-in-Publication Data
Dr. Lorenzmeier, Stefan / Dr. Miler, Dorota
The New Law
Suggestions for Reforms and Improvements of Existing Legal Norms and Principles
Dr. Stefan Lorenzmeier / Dr. Dorota Miler (eds.)
408 p.

ISBN 978-3-8487-4088-8 (Print)
978-3-8452-8397-5 (ePDF)

1st Edition 2018

Foreword

The Augsburg Graduate Conference in Law took place at the Law Faculty of the University of Augsburg on June 3 and 4, 2016. The theme of the Conference was "The New Law – Suggestions for Reforms and Improvements of Existing Legal Norms and Principles." The Conference was addressed to young academics and researchers wishing to pursue an academic career.

The editors express sincere gratitude to everyone who made this conference and the publication possible. We are very grateful to the participants of the conference for their contributions published in this volume. We would like to express our sincere gratitude to professors from the Law Faculty of the University of Augsburg, specifically: Prof. Dr. Thomas M.J. Möllers, Prof. Dr. Matthias Rossi, Prof. Dr. Christian Gomille and Prof. Dr. Luís Greco (now Humboldt University of Berlin), and Prof. Dr. Roman Petrov (National University of Kyiv-Mohyla Academy), who held chairs during the Conference and whose remarks stimulated participants to consider their theses in a broader perspective. We would also like to thank Michael Friedman for his language assistance with some of the contributions and the Augsburg Center for Global Economic Law and Regulation (ACELR) as well as the Gesellschaft der Freunde der Universität Augsburg e. V. (GdF) for the financial support that allowed publication of this book.

Augsburg, October 2018 Stefan Lorenzmeier & Dorota Miler

Contents

Abbreviations

Art. / Arts.	Article / Articles
e.g.	exempli gratia (for example)
EC	European Community
ed, eds	editor, editors
EU	European Union
ff.	and the following pages
i.e.	id est (that is)
ibid.	ibidem (in the same place)
No / no	number
p.	page
para. / paras.	paragraph / paragraphs
sec.	Section
UK	United Kingdom
UN	United Nations
v.	versus
Vol.	Volume

Introduction to The New Law – Suggestions for Reforms and Improvements of Existing Legal Norms and Principles

Stefan Lorenzmeier, Dorota Miler

A. *Augsburg Graduate Conference in Law*

The Augsburg Graduate Conference in Law provided young scholars wishing to pursue an academic career with a forum in which they could present their academic work, exchange innovative ideas and engage in a scholarly discussion. It encouraged the participants (doctoral and post-doctoral candidates) to develop an international academic network that would serve to advance their careers. It also provided a venue for taking first steps in the academic world, including a chance for a publication with a respected publisher.

As the organizers, we recognized that many young scholars and researchers are intimidated by their experienced colleges and role-models and that they are, consequently, reluctant to present new ideas that may diverge from the accepted state of affairs. Our goal was to encourage them to share these new concepts. The conference aimed at enhancing the self-confidence of ambitious young scholars by showing them: (1) that their innovative ideas can gain recognition; (2) that they can present and publish like experienced scholars and (3) that their comments and observations may advance the work of others or become a source of inspiration.

The reaction following the call for papers for the Augsburg Graduate Conference in Law exceeded our expectations. We received over 100 abstracts from scholars from Europe, Asia, North America and Australia. The chosen participants come from fourteen countries (Czech Republic, Finland, Germany, Greece, Hungary, India, Iran, Norway, Poland, Scotland, Slovenia, Thailand, Ukraine and Vietnam) from top academic institutions such as the Max Planck Institute for Comparative Public Law and International Law, Free University of Berlin and the Universities of Budapest, Edinburgh, Kiew, Krakau, Ljubljana, Oslo and Thessaloniki. The presenters and contributors are a blend of experienced and early-stage researchers with diverse legal and cultural backgrounds and with different interests and ideas about and for law. Their commonality was having forceful and original proposals for a new law.

The theme of the Augsburg Graduate Conference in Law was "The New Law – Suggestions for Reforms and Improvements of Existing Legal Norms and Principles." All laws are, by definition, imperfect, thus needing further interpretation and contextual understanding. Throughout the evolutionary development of law, many have struggled with unjust, impractical and obsolete laws, requiring practitioners and academics to seek alternative solutions when the legal rules did not keep pace with societal or technical developments, and to look for equitable principles or the spirit of the law when the letter of the law was unclear or unfair. These are only a few of the many problems legal scholars have faced and have overcome while influencing the process of reforming and improving the law. Adopting this theme aimed at stimulating a deep exploration of the mentioned issues and finding common patterns for their resolution which could be applied in different legal contexts.

A broad wording opened the Conference to all young, talented legal scholars regardless of their particular legal field. The scholars were provided with an opportunity to combine the knowledge and experience of legal academics and practitioners with their legal know-how and creativity so as to think beyond the traditional legal models and to introduce significant innovations advancing the existing body of law. Especially welcome were original approaches situated 'outside the box' of traditional legal thinking.

The young scholars participating in the Augsburg Graduate Conference were not limited to a particular question or area of law or to a specific research approach. Solutions to legal problems can be found by applying different approaches, reasoning or methodologies. However, and not surprisingly, most of the questions discussed during the conference and in the contributions have an international character extending beyond countries to regions and continents.

As innovation also entails failure, it is not necessary that the reader is always convinced by the proposed solutions. Nevertheless, we do hope that they will be helpful in advancing the legal discussion and the law.

B. *'The New Law' as Innovative and Constructive Proposals, Predictions, Evaluations and Theoretical Conceptions*

In this publication the contributions are organized according to the geographic scope of applicability of the discussed issues. There are therefore three parts in which new ideas focus on national (Part A), European (Part B) and international (Part C) laws. An additional part is dedicated to solutions influencing our understanding of general legal concepts.

The common feature shared by all the contributions is a discussion of a new law. What is 'new law'? This simple question requires a complex answer. There are four ways in which this term was understood by the contributors.

I. 'The New Law' as an original proposal for a solution to an existing legal problem

There are many recognized problems that remain unsolved in legal literature. The hitherto presented recommendations have proven unfit for a successful and definitive clarification of these matters. A new hope for solving such well-known issues looks to turn the existing discussion in a different direction by considering brand new ideas that, although building on already examined suggestions, are primarily based on an application of alternative approaches and fresh sources of inspiration.

The known controversy regarding the appropriate starting point for the period of prescription in relation to delictual claims is addressed in a revolutionary way by *Kruszyńska-Kola*. She examines the question of period of time that needs to expire before a debtor should be entitled to refuse performance in situations where Polish private law might classify rising the defence of prescription as an abuse of rights. To solve this significant problem, she proposes a novel and flexible regulation for determining the period of prescription, one that provides maximum transparency and predictability. Her recommendations are inspired by French law.[1]

The innovation that *Prostybozhenko* puts forward is to include goodwill (understood as "a favour or advantage that a person or a business controlled

---

1 In detail see *Kruszyńska-Kola*, Time, Emotions, Legal Certainty and Justice. New Period of Prescription of Delictual Claims for Damages in the Polish Civil Code, p. 47.

by a person has acquired especially owing to a number of factors, including education, knowledge, skills, contact network, intellectual property, branding, and good reputation") as a component in the process of dividing matrimonial assets acquired over the duration of validity of the matrimonial property regime. He suggests a method of determining goodwill and, depending on the type of a matrimonial regime applicable in a given country, different ways of incorporating it in a legal system. [2]

Fenkner introduces an original and radical proposal to optimize the interpretation and application of EU law. The mandatory requirement that has been imposed by the Court of Justice of the European Union to compare all twenty-four official language versions of a provision of European law to ensure uniform interpretation and application is, according to her, impractical, time-consuming, something demanding advanced language knowledge and, for most practitioners and individuals, simply, impossible to comply with. She presents an original alternative solution and analyses it.[3]

An improvement to EU law is proposed also by *Urban-Kozłowska.* She critically examines the new guidelines issued by the European Commission in 2014 on State aid to airports and airlines,[4] which provides a framework for determining whether State aid in the form of public funds granted to airports and/or airlines is compatible with the internal market. Her novel proposal significantly optimizes the Commission's decision-making process.[5]

As pointed out by *Nguyen*, the problem of jurisdictional conflicts occurring when a single dispute is submitted in parallel or consecutively to a number of fora has been studied before. However, he is the first to propose and comprehensively analyse a new approach: application of the principles

---

2 In detail see *Prostybozhenko*, Equal v. Fair: Considering Goodwill in the Division of Matrimonial Property, p. 115.

3 In detail see *Fenkner*, Multilingualism and the Uniform Interpretation of European Union Law, p. 143.

4 See: Communication from the Commission – Guidelines on State aid to airports and airlines, OJ C 99, 4.04.2014, p. 3–34.

5 In detail see *Urban-Kozłowska*, In Search of a More Effective Assessment of State Aid Measures in the Aviation Sector, p. 179.

of treaty interpretation, particularly Article 31 (3) (c) of the Vienna Convention on the Law of Treaties, as a practical and useful alternative serving to minimize the negative consequences of multiple proceedings.[6]

An original idea advocating the adoption of a multi-faceted approach to climate change refugees – defined as "refugees who are forced to leave their normal places of residence because of environmental changes adversely affecting their lives and livelihood" – by using various international instruments is proposed by *Sanyal*. As he describes, this issue is potentially of enormous concern since by 2050 as many as 200 million people could be displaced by the consequences of climate change. His proposal aims at solving the problem of there not being any effective and uniform protection of the basic human rights of these refugees.[7]

Mendelsohn has an innovative idea for how to determine whether adopted legislative and policing measures minimize systemic risks. In her contribution, she inquires whether the actions undertaken by legislators and policy makers are sufficient to prevent the next systemic crisis. In so doing, she looks at the reasons behind systemic risk – understood as "the risk that the failure of one or more financial institutions or a shock in the financial system can lead to widespread losses and consecutive failures that threaten the stability of the entire financial system and the real economy at large" – considering both the economic description and legal definition of systemic risk and also analysing the consequences of bailouts associated with such risks.[8]

II. 'The New Law' as a prediction of future developments in law

The term 'new law' can also be understood as a prediction of advancements in legal regulations, customary law or legal doctrines. These tendencies can be identified, for instance, on the basis of the evolution of the relevant area of law and the opinions on its future prospects as represented in legal liter-

6 In detail see *Nguyen*, Resolving Jurisdictional Conflicts Between WTO and RTA Dispute Settlement – Possible Roles for Article 31(3)(c) of the VCLT, p. 211.

7 In detail see *Sanyal*, Solutions to the Problem of Climate Change Refugees, p. 289.

8 In detail see *Mendelsohn*, The Theory and Principles of Banking Regulation after the Financial Crisis: No (Systemic) Risk, No Fun, p. 307.

ature. Given that the harmonization of different laws happens also in a bottom-up process, the uncertainty of the future – along with the uncertainty of what it may bring – can be further minimized by considering progressive laws that have already been adopted in other countries and by determining, where possible, how those laws came to evolve.

The direction of the development of liability principles in Polish and German tort law (in particular, the principles of fault, risk and community life) and the assessment of their potential evolution is what *Krygier* sheds light on. After comparing and analysing relevant regulations and legal literature from these two jurisdictions, she presents original suggestions for improving effectiveness in applying the principles of liability in Polish and German tort law.[9]

The task of identifying current and foreseeable trends in the reform of rules on forced succession and of estimating their future shape was undertaken by *Miler*. In her study, she poses a question: How is the freedom of testation likely to be balanced in the future in respect of a close family member's interest in receiving a portion of the testator's estate (rules of forced succession)? To answer this question, she analyses rules on forced succession in chosen civil law jurisdictions, examining both their character as well as recent reforms.[10]

III. 'The New Law' as a critical evaluation of new laws, practices, theories and proposals

In many cases, the efficiency of new legislation can be assessed only after the law is adopted, enforced and complied with. At that point, the controlling law can be scrutinized not only theoretically but also from a practical perspective. Suggestions for the improvement of such law can then be based on known outcomes that could not always be predicted in advance. Additionally, new legal practices, theories and proposals can be examined regarding their correctness, applicability or usefulness. Thanks to constructive critique, they can gain recognition, acceptance and further evolve.

---

9 In detail see *Krygier*, Principles of Liability in Tort and Their Future in the German and Polish Legal Systems – *De Lege Lata* and *De Lege Ferenda* Remarks, p. 61.

10 In detail see *Miler*, The Present and Future of Forced Succession in Chosen Civil Law Jurisdictions, p. 89.

Kotowski critically evaluates the new law regulating supplementary performance – the law includes both a right of repair as well as the right to have a defective product replaced – and identifies a number of problems in this law. For instance, there are no detailed rules explaining the enforcement of supplementary performance, there is no statutory period system for its accomplishment and customers are persistently misinformed about their rights. However, based on his analysis, commercial guarantees do not provide a sound alternative to supplementary performance. Thus, the author looks for alternate new solutions.[11]

The newest Iranian Act on debt convictions from 2015 is constructively critiqued by *Barzegar*. The Act regulates the problem of imprisoning convicted debtors. This problem, rather unknown to European scholars, has not only been considered in Iran for decades but also has significant practical importance: "78 per cent of the inmates in Iran prisons are imprisoned because of financial matters." *Barzegar* explains the legal and social-historical background of this issue, critically assesses the newest Act and recommends a number of progressive changes.[12]

An improvement of the unwritten principle prohibiting an abusive use of rights – thereby constituting a limitation on the exercise of the fundamental freedoms ensured by the European Treaties – is the goal of *Beck*. Such abuse takes place when "a factual circumstance is created that allows rights to be exercised contrary to the purposes the fundamental freedoms intend to protect." After an analysis of the principle's legal foundations and the relevant case law, he discusses the most recent developments regarding the abuse of rights doctrine.[13]

Pouikli scrutinizes the transposition, application and enforcement of Directive 2004/35/EC on Environmental Liability with Regard to the Prevention and Remedying of Environmental Damage and identifies a number of issues. She finds that the Directive is ineffective as it is difficult to reach the threshold set in it and that it is not uniformly and efficiently implemented due to its inherent ambiguity. In particular, the Member States can each de-

---

11 In detail see *Kotowski*, Effective Supplementary Performance?, p. 77.

12 In detail see *Barzegar*, A Critical Review of Iranian's New Imprisonment Policy Regarding Convicted Debtors, p. 131.

13 In detail see *Beck*, Abuse of Rights in EU Law: A General Law Principle Limiting the Exercise of Rights at the EU Level?, p. 157.

cide for themselves on the strength of the implemented measures. She considers a number of significant revisions that would allow for the creation of a powerful liability system.[14]

Puškár, on the other hand, is concerned with the almost unlimited immunity enjoyed by international organizations in a host state that allows these organizations to be excluded from the jurisdiction of the host state's courts as well as other state organs. He questions whether this immunity should not be restricted, especially in context of an individual's right of access to a court. After considering the reasons for the immunity and the current prevailing practice, he makes a strong recommendation on how jurisdictional immunity could be restricted.[15]

Current practice is also challenged by *Korošec* and *Veber*. They examine whether and under what conditions the use of force against non-state actors could be classified as an exercise of the right of self-defence under Article 51 of the United Nations Charter. Particular attention is given to the interpretation of the term 'armed attack' as used in the article as well as the role of the 'unwilling or unable doctrine', providing that the unwillingness or inability of a state to prevent the use of its territory as a shelter for terrorist activities may justify use of force against this state. The theoretical discussion is set in context of the most recent international developments, starting from the 9/11 attacks and the reaction of states and international bodies thereto, and continuing on to the US-led coalition's military intervention against ISIL (Islamic State of Iraq and the Levant) in Iraq and Syria.[16]

The ineffectiveness of international law in preventing mass atrocity crimes is criticized by *Žagar*. She argues that the primary responsibility for the maintenance and restoration of international peace and security is borne by the United Nation's Security Council. She critically examines the latest international developments and the initiatives to change 'veto as a right' to 'veto as a responsibility'.[17]

---

14 In detail see *Pouikli*, Propositions towards a Potential Revision of Directive 2004/35/EC on Environmental Liability with Regard to the Prevention and Remedying of Environmental Damage (ELD), p. 199.

15 In detail see *Puškár*, Jurisdictional Immunity of International Organizations – Should It Be Restricted?, p. 233.

16 In detail see *Korošec* and *Veber*, The Right of Self-Defence in International Law: Contemporary Developments in the Context of the Fight against Terrorism, p. 243.

17 In detail see *Žagar*, Responsibility Not to Veto, p. 275.

Kompatsiari explores a legal gap falling between the rejection of a legal obligation of people to live and the rejection of a positive right to die, a gap that forces people incapable of committing suicide to remain alive. In her contribution, she discusses the social legitimation of law and the element of 'fellowship' among members of a society. She disapproves of the current state of affairs and looks to stimulate a legal debate on the existence of and preconditions for a right to die as held by people incapable of committing suicide.[18]

IV. 'The New Law' as innovative theoretical conceptions of legal issues

The theoretical understanding of a concept leads to its better enforcement and application. To influence the entire legal system, a concept's nature, characteristics and manner of function must be explored. Only a clear understanding of the world of legal norms and rules allows improvements of a general nature and the creation of laws that not only perfectly fulfil their purpose but also are easy to enforce and comply with.

MacFarlane investigates the unique nature of the right to enforce a benefit provided by contracting parties to a party that is external to the contract (a third party right) in Scots and German law. The theoretical classification of the legally unsystematized right has practical consequences. What laws are to be complied with? What terminology is to be used? How do we make third party rights doctrinally and theoretically sound? How are they classified in German law and could this support their classification in Scots law? How do we make them theoretically apt for any future harmonization measures? To answer these questions *MacFarlane* briefly considers eight potential approaches to the nature of third party rights and discusses in detail the advantages and disadvantages of two of them (the promissory and *sui generis* analyses) in Scots and German law.[19]

18 In detail see *Kompatsiari*, Contribution of the Element of 'Fellowship' to the Recognition of a Positive Right to Die for People Incapable of Committing Suicide, p. 327.

19 In detail see *MacFarlane*, The Nature of Third Party Rights: Lessons from German Law, p. 27.

The contribution of *Salmi* disapproves of legal rules that have forms against which real life activities cannot be measured. In his opinion, it is particularly problematic when public authorities supervise and enforce rules requiring continuous compliance of the relevant activities. He correlates the difficulty of complying with norms to such norms' vagueness and indeterminacy and urges the introduction of specific, precise norms in dynamic compliance situations, especially when they are enforced by a public body.[20]

The phenomenon of 'retroactivity' in law is studied by *Tøssebro,* who discusses the principle of retroactivity specifically in context of Norwegian constitutional law. She formulates a ground-breaking hypothesis arguing that the content of the principle and the scope of its application are different than commonly accepted. Particularly, she distinguishes two different rules under the principle: The prohibition to make 'true' retroactive laws and the permission to make 'false' retroactive laws. She examines these rules' characteristics and justifications, their possible links with each other and with other relevant legal principles. Finally, she discusses the applicability of these rules to individually drafted administrative decisions.[21]

A novel approach to explaining the relationship between the world of legal norms and systems and the natural world is proposed by *Saensawatt*, who attempts to prove that legal systems, as with all the other systems existing in the nature world, have the nature and characteristics of complex adaptive systems. In his contribution, *Saensawatt* focuses on explaining the first feature, namely the complexity of a system, by discussing hierarchical organization, the concept of nonlinearity, initial conditions and their relation to the chaotic behavior of dynamical legal systems, and the emergent behaviour of dynamical legal systems. The author lists potential benefits that can be gained through the recognition of legal systems as complex adaptive systems.[22]

---

20 In detail see *Salmi*, Principles Based Regulation and Compliance with Financial Legislation, p. 343.

21 In detail see *Tøssebro*, The Principle of Non-Retroactivity and Its Application to Administrative Decisions, p. 361.

22 In detail see *Saensawatt*, On the Nature and Characteristic of Legal Systems as Complex Adaptive Systems, p. 379.

C. Concluding Remarks

Each of the contributions included in this volume embodies the idea that moved us to organize the Augsburg Graduate Conference in Law, namely that young scholars and researchers should receive a chance to present their work; propose solutions attempting to solve legal problems; critically analyse governing laws, current legal practices or academic policies and their newest developments; formulate bold theories; and, most importantly, with their novel ideas contribute to legal progress and an enhancement of the quality of law.

We hope that the new ideas envisioned and examined by the young scholars during the Augsburg Graduate Conference in Law and presented here will help solve problems that international organizations, states, populations and common people struggle with every day. The proposals for new laws that the young scholars have shared with us inspire belief in a bright future for the law. We are delighted to have contributed to advancing law by disseminating their ideas for potential reforms and for the improvement of existing legal norms and principles.

A. Lessons from National Legal Systems

The Nature of Third Party Rights: Lessons from German Law

Lorna MacFarlane

A. *Introduction*

Generally, only the parties to a contract will derive rights under that contract, due to the privity doctrine.[1] However, the contracting parties may wish to confer a benefit upon another party who is external to the contract. When the parties provide that person with a right to enforce the benefit, that person is the recipient of a third party right. This basic definition applies in both Scots[2] and German[3] law.

This article discusses the theoretical nature of third party rights in Scots and German law, and assesses whether these positions are desirable. The nature of the third party right is important in practical terms, as this determines (at least in part) various aspects of the right. For example, if third party rights are promissory in nature, the formation of the rights must comply with the laws governing the formation of promises. The terminology used to refer to the contracting parties and third party may be impacted by the right's theoretical classification.[4] Clarity on the issue is also essential in ensuring that third party rights are doctrinally and theoretically sound.

1 In Germany, this is enshrined in § 311 I BGB. See *Medicus*, Allgemeiner Teil des BGB, 2010, p. 14; *Flume*, Allgemeiner Teil des Bürgerlichen Rechts, 1992, p. 42. For discussion on the doctrine in Scotland, see *Sutherland/Johnston*, Contracts for the Benefit of Third Parties, in: Zimmermann/Visser/Reid (eds), Mixed Legal Systems in Comparative Perspectives: Property and Obligations in Scotland and South Africa, 2004, p. 208 (209); *D&J Nicol v. Dundee Harbour Trustees* 1915 SC (HL) 7 at 13 per Lord Dunedin.

2 Contract (Third Party Rights) (Scotland) Act 2017, s 1 (1). See also *Gloag*, The Law of Contract: A Treatise on the Principles of Contract in the Law of Scotland, 1929, p. 68; *McBryde*, The Law of Contract in Scotland, 2007, § 10-01.

3 The German contractual third party right is provided for in §§ 328–335 BGB.

4 The English Contracts (Rights of Third Parties) Act 1999 refers to the contracting parties as the promisor and promisee, for example. See also *Scottish Law Commission*, Discussion Paper on Third Party Rights, Scot Law Com No 157, March 2014, § 4.1.

B. An Overview of the Potential Theoretical Analyses

This section outlines the potential analyses of third party rights and identifies which of these may provide an accurate description of the theoretical nature of third party rights.

Reference is made primarily to third party rights generally, rather than providing an in-depth assessment of the suitability of the classifications to the particular characteristics of Scots and German third party rights. Commentary from both jurisdictions is however cited as necessary to illustrate the unsuitability of certain analyses. This section serves to eliminate the majority of the potential 'natures'.

I. The Promissory Analysis

According to this analysis, the third party is the recipient of a unilateral promise from the debtor.[5] Hogg defines a promise as a "statement by which one person commits to some future beneficial performance, or the beneficial withholding of a performance, in favour of another person."[6]

This seems an apt description for third party rights, save for the fact that the definition appears to apply to only bilateral relationships, whereas third party rights deal, of course, with tripartite relationships. One can however easily see that Hogg's definition could be expanded to cover cases in which two parties wish to confer a benefit on another. Further, Fried asserts than two parties may in numerous situations wish to confer a promise on a third party.[7] Third party rights need not be construed in promissory terms in order to be viewed as promises, as promises can be both verbalized and written in various ways.[8]

If promises are enforceable in some circumstances in a particular jurisdiction, it appears logical that promises should also be valid in the context of third party rights – there is no compelling reason not to enforce such

5 *Hogg*, Promises and contract law: comparative perspectives, 2011, chapter 5.
6 Ibid., p. 288.
7 *Fried*, Contract as Promise, 1982, p. 45.
8 *Hogg*, 2011, p. 287–288.

promises. Unilateral promises are enforceable in Scots law,[9] however, German law recognises such obligations only in particular circumstances, such as the promise of reward in accordance with § 657 *Bürgerliches Gesetzbuch* (German Civil Code, hereinafter BGB).[10] This obviously impedes recognition of third party rights as promissory under German law. Nonetheless, the failure of German law to recognise promises generally has been criticised,[11] and so the possibility of viewing the German third party right as promissory should not be dismissed, as the possibility of reform is always present, if remote, and German law recognises promises in some circumstances.

One potential obstacle to the promissory analysis is that promises in both Scotland[12] and Germany[13] are binding upon formation, whereas the contracting parties are permitted (or ought to be permitted) in both jurisdictions to create a revocable third party right under certain circumstances.[14] Hogg does not view this as an impediment to a promissory analysis in either jurisdiction.[15] The possibility of viewing each jurisdiction's third party right as promissory in spite of the fact that promises are generally irrevocable is assessed with reference to the particularities of Scots and German law in the following sections.

A final point is that the promissory analysis:

> "makes the doctrine of third party rights redundant: since Scots law recognises the enforceability of unilateral promises, the mere fact that such a promise occurs within a contract to which the promisee is not a party is of no particular significance in itself."[16]

Essentially, the consequence of accepting the promissory analysis is that it is not necessary to have any specific laws governing the third party right.

---

9 *McBryde*, 2007, § 2-02; *Stair*, The institutions of the law of Scotland, 1681, § 1.10.4.

10 *Hogg*, 2011, p. 152 and 159.

11 Ibid., p. 463–464.

12 *Stair*, 1681, § 1.10.4.

13 *Schuster*, The principles of German civil law, 1907, § 283.

14 The relevant German law is § 328 II BGB. In Scotland the matter of whether third party rights must be irrevocable has been subject to rigorous academic and judicial debate. An overview of the issues can be found in *Hogg*, 2011, p. 205. The Contract (Third Party Rights) (Scotland) Act 2017 clarifies that it is possible to confer a revocable third party right (s 2 (4) (a)).

15 *Hogg*, 2011, p. 308.

16 *MacQueen*, The laws of Scotland: Stair Memorial Encyclopaedia, 1995, § 827.

The same reasoning applies if the third party right fits any of the other possible natures below, with the exception of the *sui generis* analysis. It can consequently be said that the promissory approach and all of the other analyses which treat the third party right as falling within an existing doctrine are an efficient approach to categorising the right, as the consequences of such approaches is that separate laws are not needed to govern third parties.

II. The 'Full Contracting Party' Analysis

According to this view, the third party is treated as a party to the contract in the same terms as the contracting parties, and as such has the status of a full contracting party.[17] The approach is unusual, although it has been adopted in Dutch law.[18]

The analysis is perhaps suitable in jurisdictions such as the Netherlands, in which acceptance on the part of the third party is required for formation of their right. However, neither Scots nor German law contains such a requirement. Von Kübel, the editor of the BGB responsible for the law of obligations, rejected a contractual view on the grounds that the third party cannot realistically be viewed as the recipient of an offer, as acceptance on the part of the third party is not required for the constitution of the right.[19] It is clear from both case law[20] and academic commentary[21] that a contractual analysis is not accepted in German law. In Scots law, a third party right

17 *Hogg*, 2011, p. 290.
18 Dutch Civil Code, § 6:254 (1).
19 *Hogg*, 2011, p. 309.
20 See, for example, BGH 08.02.2006 – IV ZR 205/04, RGZ 71, 324 (§ 8).
21 *Gernhuber*, Das Schuldverhältnis, 1989, p. 469, 480.

is conferred on a "person who is not a party to the contract".[22] Scots academic commentary likewise disapproves of a contractual analysis,[23] and von Kübel's views apply equally in Scots law. It is simply impossible to pursue a contractual analysis in jurisdictions which do not require acceptance on the part of the third party before the right is enforceable.

Further, one cannot view the third party as a party to the contract without treating the tripartite relationship as a multi-partite contract,[24] and this is not an accurate assessment of the factual situation. Such an analysis may be unappealing in legal practice, as categorising the third party right as contractual would indicate that the third party enjoys the same weight in contractual negotiations as the contracting parties. The analysis is thus contrary to the aim of ensuring that the third party right is practically usable. Further, as third parties have no means by which to vary or rescind the entire contract, their right is inferior to those of the contracting parties. For these reasons, the analysis ought not to be followed in either jurisdiction.

III. The Assignment Analysis

A party assigns a right when they transfer it to another party: A and B may conclude a contract, and then assignor B may assign his rights to assignee C, in which case C 'steps into B's shoes' and becomes a party to the contract with A.[25] According to the assignment analysis, the third party is in the position of an assignee, and the third party right consists of the benefit originally granted to the assignor.

---

22 Contract (Third Party Rights) (Scotland) Act 2017, s 1 (1). This view was also accepted in historical Scottish case law. It was said in *Wood v. Moncur* (1591) Mor 7719 at 7719 that "albeit [the tertius] was no contractor, yet there was a provision made in the same in his favours." See also *Morton's Trustees v. Aged Christian Friend Society of Scotland* (1899) 2 F 82 at 84 per Lord Kinnear.

23 *MacQueen* (ed), Gloag and Henderson – The Law of Scotland, 2012, p. 97; *McBryde*, 2007, § 10-23; *Smith*, Jus Quaesitum Tertio – Remedies of the Tertius in Scottish Law (1956) Juridical Review, p. 3 (14); *Loewensohn, Jus quaesitum tertio*: a comparative and critical survey, (1940) 56 Scottish Law Review, p. 77 and 104 (111).

24 *Hogg*, 2011, p. 288.

25 *McBryde*, 2007, § 12-01 – 12-08 (Scots law); § 398 BGB and *Hoffmann*, Zession und Rechtszuweisung, 2012, p. 7–20 (German law).

The analysis is unsuitable in both jurisdictions, as benefits granted to external parties by assignment are originally intended for one of the contracting parties, whereas third parties possess rights initially intended for them. In other words, third party rights are original and rights obtained by assignment are derivative.

The formation requirements of the two mechanisms are also incomepatible. In Scotland, assignation is completed by intimation (i.e. A must be informed that B has assigned his rights to C);[26] this is not required for Scots third party rights.[27] Further, the BGB demands that assignors provide assignees with documents serving as proof of the right assigned,[28] and assignors are obliged, if requested by assignees, to provide a document certified by a notary evidencing the assignment.[29] Neither of these requirements apply to the German third party right.

The analysis has thus been rejected in both Scots[30] and German[31] commentary. The two mechanisms are distinct, and third parties are clearly not assignees.

IV. The Agency Analysis[32]

Agency is the "relationship, usually created by contract, in terms of which the principal instructs the agent to act on his behalf in order to produce legally binding effects for the principal."[33]

26 *McBryde*, 2007, § 12-07.
27 Contract (Third Party Rights) (Scotland) Act 2017, s 2 (4) (b).
28 § 402 BGB.
29 § 403 BGB.
30 *Hogg*, 2011, p. 313; *McBryde*, 2007, § 12-13.
31 *Gernhuber*, 1989, p. 470; *von Gierke*, Der Lebensversicherungsvertrag zugunsten Dritter nach deutschem und ausländischem Recht, 1936, p. 20, 28; *Gottschalk*, Zum Wesen des Rechtserwerbs beim Vertrag zugunsten Dritter, Versicherungsrecht, 1976, p. 797 (798); *Raab*, Austauschverträge mit Drittbeteiligung, 1999, p. 37.
32 The German concept of 'agency without specific authorisation' is discussed below.
33 *Macgregor*, The law of agency in Scotland, 2013, § 2-01 (Scots law). For the German law see §§ 164–181 BGB; *Markesinis/Unberath/Johnston*, The German Law of Contract: A Comparative Treatise, 2006, p. 109–118.

This analysis provides that the third party is a principal, for whom the stipulator has acted as an agent.[34] However, this has been discounted in Scots commentary because it is highly doubtful that a stipulator would view himself as an agent.[35] German commentators have also dismissed the analysis, because it ignores the role of the debtor in the tripartite relationship, and, further, due to the fact that principals become full contracting parties, whereas third parties do not.[36] The agency analysis therefore fits neither the Scots nor the German third party right.

V. The Negotiorum Gestio Analysis

In Scots law, *negotiorum gestio* applies where one party, through absence, ignorance, or incapacity, cannot manage their own affairs, and a second party undertakes to manage the affairs.[37] The resulting relationship is not contractual, but the first party is nonetheless liable for expenses incurred in the unauthorised management.[38] The German equivalent is "agency without specific authorisation."[39]

The analysis provides that the debtor manages the affairs of the third party without authorisation, and the third party's acceptance of this benefitcial intervention constitutes ratification of the unauthorised management.[40]

However, *negotiorum gestio* deals with bipartite relationships, and third party rights necessarily involve tripartite relationships.[41] Further, the party who improves the other's situation according to the doctrine acts on their own initiative – their performance is not contractually compelled in the manner of a stipulator obliged to fulfil a third party right. Lastly, *negotiorum gestio* involves the management of a party's existing affairs, and in the case of third party rights the 'affairs' surrounding the right do not exist

34 *Hogg*, 2011, p. 313.
35 Ibid., p. 313.
36 *Gernhuber*, 1989, p. 470; *von Gierke*, 1936, p. 29; *Raab*, 1999, p. 37–38.
37 A recent overview of the law is found in *MacQueen*, The sophistication of unjustified enrichment, (2016) 20 (3) Edinburgh Law Review, p. 312.
38 *Hogg*, Obligations, 2006, § 1.04, 1.26, and 1.33.
39 §§ 677–687 BGB.
40 *Hogg*, 2011, p. 292.
41 *Zweigert/Drobnig* (eds), International Encyclopaedia of Comparative Law, 2002, p. 9.

until the contracting parties deem them to do so.[42] The analysis is thus discounted.

VI. The Trust Analysis

The Scots law of trusts impacted upon the development of the Scots third party right,[43] as the tripartite relationships are similar: the trustor and trustee(s), and the contracting parties confer benefit on the beneficiary and *tertius* respectively. In Germany, cases where one party agrees to manage another's property under a trust, making transfers to a third party, may amount to contracts in favour of third parties under § 328 BGB.[44]

However, whilst the two concepts are certainly intertwined in some situations, the analysis is on the whole unsuitable. Trustors and trustees are under fiduciary duties to the beneficiary (this is not necessarily the case in relationships involving third party rights),[45] and the formation of the trust requires the transfer of property between the trustor and trustee (this is not required in the formation of third party rights).[46]

VII. The Donation Analysis

This analysis is appropriate where the contracting parties wish to confer a third party right as a gift. However, the stipulator may use the right to settle a debt owed to the third party, in which case the third party is in the position of a creditor.[47]

---

42 *Hogg*, 2011, p. 291.

43 *MacQueen/Sellar*, Scots Law: Ius quaesitum tertio, Promise and Irrevocability, in: Schrage (ed), Ius Quaesitum Tertio, 2008, p. 357 (383).

44 *Schermaier*, Contracts for the Benefit of a Third Party in German Law, in: Schrage (ed), Ius Quaesitum Tertio, 2008, p. 289 (295–296).

45 *Scottish Law Commission*, March 2014, § 2.20.

46 *Allan's Trs v. Lord Advocate* 1971 SC (HL) 45; *Scottish Law Commission*, March 2014, § 2.20 (Scots law); *de Waal*, Trust law, in: Smits (ed), Elgar encyclopaedia of comparative law, 2012, p. 926 (931) (German law).

47 *Smith*, (1956) Juridical Review, p. 3 (14–15).

According to German law, donations must be evidenced in writing and authenticated by a court or notary public.[48] It would be commercially inconvenient if this was required for the formation of all third party rights, and so the analysis has been dismissed in commentary.[49] Scots commentators have also spoken unfavourably of a donation analysis.[50]

Thus, whilst the analysis may be appropriate under certain circumstancees, it is too restrictive to apply to third party rights generally.

VIII. The Sui Generis Analysis

The term *'sui generis'* means 'of its own kind.'[51] The analysis provides that third party rights are unique in nature, though they may share various properties with other rights. This is equally possible in Scots and German law, as neither restrict the classification of third party rights as necessarily falling within a particular category. Advocates of the analysis include Sutherland and Johnson,[52] and Hallebeek and Dondorp.[53]

Hogg states that such analyses should be avoided unless none of the existing characterisations are capable of describing the right, although he acknowledges that a *sui generis* classification of third party rights is 'perfectly possible.'[54] If third party rights do fit neatly into an existing category of right, this should be adopted in the interests of avoiding the development of a separate obligation at the expense of academic and judicial time and energy. However, a *sui generis* analysis can be avoided only if there is another suitable alternative.

---

48 § 518 BGB.

49 *Wesenberg*, Verträge zugunsten Dritter, 1949, p. 29–35; *Schlechtriem*, Schuldrecht: Besonderer Teil, 1998, § 168.

50 *McBryde*, Jus Quaesitum Tertio, (1983) Juridical Review, p. 137 (138).

51 *Garner*, Garner's dictionary of legal usage, 2011, p. 862.

52 *Sutherland/Johnston*, in: Zimmermann/Visser/Reid, p. 208 (217); *Sutherland*, Third-Party Contracts, in: MacQueen/Zimmermann (eds), European Contract Law: Scots and South African Perspectives, 2006, p. 203 (209).

53 *Hallebeek/Dondorp*, Contracts for a Third-Party Beneficiary: A Historical and Comparative Perspective, 2008, p. 256.

54 *Hogg*, 2011, p. 291.

IX. Summary

This section has considered eight potential approaches to the nature of third party rights. Six of these are evidently incorrect. The third party is not a full contracting party in Scots or German law, and whilst assignment, agency, *negotiorum gestio*, trust, and donation all share similarities with third party rights, none fully account for the characteristics of the Scots or German third party rights. These analyses are not discussed further.

The remaining options are the promissory and *sui generis* analyses. Whilst Hogg is correct in his view that *sui generis* classifications should be avoided where possible, the promissory analysis must be analysed to ascertain whether this is indeed a robust theory of Scots and German third party rights. The following sections assess the merits and disadvantages of these approaches in each jurisdiction.

C. *The Nature of the Scots Third Party Right*

This section discusses whether the Scots third party right is promissory, and, if not, whether a *sui generis* analysis is appropriate.

I. The Promissory Analysis in Scots Law

The promissory analysis enjoys significant academic support in Scotland. Notable proponents include Smith,[55] MacQueen,[56] and more recently, Hogg,[57] amongst others.[58] It is thought that the canon law's emphasis on enforcing promises influenced the development of the right,[59] and Stair certainly viewed third party rights as promissory.[60] Whilst the theoretical nature of third party rights has not been the subject of a great deal of judicial

55 *Smith*, Studies Critical and Comparative, 1962, p. 172–197.
56 *MacQueen*, 1995, § 827.
57 *Hogg*, 2011, chapter 5.
58 *Baron Keith of Avonholm*, The Spirit of the Law of Scotland, 1957, p. 25–27.
59 *MacQueen/Sellar*, in: Schrage, p. 357 (361–369).
60 *MacQueen*, 1995, § 827; *Hogg*, 2011, p. 305.

discussion in Scots law,[61] the promissory analysis also has at least a degree of acceptance in the courts. Early cases on third party rights indicate a preference for promissory language,[62] and a promissory approach is also reflected in several more recent decisions.[63] Further, Scots law has long accepted the admissibility of unilateral obligations.[64]

Third party rights and promises share numerous characteristics. Neither need be communicated to their recipients in order to bind,[65] and recipients of promises and third party rights are not required to accept.[66] Both promises and third party rights require intention on the part of their makers to be legally bound,[67] and both may be made conditionally.[68]

However, there is also a significant body of academic opposition to the analysis. McBryde claims that whilst Stair adopted a promissory analysis to explain third party rights, such reliance is no longer necessary, and the 'specialties' of the law on promise may not be suited to an analysis of third party rights.[69] Rodger views the promissory approach as 'purely fanciful,'[70] and it is Sutherland's opinion that the analysis is 'unconvincing.'[71] Further, whilst the promissory analysis certainly has a foothold in Scots case law, it

---

61 *MacQueen*, Third Party Rights in Contract – Jus Quaesitum Tertio, in: *Reid/Zimmermann* (eds), A History of Private Law in Scotland, 2000, p. 220 (243).

62 See, for example *Auchmoutie v. Hay* (1609) Mor 12126 at 12126: "the pursuer had promised to [the third party]."

63 *Morton's Trustees v. Aged Christian Friend Society of Scotland* (1899) 7 SLT 220 at 85–89 per Lord Kinnear. See also *Lamont v. Burnett* (1901) 3 F 797 per Lords Young and Trayner.

64 The oldest recorded case in which the Court of Session upheld a claim on the basis of unilateral promise is *Drummond v. Bisset* (1551) Mor 12381. See also *Kintore v. Sinclair* 1623 Mor 9425; *Stonehewer v. Inglis* (1697) Mor 7724.

65 *Regus (Maxim) Ltd v. Bank of Scotland plc* 2013 SC 331 at para. 34 per Lord President (Gill); Contract (Third Party Rights) (Scotland) Act 2017, s 2 (4) (b).

66 *McBryde*, 2007, § 2-28; Contract (Third Party Rights) (Scotland) Act 2017, s 1 (4).

67 *Hogg*, 2006, § 2.13; Contract (Third Party Rights) (Scotland) Act 2017, s 1 (1) (b).

68 *Gloag*, 1929, p. 20; *Walker*, The law of contracts and related obligations in Scotland, 1995, § 29.15; Contract (Third Party Rights) (Scotland) Act 2017, s 2 (2).

69 *McBryde*, 2007, § 10-07; *McBryde*, (1983) Juridical Review, p. 137 (138).

70 *Rodger*, Molina, Stair and the Jus Quaesitum Tertio, (1969) Juridical Review, p. 128 (143–144).

71 *Sutherland*, in: MacQueen/Zimmermann, p. 203 (209).

would be an exaggeration to say that such an approach is widely and unanimously accepted amongst the judiciary. It is unfortunate that the views of those who disagree with the promissory analysis are not fully explained. Rather, there is a tendency amongst these commentators to state their opinion without much explanation as to why third party rights ought to be so classified. This has perhaps contributed to the lack of clarity in Scots law regarding the nature of third party rights.

These concerns are perhaps related to the matter of gratuitousness. Although Gloag opines that promises are not required in Scots law to be gratuitous,[72] and Atiyah writes that although promises may be made entirely benevolently, it is highly likely that most "are promises given as the price of something the promisor wants,"[73] Scots law currently lacks consensus on the issue of whether a promise must always be gratuitous, or whether it is possible for it to be gratuitous or onerous.[74] The acknowledgement in the Requirements of Writing (Scotland) Act 1995 (hereinafter RoWSA) that promises may be made in the course of business[75] would suggest that Scots law also encompasses the making of promises for reasons which may not be altruistic, and so it does appear that Gloag's approach is correct. However, the matter is clearly not settled, and this lack of clarity would affect the Scots third party right, should it be classed as promissory.

If the promissory analysis were adopted in Scotland, third party rights must comply with the promissory requirements of formation. This would entail adherence to the relevant rules contained in RoWSA, namely, that the third party right must be in writing unless it is made in the course of business.[76] Enforcing such a requirement for the formation of third party rights in domestic contexts would be undesirable. Recent legislation on Scots third party rights does not require formal writing. One of the Scots third party right's attributes is accordingly the flexibility of its requirements of formation, which allow for third party rights to be validly constituted orally in all contexts, or for the parties to create written proof of the right if they

72 *Gloag*, 1929, p. 25.

73 *Atiyah*, Promises, Morals and Law, 1983, p. 143.

74 For further discussion of the views of MacQueen, Black, and Sellar (who feel that promises must always be gratuitous), and Thomson and McBryde (who disagree), see *Hogg*, 2006, § 2.06.

75 RoWSA 1995, s 1 (2) (a) (ii) provides that a gratuitous unilateral obligation must be constituted in writing unless it was made in the course of business.

76 RoWSA 1995, s 1 (2) (a) (ii).

choose to do so. Unambiguous provision that third party rights are promissory would result in a loss of flexibility in the formation of the third party right, and this is unnecessarily restrictive.

It seems that, although the third party right shares a number of qualities with promises, adhering to a promissory analysis would be problematic in terms of the requirements of RoWSA pertaining to promises, and the lack of coherence on the matter of when the right is binding. The *sui generis* analysis should thus be considered as an alternative to the promissory analysis.

II. The Sui Generis Analysis in Scots law

This approach is well supported academically. McBryde describes the nature of third party rights as "uncertain,"[77]stating that it is best to treat it as "an independent right which shares some of the characteristics of other contractual rights but also has special features."[78] Similarly, Rodger opines that the right will "defy neat analysis," such that "little purpose will be served and much time will be wasted if we try to work out an elegant theory to cover the facts."[79] The approach is affirmed judicially by Lords Dunedin[80] and Penrose.[81]

III. Summary

There are certainly several convincing elements of the promissory analysis. However, it is not a feasible view of the nature of the Scots third party right. Consequently, the right ought to be described as *sui generis*.

The Scottish Law Commission, in their recent work on third party rights,[82] considers that

77 *McBryde*, 2007, § 10-07.

78 *McBryde,* (1983) Juridical Review, p. 137 (138).

79 *Rodger*, (1969) Juridical Review, p. 128 (143–144).

80 *Maguire v. Burges* 1909 SC 1283 at 1290–1291 per Lord Dunedin.

81 *Beta Computers (Europe) Ltd v. Adobe Systems (Europe) Ltd* 1996 SLT 604 at 611 per Lord Penrose.

82 A team at the Scottish Law Commission, headed by Professor Hector MacQueen, produced the Report which ultimately lead to the enactment of the

> "there is considerable benefit in a reformed third party right being placed as far as possible within existing categories in the law of obligations, rather than being a 'standalone' right, the nature and implications of which have to be fully worked out in a complete legislative scheme."[83]

Following consultation, they concluded that specific juristic characteristics of the Scots third party right in any future legislation was unnecessary.[84] This was a sensible approach: the legislation[85] resulting from the project is intended to modernise Scots law and ensure it is practically fit for purpose, and legislative statement on the nature of the right is unnecessary in respect of this aim – adding a provision on the nature of third party rights would not be of direct use to practitioners. Nonetheless, in order to preclude application of RoWSA, and to ensure that the Scots third party right is soundly classified, academic and judicial authority ought to recognise that the right is *sui generis* where the matter arises.

D. *The Nature of German Third Party Rights*

This section ascertains the compatibility of the promissory and *sui generis* theories with German third party rights.

I. The Promissory Analysis in German Law

Although the BGB's provisions on third party rights are found under the heading "The promise of performance to a third party," the provisions therein use promissory language to refer to the relationship between the contracting parties, rather than between either of the contracting parties and the third party.[86] This reflects the fact that contracting parties generally are seen as making reciprocal promises to one another in German law,[87] but this has no implications for the nature of third party rights. The heading is the

---

Contract (Third Party Rights) Scotland Act 2017. See further *Scottish Law Commission*, Report on Third Party Rights, Scot Law Com No 245, July 2016.

83 *Scottish Law Commission*, March 2014, § 4.18.

84 *Scottish Law Commission*, July 2016, § 3.17.

85 *Scottish Law Commission*, July 2016, Appendix A.

86 For example, §§ 331, 333–334 BGB.

87 *Markesinis/Unberath/Johnston*, 2006, p. 55.

only reference in the BGB which could be construed as describing the right as promissory: it clearly cannot be said that the BGB definitively provides that third party rights are promises.

A promissory analysis was initially advocated by von Kübel, but this approach was not eventually followed,[88] and the analysis has not been considered in recent commentary.

In light of the fact that gratuitous unilateral obligations are not generally enforceable in German law, and considering the lack of strong academic or judicial impetus to include third party rights within the small group of exceptions to the principle that such obligations are invalid, it cannot be said that German third party rights are promissory.

II. The Sui Generis Analysis in German Law

The *sui generis* approach is the dominant view in German commentary. The German Federal Court of Justice (*Bundesgerichtshof*, hereinafter BGH) describes third party rights as "vertragsähnlich" ('quasi-contractual').[89] Other commentators remark that attempts to explain the German third party right dogmatically have proved unsatisfactory and unnecessary,[90] and Gernhuber opines that attempts at categorisation should be regarded with scepticism in light of the diversity of uses of the right.[91] Wesenberg remarks that the right is a legal curiosity.[92]

III. Summary

The academic and judicial support for the *sui generis* analysis, and the unsuitability of the promissory analysis, indicate that German third party rights are unique in nature.

---

88 *Hogg*, 2011, p. 151–152, 309.
89 BGH 29.04.1953 – VI ZR 63/52, BGHZ 9, 316 (§ 8).
90 *Hallebeek/Dondorp*, 2008, p. 256. The authors comment in relation to European third party rights generally, including the German right.
91 *Gernhuber*, 1989, p. 468.
92 *Wesenberg*, 1949, p. 133.

E. Concluding Remarks

Various circumstances in which obligations arise in bi- or tripartite relationships do not fit any neat categorisations of the law of obligations: for example, agency, assignment, and *negotiorum gestio*. It is neither necessary nor beneficial to 'shoehorn' third party rights into an existing analysis simply on the grounds that *sui generis* categorisations allow rights to escape neat allocation to a particular category of right. The added complexity to the map of private law may be undesirable, but this is preferable to allowing a theoretically unsound classification. As neither the promissory analysis nor any of the other analyses discussed above adequately account for the nature of the Scots or German third party rights, both are best described as *sui generis*. Whilst the Scots third party right more narrowly escapes a promissory analysis than its German counterpart, both ultimately possess the same inherent nature of being unique rights.

If the contracting parties wish to confer a third party right by way of a promise, there seems to be no reason to prohibit such a transaction in jurisdictions which permit the formation of legally enforceable gratuitous obligations. This presently could not include Germany, although reform in this respect could perhaps be useful in the future, should there be demand for recognition of promises generally. Essentially, there is nothing theoretically unsound in claiming that third party rights *can* be promissory, but they need not always fit the mould of a promise. The fact that third party rights may in many instances appear to be very similar to promises ought not to lead to the adoption of a promissory analysis generally, as this does not account for the diversity of third party rights which may be constituted under the current laws of both jurisdictions.

It is also relevant that a promissory approach to the nature of the right in either jurisdiction may impede future harmonisation at European or global level. If various jurisdictions choose to view their third party rights as promissory, then harmonisation must account for these jurisdictions' laws on promises. Any proposed harmonisation measure on third party rights which contradicted a jurisdiction's laws on promises may be rejected on this ground, whereas deviations to the law on third party rights only may be more readily accepted.

In essence, it is important both for the doctrinal coherence of Scots contract law as it currently stands, and its influence in any future harmonization measures, that third party rights are classed as *sui generis*. Scots commentary is not unified on this point, and reference could be made in the course of any future reform of the Scots third party right to the fact that the German third party right is widely considered to be *sui generis*, in asserting that that the Scots third party right ought to be so classified.

Bibliography

Allan's Trs v. Lord Advocate 1971 SC (HL) 45

Patrick Atiyah, *Promises, Morals and Law* (Oxford University Press, Oxford 1983)

Auchmoutie v. Hay (1609) Mor 12126 at 12126

Beta Computers (Europe) Ltd v. Adobe Systems (Europe) Ltd 1996 SLT 604

BGH 08.02.2006 – IV ZR 205/04 (RGZ 71, 324, RGZ 82, 99)

BGH 29.04.1953 – VI ZR 63/52 (BGHZ 9, 316)

D&J Nicol v. Dundee Harbour Trustees 1915 SC (HL) 7

Marius de Waal, 'Trust law' in Jan Smits (ed), *Elgar encyclopaedia of comparative law* (2nd Edition, Edward Elgar Publishing, Cheltenham 2012), 926

Drummond v. Bisset (1551) Mor 12381

Werner Flume, *Allgemeiner Teil des Bürgerlichen Rechts*, Vol. 2 (4th Edition, Springer Verlag, Berlin 1992)

Charles Fried, *Contract as Promise* (Harvard University Press, Massachusetts 1982)

Bryan Garner, *Garner's dictionary of legal usage* (3rd Edition, Oxford University Press, Oxford 2011)

Joachim Gernhuber, *Das Schuldverhältnis* (Mohr Siebeck, Tübingen 1989)

William Murray Gloag, *The Law of Contract: A Treatise on the Principles of Contract in the Law of Scotland* (2nd Edition, W. Green & Son, Edinburgh 1929)

Hans-Joachim Gottschalk, Zum Wesen des Rechtserwerbs beim Vertrag zugunsten Dritter, Versicherungsrecht 1976, 797

Jan Hallebeek and Harry Dondorp, *Contracts for a Third-Party Beneficiary: A Historical and Comparative Perspective* (Martinus Nijhoff Publishers, Leiden 2008)

Jan Felix Hoffmann, *Zession und Rechtszuweisung* (Mohr Siebeck, Tübingen 2012)

Martin Hogg, *Obligations* (2nd Edition, Avizandum Publishing Ltd, Edinburgh 2006)

Martin Hogg, *Promises and contract law: comparative perspectives* (Cambridge University Press, Cambridge 2011)

Baron Keith of Avonholm, *The Spirit of the Law of Scotland* (Holdsworth Club of the University of Birmingham, Birmingham 1957)

Kintore v. Sinclair 1623 Mor 9425

Lamont v. Burnett (1901) 3 F 797

Leo Loewensohn, '*Jus quaesitum tertio*: a comparative and critical survey' (1940) 56 Scottish Law Review, 77 and 104

Laura Macgregor, *The law of agency in Scotland* (W. Green, Edinburgh 2013)

Hector MacQueen (ed), *Gloag and Henderson – The Law of Scotland* (13th Edition, W. Green, Edinburgh 2012)

Hector MacQueen, *The laws of Scotland: Stair Memorial Encyclopaedia*, Vol. 22, (LexisNexis, London Reissue 1995)

Hector MacQueen, 'The sophistication of unjustified enrichment' (2016) 20 (3) Edinburgh Law Review, 312

Hector MacQueen, 'Third Party Rights in Contract – *Jus Quaesitum Tertio*' in Kenneth Reid and Reinhard Zimmermann (eds), *A History of Private Law in Scotland*, Vol. 2 (Oxford University Press, Oxford 2000), 220

Hector MacQueen and William D.H. Sellar, 'Scots Law: *Ius quaesitum tertio*, Promise and Irrevocability' in Eltjo Schrage (ed), *Ius Quaesitum Tertio* (Duncker and Humblot, Berlin 2008), 357

Maguire v. Burges 1909 SC 1283

Basil Markesinis, Hannes Unberath, and Angus Johnston, *The German Law of Contract: A Comparative Treatise* (2nd Edition, Hart Publishing, Oxford 2006)

Dieter Medicus, *Allgemeiner Teil des BGB* (10th Edition, C.F. Müller, Heidelberg 2010)

William McBryde, *The Law of Contract in Scotland* (3rd Edition, W. Green, Edinburgh 2007)

William McBryde, '*Jus Quaesitum Tertio*' (1983) Juridical Review, 137

Morton's Trustees v. Aged Christian Friend Society of Scotland (1899) 7 SLT 220

Regus (Maxim) Ltd v. Bank of Scotland plc 2013 SC 331

Thomas Raab, *Austauschverträge mit Drittbeteiligung* (Mohr Siebeck, Tübingen 1999)

Alan Rodger, 'Molina, Stair and the Jus Quaesitum Tertio' (1969) Juridical Review, 128

Martin Schermaier, 'Contracts for the Benefit of a Third Party in German Law' in Eltjo Schrage (ed), *Ius Quaesitum Tertio* (Duncker and Humblot, Berlin 2008), 289

Peter Schlechtriem, *Schuldrecht: Besonderer Teil* (5th Edition, Mohr Siebeck, Tübingen 1998)

Ernest Joseph Schuster, *The principles of German civil law* (Clarendon Press, London 1907)

Scottish Law Commission, 'Discussion Paper on Third Party Rights' Scottish Law Commission No 157 (March 2014)

Scottish Law Commission, 'Report on Third Party Rights' Scottish Law Commission No 245 (July 2016)

Thomas Broun Smith: '*Jus Quaesitum Tertio* – Remedies of the Tertius in Scottish Law' (1956) Juridical Review, 3

Thomas Broun Smith, *Studies Critical and Comparative* (W. Green, Edinburgh 1962)

James Dalrymple Stair, *The institutions of the law of Scotland* (3rd Edition, G Hamilton and J Balfour, Edinburgh 1681)

Stonehewer v. Inglis (1697) Mor 7724

Philip Sutherland, 'Third-Party Contracts' in Hector MacQueen and Reinhard Zimmermann (eds), *European Contract Law: Scots and South African Perspectives* (Edinburgh University Press, Edinburgh 2006), 203

Philip Sutherland and David Johnston, 'Contracts for the Benefit of Third Parties' in Reinhard Zimmermann, Daniel Visser and Kenneth Reid (eds), *Mixed Legal Systems in Comparative Perspectives: Property and Obligations in Scotland and South Africa* (Oxford University Press, Oxford 2004), 208

Otto von Gierke, *Der Lebensversicherungsvertrag zugunsten Dritter nach deutschem und ausländischem Recht* (Ferdinand Enke Verlag, Stuttgart 1936)

David Maxwell Walker, *The law of contracts and related obligations in Scotland* (3rd Edition, T&T Clark, London 1995)

Gerhard Wesenberg, *Verträge zugunsten Dritter* (Hermann Bölhaus, Weimar 1949)

Wood v. Moncur (1591) Mor 7719

Konrad Zweigert and Ulrich Drobnig, (eds), *International Encyclopaedia of Comparative Law*, Vol. 7 (Brill, Leiden 2002)

Time, Emotions, Legal Certainty and Justice. New Period of Prescription of Delictual Claims for Damages in the Polish Civil Code

Joanna Kruszyńska-Kola

A. *Introduction*

In his well-know paper, published in 1996, Bénabent discussed the status of the French provisions concerning prescription (*prescription extinctive*), employing such expressions as 'chaos', 'lumber room', 'Achilles' heel', 'pitfall', 'mystery', 'enigma', or 'surprises'.[1] Such words used with respect to prescription are hardly astonishing, not only in France. As the comparative examination by Borghetti demonstrated,

> "it seems that a few decades ago the main thing that the various national legal systems had in common on the issue of prescription was the great disorder of existing rules and the criticism they attracted."[2]

Regrettably, prescription is still a matter of criticism and controversy in many European countries, often notwithstanding the profound reforms effected there.[3] One of the most problematic issues (also in the universal perspective), is prescription of delictual claims. The latter entail numerous detailed quandaries, which are mainly associated with questions about the appropriate starting point of the period of prescription.[4]

This paper presents one of the issues which arises from the Polish regulation on prescription of delictual claims when the institution of abuse of rights is applied, as well as suggests a solution relying on a different manner

---

* English translation: Joanna Kruszyńska-Kola, Szymon Nowak.

1 *Bénabent*, Le chaos du droit de la prescription extinctive [Chaos of the Law of Liberative Prescription], in: Mélanges dédiés à Louis Boyer, 1996, p. 123 (123–133).

2 *Borghetti*, Prescription, Zeitschrift für Europäisches Privatrecht (hereinafter ZEuP) 2016, p. 167 (170).

3 See e.g. *Casson/Pierre* (eds), La réforme de la prescription en matière civile. Le chaos enfin régulé? [Reform of the Liberative Prescription in Civil Law. Chaos Finally Regulated?], 2010; *Borghetti*, ZEuP 2016, p. 167 (167–182).

4 See *von Bar*, The Common European Law of Torts, 2000, p. 576–592.

of determining the period of prescription, inspired by Art. 1648 of the French Civil Code (hereinafter FCC) in its original version.

B. Prescription of Delictual Claims in the PCC

In the current Polish Civil Code of April 23, 1964 (hereinafter PCC), prescription of delictual claims for damages is regulated by Art. 442[1] (in force since August 10, 2007). Its § 1 provides that delictual claim for damages is subject to prescription after three years from the day on which the injured party has learnt or with due diligence could has learnt about the damage and the person liable for the redress of the damage (*a tempore scientiae*). However, this period may not be longer than ten years from the day on which the damaging event took place (*a tempore facti*). Further paragraphs stipulate a simple 20-year period of prescription, *a tempore facti*, if the damage resulted from a crime or petty crime (§ 2), a postponement of the expiry of the period of prescription if the damage was inflicted on a person, so that the prescription period may not end earlier than upon the lapse of three years, *a tempore scientiae* (§ 3), and a postponement of the expiry of the period of prescription of a minor's claim for redress of the injury to a person (§ 4). Thus, it is a regulation which tallies with a range of legislative solutions known in other European legal systems and in EU law as well.[5]

Article 442[1] of the PCC is considered to be a specific regulation, but only with respect to certain provisions concerning prescription, set out in the General Part of the PCC. Namely, it excludes the general regulation of the period of prescription, the moment at which prescription begins to run and the moment at which prescription of some claims ends its run.[6] Within the remaining scope, provisions of Arts. 117–125 of the PCC (Title VI – Prescription of Claims) apply. One of them is Art. 117 § 2 of the PCC, in which the legislator describes the essence of the prescription mechanism[7]: after the expiry of the prescription period, the debtor is entitled to refuse performance, provided that they have not renounced the right to raise defence

5 See ibid., p. 578–581.

6 See *Gutowski* (ed), Kodeks cywilny. Tom I. Komentarz do Art. 1–449[11] [Civil Code. Volume I. Commentary on Arts. 1–449[11]], 2016, Art. 442[1] (2).

7 This regulation does not apply to claims against consumers (see Art. 117 § 2[1] of the PCC).

based on a time-barred claim. In other words, the lapse of time determined by law has no influence on the existence of the claim, but leads to granting the debtor the defence of prescription (i.e. a more widely adopted 'weak effect'[8]). Whereas "the defence in civil law is understood as specific right to refuse performance. Therefore, it serves to protect the interests of the person against whom the claim is filed."[9] Hence, it is a form of right which constitutes an element of the subjective right, defined by Polish legal science as a "legal situation, determined in favour of legal entities by applicable legal norms and protecting lawful interests of these entities."[10]

C. *Abuse of the Defence of Prescription*

Classification of the defence of prescription as an element of subjective right has significant consequences. One of the initial provisions of the PCC, Art. 5, sets out a prohibition of abuse of rights (subjective rights): one may not use their right in a manner which is contrary to its social and economic purpose or to the principles of community coexistence; any such act or refraining from acting by the entitled person shall not be treated as the exercise of the right and shall not be protected.[11] Therefore, "in judicial decisions of the Supreme Court and in legal doctrine, there is no doubt that Art. 5 of the PCC applies also in the case of raising the defence of prescription by the defendant,"[12] which in such situation is not allowed and has no effect.

Importantly enough, in each case the court examines *ex officio* if there any abuse of rights has occurred.[13] It is especially justified in view of the so-called internal theory of abuse of rights, according to which the prohibition of using a right in a manner contrary to the social and economic purpose of this right or contrary to the principles of community coexistence also determines the scope of subjective right.[14] Therefore, abuse of rights

8 *Zimmermann*, Comparative Foundations of a European Law of Set-Off and Prescription, 2010, p. 72–73.

9 *Radwański*, Prawo cywilne – część ogólna [Civil Law – General Part], 2009, p. 91.

10 Ibid., p. 88.

11 Translation by the System of Legal Information LEX.

12 Judgment of the Supreme Court dated 20.10.2011, IV CSK 16/11.

13 See Judgment of the Supreme Court dated 23.5.2013, IV CSK 660/12.

14 See *Radwański*, 2009, p. 106.

does not mean that the entity uses its right improperly (as it is asserted in the external theory of abuse of rights), but in fact it does not perform the right at all.[15]

According to Pyziak-Szafnicka, Art. 5 of the PCC is not very commonly applied in practice by the courts *ex officio*, because the parties usually raise the defence based on abuse of rights on their own.[16] However, regarding the defence of prescription, it is generally speaking crucial that the defence provided for in Art. 5 of the PCC is raised very often, and many times successfully. The author of one of the most recent Polish monographs on prescription claims expressly that "... the courts should show much more restraint in refusing to allow the defence of prescription pursuant to Art. 5 of the PCC."[17] It is worth noting that the significant part of these judgments concerns the disputes arising from delictual claims.[18]

To illustrate the broad range of behaviours which are considered an example of abuse of the defence of prescription, one may cite one of the latest judgements of Supreme Court. The case number V CSK 516/12 concerned the claim of a minor daughter and a widow of one of two victims of a traffic accident, filed against the road administrator for damages and pension. After the accident, the plaintiff became ill and did not wish to return to the issue of her husband's death in any way. Following a conversation with the widow of the second victim of the accident, the plaintiff decided to bring an action after almost two years from the expiry of a 3-year period of prescription of her claim. In the judgment dated November 27, 2013, the Supreme Court stated that

> "the state of health of the plaintiff could not be ignored only because she had started working, and had been taking care of the household and the orphaned baby. Those behaviours, providing only satisfaction of elementary needs, had not been tantamount, in her state of health, to emotional readiness to file the action for damages. The defendant's attitude, which in fact was crucial for assessing the effects of the

15 See *Kidyba* (ed), Kodeks cywilny. Komentarz. Tom I. Część ogólna [Civil Code. Commentary. Volume I. General Part], 2012, Art. 5 (4).

16 See Księżak (ed), Kodeks cywilny. Komentarz. Część ogólna [Civil Code. Commentary. General Part], 2014, Art. 5 (57).

17 *Pałdyna*, Przedawnienie w polskim prawie cywilnym [Prescription in Polish Civil Law], 2012, p. 331.

18 See e.g.: Judgment of the Supreme Court dated 4.10.2011, I PK 48/11; Judgment of the Supreme Court dated 4.4.2013, II PK 236/12; Judgment of the Supreme Court dated 24.2.2015, II PK 88/14.

> defence of prescription, should not be ignored either – a dispute initiated by the widow of the second victim of the accident had been conducted and ended (unfavourably for the defendant). The defendant had known that two victims were involved in the accident, but contrary to the principles of ethical and fair dealing, they had not paid any attention to the members of the closest family of the second victim."

On the other hand, Warciński poses a "... question about the possibility of certain 'objectivisation' and – in consequence – 'automatism' in applying Art. 5 of the PCC in the case of raising the defence of prescription of claim for damages."[19] Subsequently, the author cites Wójcik: "The regulation of prescription in particular has to be maximally transparent, clear and precise."[20]

D. The Existing Problem

The above cited assertions can still provide basis for determining a problem here. First of all, it is apparent that through extensive use of the institution of abuse of rights in instances involving prescription of claims, especially delictual claims, the courts recognize and satisfy a practical need for making the regulation of prescription more flexible. Secondly, one discerns a kind of tension between the striving to ensure fairness in applying relatively clear and precise regulation and the tendency to ensure highest transparency and predictability of rules related to the effects of the passage of time (especially that the means to achieve the first aim, the institution of abuse of rights, is extraordinary by its nature).[21]

Balwicka-Szczyrba appears to have identified the crux of this problem. Against the background analysis concerning historical evolution of the Supreme Court's case law, she observed that the rules related to the prescription of delictual claims had been

---

19 *Sobolewski/Warciński*, Przedawnienie roszczeń deliktowych [Prescription of Delictual Claims], 2007, p. 81.

20 See ibid.; *Wójcik*, Zagadnienia etyczne przedawnienia roszczeń [Ethical Issues of Prescription], in: Sawczuk (ed), Z zagadnień cywilnego prawa materialnego i procesowego, 1988, p. 141 (147).

21 See e.g. *Sobolewski/Warciński*, 2007, p. 74.

> "... the subject of discussion, which had revealed a kind of contradiction between *ratio legis* of prescription and a principle of protecting the interests of injured persons."[22]

Indeed, social relationships governed by the so-called delict law are by default characterised by a certain singularity.[23] The magnitude of the latter is reflected in the division of obligation into those arising under contracts and those of delictual provenance. This division

> "... has remained fundamental ever since and is a reflection of the fact that different rules are needed to govern the voluntary transfer of resources between two members of the legal community on the one hand, and possible collisions between their private spheres on the other: the one body of rules being concerned with the fulfilment of expectations engendered by a binding promise, the other with the protection of the status quo against wrongful harm."[24]

Meanwhile, prescription is a mechanism which proves exceedingly embittering for the plaintiff,[25] particularly considering legal provisions concerning prescription of delictual claims, which throughout the entire history of Polish civil codifications (since 1933) have ultimately served finally the interest of the debtor.[26] In fact, were it the aim of the legislator to protect the injured persons, would they make use of e.g. a special period of prescription, significantly shorter than the general period (ten years)? Still, historical experience shows that even in the sphere of delictual obligations the existence of prescription is justified.

22 *Balwicka-Szczyrba*, Przedawnienie roszczeń o naprawienie szkody wyrządzonej czynem niedozwolonym [Prescription of Delictual Claims for Damages], (2007) 24 Monitor Prawniczy, p. 1343 (1344).

23 Among other things, the specificity of delicts owes to the fact that a damaging event is often unpredictable, the person liable for the redress of the damage cannot be easily determined or identified, the injured party fails to take the necessity of future legal action into account (in that they have not secured sufficient means/have not gained knowledge concerning the manner of pursuing claims) etc.

24 *Zimmermann*, The Law of Obligations. Roman Foundations of the Civilian Tradition, 1996, p. 11.

25 See *von Bar*, 2000, p. 467.

26 Aspects entailed by the public interest (evidence-related issues and efficiency of the judicial system) are not of material importance, at least not in the light of case law discussed here.

E. A Solution to the Problem

This problem could therefore be solved by way of a considerable extension of prescription periods. However, the introduction of the period that would be applicable to the majority of different cases classified as abuse of rights is probably neither possible nor appropriate (taking into consideration the manner of applying general clauses from Art. 5 of the PCC). Nonetheless, the fact that the defence of abuse of rights used to be allowed not only in the context of delictual claims but also claims which are subject to other prescription periods, shows that the length of prescription period is not problematic. This issue may only be more apparent with respect to Art. 442^1 of the PCC.

A different method of determining the period of prescription may thus offer an alternative. In this respect, a very interesting and inspiring example may be found in Art. 1648 of the FCC in its original version (which remained in force between 1804 and 2005).

This article stated that an action resulting from redhibitory defects (*vices rédhibitoires*[27] – physical defects of a sold item which the seller supplies with a warranty) shall be brought by the buyer within a short period, according to the nature of the defects and the custom of the place where the sale took place.[28] It can be seen that the extended expression containing an indefinite phrase (the nature of the defects) and a reference to local custom was used to establish the time-frames for actions granted to the buyer

27 See *Aubry/Rau*, Cours de droit civil français d'après l'ouvrage allemnad de C.-S. Zachariae [Course of French Civil Law According to the German Work of C.-S. Zachariae], 1856, p. 274.

28 L'action résultant des vices rédhibitoires doit être intentée par l'acquéreur, dans un bref délai, suivant la nature des vices rédhibitoires, et l'usage du lieu où la vente a été faite.

against the seller.[29] Thus, the traditional manner of determining the prescription period[30] by providing a number of years or months (applied either in the Title XX of the FCC which concerns prescription or in the remedies invented by *aediles curules*,[31] which inspired the French legislator[32]) was rejected.

This raises the question of why it was decided that such a solution should be introduced. The aim of the French legislator (corresponding with the Roman experience concerning *actio redhibitoria* and *actio quanti minoris*) was to determine the shortest possible period. It was believed that this aim could accomplished by virtue of reference to 'local custom' and 'prudence of judges', instead of implementing a compromise (i.e. one which would not have been fitting in each and every case), uniform period of prescription.[33] The conclusion occasioned by the analysis of Art. 1648 of the FCC is that when one strives to adapt the period of prescription as precisely as possible to match the circumstances of the concrete case, it is possible to determine only a limited number of criteria and leave at the discretion of

---

29 Art. 1644 FCC (original version). Under Articles 1641 and 1643, the buyer may choose either to return the item and to have the amount paid at purchase reimbursed or to keep the item and to have a fraction of the price returned to them, as decided by experts. (Dans le cas des articles 1641 i 1643, l'acheteur a le choix de rendre la chose et de se faire restituer le prix, ou de garder la chose et de se faire rendre une partie du prix, telle qu'elle sera arbitrée par experts).

30 On the period being classified as a period of prescription see e.g. *Baudry-Lacantinerie/Tissier*, Traité théorique et pratique de droit civil. XXVIII De la prescription [Theoretical and Practical Civil Law Treatise. XXVIII Prescription], 1924, p. 566.

31 See *Zimmermann*, 1996, p. 317–318.

32 See *Dard*, Code civil des Français avec des notes indicatives des lois romaines, coutumes, ordonnances, édits et déclarations, qui ont rapport à chaque article [Civil Code of the French with the Guidance Notes of the Roman Laws, Customs, Ordinances, Edicts and Declarations that Relate to Each Article], 1807, p. 354.

33 "La loi proposée veut que l'action soit intentée dans le plus court délai: elle ne pouvait établir à cet égard un délai commun. L'usage des lieux et la prudence des juges y suppléeront" (The aim of the proposed provision is that the action is brought within the shortest possible period: in this respect it was not possible to establish a uniform period. Local custom and prudence of judges would substitute it) – *Fenet*, Recueil complet des travaux préparatoires du Code civil [Comprehensive Digest of the Preparatory Works of the Civil Code], 1836, Vol. 14, p. 169.

the judges to make a sovereign decision (concerning either the length or the run of the period of prescription).[34]

Exactly the same situation exists under Polish law; as it was demonstrated above, the extensive use of the institution of abuse of rights where prescription of delictual claims is involved satisfies the need to make the regulation more flexible. Now, in what fashion could the aforementioned innovative concept be transferred from Art. 1648 of the FCC to Art. 442[1] of the PCC?

It is rational to restrict the freedom of the courts by selecting appropriate criteria, based on judgments concerning the rules of assessing the abuse of defence of prescription raised in the course of disputes which had arisen from delictual claims. Relevant jurisprudence is well-established and may be summarized in the following way: all circumstances of the case must be considered and the reasons for the delay in pursuing claims, the length of the delay, the nature of the damage, the behaviour of the creditor and the debtor, as well as the interests of both parties must be examined.[35]

Hence, one of the possible new versions of Art. 442[1] § 1 of the PCC would stipulate as follows: delictual claim for damages is subject to prescription upon the expiry of an appropriate period given all circumstances of the case, in particular: the circumstances of bringing an action, the nature of the damage, the behaviours of the creditor and the debtor as well as the interests of both parties, whereby the period must be no shorter than three years from the day on which the injured party has learnt or with due diligence could has learnt about the damage and the person liable for the redress of the damage or ten years from the day on which the damaging event took place.

Obviously, practical applicability of such a mode of determining the period of prescription needs to be considered. In France, Art. 1648 of the FCC had been controversial from the very beginning (even before the final version of the project was drafted). During the consultation stage, the solution was critically assessed e.g. by the tribunals of appeal. Majority of the tribunals noted the necessity of establishing a precise period of prescription due

---

34 See Com. 18.07.1966: Bull. civ. III, n° 362; Cass. 3e civ., 16.05.1973: JCP 75, II, 17932.

35 See *Sobolewski/Warciński,* 2007, p. 80–82; *Gutowski*, 2016, Art. 442[1] (I) (4); Judgment of the Supreme Court dated 8.05.2014, V CSK 322/13; Judgment of the Supreme Court dated 24.02.2015, II PK 88/14.

to possible inconveniences and lack of legal certainty.[36] Also, the reports from the preparatory works of the French Parliament concerning a draft amendment act dated 2005 described the expression contained in Art. 1648 of the FCC to be imprecise, offering an opportunity to be disputed.[37]

However, the state of jurisprudence is the reality of law. The proposed solution would not necessarily cause a significant decline in legal certainty,[38] as the achievements of case law would be incorporated in the text of the code. In fact, even now, the provision contained in Art. 442^1 of the PCC is relatively clear, but the wide scope of application of the institution of abuse of rights in practice does not enable any debtor to determine when the claim would be prescribed. In contrast, the version presented above, containing a comprehensive indication of criteria as established by the courts, satisfies the demand of maximal transparency and prevents an institution of exceptional nature from being abused. It would still be applicable, though in a much narrower scope. Relying on the text of the Code one would be able to identify the circumstances which determine prescription of claims. In this context, attention should be paid to the judgment in which the French Supreme Court asserted that

> "the notion of a brief period of prescription set out in Art. 1648, if it does not indicate the precise duration, is no less clear in its objective and straightforward application according to the well-established jurisprudence."[39]

In addition, the minimum period reduces the extent of potential uncertainty.

Arguments relating to the necessity of adopting 'arithmetical' solutions are understandable given the viewpoint of legal practice, yet in the light of issues discussed here they lack the power to convince. This is due to the fact that it is the current, traditionally 'arithmetical' regulation governing the period of prescription of delictual claims which constitutes a problem.

---

36 See *Fenet*, 1836, Vol. 3, p. 23, 139, 201, 246–247, 452–453, 526, 629; Vol. 4, p. 186, 615; Vol. 5, p. 83.

37 See http://www.assemblee-nationale.fr/12/rapports/r2836.asp (visited: 30.04. 2016).

38 The substantial part of arguments against such substance of Art. 1648, which were advanced by the French tribunals of appeal, concerns the reference to the immensely varied local customs; see footnote 35.

39 La notion de bref délai de l'art. 1648, si elle n'indique pas une durée précise, n'en est pas moins claire dans son objectif et d'application simple selon une jurisprudence constante (Civ. 1re, 21.03.2000: Bull. civ. I, no 97).

When one examines the transformations of the laws concerning prescription of claims which took place over the recent decades in other legal systems of Europe, it becomes evident that the hitherto predominant technical[40] approach to prescription, especially from the standpoint of public interest (interest of the judiciary) or ease of application of law is becoming exhausted. Instead, there is increasing room for notions in which prescription is an instrument to regulate relationships between creditors and debtors, which is yet another territory for a play of interests of both parties to the obligation. This leads to greater flexibility of the rules, including introduction of a subjective starting point of the prescription period ('the date of knowledge'),[41] negotiation as a premise underlying suspension of the course of prescription, and admissibility of contractual modification of the period of prescription.[42] This tendency is manifested in the concept of 'delay of completion of prescription', which Borghetti advanced recently in response to the problem of determining the starting point of prescription of delictual claims.[43] Also, the English *Limitation Act 1980* (Sec. 33) encompassed a solution defined as "discretionary exclusion of time limit for actions in respect of personal injuries or death."[44]

40 See *Borghetti*, ZEuP 2016, p. 167 (168).

41 See ibid., p. 167 (176).

42 See e.g. § 202 of the BGB, Art. 2254 of the FCC. As regards the latter Code, one should also mention the incorporation of a premise which had previously been permanently present in case law (Art. 2234 of the FCC), namely that the course of the period of prescription is suspended due to impossibility to act (*impossibilité d'agir*).

43 See *Borghetti*, ZEuP 2016, p. 167 (181).

44 For more on that issue see *von Bar*, 2000, p. 591–592; (a notable item in Sec. 33 (3) of the *Limitation Act 1980* is the enumeration of circumstances that the court should take into account while applying Sec. 33; to a substantial degree, the circumstances in question coincide with the aforementioned criteria for assessing the abuse of defence of prescription which emerged in Polish case law). Incidentally, it should be noted is that the solution suggested in this paper would make it possible to solve problems of determining the starting point of the prescription period and the length of the period itself, without resorting to solutions whose structuring is doubtful ('delay of completion of prescription' in the case of expired period), or creating a separate exceptional institutions like in the *Limitation Act 1980*.

F. Summary

All elements of this kind gradually contribute to situation, where prescription performs a function corresponding with the general idea which laid the foundation for its adoption in the first place. After all, the crux of the matter is to make law reflect[45] the effects of the passage of time, especially psychological ramifications, in interpersonal relationships. Since in an overwhelming majority of cases prescription favours the debtor (in that it 'emulates' the sense of being released from a liability which the creditor forgoes to recoup – "long dormant claims, as a rule, 'have more cruelty than justice in them'"[46]), it is in the intrinsically exceptional cases of delictual claims that perhaps one could make the worthwhile attempt at non-standard 'emulation' of the virtually incomputable 'emotions', as a result of which the interest of the creditor could be protected to a greater degree.

Trying to balance the values of protecting persons who suffer damage or incur loss as a result of delict, the consideration due to the effects of the passage of time and finally legal certainty, the proposed version of Art. 442^1 § 1 of the PCC would facilitate meeting the needs of practice, resolve the problem of e.g. the appropriate starting point of the period of prescription as well as make law and the process of its application more transparent.

Bibliography

Charles Aubry and Charles-Fréderic Rau, *Cours de droit civil français d'après l'ouvrage allemnad de C.-S. Zachariae*, Vol. 3. (3rd Edition, Cosse, Paris 1856)

Christian Baldus and Thomas Raff, 'La capacité du «système des pandectes»' (2008) 2 Studia Universitatis Babes-Bolyai – Iurisprudentia, 101

Małgorzata Balwicka-Szczyrba, 'Przedawnienie roszczeń o naprawienie szkody wyrządzonej czynem niedozwolonym' (2007) 24 Monitor Prawniczy, 1343

Christian von Bar, *The Common European Law of Torts*, Vol. 2 (Clarendon Press, Oxford 2000)

---

45 At the same time, this is not a postulate of 'emulation' which would distort the function of law as an instrument of regulating social relationships; see *Baldus/Raff*, La capacité du «système des pandectes» [Capacity of the «pandectic system»], (2008) 2 Studia Universitatis Babes-Bolyai – Iurisprudentia, p. 101 (103).

46 *Zimmermann*, 1996, p. 768.

Gabriel Baudry-Lacantinerie and Albert Tissier, *Traité théorique et pratique de droit civil. XXVIII De la prescription* (4th Edition, Librairie de la Société du recueil Sirey, Paris 1924)

Alain Bénabent, 'Le chaos du droit de la prescription extinctive' in *Mélanges dédiés à Louis Boyer* (Presses de l'Université des sciences sociales de Toulouse, Toulouse 1996), 123

Jean-Sébastien Borghetti, Prescription, Zeitschrift für Europäisches Privatrecht 2016, 167

Philippe Casson and Philippe Pierre (eds), *La réforme de la prescription en matière civile. Le chaos enfin régulé?* (Dalloz, Paris 2010)

Henri-Jean-Baptiste Dard, *Code civil des Français avec des notes indicatives des lois romaines, coutumes, ordonnances, édits et déclarations, qui ont rapport à chaque article* (New Edition, J.A. Commaille, Paris 1807)

Pierre-Antoine Fenet, *Recueil complet des travaux préparatoires du Code civil* (Videcoq, Paris 1836)

Maciej Gutowski (ed), *Kodeks cywilny. Tom I. Komentarz do art. 1-449[11]* (System of Legal Information Legalis 2016)

Andrzej Kidyba (ed), *Kodeks cywilny. Komentarz. Tom I. Część ogólna* (System of Legal Information LEX 2012)

Paweł Księżak (ed), *Kodeks cywilny. Komentarz. Część ogólna* (System of Legal Information LEX 2014)

Tomasz Pałdyna, *Przedawnienie w polskim prawie cywilnym* (3rd Edition, LexisNexis, Warszawa 2012)

Zbigniew Radwański, *Prawo cywilne – część ogólna* (10th Edition, Wydawnictwo C.H. Beck, Warszawa 2009)

Przemysław Sobolewski and Michał Warciński, *Przedawnienie roszczeń deliktowych* (Wolters Kluwer SA, Warszawa 2007)

Sylwester Wójcik, 'Zagadnienia etyczne przedawnienia roszczeń' in Mieczysław Sawczuk (ed), *Z zagadnień cywilnego prawa materialnego i procesowego* (Uniwersytet Marii Curie-Skłodowskiej. Wydział Prawa i Administracji, Lublin 1988), 141

Reinhard Zimmermann, *Comparative Foundations of a European Law of Set-Off and Prescription* (Reprint Edition, Cambridge University Press, Cambridge 2010)

Reinhard Zimmermann, *The Law of Obligations. Roman Foundations of the Civilian Tradition* (Reprint Edition, Oxford University Press, Oxford 1996)

Principles of Liability in Tort and Their Future in the German and Polish Legal Systems – *De Lege Lata* and *De Lege Ferenda* Remarks

Agata Krygier

A. *Introduction*

The principles of liability[1] in tort[2] (or the principles of compensatory liability) pose significant difficulties in different legal systems all over the world and are subject to constant change. They not only determine the basis of liability in tort law but also indicate the direction of developments in this area of law.

The main aim of this paper is to consider in what direction these principles will develop in German and Polish civil law in the future by comparing and analysing currently applicable regulations as well as legal doctrines in the above-mentioned legal systems.

---

1 E.g. in Polish law the principle of compensatory liability is defined as a rule which indicates who should assume liability for caused damages. See: *Radwański/ Olejniczak*, Zobowiązania. Część ogólna, 2014, p. 85. Compare: *Banaszczyk*, in: Pietrzykowski (ed), Kodeks cywilny. Komentarz, 2008, p. 1209.

2 Nowadays the word 'tort' has a wider meaning than the word 'delict'. The former includes acts that were conducted not only by people. However, in practice the two terms are very often used interchangeably. See: *Kolańczyk*, Prawo rzymskie, 2001, p. 432.

B. Comparative Historical Analysis

Roman law laid the foundation for the development[3] of principles of liability in tort. In an early stage *delicts* had a penal character because there was no strict distinction between civil wrongs and crimes.[4] This explains why compensatory liability was initially related to penal liability and took the form of *ius talionis* (an eye for an eye, a tooth for a tooth).[5] With the passing of time delicts (delicta privata)[6] were separated from crimes (crimina publica)[7] but they never lost their penal character.[8] Delictual liability was generally based on unlawfulness and later on fault.[9] However, Roman law provided some exceptions in this regard.[10]

---

3 The principles of compensatory liability developed in each period under the influence of different factors. See: *Warkałło*, Przemiany odpowiedzialności cywilnej, in: Łętowska (ed), Tendencje rozwoju prawa cywilnego: zbiór studiów, 1983, p. 283 (329).

4 *Borkowski*, Textbook on Roman Law, 1994, p. 302. *Thomas*, Introduction to Roman Law, 1986, p. 119.

5 As in the Law of the Twelve Tables. On the other hand, it can be observed that the Roman law of *talion* reduced to some extent the private punishment (financial penalty). In reference to *maleficio*, the above-mentioned methods of punishment were in force together with the obligation to compensate up until the Iustinian era. Penalty payments in connection with delicts lost their meaning in the 18th century as a result of the codification process in penal law. See: *Kolańczyk*, 2001, p. 424. *Dajczak/Giaro/ Longchamps de Bérier*, Prawo rzymskie. U podstaw prawa prywatnego, 2014, p. 447, 453, 468, 478, 553, 555, 563. *Warkałło*, Odpowiedzialność odszkodowawcza. Funkcje, rodzaje, granice, 1962, p. 23 ff.

6 On the meaning of delict and its functions in practice, see: *Kolańczyk*, 2001, p. 426. It is also interesting that in Roman law delicts under Praetorian law resulted in the same legal consequences as those in civil law. *Kolańczyk*, 2001, p. 435, 437.

7 Ibid., p. 424. *Rozwadowski*, Prawo rzymskie. Zarys wykładu wraz z wyborem źródeł, 2008, p. 194; *Lee*, The Elements of Roman Law, 1956, p. 377.

8 Ibid., p. 377. Kolańczyk emphasizes that in the Dominate period some private delicts (*delicta privata*) were pursued vigorously by the state. *Kolańczyk*, 2001, p. 425.

9 As mentioned above, initially (in the archaic period) the liability for delictual damages was connected with *ius talionis* and later with a penalty payment. This situation lasted until 287/286 B.C. when the *Lex Aquilia* was passed. In itself the act determined only the objective prerequisites for the compensatory liability associated with a delict, mainly damage and a causal connection between the

Over the course of time, it transpired that the process of generalizing compensatory liability did not bring about the desired effects.[11] That is the reason why changes occurred. Owing to canonical law, a general clause of fault was developed[12], this encompassing all kinds of damages and behaviour.[13] What is more important, having been in force for many years, it was reflected in then codifications and was the only basis of compensatory liability.[14] However, the person who caused the damage was responsible only

---

damage and unlawful action. The activity of Roman lawyers caused the *Lex Aquilia* to be interpreted more strictly than previously, because they identified as prerequisites damage and the culpable – as opposed to merely unlawful – act of the perpetrator. It can be said that from that point the principle of fault in tort law started to evolve (D. 9,2,52,3). As to the way that culpa was understood, see: I. 4,3,2–9. *Dajczak/Giaro/Longchamps de Bérier*, 2014, p. 469–470, 560–561. *Kaser/Knütel*, Römisches Privatrecht, 2005, p. 250. *Hausmaninger/Selb*, Römisches Privatrecht, 1997, p. 355. *Borkowski*, 1994, p. 303. However, Kowalewski does not fully agree with the statement that the principle of fault has its roots in the *Lex Aquilia.* See: *Kowalewski*, Prawo ubezpieczeń gospodarczych. Ewolucja i kierunki przemian, 1992, p. 198.

10 In such cases the liability was based on a principle of strict liability. As examples one can mentioned an individual's liability for damages caused by animals and quasi-delicts. *Dajczak/Giaro/Longchamps de Bérier*, 2014, p. 472–476.

11 *Lewaszkiewicz-Petrykowska*, Deliktowa odpowiedzialność za własne czyny w prawie cywilnym krajów europejskich (1998) 2 Kwartalnik Prawa Prywatnego, p. 207 (208 ff.).

12 The legal solution appearing in the *Lex Aquilia* initiated fruitful debate over the next centuries. The term 'clausula generalis' was used for the first time by Baldus de Ubaldis (Commenataria I, 335,27). In turn, Grotius stated that a person is always assigned compensatory liability when he acted in a culpable way. (De iure belli II.17,1). The idea of a general clause for delicts was criticized in the 19th century by Jehering. Today, this principle is regulated in the Polish civil code (art. 415) and the French Code Civil (art. 1382), where damage is understood in a broad way. On the other hand, in Germany (§ 823 I BGB) it is interpreted much more strictly. *Dajczak/Giaro/Longchamps de Bérier*, 2014, p. 453–454, 560–561.

13 *Lewaszkiewicz-Petrykowska*, (1998) 2 Kwartalnik Prawa Prywatnego, p. 207 (209). The establishment of a general clause regarding fault was the result of the process which aimed to individualize legal liability. See: *Kowalewski*, 1992, p. 199.

14 The best example is the French Napoleonic Code from 1804, in which the fundamental principle was the principle of fault. R. Von Jhering described it as: 'the most valuable jewel inherited from Roman lawyers'. See: *Sójka-Zielińska*, Kodeks Napoleona – Historia i współczesność, 2008, p. 183. Concerning the development of tort liability in French law, see: *Nesterowicz*, Ewolucja odpowie-

when he acted (i) intentionally and illegally or (ii) negligently. In cases not fulfilling these prerequisites, the damage had to be compensated by the victim. It was evident that such a state of affairs in civil law could not last *ad infinitum*. Ultimately, it was the process of industrialization, the progress of technology and social transformations which led to judges and legislators being faced with new legal problems in this area of law in the 19th century, especially with reference to provisions on compensatory liability.[15] Despite significant opposition, in many legal systems in Europe (e.g. in Germany and Poland) the catalogue of principles for compensatory liability was broadened by the principle of risk.[16]

---

dzialności deliktowej w prawie francuskim, (2007) 12 Państwo i Prawo, p. 10 (10 ff).

15 *Szpunar*, Perspektywy dalszego rozwoju odpowiedzialności cywilnej, (1979) 8–9 Państwo i Prawo, p. 53. See also: *Warkałło*, in: Łętowska, p. 283 (283).

16 *Kötz/Wagner*, Deliktsrecht, 2010, p. 19.

C. Analysis of Currently Applicable Principles of Liability in Tort in Polish and German Civil Law

Generally, Polish scholars have developed the following principles of liability in tort[17]: principle of fault (I),[18] principle of risk and principle of community life (II).[19]

I. Principle of Fault

With regard to the principles of fault, risk and community life, legal scholars are in full agreement. The principle of fault, regulated in art. 415 of the Polish civil code (KC), is the most important in practice.[20] Furthermore, it

---

17 The currently applicable Polish civil code came into force in 1964. It is mainly based on the French and German civil codes. See: Ustawa z dnia 23 kwietnia 1964 r. Kodeks cywilny (Dz.U. 1964 nr 16 poz. 93 with subsequent amendments). On the history of the Polish civil code see: *Radwański*, Kodyfikacja prawa cywilnego, (2009) 2 Ruch Prawniczy, Ekonomiczny i Socjologiczny, p. 131. *Radwański*, Wprowadzenie, in: Kodeks cywilny i inne akty prawne, 2013, IX ff. *Giaro*, Westen im Osten. Moderniesierung osteuropäischer Rechte bis zum Zweiten Weltkrieg, (2003) 2 Rechtsgeschichte, p. 123. *Liebscher/Zoll*, Einführung in das polnische Recht, 2005.

18 In the contemporary Polish and German legal systems there is no legal definition of 'fault'. That is the reason why this term was developed by scholars and in jurisprudence. See: *Czachórski/Brzozowski/Safjan/Skowrońska-Bocian*, Zobowiązania. Zarys wykładu, 2009, p. 215. Compare *Joussen*, Schuldrecht I – Allgemeiner Teil, 2013, p. 115. *Kötz/Wagner*, 2010, p. 54. With regard to this principle Polish law patterned itself upon French law. In the Polish civil code, as in the French civil code, Art. 415 regulates the liability for one's own acts based on the principle of fault. See: *Kuźmicka-Sulikowska*, Odpowiedzialność deliktowa w prawie wybranych państw obcych, 2011, p. 331.

19 *Radwański/Olejniczak*, 2014, p. 85. *Czachórski/Brzozowski/Safjan/Skowrońska-Bocian*, 2009, p. 211–212. *Olejniczak* (ed), System prawa prywatnego. Prawo zobowiązań – część ogólna, 2014, p. 38–48.

20 Art. 415 of Polish Civil Code provides: 'Anyone who by a fault on his part causes damage to another person is obliged to remedy it.' See: *Czachórski/Brzozowski/Safjan/Skowrońska-Bocian*, 2009, p. 212. Here, it cannot be omitted that this norm refers only to damages caused by natural persons, whereas Art. 416 KC regulates the liability of legal persons and acts done under their authority (art. 416 KC states that: "A legal person is obliged to remedy any damage caused through a fault occurring on the basis of its authority"). Concerning Art. 416 KC,

is applicable when other principles of tort law liability do not apply (like art. 436 § 2 KC).[21] Besides these regulations, art. 427 KC (fault in supervision – *culpa in custodiendo*), art. 429 KC (fault in selection – *culpa in eligendo*) and art. 431 KC (damages caused by animals)[22] refer to this principle.[23]

---

there have been many discussions in legal literature not only about relations between legal persons and acts done under their authority but also in what way compensatory liability comes into being. For more information, see: *Safjan*, Odpowiedzialność deliktowa osób prawnych. Stan obecny i kilka uwag de lege ferenda, in Studia Iuridica. Z zagadnień współczesnego prawa cywilnego. Księga pamiątkowa ku czci Profesora Tomasza Dybowskiego, 1994; *Dąbrowa*, Odpowiedzialność deliktowa osoby prawnej, 144 Acta Universitatis Wratislaviensis, Przegląd Prawa i Administracji, 1972.

21 The expression 'on general terms' indicates that Art. 436 § 2 KC refers to the principle of fault. In practice, this legal rule is interpreted very strictly and exceptionally. In some situations a collision of vehicles propelled by natural forces can be based on the principle of risk. See: *Kuźmicka-Sulikowska*, Zasady odpowiedzialności deliktowej w świetle nowych tendencji w ustawodawstwie polskim, 2011, p. 42, 50–51. Concerning compensatory liability for damages caused to people transported out of courtesy, the solution based on the principle of fault is often criticized by scholars. That is the reason why some of these critics would like to relate this case to the principle of risk. See: *Ludwichowska*, Odpowiedzialność cywilna i ubezpieczeniowa za wypadki samochodowe, 2008, p. 174.

22 In order to understand Art. 427 KC in an appropriate way and differentiate between a responsible person and a person who caused damages, both Art. 425 KC (which determines in which cases somebody is insane) and Art. 426 KC (which provides that a 'minor under thirteen years of age is not liable for damage caused') must be taken into account. Further discussions have arisen as to whether, Art. 427 KC establishes liability for one's own or somebody else's acts. As we can see, opinions differ in legal literature. See: *Szpunar*, Odpowiedzialność osób zobowiązanych do nadzoru, 1978, p. 151, 156; *Śmieja*, Odpowiedzialność odszkodowawcza z tytułu nienależytego sprawowania nadzoru nad małoletnim, 512 Acta Universitatis Wratislaviensis, Prawo XC, 1982, p. 45–47.
Despite the fact that Art. 431 KC is based on the principle of fault, there are some commentators who claim that this provision should be understood as referring to the principle of risk. Opponents maintain that such a solution would not make any sense because animal threats are limited to rare and exceptional situations. See: *Kuźmicka-Sulikowska*, Zasady, 2011, p. 64–65.

23 *Bieranowski/Bogdalski/Goettel*, Prawo cywilne. Zarys wykładu, 2016, p. 211–212, 218–19.

The situation in German tort law looks quite similar because the principle of fault plays the most significant role in compensatory liability.[24] § 823 (1), § 823 (2) (liability in damages) and § 826 (intentional damage contrary to public policy) of the German civil code (hereinafter BGB)[25] set out three general clauses, which are also known as 'small clauses'.[26] Each of these rules is connected to the principle of fault. At this point it is also necessary to mention that this principle is also referred to by § 832 BGB (liability of a person with a duty of supervision), § 833 s. 2 BGB (liability of an animal keeper) and § 836 BGB (responsibility of the owner of a plot of land).[27]

II. Principle of Risk and Principle of Community Life

In Polish literature it is often stressed that the principle of risk and the principle of community life perform functions subsidiary to the principle of fault.[28] Articles 430 KC (responsibility for damages caused by a subordinate), 433 KC (responsibility for damages caused by ejection, effusion or the falling of any object from premises), 434 KC (responsibility for damages caused by the collapse of a structure), 435 KC (responsibility for damages caused by the operation of an enterprise or establishment), and 436 KC

---

24 *Kuźmicka-Sulikowska*, Odpowiedzialność 2011, p. 83. However, in legal literature authors sometimes emphasize that this principle can cause some difficulties in determining the scope of liability. See: *Larenz/Canaris*, Lehrbuch des Schuldrechts, Besonderer Teil, 1994, p. 352.

25 Bürgerliches Gesetzbuch vom 18.2.1896 in der Fassung der Bekanntmachung vom 2.1.2002 with subsequent amendments. § 823 BGB states:
"(1) A person who, intentionally or negligently, unlawfully injures the life, body, health, freedom, property or another right of another person is liable to provide compensation to the other party for the damage arising from this.
(2) The same duty is held by a person who commits a breach of a statute that is intended to protect another person. If, according to the contents of the statute, it may also be breached without fault, then compensation liability only exists in the case of fault."

26 *von Bar*, The Common European Law of Torts, 1998, p. 25. See also: *Larenz/Canaris*, 1994, p. 354–355; *Medicus*, Schuldrecht I, Allgemeiner Teil, 2004, p. 366; *Brox/Walker*, Besonderes Schuldrecht, 2016, p. 522.

27 See: *Deutsch/Ahrens*, Deliktsrecht, 2014, p. 153–160.

28 *Czachórski/Brzozowski/Safjan/Skowrońska-Bocian*, 2009, p. 212. See also: *Radwański/Olejniczak*, 2014, p. 87.

(responsibility of an owner-like possessor) refer to the principle of risk.[29] Whereas art. 428 KC (liability of a perpetrator) and art. 431 § 2 KC (liability of a person who keeps animals according to the principles of community life in a case where he is not responsible under the principle of fault) concern the principle of right.[30]

In German legal literature the principle of risk is also distinguished from the principle of fault and refers to the liability for the damages arising from threat or danger.[31] Many legal rules, regulated in specific legal acts, relate to this provision, whereas in the BGB only § 833 s. 1 BGB (liability for animals) is specifically based on it.[32]

A further principle that should be mentioned is that of equitable liability (§ 829 BGB). However, as in Polish tort law, it does not play any significant role in practice.[33]

D. *The Future of Principles of Compensatory Liability in Polish and German Tort Law – De Lege Ferenda Remarks*

The above-mentioned principles of liability in tort play the most important roles in Polish and German legal systems. However, we cannot forget about other principles of liability whose significance increases in practice. For instance, thanks to the development of insurance law in recent years, the guarantee-pay-as-you-go principle has been identified as a distinct principle in Polish legal literature. The development of this principle took place in the last decade. However, Radwański emphasizes that despite the fact that this principle is developing gradually, lawmakers use it very often in relation to legal norms which are not regulated in the Polish Civil Code but in other

29 Ibid., p. 85–86. *Czachórski/Brzozowski/Safjan/Skowrońska-Bocian*, 2009, p. 234, 256–257.

30 *Radwański/Olejniczak*, 2014, p. 87. Compare *Czachórski/Brzozowski/Safjan/Skowrońska-Bocian*, 2009, p. 212.

31 However, in the BGB there are no general clauses making reference to this principle. *Kuźmicka-Sulikowska*, Odpowiedzialność, 2011, p. 84.

32 Ibid., p. 85.

33 Ibid., p. 91.

civil law acts.[34] Also under German tort law, a person or entity can be liable for damage caused without fault, e.g. liability for unlawful interference with private property by a government agency or liability for an accidental event.[35]

These reflections lead to the questions: 'What is the future of principles of tort liability in the Polish and German legal systems? In which direction are they evolving?' The answers can be provided on the basis of the initial developments. It is stressed in German doctrine that in the future the role of the principle of risk will increase.[36] The same situation can be observed under Polish law, as there are many situations in which the legislature has established that a compensatory obligation exists even the where the damage occurred in the absence of fault. The author of this article absolutely agrees with this determination, because each legal system and its rules have to systematically adapt to changes which occur in all areas of life. As mentioned above, the development of industry in the 19th century led to the creation of the principle of risk. Therefore, it can be assumed that in the coming years new principles of compensatory liability will emerge in legal literature.

In my opinion, the fact that in the future other principles regarding liability in tort will develop does not necessarily mean that the principle of fault is losing or will lose its significance in practice. However, in order to increase its effectiveness, it should be modified. As mentioned above, in Polish and German tort law there is no legal definition of fault. Admittedly,

---

34 Compare e.g. *Brzozowski/Jastrzębski/Kaliński/Skowrońska-Bocian*, Zobowiązania. Część ogólna, 2013, p. 56–60 with *Radwański/Olejniczak*, 2014, p. 185 and 87. In the former book the authors do not recognize such principle.

35 *Kuźmicka-Sulikowska*, Odpowiedzialność, 2011, p. 89–90. In relation to a government agency's liability for unlawful interference with private property see e.g.: judgement of the BGH 29.03.1971 – III ZR 110/68, NJW 1971, 1172–1174. Liability for an accidental event is regulated, inter alia in section 945 of the German Code of Civil Procedure, which provides that:
"Should the order of a seizure or an injunction prove to have been unfounded from the start, or should the measure directed be repealed pursuant to section 926 subsection (2) or section 942 (3), the party that has obtained the order is under obligation to compensate the opponent for the damages that he has suffered as a result of the measure directed having been enforced, or as a result of the opponent having provided security in order to avert the enforcement or to obtain the repeal of the measure."

36 *Larenz/Canaris*, 1994, p. 352.

scholars and jurisprudence try to remedy this problem, but unfortunately a unanimous solution has not been reached so far.[37] This is the reason why lawmakers should think about defining the word 'fault' in a legal act. The same applies for the terms: 'intention' and 'negligence' as in this area Polish civil law, for instance, follows the interpretation laid out by Polish criminal law. At present this solution seems to be the best, but it should not be applied for ever. Of course, as defining legal terms is difficult, the legislature has to be very careful. Nevertheless, I think that creating legal definitions for these legal terms would improve the effectiveness of the application of the principle of fault.[38]

In searching for a suitable definition of 'fault', the Principles of European Tort Law could be of aid.[39] Art. 4:101 states that: "A person is liable on the basis of fault for intentional or negligent violation of the required standard of conduct." At this point it should be added that the required standard of conduct is regulated in Art. 4:102:

> "(1) The required standard of conduct is that of the reasonable person in the circumstances, and depends, in particular, on the nature and value of the protected interest involved, the dangerousness of the activity, the expertise to be expected of a person carrying it on, the foreseeability of the damage, the relationship of proximity or special reliance between those involved, as well as the availability and the costs of precautionary or alternative methods.
>
> (2) The above standard may be adjusted when due to age, mental or physical disability or due to extraordinary circumstances the person cannot be expected to conform to it.
>
> (3) Rules which prescribe or forbid certain conduct have to be considered when establishing the required standard of conduct."

The principle of fault is inseparably connected with the notion of illegality. However, it is emphasized in legal doctrine that the word 'illegality' should also have a legal definition because neither Polish commentators nor jurisprudence has developed an unambiguous definition so far. There are, however scholars who claim that 'illegality' should be considered as a separate

37 For more on the concept of fault in Polish civil law see: *Kuźmicka-Sulikowska*, 2011, p. 67–77.

38 Ibid., p. 472–473.

39 See: http://www.egtl.org/ (visited 30.04.2016).

principle of compensatory liability in Polish tort law.[40] This statement seems to be correct, in particular in respect of liability for damages caused by an unlawful act or omission while exercising public authority, which is regulated in art. 417 KC.[41] It is discussed in legal literature which principle should apply in this case: the principle of risk or the principle of illegality. There are more and more supporters for the second concept, so there is

40 What is more interesting, this idea has been met with constantly rising support among lawyers in recent years.

41 Art. 417 KC states that:
"§ 1. The State Treasury or a local government unit or another person exercising public authority by force of law is liable for any damage caused by an unlawful action or omission while exercising public authority.
§ 2. If performance of public authority tasks is contracted under an agreement to a local government unit or another legal person, joint and several liability for any damage caused is borne by the contractor and the local government unit contracting the tasks or the State Treasury."
In turn, in German law, state liability (German: *Amtshaftung*) is regulated in § 839 BGB which provides:
"(1) If an official intentionally or negligently breaches the official duty incumbent upon him in relation to a third party, then he must compensate the third party for damage arising from this. If the official is only responsible because of negligence, then he may only be held liable if the injured person is not able to obtain compensation in another way.
(2) If an official breaches his official duties in a judgment in a legal matter, then he is only responsible for any damage arising from this if the breach of duty consists in a criminal offence. This provision is not applicable to refusal or delay that is in breach of duty in exercising a public function.
(3) Liability for damage does not arise if the injured person has intentionally or negligently failed to avert the damage by having recourse to appeal."
This norm has to be read together with Art. 34 of the Basic Law of the Federal Republic of Germany from 1949. Art. 34 states that:
"If any person, in the exercise of a public office entrusted to him, violates his official duty to a third party, liability shall rest principally with the state or public body that employs him. In the event of intentional wrongdoing or gross negligence, the right of recourse against the individual officer shall be preserved. The ordinary courts shall not be closed to claims for compensation or indemnity."
In German law, this kind of liability is mainly based on the principle of fault. For more information see: *Brox/Walker*, 2016, p. 581–592.

a high probability that the principle of illegality and the principle of absolute liability (e.g. in nuclear law) will be singled out in the future.[42]

It must also be admitted that in Polish literature we can see that some authors separate out the principle of absolute liability while in German law this principle is specified in some acts but is mostly not given independent applicability. Many authors state that delicts connected with nuclear or aviation law are based on the principle of risk. Concerning this principle, literature often stresses that art. 431 KC (liability for damages caused by animals) should be based on the principle of risk rather than the principle of fault.[43]

E. Summary

To sum up, the principles of compensatory liability in tort law do not comprise an easy issue. On the one hand there are no legal definitions of those principles of compensatory liability which are identified in Polish and German doctrine; on the other hand new principles are being identified in both

---

42 *Kuźmicka-Sulikowska*, Zasady, 2011, p. 328–352. Some legal books distinguish these principles, e.g. *Czachórski/Brzozowski/Safjan/Skowrońska-Bocian*, 2009, p. 212. *Olejniczak*, 2014, p. 44–45, 47.

43 It is interesting that chapter 5 of the Principles of European Tort Law specifies in which cases the principle of risk finds application:
Art. 5:101
"(1) A person who carries on an abnormally dangerous activity is strictly liable for damage characteristic to the risk presented by the activity and resulting from it.
(2) An activity is abnormally dangerous if
a) it creates a foreseeable and highly significant risk of damage even when all due care is exercised in its management and
b) it is not a matter of common usage.
(3) A risk of damage may be significant having regard to the seriousness or the likelihood of the damage.
(4) This Article does not apply to an activity which is specifically subjected to strict liability by any other provision of these Principles or any other national law or international convention."
Art. 5:102
"(1) National laws can provide for further categories of strict liability for dangerous activities even if the activity is not abnormally dangerous.
(2) Unless national law provides otherwise, additional categories of strict liability can be found by analogy to other sources of comparable risk of damage."

legal systems. Furthermore, the reader can see that each national law is imperfect and that its legislators are constantly faced with different legal problems. However, such challenges also allow each legal system to continue to develop and to reduce the number of impractical regulations, this being true also in respect of the principles governing compensatory liability in tort law. As mentioned above, the Principles of European Tort Law can be helpful in solving these problems because in some ways it is a reference work that summarizes the outcomes developed and reached in European legal systems and indicates how such principles could evolve.

Bibliography

Christian von Bar, *The Common European Law of Torts*, Vol. 1 (Clarendon Press, Oxford 1998)

BGH 29.03.1971 – III ZR 110/68, NJW 1971

Adam Bieranowski, Piotr Bogdalski and Mieczysław Goettel, *Prawo cywilne. Zarys wykładu* (4th Edition, Wolters Kluwer, Warszawa 2016)

Andrew Borkowski, *Textbook on Roman Law* (Blackstone, London 1994)

Hans Brox and Wolf-Dietrich Walker, *Besonderes Schuldrecht* (41st Edition, C.H. Beck, München 2016)

Adam Brzozowski, Jacek Jastrzębski, Maciej Kaliński and Elżbieta Skowrońska-Bocian, *Zobowiązania. Część ogólna* (LexisNexis, Warszawa 2013)

Witold Czachórski, Adam Brzozowski, Marek Safjan and Elżbieta Skowrońska-Bocian, *Zobowiązania. Zarys wykładu* (11th Edition, LexisNexis, Warszawa 2009)

Wojciech Dajczak, Tomasz Giaro and Franciszek Longchamps de Bérier, *Prawo rzymskie. U podstaw prawa prywatnego* (2nd Edition, Wydawnictwo Naukowe PWN S.A., Warszawa 2014)

Janina Dąbrowa, 'Odpowiedzialność deliktowa osoby prawnej', 144 Acta Universitatis Wratislaviensis, Przegląd Prawa i Administracji, Vol. 1, Wrocław 1972, 95

Erwin Deutsch and Hans-Jürgen Ahrens, *Deliktsrecht* (6th Edition, Vahlen, München 2014)

Tomasz Giaro, Westen im Osten. Moderniesierung osteuropäischer Rechte bis zum Zweiten Weltkrieg, 2 Rechtsgeschichte 2003, 123

Herbert Hausmaninger and Walter Selb, *Römisches Privatrecht* (8th Edition, Böhlau, Wien-Köln-Weimar 1997)

Jacob Joussen, *Schuldrecht I – Allgemeiner Teil* (2nd Edition, Stuttgart 2013)

Max Kaser and Rolf Knütel, *Römiches Privatrecht* (18th Edition, C.H. Beck, München 2005)

Kazimierz Kolańczyk, *Prawo rzymskie* (5th Edition, LexisNexis, Warszawa 2001)

Eugeniusz Kowalewski, *Prawo ubezpieczeń gospodarczych. Ewolucja i kierunki przemian* (Oficyna Wydawnicza Branta, Bydgoszcz 1992)

Hein Kötz and Gerhard Wagner, *Deliktsrecht* (11th Edition, Vahlen, München 2010)

Joanna Kuźmicka-Sulikowska, *Odpowiedzialność deliktowa w prawie wybranych państw obcych* (Prawnicza i Ekonomiczna Biblioteka Cyfrowa, Wrocław 2011)

Joanna Kuźmicka-Sulikowska, *Zasady odpowiedzialności deliktowej w świetle nowych tendencji w ustawodawstwie polskim* (Wolters Kluwer, Warszawa 2011)

Karl Larenz and Claus-Wilhelm. Canaris, *Lehrbuch des Schuldrechts*, Vol. II, Halbband 2, Besonderer Teil (13th Edition, C.H. Beck, München 1994)

Robert W. Lee, *The Elements of Roman Law* (4th Edition, Sweet & Maxwell, London 1956)

Biruta Lewaszkiewicz-Petrykowska, 'Deliktowa odpowiedzialność za własne czyny w prawie cywilnym krajów europejskich' (1998) 2 Kwartalnik Prawa Prywatnego, 207

Marc Liebscher and Fryderyk Zoll, *Einführung in das polnische Recht* (C.H. Beck, München 2005)

Katarzyna Ludwichowska, *Odpowiedzialność cywilna i ubezpieczeniowa za wypadki samochodowe* (Towarzystwo Naukowe Organizacji i Kierownictwa „Dom Organizatora", Toruń 2008)

Dieter Medicus, *Schuldrecht I, Allgemeiner Teil* (16th Edition, C.H. Beck, München 2004)

Mirosław Nesterowicz, 'Ewolucja odpowiedzialności deliktowej w prawie francuskim' (2007) 12 Państwo i Prawo, 10

Adam Olejniczak (ed), *System prawa prywatnego. Prawo zobowiązań – część ogólna*, Vol. 6 (2nd Edition, C.H. Beck, Warszawa 2014)

Krzysztof Pietrzykowski (ed), *Kodeks cywilny. Komentarz*, Vol. I (5th Edition, C.H. Beck, Warszawa 2008)

Zbigniew Radwański, 'Kodyfikacja prawa cywilnego' (2009) 2 Ruch Prawniczy, Ekonomiczny i Socjologiczny, 131

Zbigniew Radwański, 'Wprowadzenie', in Kodeks cywilny i inne akty prawne (34th Edition, C.H. Beck, Warszawa 2013)

Zbigniew Radwański and Adam Olejniczak, *Zobowiązania. Część ogólna* (11th Edition, C.H. Beck, Warszawa 2014)

Władysław Rozwadowski, *Prawo rzymskie. Zarys wykładu wraz z wyborem źródeł* (2nd Edition, Ars boni et aequi, Poznań 2008)

Marek Safjan, 'Odpowiedzialność deliktowa osób prawnych. Stan obecny i kilka uwag de lege ferenda', in *Studia Iuridica. Z zagadnień współczesnego prawa cywilnego. Księga pamiątkowa ku czci Profesora Tomasza Dybowskiego*, Vol. 21 (Warszawa 1994)

Katarzyna Sójka-Zielińska, *Kodeks Napoleona – Historia i współczesność* (2nd Edition, LexisNexis, Warszwa 2008)

Adam Szpunar, *Odpowiedzialność osób zobowiązanych do nadzoru* (Wydawnictwo Prawnicze, Warszawa 1978)

Adam Szpunar, 'Perspektywy dalszego rozwoju odpowiedzialności cywilnej' (1979) 8–9 Państwo i Prawo, 53

Andrzej Śmieja, 'Odpowiedzialność odszkodowawcza z tytułu nienależytego sprawowania nadzoru nad małoletnim', 512 Acta Universitatis Wratislaviensis, Prawo XC, Wrocław 1982

P.J. Thomas, *Introduction to Roman Law* (Kluwer Law and Taxation Publ., Deventer 1986)

Witold Warkałło, *Odpowiedzialność odszkodowawcza. Funkcje, rodzaje, granice* (Państwowe Wydawnictwo Naukowe (Warszawa 1962)

Witold Warkałło, 'Przemiany odpowiedzialności cywilnej', in Ewa Łętowska (ed), *Tendencje rozwoju prawa cywilnego: zbiór studiów* (Zakład Narodowy Imienia Ossolińskich Wydawnictwo Polskiej Akademii Nauk, Wrocław – Warszawa – Kraków – Gdańsk – Łódź 1983), 283

Effective Supplementary Performance?

Markus Kotowski

A. *The Law*

To understand the problems discussed in this article it is necessary to understand the differences between warranties and guarantees in German Law.

I. Statutory Warranties (*gesetzliche Gewährleistung*)

Throughout the European Union, laws based on the "Directive 1999/44/EC of the European Parliament and of the Council of 25 May 1999 on certain aspects of the sale of consumer goods and associated guarantees"[1] grant consumers so called statutory warranties (in German law we speak of *gesetzliche Gewährleistungsrechte*) in regards to sales contracts. According to this directive, the seller of a product is liable to the consumer for any lack of conformity which exists at the time when the goods were delivered.[2] In the case of lack of conformity, the consumer is entitled to have the goods brought into conformity free of charge by repair or replacement.[3] These statutory warranties are mandatory for each sales contract between the seller and a buyer who is a consumer. Statutory warranties only stipulate rules between sellers[4] and buyers, but do not create obligations for the manufacturer.[5]

---

1 Full text available at: http://eur-lex.europa.eu/LexUriServ/LexUriServ.do?uri=CELEX:31999L0044:en:HTML (visited 21.03.2017).

2 Council Directive 99/44/EC, Art. 3, para. 1.

3 Council Directive 99/44/EC, Art. 3, para. 2.

4 Unless stated otherwise, the term 'trader' is used interchangeably with the term 'seller'.

5 That is, unless the manufacturer is identical with the seller.

In 2002 the directive 1999/44/EC was implemented into the German Civil Code (hereinafter BGB).[6] By integrating the rules into the BGB, German lawmakers decided not to create a separate Consumer Code like in other European jurisdictions.[7] They also chose to set those rules as the new standard, meaning that most provisions apply for all sales contracts (Business to Business, hereinafter *B2B*; Customer to Customer, hereinafter *C2C*; Business to Consumer, hereinafter *B2C*),[8] only some extra provisions, §§ 474–479 BGB apply solely to B2C contracts.

In German law the newly created right to repair and the right to receive a replacement are now combined under the term supplementary performance[9] (*Nacherfüllung*), laid down in §§ 437, 439 BGB. The term refers to the original duty of the seller in a sales contract, the so called *Erfüllung* (performance): According to § 433 I BGB, the seller has the duty to transfer the goods free of defects. If the goods are nonetheless defective, it is deemed as a violation of this original duty. Since the original duty to perform free from defects cannot be fulfilled, the buyer can, as a consequence, only claim for supplementary performance (*Nacherfüllung*).

On a first level, §§ 433 et seq. BGB gives the buyer a prior-ranking right to supplementary performance if goods are defective. According to §§ 437, 439 BGB, the buyer can chose whether he wants the defect to be remedied (repair of the goods) or the supply of a product free of defects (replacement of goods). These duties have to be performed by the seller free of charge.

Only if the seller fails to do so or if the repair is impossible, the buyer can access the subsidiary rights to revoke the contract, §§ 437 No.1, 440 BGB, to reduce the purchase price, §§ 437 No 2, 441 BGB and to claim damages §§ 437 No.3, 440 BGB.

---

6 The official English translation of the German Civil Code (BGB) is available at the website of the Ministry of Justice and Consumer Protection: http://www.gesetze-im-internet.de/englisch_bgb/ (visited 21.03.2017).

7 E.g. Austria's *Konsumentenschutzgesetz.* Full text available in German at: https://www.ris.bka.gv.at/GeltendeFassung.wxe?Abfrage=Bundesnormen&Gesetzesnummer=10002462 (visited 21.03.2017).

8 However, e.g. in B2B contract it its possible and common practice to waive certain provisions.

9 The official translation of the German Civil Code uses the term 'cure' for supplementary performance.

The statute of limitations sets a time limit of 2 years from the time of delivery for making a claim, § 438 BGB.[10] Furthermore, the law provides for a shifted burden of proof, § 476 BGB. Therefore any lack of conformity which becomes apparent within six months of delivery of the goods is presumed to have existed at the time of delivery unless this presumption is incompatible with the nature of the goods or the nature of the lack of conformity.[11]

This provision is only applicable to B2C contracts and can be seen as a major advantage for consumers in comparison to the general principles, according to which each party has the burden of proving the facts to support its claim.

II. Commercial Guarantees (*Herstellergarantien*)

Apart from 'statutory warranties' (*gesetzliche Gewährleistung*), so called 'commercial guarantees' (*Garantien*) are very common throughout the German consumer retail market.

Commercial guarantees are mostly offered by manufacturers to consumers as a special service and buying incentive. Since seller and manufacturer are in most cases not identical, guarantees are fully independent of statutory warranties. A commercial guarantee is an autonomous contract between the consumer and the guarantor (here: the manufacturer). This happens on a voluntary (non-obligatory) basis, manufacturers are not required to give commercial guarantees under German law. If a commercial guarantee exists, a guarantee contract is typically established between the manufacturer and the consumer when the latter purchases the product.

German law only stipulates some rules on how a commercial guarantee has to look like if it is granted, e.g. the guarantor is only under obligation to provide a written document in the case of off-premises and distance contracts.[12] § 477 BGB further stipulates that a commercial guarantee has to provide a reminder of the existence of the legal guarantee.

---

10 According to § 475 III BGB this can only be reduced to one year for used goods in B2C contracts. However, in B2B contracts, the parties are free to agree on a shorter period.

11 § 476 BGB.

12 § 477 II BGB.

It should be noted that there is no legal link between the guarantee contract and the sales contract between seller and buyer.[13] A claim for repairs based on a commercial guarantee has no effect on the statutory warranty and *vice versa*. Furthermore, German law does not foresee any possibility for the consumer to make a claim against any other intermediary in the sale chain, thus, the consumer can only make a claim against the manufacturers if they offer their own commercial guarantee.

B. *Legal Obstacles*

I. No Detailed Rules, No Easy Statutory-Period System

Since the provisions about supplementary performance[14] are very general, they apply to all sale contracts. Unlike in other member states,[15] there are no precise, easy-to understand written rules about 'how' the supplementary performance has to be performed.

For example, some member states require the repairs to be done within a statutory period: The Czech Republic as well as Slovakia oblige the repair works to be performed within '30 days'.[16] This easy to remember '30 days maximum' concept can also be found in the draft for a European Sales Law.[17] In Hungarian Law, the period is laid down in a special governmental decree and normally amounts to 15 days.[18] The aim of these concepts is clear: they give the consumers some kind of orientation about how long repairs should take at the most.

In Germany, however, no statutory period exists. The system can be seen as more flexible – but also as more complicated. At first, the consumer has

---

13 Only if the seller and guarantor are identical the statutory warranty rights and commercial warranty have an effect on each other.

14 § 439 BGB.

15 For example Slovakia, the Czech Republic and Hungary.

16 Section 19 para. 3 634/1992 Sb. Zákon ze dne 16. prosince 1992 o ochraně spotřebitele (Consumer Protection Act No 634/1992 Coll.as of 16.12.1992).

17 Proposal for a Regulation of the European Parliament and of the Council on a Common European Sales Law, COM (2011) 635 final, Section 111 No 3.

18 Decree No 49/2003/GKM on the handling of guarantee and mandatory warranty claims in consumer contracts lays down that the seller shall endeavor to complete the repair or replacement within maximum 15 days.

to request supplementary performance. He can – afterwards or at the same time – set a period until the repair has to be done. This deadline set by the customer has to be 'reasonable' (*'angemessene Frist setzen'*). If the seller fails to perform the repairs within the reasonable period, the buyer can, as a consequence, withdraw from the contract. Recent legislation[19] of the German Federal Court of Justice (*Bundesgerichtshof*, hereinafter BGH) dealing with the requirements for a successful setting of a reasonable deadline has been in favor of the customer, but has created legal uncertainty. On the one hand, it is now no longer necessary for the consumer to set a specific date, on the other hand it is now less clear what the minimal requirements for successfully setting a period are.

Since this specific German prerequisite has no basis in the Customer Sales Directive, it has been disputed if this requirement is in accordance with EU Law. Recently, the Regional Court of Hannover therefore referred a dispute about this question to the European Court of Justice for a preliminary ruling.[20]

II. No Direct Manufacturer's Liability for Non-Conformity

Also, unlike German law, other legislations provide consumers with direct statutory provisions against the manufacturer in case of a defective product. In France, the *'action directe'*[21] has a long legal tradition, and also e.g. Portugal's, Spain's and Hungary's civil codes feature similar rules. The German product liability act (*Produkthaftungsgesetz 'ProdHaftG'*),[22] however, only covers liability for damage to life and limb and other things than the product itself.

---

19 BGH 12.08.2009 – VIII ZR 254/08; BGH 18.03.2015 – VIII ZR 176/14; BGH 13.07.2016 – VIII ZR 49/15.

20 LG Hannover 22.04.2016 – 17 O 43/15; *Schottelius v. Seifert*, 1 August 2016, Case C-247/16, OJ 279.

21 See *Cannarsa/Moréteau*, The French Action Directe, in: Ebers/Janssen/Meyer (eds), European Perspectives on Producers' Liability: Direct Producers' Liability for Non-conformity and the Sellers' Right of Redress, 2009, p. 311.

22 Full text available in German at: https://www.gesetze-im-internet.de/prodhaftg/ (visited 21.03.2017).

C. *Reality Check – The Consumer Protection Field Study 2012*

A study of the German Federal Consumer Agency *(Verbraucherzentrale Bundesverband)* in 2012 tried to ascertain what happens if consumers make a claim for supplementary performance.

The survey took place throughout Germany in more than 550 shops of large retailers that sell consumer products (*Media Markt, Aldi, Obi etc.*). The testers went to the shops claiming that a product, which they had bought before in that certain shop, was defective and requested the rectification or the exchange of the product. However, in almost 60% of all cases, the shop assistants rejected the claims for supplementary performance contrary to the law.

The study listed the most common reasons for rejection that were communicated to the customers: Most of the time the retailers claimed they were not liable at all and told the customers that they would have to contact the manufacturer of the product directly instead. Another reason given for rejection was that the claim had expired due to a 'claim deadline' *('Ausschlussfrist')* of two or four weeks. Sometimes, instead of supplementary performance or reimbursement, only a voucher was offered to the customers. Also, customers were told that they would always have to prove the defect by a technical report at their own expense.

None of those reasons have a legal basis, in fact they are all contrary to the law. Statutory warranties exist for all customer sales contracts no matter if a commercial guarantee is given by the manufacturer; a 'claim deadline' does not exist; customers do not have to accept vouchers and § 476 BGB shifts the burden of proof within the first 6 months.

In general, the authors of the study noted, that the shop employees acted, in most cases, very self-consciously. The testers therefore suspected that the misinformation of customers was 'systematic behavior'.

D. *(Legal) Consequences of the Findings of the Survey*

I. Consumers Do Not Know About Their Rights

The study showed that consumers who do not know precisely about their rights are regularly misinformed. Even if consumers know about the existence of their rights, they are not always aware of how to use them. And even if they do know, that does not mean they will successfully exercise their rights. One reason for this is that the dispute value is usually too low to consult legal advice. Consumer products for everyday life typically cost only a few to a few hundred Euros. Naturally, it is neither cost nor time-effective to sue the seller when the legal costs easily exceed the amount in dispute. Other ways of dispute resolution exist,[23] but are rarely relied on by German consumers. As a consequence, this can lead to non-use or loss of statutory warranty rights. The misinformed consumers might therefore pay off for the seller. It is still cheaper to settle a few number of disputes than to grant every customer his statutory rights right away.

II. Guarantees Are Not Always Better

One may ask if it is really a disadvantage for the customer if he is – due to misguidance – referring to a commercial guarantee granted by the manufacturer instead of relying on his statutory rights granted by the seller.

1. Conditions of Commercial Guarantees are Up to the Manufacturers

It is true that the customer will not even notice the difference in many cases.

However, if a commercial guarantee exists and the customer only relies on the manufacturer, he might be worse off. The main reason for this is that commercial guarantees are voluntary. As there is no law in Germany requiring manufacturers to grant guarantees to customers, the content of those guarantees is mostly up to manufacturers.

As a consequence, the duration of a commercial guarantee can be shorter than the two-year period set by the law for the use of statutory rights. Therefore, it is quite common and legal to grant only a 'one-year-guarantee' (e.g. Apple, Pioneer). Some manufacturers also use the possibility to exclude some defects, for example damages to the display glass of mobile phones, from the guarantee. It is also common to offer customers the option to extend those guarantees to two or more years. Especially if these guarantees do not exceed the conditions of the statutory rights, customers might often end up paying for guarantee-extensions they would never have bought, if they had known of the existence of their statutory warranty rights.

23 See e.g. the recent *Gesetz über die alternative Streitbeilegung in Verbrauchersachen* available in Germana at: https://www.gesetze-im-internet.de/bundesrecht/vsbg/gesamt.pdf based on Council Directive 2011/11/EU on consumer ADR.

2. Possible Loss of Rights When Relying on the Commercial Guarantee

But not only from a commercial, but also from a legal perspective there are disadvantages: most of them stem from the fact that there is no link between commercial guarantees and statutory warranties. This leads, for example, to the risk of loss of rights due to the statute of limitation. Warranty rights become time-barred after two years. When repairs are carried out during this time the limitation period is interrupted.

During guarantee repairs, however, the statute of limitation in regards to warranty rights is not suspended. If repairs are unsuccessful and / or take a long time, this can trigger a considerable negative effect.

The consumer might also risk losing the advantage of the reversed burden of proof, § 476 BGB, if he only refers to the manufacturer. Furthermore, he might have to bear extra costs since the manufacturer is not bound to the strict rules applying to sales contracts when defining the scope and the extent of his voluntary guarantee: whereas § 439 para. II BGB states that repairs have to be 'completely free of charge'[24], consumers relying on a commercial guarantee might have to pay ancillary costs, for example for de- / re-installation.

III. Current Information Duties are Too Weak

Since the study displayed a major knowledge gap between traders and their customers, one approach could be to impose duties on sellers or manufacturers to inform consumers about their rights. In fact, there are already existing duties to inform, but their scope is in most cases very limited and the remedies for non-compliance are weak.

1. Existing Information Duties

Once more, most of the duties to inform stem from European consumer laws. The Consumer Rights Directive of 2011[25] sets information require-

24 This includes ancillary costs, see *Weber v. Wittmer / Putz v. Medianess Electronics GmbH*, 16 June 2011, Joined Cases C-65/09 and C-87/09, ECLI:EU:C: 2011:396.

25 Council Directive on Consumer Rights 2011/83/EU.

ments for contracts other than distance or off-premises contracts. These provisions have been implemented into German law only recently. The most important provision in regards to statutory warranties and guarantees reads as follows:

> "Before the consumer is bound by contract … the trader shall provide the consumer with the following information in a clear and comprehensible manner, if that information is not already apparent from the context
>
> (e) … a reminder of the existence of a legal guarantee [i.e: statutory warranty] of conformity for goods, and the conditions of after-sales services and commercial guarantees, where applicable … ."[26]

It is obvious that those duties to inform the consumer are quite limited. The above cited new provision is the current maximum in terms of information duties in regards to guarantees and warranties. And even this regulation is unclear: it is hard to determine what "already apparent from the context" is supposed to mean.

2. Sanctioning Non-Compliance under Competition Law

The biggest problem remains, however, that if duties to inform are not fulfilled, no effective sanctions kick in. This is mainly due to strict separation between public and private law in Germany.

Legal non-compliance could be combated under the competition law. Unlike other countries Germany has no specific public consumer protection authority, the enforcement is mostly organized under private law.

There are no government bodies that overlook those rules and have the power to fine traders for breaking them. The government instead funds the *'Verbraucherschutzzentralen'* (consumer protection organizations), which are nonprofit organizations. Due to this fact, consumer protection organizations have only quite limited capacity to act. They can sue companies e.g. for illegal terms and conditions, but they cannot fine them directly.

---

26 Council Directive on Consumer Rights 2011/83/EU, Art. 5 I lit. e 7; German implementation: § 312 a II 1 BGB, Art. 246 I No 5 Einführungsgesetz zum Bürgerlichen Gesetzbuch (Introductory Act to the German Civil Code).

Competition law in Germany (especially the UWG[27]) prohibits unfair commercial practices, if they are capable of affecting interests of consumers.[28] Misinformation about guarantees and warranties therefore could fall under the scope of the law.[29] However, only competitors, the aforementioned consumer organizations and the chambers of commerce, but not the consumers themselves are entitled to make a claim.[30] As the misbehavior of traders happens mostly in direct private communication with the customer, chambers and associations become only aware of violations by studies, such as the field study mentioned above.

Naturally, one can argue that this does not really matter since duties to inform are unnecessary as they create administrative work and extra costs for the traders. In the end this might result in higher prices for the consumers. Detailed strict duties to enforce could therefore also 'punish' well-informed customers who would also have to bear those costs.

However, these same arguments were raised in 2002 in an early discussion about introducing the right to repairs into German Law. Yet, 16 years later, not many people would doubt that the implementation of this right into general sales law was a good idea.

Though, there are examples showing that duties to inform can work. The EU Regulation on air passenger rights[31] would not be as effective, as it is if it would not include duties to inform the passengers about their rights before the flight, at the airport and in case of delays.[32]

And even within consumer sales law role models already exist. France just recently introduced a law[33] that requires traders to inform their customers with an 'Infobox' on every distance contract with information about

27 *Gesetz gegen den unlauteren Wettbewerb* (hereinafter UWG; The Act Against Unfair Competition, English translation of the Act available at: http://www. gesetze-im-internet.de/englisch_uwg/).

28 § 3 I UWG.

29 § 5 I No 1 UWG.

30 § 8 III, § 9, § 10 I UWG.

31 Council Regulation (EC) No 261/2014 Regulation establishing common rules on compensation and assistance to passengers in the event of denied boarding and of cancellation or long delay of flights.

32 Regulation (EC) No 261/2004, Art. 14 (Obligation to inform passengers of their rights).

33 "Loi Hamond" / LOI n° 2014-344 du 17 mars 2014 relative à la consommation (1), full text available at: https://www.legifrance.gouv.fr/affichTexte.do?cidTexte=JORFTEXT000028738036&categorieLien=id (visited 21.03.2017).

their most important statutory warranty rights. Sanctions for noncompliance can go up to € 15.000. One could think about fulfilling this duty of the seller by requiring the customer to tick a box like it is already common practice in regards to the 14 days right of withdrawal for distance and off-premises contracts.

In stationary trade, mandatory posters in shops displaying the most important information in an easy-to-understand way could be a further option.

3. Judicial Remedies of the Consumer?

For consumers themselves, judicial remedies for misinformation play only a limited role. In theory, willful deceit (*arglistige Täuschung*) can entitle the buyer to cancellation of the contract[34] and damages[35]. Also, under the rules of contract law, misinformation can be seen as a breach of contract and lead to cancellation of the contract as well as damages.

In practice, consumers would face two problems in front of the court. First, there is the evidence problem. The customer has the burden of proof. When claiming for willful deceit it will be hard to prove that the trader acted deliberately. Furthermore, there is also a 'damages problem'. Under German law, a successful claim for damages restores the position that would exist if the breach of contract (e.g. the misinformation) had not occurred. That means, if the breach of contract did not result in a direct monetary disadvantage for the consumer, their claim for damages would not be successful.

E. Conclusion

Consumer protection matters and the legal framework are constantly changing. The implementation of a mandatory right to repair into German sales law can be seen as a consequence of the rapid development of consumer law in Europe. The fact that this right has gained importance within the least decades is due to the prevalence of customizable products like laptops and smart phones.

---

34 § 123 BGB.

35 § 823 II BGB in conjunction with § 263 Strafgesetzbuch (German Criminal Code).

However, the current legal situation is unsatisfying. The aim of the developments and changes resulting from new EU directives is clear, but in practice the laws do not reach what they aim for.

Customers do not know about the difference between guarantees and warranties, they are regularly misinformed, and most cases do not go to trial. The information divide between traders and consumers is obvious.

It is therefore necessary to think about reforms and improvements of the existing legal provisions in German consumer sales law.

An amendment of information requirements as well as precise statutory provisions, for example easy to remember fixed deadlines with possible exceptions, could help to improve knowledge about the legal framework. Furthermore, a specialized government body with the power to effectively sanction non-compliance could keep traders from deliberately misinforming consumers.

Bibliography

BGH 12.08.2009 – VIII ZR 254/08

BGH 18.03.2015 – VIII ZR 176/14

BGH 13.07.2016 – VIII ZR 49/15

Michel Cannarsa and Olivier Moréteau, 'The French Action Directe' in Martin Ebers, André Janssen and Olaf Meyer (eds), *European Perspectives on Producers' Liability: Direct Producers' Liability for Non-conformity and the Sellers' Right of Redress* (Sellier, Munich 2009), 31

LG Hannover 22.04.2016 – 17 O 43/15

Schottelius v. Seifert, 1 August 2016, Case C-247/16, OJ 279

Weber v. Wittmer / Putz v. Medianess Electronics GmbH, 16 June 2011, Joined Cases C-65/09 and C-87/09, ECLI:EU:C:2011:396

The Present and Future of Forced Succession in Chosen Civil Law Jurisdictions

Dorota Miler

A. *Introduction*

When regulating succession law, every legislator has the difficult but important task of balancing a testator's freedom of testation against the protection of the testator's family members' property interest in inheriting a portion of the testator's estate. Balancing these concerns is a continuous process that entails responding to new developments. As a result, even succession law, which is considerably resistant to change, has been reformed and is bound to be further changed in the future.

Freedom of testation can be defined as an individual's freedom to – according to his[1] wishes – make dispositions of his property that will be effective on his death. It is limited in a number of ways. Hereinafter, consideration is given only to limitations of that freedom which influence the final disposition of an estate by way of providing a testator's close family members with a portion of the estate.[2] The purpose of these limitations is to protect the interests of the testator's close family members. Instruments meeting these requirements can be defined as forced succession.[3]

This paper has two aims: (1) to identify the current and foreseeable trends in reforming rules of forced succession in chosen civil law jurisdictions and (2) to estimate the future shape of these limitations. To achieve the first

1 To improve readability and to avoid awkward constructions of "he or she" and "his or her", only masculine pronouns are used. When masculine pronouns are used, readers should assume a reference to the feminine gender, or to both genders, as appropriate.

2 Other instruments restricting the freedom of testation, such as formalities regarding the form, content or revocability of testamentary dispositions or the mental capacity of the testator will not be considered in this paper.

3 See *Friedman*, The Law of the Living, the Law of the Dead: Property, Succession and Society, (1966) 29 Wisconsin Law Review, p. 340 (366).

goal, three instruments (compulsory portion, reserved portion and family provisions) implemented by legislators from chosen European common and civil jurisdictions[4] are briefly introduced. This is followed by a discussion of recent reforms of forced succession, as illustrated with examples from chosen civil law jurisdictions. The discussion subsequently presents an analysis of the trends seen in current reform of the rules of reserved and compulsory portion. The paper concludes with an estimate on foreseeable developments in the reform of rules of forced succession.

B. Types of Forced Succession Rules

There is no developed legal system that provides unlimited freedom of testation.[5] In each jurisdiction there is always a claim or a right to a part of the testator's estate that is available to certain members of a testator's close family. The regulations and the forms of limitations vary between jurisdictions. Generally speaking, there are three types of limitations identifiable in European civil and common legal systems: reserved portions, compulsory portions and family provisions. The first two types of forced succession limitations can be found in civil law jurisdictions; the third one is characteristic of common law jurisdictions.

I. Reserved Portion

The first type of limitation, a reserved portion, originated in Roman law and is provided, for example, under French law (Arts. 913–917 Code civil), Italian law (Arts. 553 ff. Codice civile), Spanish law (Art. 806 Código civil)[6]

---

4 Succession law from Austria, England and Wales, France, Germany, Italy, Netherlands, Poland, Spain and Switzerland is considered for this purpose.

5 *De Waal*, Comparative Succession Law, in: Reimann/Zimmermann (eds), The Oxford Handbook of Comparative Law, 2008, p. 1071 (1080). Even in the USA, the freedom of testation has limitations, see *Scalise Rd.*, Freedom of Testation in United States, in: Zimmermann (ed), Freedom of Testation/Testierfreiheit, 2012, p. 143 (158 ff.).

6 In Spain certain territories, e.g. Catalonia or Aragón, maintain separate private law systems, including autonomous regulations on succession law. Hereinafter references are made only to the regulations included in the Código civil.

and Swiss law (Arts. 470 ff. Schweizerisches Zivilgesetzbuch). Under the laws of these countries, a certain part of the testator's estate is reserved for certain predefined relatives and cannot be effectively disposed of by a testator.[7] Therefore, the portion of the estate that a testator can dispose of, called the "disposable portion", is limited.[8] For instance, under French law a testator cannot dispose of more than ½ of his estate if he is survived by one child, more than ⅓ if he is survived by 2 children, more than ¼ if he is survived by 3 or more children (Art. 913 Code civil)[9] or more than ¾ of his estate if he has left no descendants but has a surviving spouse (Art. 916 Code civil). If a testator's testamentary dispositions exceed the disposable portion of his estate, the legacies the testator has made will, in most cases, be reduced (e.g. Art. 920 French Code civil, Art. 814 Spanish Código civil, Art. 486 Schweizerisches Zivilgesetzbuch). In most jurisdictions providing for a reserved portion, a person entitled to the portion is a testator's forced heir.[10]

II. Compulsory Portion

In jurisdictions that provide for the second type of limitation, a compulsory portion, a testator can dispose of his entire estate, but after his death, on a claim brought by a person entitled to this portion, the testator's heirs will have to pay the equivalent of a fraction of the inheritance that the person entitled to a compulsory portion would have received on intestacy (e.g. §§ 2303–2338 Bürgerliches Gesetzbuch, hereinafter BGB, §§ 756–792

7 E.g. Art. 912 French Code civil defines the reserved portion as "that part of the assets and rights of the succession whose devolution, free of charges, legislation assures to certain heirs, called forced heirs, if they are called to the succession and if they accept." An English translation of French Code civil is available at: http://lexinter.net/ENGLISH/civil_code.htm (visited 23.03.2017).

8 E.g. Art. 912 French Code civil defines the disposable portion as "that part of the assets and rights of the succession that is not reserved by legislation and of which the deceased can freely dispose by liberalities."

9 "Included under the name of children, as used in Article 913, are descendants in whatever degree, although they must be counted only for the child whose place they take in the succession of the disposing party." (Art. 913-1 Code civil).

10 E.g. in Swiss law, see *Hausheer/Aebi-Müller*, Familienerbrecht und Testierfreiheit in der Schweiz, in: Henrich/Schwab (eds), Familienerbrecht und Testierfreiheit im europäischen Vergleich, 2001, p. 213 (219).

Allgemeines bürgerliches Gesetzbuch, hereinafter ABGB, Arts. 991–1011 Polish civil code).

Under German law a testator's spouse (or registered partner), descendants and parents are, if they outlive the testator,[11] entitled to a compulsory portion equaling ½ of what would have been their intestate portion in cases where they are excluded from inheriting from the testator in his testamentary dispositions and there are assets in the estate (§ 2303 BGB).[12] The abstract right to the portion exists already during the deceased's life, but the portion itself can be demanded only after the testator's death.

III. Family Provisions

Also in common law jurisdictions, a testator's freedom is limited. The limitation, which usually falls under the heading of family provisions, prevails in common law jurisdictions, e.g. in Australian states and territories, in Canadian common law provinces and territories and in England and Wales.[13] Pursuant to the law of these jurisdictions, a testator can dispose of his entire estate through his testamentary provisions, but a court can vary these provisions subsequent to his death if it decides that the testator did not make reasonable provision for his family.[14] Therefore, unlike the limitations binding in civil law jurisdictions, the entitlement that a member of a testator's family may receive is not automatic, and receiving provision out of the testator's estate will depend on the case circumstances. Specific statutes regu-

---

11 *Heisel*, in: Dauner-Lieb/Grziwotz/Hohmann-Dennhardt, Pflichtteilsrecht. Bürgerliches Recht/Prozessrecht/Wirtschaftsrecht. Handkommentar, § 2303, para. 26. Exception: nasciturus, if born alive, see e.g. *Otte*, in: von Staudingers, Kommentar zum Bürgerlichen Gesetzbuch mit Einführungsgesetz und Nebengesetzen, Vol. V, § 2303, paras. 2, 7.

12 For brief comparison of the size of compulsory portions in different jurisdictions see *Pintens*, Tendencies in European Succession Law, in: Frantzen (ed), Inheritance Law – Challenges and Reform. A Norwegian-German Research Seminar, 2013, p. 9 (14–21).

13 Only the law of England and Wales will be further considered. For a brief summary of the history of the introduction of family provisions in England and Wales see *Meston*, Familienerbrecht und Testierfreiheit in Schottland und England, in: Henrich/Schwab (eds), Familienerbrecht und Testierfreiheit im europäischen Vergleich, 2001, p. 73 (81–82).

14 Inheritance (Provision for Family and Dependants) Act 1975, sec. 2.

late who can apply for provision and what circumstances should be considered by a court.[15]

If a court decides that reasonable financial provisions were not made for the applicant in a testator's will, or did not result on intestacy,[16] the court can depending on the applicable law order periodic payments or a lump sum payment out of any relevant property or order a transfer of the relevant property.[17]

IV. Conclusions

All three limitations serve the same purpose, i.e. they limit a testator's freedom of testation by influencing the final disposition of his assets in order to protect the interests of his close family members by providing them with a portion of the testator's estate. However, the limitations fulfill this task in substantially different ways.

The reserved and compulsory portions balance a testator's freedom of testation and the interests of his family members in the most time and cost efficient way possible, an approach that is suitable especially for large populations. They provide an actual right to receive either a part of the testator's estate or its monetary equivalent. The strict rules allow almost complete elimination of the court's involvement in determining the size and form of the provision that is due. The predictability in calculating the size of the portion is traditionally based on the rejection of any subjective factors, such as the conduct of the person entitled to the portion, his wealth or financial needs, or the quality and length of his relationship with the testator. Therefore, the extent to which a testator's freedom is limited is almost always entirely predictable. As a result, a testator's will remains unvaried and at least a part of the value of the testator's estate is disposed of in accordance with this will. Nevertheless, the solutions adopted in civil law jurisdictions can be criticized for their rigidness and inflexibility.

Under family provisions, persons listed in the relevant Act have only a claim to receive a portion of a testator's estate. A court decides whether any person who has made a claim is to receive any additional provision. In

15 Ibid., sec. 1 (1) determines who can apply under the Act. Section 3 (1) of the Act determines the circumstances a court should consider.

16 Ibid., sec. 1 (1).

17 Ibid., sec. 6 (2).

order to provide the most just outcome, a court adjusts the division of the estate on the basis of all the (subjective and objective) case circumstances that it finds relevant. If any provision is ordered, the court decides on its form and on the method of its transfer. Thus, family provisions provide flexibility, but they also create (a risk of) inconsistent outcomes from one case to the next due to strong reliance on particular case circumstances and their case-dependent evaluation. Therefore, the effectiveness of this limitation is comparably lower because it is time and resource consuming. Nevertheless, it can be appropriate for small populations. Further, due to the unlimited discretion of courts and the lack of clear, unambiguous rules, its adoption in a legal system depends on the confidence one has in the court system. The protection of testator's freedom also seems limited, if at all existent. There is, namely, no portion of a testator's estate that is safe from redistribution by a court and that will always be distributed according to the testator's will binding at the time of his death.[18] Also, there is no portion of the testator's will that cannot be rewritten in a court's order.

18 Extreme examples of the extent to which a court may exercise its discretion in imposing family provisions by varying a testator's will can be found in, for example, the case law of British Columbia. In some cases, to "make adequate provision for the proper maintenance and support of the will-maker's spouse or children", British Columbia courts have entirely changed testator's wills, ordering provision out of the testator's estate that they thought were "adequate, just and equitable in the circumstances" (Wills, Estates and Succession Act, SBC 2009, Chapter 13, sec. 60). Courts in other Canadian provinces and territories do not have such a wide discretion (see Wills, Estates and Succession: A Modern Legal Framework, (2007–2008) 27 Estates, Trusts and Pensions Journal, p. 5 (8–9) and *Miler*, Dependants' Relief Legislation and Compulsory Portion. Limitations of Freedom of Testation in British Columbia and Germany in Comparative Perspective, 2017).

C. *Examples of Recent Reforms of Rules on Forced Succession in Chosen European Countries*

Succession law has always been considered to be very stable and resistant to change.[19] This opinion might once have been true, but it can no longer be used to describe the current stage of reforms of succession law.[20]

As succession law does not have to address rapid business and economic changes, there is no apparent driving force for very quick or frequent reform of this area of law.[21] Rather, succession law must respond to the complex and varied societal transformations.[22] Therefore, although this law is undergoing constant development, because it takes place "usually in long waves and step by step, … [the] profound change may only be established after long periods when the little steps have led to something really new."[23] Two such developments, adopted over the span of the twentieth century in European countries, are the equalization of succession rights of legitimate and illegitimate children (children born out of wedlock) and the increase in the intestate inheritance rights of a deceased's surviving spouse.[24]

---

19 *Zimmermann*, The Present State of European Private Law, (2009) 57 No 2 American Journal of Comparative Law, p. 479 (504).

20 As early as 1984 Langbein observed that "[o]ver the course of the twentieth century, persistent tides of change have been lapping at the once-quiet shores of the law of succession." *Langbein*, The Nonprobate Revolution and the Future of the Law of Succession, (1984) 97 Harvard Law Review, p. 1108 (1108).

21 *Spellenberg*, Recent Developments in Succession Law, in: Blanpain (ed), Law in Motion, 1997, p. 711 (713).

22 *De Waal*, The social and economic foundations of the law of succession, (1997) Stellenbosch Law Review, p. 162 (165); *Beckert*, Familiäre Solidarität und die Pluralität moderner Lebensformen, in: Röthel (ed), Reformfragen des Pflichtteilsrechts, 2007, p. 1 (2); *van Erp*, New Developments in Succession Law, (December 2007) 11.3. Electronic Journal of Comparative Law (hereinafter EJCL), p. 1 (7).

23 *Spellenberg*, in: Blanpain, p. 711 (713); see also *Langbein*, (1984) 97 Harvard Law Review, p. 1108 (1108).

24 *Pintens*, Die Europäisierung des Erbrechts, Zeitschrift für Europäisches Privatrecht (hereinafter ZEuP) 2001, p. 628 (629); *Spellenberg*, in: Blanpain, p. 711 (720, 728–737); *Leipold*, Europa und das Erbrecht, in: Europas universale rechtsordungspolitische Aufgabe im Recht des dritten Jahrtausends: Festschriften für Alfred Söllner zum 70. Geburtstag (hereinafter FS Söllner), 2000, p. 647 (658).

Some authors take the position that succession law varies in different jurisdictions as it is "influenced by socio-cultural, socio-economic and, sometimes, religious factors."[25] It is possible that these differences are caused by the diverse legal origins of particular legal systems and rejection (or acceptance) of certain legal concepts during their development and evolution. Nevertheless, even if it cannot be denied that succession law is regulated to a greater or lesser degree in different ways in various jurisdictions,[26] some developments are common to jurisdictions of similar cultural, economic and social background, such as Austria, France, Germany, Italy, Netherlands and Spain. Identifying recent reforms made to rules of forced succession in these countries suggests potential future trends in other countries having a comparable background.

I. Reforms of the Reserved and Compulsory Portion

As a result of reforms of the reserved portion under French law, which came into force in July 2002 and on January 1, 2007, the group of people entitled to a reserved portion has changed. Since 2002, a testator's surviving spouse has become a forced heir for the first time since the enactment of the French Civil Code in 1804 (Art. 914-1 Code civil);[27] since 2007, a testator's parents are no longer entitled to a portion. Therefore, under currently binding French law, a testator is obligated to leave a certain part of his estate only to his descendants and to his spouse (Art. 916 Code civil). Further, since January 2007, a child that rejects the reserved portion is generally not counted as a forced heir (Art. 913 Code civil).[28] In that case, the disposable portion of the estate increases.

25 E.g. *van Erp*, (December 2007) 11.3. EJCL, p. 1 (1). Against: *Leipold*, in: FS Söllner, p. 647 (650–651).

26 Ibid., p. 647 (653).

27 However, the reform not only provided a surviving spouse with the reserved portion but also increased his rights to succession in intestacy, see Arts. 756–767 Code civil.

28 *Gresser*, Pflichtteilsrecht in Frankreich, in: Röthel (ed), Reformfragen des Pflichtteilsrechts, 2007, p. 227 (229). Exceptions: "A child who renounces the succession is counted among the number of children left by the deceased only if he is represented or if he is bound to collate a liberality by application of the dispositions of Article 845." (Art. 913 Code civil).

Similarly, the group of persons entitled to a reserved portion has been modified also in other jurisdictions that provide for a reserved portion. In Italy, since 1975, a reserved portion has been guaranteed for a testator's surviving spouse.[29] In Spain, a spouse is not entitled to a portion but "to the usufruct of a portion of the deceased's property" (Art. 834 Código civil).[30] In Switzerland, since January 1, 1988, reform modification has increased the disposable portion of the estate and deprived testator's siblings of a right to the portion.[31]

In some jurisdictions the form of the reserved portion was restructured. To increase legal certainty and prevent restitution of gifts,[32] under some circumstances French law provides forced heirs with a monetary claim against beneficiaries of a testator's *inter vivos* gifts (Arts. 866–867, 924 Code civil). In Spain, since 1981 and under certain situations, the forced share can be paid in cash rather than involve the transfer of property belonging to the estate of the deceased (Arts. 808, 841–847 Código civil). Moreover, under Spanish law a testator can since the reform of 2003 protect the unity of his company in the interest of his family by ordering that the company is to be inherited by a certain person and that other heirs are to receive payment of the reserved portion, which, in the case of insufficient cash, can be delayed up to five years after the testator's death (Art. 1056 Código civil).[33]

In jurisdictions providing a compulsory portion, the relevant laws have been made more flexible. Since 1969 a court in Germany has been permitted to order a delay of payment of the compulsory portion or a payment in installments. Since January 1, 2010, under the law that widened the scope of applicability of the relevant paragraph, the order can be made on a claim made by any heir (and, not as earlier, only on a claim made by an heir entitled to a compulsory portion) "if the immediate satisfaction of the entire [compulsory portion] claim would constitute an inequitable hardship for the

---

29 *Braun*, Testamentary Freedom and its Restrictions in French and Italian Law: Trends and Shifts, in: Zimmermann (ed), Freedom of Testation/Testierfreiheit, 2012, p. 57 (66 footnote 39).

30 *Vaquer*, Freedom of Testation in Spain and Catalonia, in: Zimmermann (ed), Freedom of Testation/Testierfreiheit, 2012, p. 85 (106–107).

31 *Hausheer/Aebi-Müller*, in: Henrich/Schwab, p. 213 (218).

32 *Gresser*, in: Röthel (ed), p. 227 (230).

33 *Arroyo i Amayuelas*, Pflichtteilsrecht in Spanien, in: Röthel (ed), Reformfragen des Pflichtteilsrechts, 2007, p. 257 (260).

heir" (§ 2331a BGB).[34] Under Austrian law, discretion to delay the payment of the compulsory portion is given not only to courts but also to testators. As of January 1, 2017, Austrian law provides that a testator can order in his will that a compulsory portion is to be paid in installments or that the payment should be delayed up to five years (§ 766 ABGB). However, after considering the circumstances of the heir and the person entitled to the compulsory portion, a court can change this disposition, if required, and order what is equitable under the circumstances.[35] Also, if a testator did not order the delay of payment, a court may order such delay for up to five years or, in special cases, up to ten years after the testator's death (§ 766 (3) ABGB).[36]

The grounds for completely disinheriting a person entitled to a compulsory portion have seen revisions as well. As of January 2017, a testator is able to deprive a person entitled to the compulsory portion of the portion under Austrian law if that person inflicted heavy emotional harm to the testator or grossly neglected his family obligations towards him (§ 770 No. 4).[37] The reform that came in force in 2010 in Germany revised the number of situations under which a testator is entitled to deprive a person of a portion. For instance, a testator can now disinherit a person for committing a crime against a broader circle of people, e.g. also a person not related but close to the testator (§ 2333 (1) point 1 BGB). Since January 1, 1991, in Austria a testator has the additional option of decreasing the size of the compulsory portion to be received by a person entitled to the portion on the grounds of distant family relations with this person.[38] Namely, he can deprive a person of ½ of the portion in his testamentary provisions. As of January 1, 2017, a testator is able to do that if a person entitled to the portion has failed to maintain a family relationship with the testator for

34 An English translation of the BGB is available at: https://www.gesetze-im-internet.de/englisch_bgb/ (visited 23.03.2017).

35 *Kerschbaum*, Österreich: Reform des Erbrechts, Zeitschrift für Erbrecht und Vermögensnachfolge (hereinafter ZEV) 2015, p. 575 (576).

36 *Steiner*, Reform des österreichischen Erbrechts und ihre Auswirkungen auf die deutsche kautelarjuristische Praxis, ZEV 2016, p. 131 (133).

37 Ibid., p. 131 (133).

38 Initially a testator could limit only the compulsory portion of his child, see Bundesgesetz: Erbrechtsänderungsgesetz 1989 – ErbRÄG 1989 (NR: GP XVII AB 1158 S. 125. BR: AB 3774 S. 523); *Edenfeld*, Europäische Entwicklungen im Erbrecht, ZEV 2001, p. 457 (460).

a long period of time (at least ten years)[39] (§ 776 (1), (3) ABGB) rather than, as it was introduced in 1991, for not maintaining a relationship with the testator at any time (§ 773a (1) ABGB).[40] Since 2001, a testator can exercise this right, not only with regard to his children but also with regard to any person entitled to a compulsory portion. The right is limited if the testator avoided contact with that person or if there is a justified ground for the lack of the relationship (§ 773a (2) ABGB; from January 1, 2017: § 776 (2) ABGB).[41] Reducing the compulsory portion increases the part of the value of the estate that can be freely disposed of by a testator.[42]

II. New Succession Law in Netherlands

A legal solution that could be seen as a bridge between, on one hand, reserved and compulsory portions and, on the other hand, family provisions was adopted in the Netherlands as a part of succession law in 2003. Even though the new succession law provides for a compulsory portion, it exhibits certain features of the limitation implemented in common law countries.

---

39 *Steiner*, ZEV 2016, p. 131 (132).

40 This paragraph was partially in force as § 733a ABGB before the reform in 2016. However, a testator could decrease a compulsory portion of a person entitled thereto only if they did not have a traditional family relationship at any point.

41 *Ferrari*, Familienerbrecht und Testierfreiheit in Österreich, in: Henrich/Schwab (eds), Familienerbrecht und Testierfreiheit im europäischen Vergleich, 2001, p. 173 (183).

42 The difference between what a person entitled to a compulsory portion receives after the reduction and what he would have received otherwise does not pass to other persons entitled to compulsory portions (§ 767 (2) ABGB) and cannot be demanded by descendants of a person whose compulsory portion was reduced and who has predeceased the testator (§ 767 (2) ABGB), see Rummel-ABGB /*Welser*, 2000, § 767, para. 6; *Wirner*, Erbrechtsänderungsgesetz in Österreich, Mitteilungen des Bayerischen Notarvereins, der Notarkasse und der Landesnotarkammer Bayern 1991, p. 16 (16); *Paliege*, Neues im österreichen Erbrecht, 32 Zeitschrift für Europarecht, Internationales Privatrecht und Rechtsvergleichung 1991, p. 169 (180).

This transitional character of the Dutch succession law is a result of influences of legal solutions adopted under, for example, German, Austrian, Swiss, French, English and American law.[43]

According to the new law, only a testator's descendants may make a monetary claim to a portion of a testator's estate (Art. 4:63 (2) Dutch Civil Code, hereinafter BW). A testator can weaken this right by including in his will a clause, under which "the claim of a forced heir, as far as it has to be performed (satisfied) at the expense (for account) of the spouse, will only become due and demandable (exigible) after the death of that spouse" (Art. 4:82 BW).[44] Further, a claim for the portion is not demandable with regard to assets that are encumbered with a usufruct and, if the testator's spouse is liable for paying the portion, it can be claimed only as long as the spouse is alive or not bankrupt (Art. 4:81 (3–5) BW). Nevertheless, the outcome of the application of the succession law regulations may be corrected in "extreme circumstances" by the "overreaching principle of reasonableness and fairness."[45]

The testator's spouse is not provided with a right to a compulsory portion.[46] However, the spouse has, apart from the right to use the testator's home and household effects at the expense of the estate for the first six months after testator's death (Art. 4:28 BW),[47] a right of usufruct as to the residential space and its household effects as well as potentially having

43 *Reinhartz*, Recent Changes in the Law of Succession in the Netherlands: On the Road towards a European Law of Succession?, (May 2007) 11.1 Electronic Journal of Comparative Law (hereinafter EJCL), p. 1 (10–12).

44 The same case can be made for "a disposition in favour of another life companion of the testator, provided that this other life companion maintained a joint household with the testator and that he and the testator had entered into a cohabitation agreement that is documented in a notarial deed" (Art. 4:82 BW). An English translation of BW is available at: http://www.dutchcivillaw.com/civilcodebook044.htm (visited 23.03.2017).

45 *Milo*, Acquisition of Property by Succession in Dutch Law, Tradition between Autonomy and Solidarity in a Changing Society, in: Anderson/Arroyo i Amayuelas (eds), The Law of Succession: Testamentary Freedom, 2011, p. 203 (226).

46 A surviving spouse did not have a right to a reserved portion also under the earlier succession law, see *Fischer*, Reform des Erbrechts im Niederländischen "Burgerlijk Wetboek", 1976, p. 63–64.

47 All other "persons who lived in a joint household with the deceased up until his death" have the same right (Art. 4:28 (2) BW).

a usufruct right in other property "as far as the spouse, considering all circumstances, is in need of (the provision of) care and support"[48] (Arts. 4:29–4:30 BW). A testator's spouse is entitled thereto, as far as he requests it, if he does not "become the sole proprietor of a residential space in which that spouse, up until the death of the deceased, lived alone or together with the deceased, which residential space now belongs to the deceased's estate" (Art. 4:29 (1) BW). The same applies to the household effects (Art. 4:29 (1) BW). For the first six months, during which the testator's spouse may apply for establishing the usufructs, the testator's heirs' right to dispose of the estate is limited (Art. 4:29 (2) BW). Further, "[u]pon the request of the spouse of the deceased, the heirs must cooperate in establishing a usufruct on behalf of that spouse on other assets of the deceased's estate … , as far as the spouse, considering all circumstances, is in need of (the provision of) care and support" and if there are no other means available to him (Art. 4:30 (1) BW).[49] Dutch law does not limit this right to any part of testator's estate; thus, as a result, a usufruct can be ordered on the testator's entire estate.[50] Further, as decided in 2007 by the Dutch Supreme Court, all the relevant circumstances must be considered by a court when assessing the need for support.[51] A spouse is not afforded the rights provided in Arts. 4:29–4:30 BW only "when an application for a divorce or legal separation was lodged in court at least one year prior to the devolvement of the deceased's estate and the divorce or legal separation could not be effectuated as a result of the death of the deceased" (Art. 4:32 BW).[52]

Also, as far as it is necessary, a testator's child who is not yet eighteen years of age can apply for a lump sum that will cover expenses for his care

48 *Kolkman*, Freedom of Testation in the Netherlands, in: Zimmermann (ed), Freedom of Testation/Testierfreiheit, 2012, p. 25 (40–41). This right of the surviving spouse is seen as fairly problematic, see: *van Erp*, The New Dutch Law of Succession, in: Reid/de Waal/Zimmermann (eds), Exploring the Law of Succession: Studies National, Historical and Comparative, 2007, p. 193 (198–202).

49 *Milo*, in: Anderson/Arroyo i Amayuelas, p. 203 (225).

50 A testator's heirs are limited in their distribution of the estate during the time that the spouse may claim the right to usufructs (Art. 4:29 (2) BW).

51 Dutch Supreme Court 8.06.2007, LJN BA2507; See *Kolkman*, in: Zimmermann, p. 25 (41).

52 This holds unless "the [surviving] spouse is not mainly to blame for the circumstances which caused that the divorce or legal separation could not be effectuated within the applicable period prior to the devolvement of the deceased's estate" (Art. 4:32 BW).

and upbringing and, until he becomes twenty-one years of age, also for maintenance and education (Art. 4:35 (1) BW). As this provision is supposed to provide for a child only in financially necessitous circumstances, this right cannot be exercised by a child for whom a testator's heir or spouse is obligated to provide for (Art. 4:35 (2) BW). A testator's child may apply for compensation for long-term work performed for the testator that has economic value (Art. 4:36 BW).[53] The size of the lump sum in this case depends on what is fair in context of the family relationship.[54] Nevertheless, a maximum of ½ of the testator's estate can be disposed of to provide lump sums to his children (Art. 4:37 (4) BW).

Additionally, a court has the power to order that "assets which were subservient to the professional practice or business of the deceased" be transferred "for a reasonable and fair price to that child or stepchild or to the spouse of this child or stepchild because ... [a testator's] child or stepchild or ... spouse shall continue the professional practice or business of the deceased" (Art. 4:38 (1) BW). The proprietor of the estate cannot be "harmed seriously as a result" of this transfer (Art. 4:38 (1) BW).[55]

Even though the succession law adopted in 2003 creates a significant contrast with other succession law regulations in European continental jurisdictions, some solutions are not new to Dutch succession law. For example, children were already considered forced heirs under the legislation adopted in 1838, and in the 1960s legislators developed the solution that gave the grounds for limiting a testator's children rights to a testator's estate

53 *Kolkman*, in: Zimmermann, p. 25 (47–48).

54 Ibid., p. 25 (48).

55 "The ... paragraph applies accordingly to stocks and shares in a limited liability corporation (*'Naamloze Vennootschap'*) or in a private limited company (*'Besloten Vennootschap'*) of which the deceased was the director and in which he, alone or together with the other directors, held the majority of the shares, provided that the child or stepchild or the spouse of this child or stepchild, at the time of death of the deceased, already was a director of that corporation or company or that this child or stepchild or this spouse takes over the deceased's position of director in that corporation or company" (Art. 4:38 (2) BW).

until the testator's surviving spouse's death, bankruptcy or remarriage.[56] A testator's parents were forced heirs only until 1996.[57]

III. Conclusions

Recent reforms regarding rules of forced succession in chosen European civil law jurisdictions show that there is a tendency to adopt laws that change the original character of the limitations. In the case of a reserved portion, some of the features traditionally associated with this limitation, e.g. the weak position of a surviving spouse or the inadmissibility of monetary equivalents for the reserved portion under any circumstances, are not as strong as they used to be. In jurisdictions providing for a compulsory portion, the rigidness of this portion was weakened by introducing exceptions, under which, for instance, a court or even a testator may postpone the payment of the portion.

Seen from a long-term perspective, it is possible that the number of differences between the different limitations will further decrease. The recent reforms of the reserved portion show that the portion has a growing number of similarities with the compulsory portion. This holds true, for instance, in the case of providing a monetary equivalent of the reserved portion.

As legislators from civil law jurisdictions adopt solutions well-known in common law jurisdictions, the differences in how a testator's freedom of testation is limited – by means of forced succession – are becoming noticeably less pronounced as between civil and common law jurisdictions. Dutch succession law supplies the highest number of examples of regulations that seem to be borrowed from common law jurisdictions, allowing, for instance, a court to interfere with strict succession law regulations on the basis of the general clause of 'reasonableness and fairness'. But also in other civil law jurisdictions, we can identify new laws that increase the testator's freedom of testation and the courts' discretion in ordering a portion, as well as

---

56 *Milo*, in: Anderson/Arroyo i Amayuelas, p. 203 (212–213); *Reinhartz*, (May 2007) 11.1 EJCL, p. 1 (2–3); *Breemhaar*, Familiäre Bindung und Testierfreiheit im neuen niederländischen Erbrecht, in: Henrich/Schwab (eds), Familienerbrecht und Testierfreiheit im europäischen Vergleich, 2001, p. 147 (168 footnote 29).

57 *Reinhartz*, (May 2007) 11.1 EJCL, p. 1 (9); *Pintens*, Pflichtteilsrecht in Belgien und in den Niederlanden, in: Röthel (ed), Reformfragen des Pflichtteilsrechts, 2007, p. 215 (219).

laws decreasing the rights of a testator's children. Nevertheless, the limitations adopted in common law jurisdictions and in civil law jurisdictions are still essentially different.

D. *Specific Trends in the Reform of the Reserved and Compulsory Portion*

I. Increasing the Testator's Freedom of Testation

The recent reforms of rules of forced succession in chosen European civil law jurisdictions have increased a testator's freedom of testation in a number of ways.[58]

The freedom of testation is increased by limiting the number of groups of people who can apply for a reserved or compulsory portion.[59] French as well as Dutch law no longer prescribes a portion for the testator's parents. In none of the discussed jurisdictions are a testator's siblings provided with a right to a portion. This trend benefits the testator because, in a growing number of jurisdictions, if he is not survived by a child or spouse, he is free to decide on the disposition of his entire estate.

The latest reform of the Austrian succession law provides a solution that grants a testator limited discretion to decide when and how a compulsory portion should be paid. Similarly, a testator under Dutch law can delay the payment of a compulsory portion until the death of his surviving spouse. Historically, this was regulated exclusively by law, or, under very specific and limited circumstances, it could be decided by a court. Providing a testator with this new power increases the control he has over the final distribution of his estate and, most of all, allows him to better protect his surviving spouse from claims of persons entitled to a portion.

Also, increasing the number of situations under which a testator can disinherit a person entitled to a portion increases the testator's testamentary

58 Some scholars claim that even though the freedom of testation is increasing in civil law jurisdiction, an opposite trend can be identified in common law jurisdictions, see *Spellenberg*, in: Blanpain, p. 711 (737–738).

59 See also *Pintens*, Grundgedanken und Perspektiven einer Europäisierung des Familien- und Erbrechts – Teil 2, Zeitschrift für das gesamte Familienrecht (hereinafter FamRZ) 2003, p. 417 (418).

freedom.[60] Allowing a testator under Austrian law to decrease the compulsory portion to half of its value, in the event a person entitled to the portion did not maintain a family relationship with the testator for a long period of time, is a novelty in civil law jurisdictions. The most popular solutions, adopted for example under German and Austrian law, amount to expanding the list of circumstances under which a person can be completely deprived of the compulsory portion. Every additional circumstance that allows a testator to deprive a person of the portion enlarges the testator's freedom by giving him another chance to escape the rigid regulations of the compulsory or reserved portion.

Thus, the existence of a trend to increase a testator's freedom of testation is generally recognized.[61] It is even argued that there has been a shift and that a testator's estate is no longer seen as a family estate.[62]

II. Weakening the Position of Persons Entitled to a Portion

Allowing a testator or a court to delay the payment of a compulsory portion or to change the payment of a lump sum to payment in installments has weakened the rights of persons entitled to compulsory portion. The trend to reduce the strength of the position of persons entitled to a portion can also be identified in jurisdictions providing for a reserved portion. In these jurisdictions, as it has been acknowledged in academic literature, there is a tendency to replace a right to a share in goods belonging to the estate with a claim for a monetary payment.[63] And in the Netherlands, introducing a compulsory portion in place of a reserved portion has aimed at weakening the position of persons entitled to the portion.[64] This idea was grounded in the thought that testators usually have good reasons for not leaving a portion of their estate to a specific person and, therefore, their decision should be

---

60 See also ibid., p. 417 (424).

61 E.g. *Braun*, in: Zimmermann, p. 57 (83); *Vaquer*, in: Zimmermann, p. 85 (121).

62 E.g. *Spellenberg*, in: Blanpain, p. 711 (726).

63 *Van Erp*, (December 2007) 11.3 EJCL, p. 1 (12); *Pintens*, FamRZ 2003, p. 417 (423); *Pintens*, ZEuP 2001, p. 628 (642); *Pintens*, Need and Opportunity of Convergence in European Succession Laws, in: Anderson/Arroyo i Amayuelas (eds), The Law of Succession: Testamentary Freedom, 2011, p. 3 (16); *Leipold*, in: FS Söllner, p. 647 (659).

64 *Breemhaar*, in: Henrich/Schwab, p. 147 (168).

respected.[65] But a compulsory portion is provided under the new Dutch law, because there was a fear that eliminating the portion completely could lead to the unequal treatment of children by a testator.[66]

III. Strengthening the Position of a Testator's Spouse

The most significant improvement of the legal position of a testator's surviving spouse (or civil or registered partner) has been adopted in civil law jurisdictions providing for reserved portion.[67] In these jurisdictions, the most recent reforms have guaranteed the surviving spouse a right to a portion or to the usufruct of a portion of a testator's estate. Also in jurisdictions that grant a compulsory portion, the testator's surviving spouse has a strong position. For example, under Dutch law, not only is a surviving spouse provided with a claim to usufruct that can be established even on the testator's entire estate, but the payment of the compulsory portion can also be postponed until his death. Such extensive rights provide a safety net for the spouse and aim, for example, at allowing the testator's surviving spouse to enjoy the same living standard he had during the testator's life.[68] It is possible that in the case of small estates, the entire estate can be depleted during the surviving spouse's life and, therefore, the right of the testator's children to a compulsory portion might be purely theoretical. The tendency to favour the surviving spouse over the children of the deceased is commonly agreed

---

65 *Pintens*, in: Röthel, p. 215 (216–217).

66 *Breemhaar*, in: Henrich/Schwab, p. 147 (169).

67 The slow increase in the succession rights held by surviving cohabitants has been discussed e.g. by *Kroppenberg*, Should the Surviving Cohabitant Be Given Hereditary Rights to the Estate of the Deceased? A European quest, in: Frantzen (ed), Inheritance Law – Challenges and Reform. A Norwegian-German Research Seminar, 2013, p. 73 (76–81).

68 *Breemhaar*, in: Henrich/Schwab, p. 147 (167); *Mincke*, Einführung in das niederländische Recht, 2002, p. 170.

upon.[69] Some scholars explain this development by arguing that the testator's spouse is no longer seen as a stranger to the testator's family but as a contributor to the growth of the family's assets.[70]

IV. Increasing Courts' Discretion in Determining a Portion

The tendency to provide courts with wider discretion with regard to the time and form of payment of a portion is identifiable in jurisdictions providing a compulsory portion. Under specific circumstances, e.g. in Austria and Germany, courts can modify the outcome of the application of the statutory provisions if the situation of a testator's heir requires it. This discretion is not as far reaching as the discretion of courts in common law jurisdictions, but it allows courts to, at least to some extent, make the rigid rules more flexible.

E. Foreseeable Developments in the Reform of Rules of Forced Succession

I. New Limitation

On the basis of trends that can be deduced from recent reforms that have taken place in civil law jurisdictions, a new type of rules of forced succession can be predicted.

Recent reforms in civil law jurisdictions allow for the prediction that it is likely that the classic division of the estate, between the part that is always disposed of according to the testator's will and the part that can be demanded by the testator's family members in nature or in the form of a monetary equivalent, will gradually be rejected. It will be replaced by a tripartite division of the testator's estate. The first part will be comparable to the present compulsory portion or, alternatively, a reserved portion, but which at

---

69 *Pintens*, ZEuP 2001, p. 628 (629, 642); *de Waal*, in: Reimann/Zimmermann, p. 1071 (1078); *Pintens*, in: Anderson/Arroyo i Amayuelas, p. 3 (16); *van Erp*, (December 2007) 11.3 EJCL, p. 1 (7, 11).

70 Ibid., p. 1 (7); *Dutta*, The Legal Protection of the Surviving Spouse – German Law in Comparative Perspective, in: Frantzen (ed), Inheritance Law – Challenges and Reform. A Norwegian-German Research Seminar, 2013, p. 35 (35, 38–41).

least under certain circumstances will be paid in cash (this development is already present in jurisdictions providing for a reserved portion). The second part will be a portion on which a court will be able to establish usufructs or to distribute so as to provide additional support for members of the testator's family in need of extra provisions from the testator's estate. That can be deduced not only on the basis of the law applicable in Netherlands but also, for instance, in view of the law allowing a German court to delay payment of the compulsory portion or to make payment in installments on account of an heir's financial circumstances. The third part will be, as is the case now, disposed of according to the testator's will.

It is not possible to predict how large each part will be. It is likely that the size of both the part disposable freely by the testator and the part guaranteed to members of his family in the form of a compulsory or reserved portion will be affected as a result of establishing the part distributed by a court to testator's family members in need. However, it cannot be excluded that, as can happen under the current Dutch succession law, the entire part of the testator's estate that would normally be disposed of according to the testator's will, will at least temporarily be used to provide for the needs of his family member(s). Determining the size of this portion could be more predictable if it were correlated with the relevant family provisions regulating spousal and / or child support. However, the size of the portion could further increase due to the fact that, unlike in the case of divorce, a testator does not need any of his assets after his death.

Considering the legislation adopted in the Netherlands and the reforms depriving a testator's parents or siblings of the right to a fixed share, one can assume that the extra provision will be extended to persons belonging to testator's close family (his spouse and children) that might be in need at the time of his death. At least at this stage, the making of additional provisions by a court to benefit persons who deserve to be rewarded for their behavior towards the testator cannot be predicted.

It is probable that an increase in a court's discretion over the division of the estate would go along with increasing the number of circumstances under which a testator can foreclose members of his family from inheriting from him. That can be assumed on the basis of the recent reforms extending the grounds for depriving a person of a compulsory portion in civil law jurisdictions.

Replacing a reserved or compulsory portion by pure safety net provisions is rather unlikely in the foreseeable future. The right to a certain portion of the testator's estate is based on the legal relation between the testator and his spouse or children. The testator's solidarity with the members of his close family requires him to provide for them and to continue to care for them after his death, even though it is often argued that this is no longer necessary due to the enhancement of life expectancy.[71] There is a long tradition of leaving at least part of the testator's assets to his family by providing a fixed portion of the testator's estate to certain members of the testator's close family.[72] Equal distribution of the compulsory or reserved portion between testator's descendants guarantees equal treatment of the children at least to some extent.[73]

Adopting the proposed solution would limit the rigidness and inflexibility of the limitations imposed in civil law jurisdictions without completely depriving the final distribution of its predictability.

Even though there are no signs that legislators in common law jurisdictions intend to introduce a compulsory or reserved portion, the above-described solution could also be advisable in their jurisdictions. Implementing a solution that divides an estate into three parts in common law jurisdictions would provide a testator with a more limited freedom of testation, but it would also prevent courts from infringing upon his freedom and changing his decisions as to the disposable portion. At a minimum, consideration should be given to introducing a legislative guarantee that would provide a testator with a certain significant part of his estate (e.g. ½ thereof) that could not be redistributed by a court.

II. Gradual Unification of Rules of Forced Succession

Further reforms of the rules of forced succession are to be expected. As there is a clear tendency to adopt legal solutions borrowed from other jurisdictions,[74] more comparative research and legal transplants in this area of succession law are also to be expected. It is also likely that jurisdictions will continue to adopt and take advantage of solutions reached by other jurisdic-

71 See *Pintens*, in: Anderson/Arroyo i Amayuelas, p. 3 (12–13).
72 See ibid., p. 3 (12–16).
73 *Edenfeld*, ZEV 2001, p. 457 (460).
74 *Pintens*, Grundgedanken und Perspektiven einer Europäisierung des Familien- und Erbrechts – Teil 1, FamRZ 2003, p. 329 (331).

tions having comparable social and familial developments.[75] However, if a spontaneous complete convergence of the limitations of testator's freedom imposing forced succession is to ever take place, it will be a rather slow process.

It is highly unlikely that in the near future there will be a complete unification of the rules of forced succession in civil law jurisdictions or in civil and common law jurisdictions. The discrepancies between the different types of limitations are too significant to be overcome without a deliberate policy aiming to unify them. However, such a harmonization "from above" is also unlikely because countries have "sovereignty-based concerns and see the harmonization of this area as encroachment upon their sovereignty."[76] Even though it is an oversimplification to say that national succession law is grounded in "local rules, customs, moral values, and cultural conventions,"[77] succession law seems to be looked upon as belonging to "the legal 'lifeblood' of a national culture and does not easily lend itself to comparative study, let alone to legal harmonization or unification",[78] behaving as if it were "a part of a country's cultural heritage."[79]

Bibliography

Esther Arroyo i Amayuelas, 'Pflichtteilsrecht in Spanien' in Anne Röthel (ed), *Reformfragen des Pflichtteilsrechts* (Carl Heymanns Verlag, 2007), 257

---

75 *De Waal*, in: Reimann/Zimmermann, p. 1071 (1075); *Pintens*, FamRZ 2003, p. 417 (424); *Terner*, Perspective of a European Law of Succession, (2007) 2 Maastricht Journal of European and Comparative Law (hereinafter MJ), p. 147 (151 footnote 17, 160). See *Vaquer*, Wills, Divorce and the Fate of the Dispositions in Favour of the Spouse: A Common Trend in European Laws of Succession, (2003) 6 European Review of Private Law, p. 782 (782 ff.).

76 *Gray*, Identifying the Impetus behind the Europeanization of the Private International Law Rules on Family Matters and Succession, (2015) 17 European Journal of Law Reform, p. 341 (350).

77 *De Waal*, in: Reimann/Zimmermann, p. 1071 (1076); see also *Henrich*, Parteiautonomie, Privatautonomie und kulturelle Identität, in: Festschrift für Erik Jayme, 2004, p. 321 (321–322).

78 *Zimmermann*, (2009) 2 American Journal of Comparative Law, p. 479 (504–505); *Milo*, in: Anderson/Arroyo i Amayuelas, p. 203 (207).

79 *De Waal*, in: Reimann/Zimmermann, p. 1071 (1073). For a discussion of the possibility of unifying succession law in Europe see *Kuchinke*, Über die Notwendigkeit, ein gemeineuropäisches Familien- und Erbrecht zu schaffen, in: FS Söllner, p. 589. See also *Terner*, (2007) 2 MJ, p. 147 (160).

Jens Beckert, 'Familiäre Solidarität und die Pluralität moderner Lebensformen' in Anne Röthel (ed), *Reformfragen des Pflichtteilsrechts* (Carl Heymanns Verlag, 2007), 1

Alexandra Braun, 'Testamentary Freedom and its Restrictions in French and Italian Law: Trends and Shifts' in Reinhard Zimmermann (ed), *Freedom of Testation / Testierfreiheit* (Mohr Siebeck, 2012), 57

Willem Breemhaar, 'Familiäre Bindung und Testierfreiheit im neuen niederländischen Erbrecht' in Dieter Henrich and Dieter Schwab (eds), *Familienerbrecht und Testierfreiheit im europäischen Vergleich* (Verlag Ernst und Werner Gieseking, Bielefeld 2001), 147

Barbara Dauner-Lieb, Herbert Grziwotz and Christine Hohmann-Dennhardt (eds) *Pflichtteilsrecht. Bürgerliches Recht / Prozessrecht / Wirtschaftsrecht. Handkommentar* (Nomos, Baden-Baden 2010)

Marius J. de Waal, 'The social and economic foundations of the law of succession' (1997) Stellenbosch Law Review, 162

Marius J. de Waal, 'Comparative Succession Law' in Mathias Reimann and Reinhard Zimmermann (eds), *The Oxford Handbook of Comparative Law* (Oxford University Press, 2008), 1071

Anatol Dutta, 'The Legal Protection of the Surviving Spouse – German Law in Comparative Perspective' in Torstein Frantzen (ed), *Inheritance Law – Challenges and Reform. A Norwegian-German Research Seminar* (Berliner Wissenschafts-Verlag, 2013), 35

Stefan Edenfeld, Europäische Entwicklungen im Erbrecht, Zeitschrift für Erbrecht und Vermögensnachfolge 2001, 457

Susanne Ferrari, 'Familienerbrecht und Testierfreiheit in Österreich' in Dieter Henrich and Dieter Schwab (eds), *Familienerbrecht und Testierfreiheit im europäischen Vergleich* (Verlag Ernst und Werner Gieseking, Bielefeld 2001) 173

Bernd Fischer, *Reform des Erbrechts im Niederländischen "Burgerlijk Wetboek"* (1976)

Lawrence M. Friedman, 'The Law of the Living, the Law of the Dead: Property, Succession and Society' (1966) 29 Wisconsin Law Review, 340

Jacqueline Gray, 'Identifying the Impetus behind the Europeanization of the Private International Law Rules on Family Matters and Succession' (2015) 17 European Journal of Law Reform, 341

Edmond Gresser, 'Pflichtteilsrecht in Frankreich' in Anne Röthel (ed), *Reformfragen des Pflichtteilsrechts* (Carl Heymanns Verlag, 2007), 227

Heinz Hausheer and Regina Aebi-Müller, 'Familienerbrecht und Testierfreiheit in der Schweiz' in Dieter Henrich and Dieter Schwab (eds), *Familienerbrecht und Testierfreiheit im europäischen Vergleich* (Verlag Ernst und Werner Gieseking, Bielefeld 2001), 213

Dieter Henrich, 'Parteiautonomie, Privatautonomie und kulturelle Identität' in Heinz P Mansel, Thomas Pfeiffer, Herbert Kronke, Christian Kohler and Rainer Hausmann (eds), *Festschrift für Erik Jayme* (Sellier European Law Publishers, 2004), 321

Sonja Kerschbaum, Österreich: Reform des Erbrechts, Zeitschrift für Erbrecht und Vermögensnachfolge 2015, 575

Wilbert D. Kolkman, 'Freedom of Testation in the Netherlands' in Reinhard Zimmermann (ed), *Freedom of Testation / Testierfreiheit* (Mohr Siebeck, 2012), 25

Inge Kroppenberg, 'Should the Surviving Cohabitant Be Given Hereditary Rights to the Estate of the Deceased? A European quest' in Torstein Frantzen (ed), *Inheritance Law – Challenges and Reform. A Norwegian-German Research Seminar* (Berliner Wissenschafts-Verlag, 2013), 73

Kurt Kuchinke, 'Über die Notwendigkeit, ein gemeineuropäisches Familien- und Erbrecht zu schaffen' in Gerhard Köbler, Meinhard Heinze and Wolfgang Hromadka (eds), *Europas universale rechtsordungspolitische Aufgabe im Recht des dritten Jahrtausends: Festschriften für Alfred Söllner zum 70. Geburtstag* (C.H. Beck, München 2000), 589

John H. Langbein, 'The Nonprobate Revolution and the Future of the Law of Succession' (1984) 97 Harvard Law Review, 1108

Dieter Leipold, 'Europa und das Erbrecht' in Gerhard Köbler, Meinhard Heinze and Wolfgang Hromadka (eds), *Europas universale rechtsordungspolitische Aufgabe im Recht des dritten Jahrtausends: Festschriften für Alfred Söllner zum 70. Geburtstag* (C.H. Beck, München 2000), 647

Michael Meston, 'Familienerbrecht und Testierfreiheit in Schottland und England' in Dieter Henrich and Dieter Schwab (eds), *Familienerbrecht und Testierfreiheit im europäischen Vergleich* (Verlag Ernst und Werner Gieseking, Bielefeld 2001), 73

Dorota Miler, *Dependants' Relief Legislation and Compulsory Portion. Limitations of Freedom of Testation in British Columbia and Germany in Comparative Perspective* (Mohr Siebeck, Tübingen 2017)

J. Michael Milo, 'Acquisition of Property by Succession in Dutch Law, Tradition between Autonomy and Solidarity in a Changing Society' in M. Anderson and E. Arroyo I Amayuelas (eds), *The Law of Succession: Testamentary Freedom* (European Law Publishing, 2011), 203

Wolfgang Mincke, *Einführung in das niederländische Recht* (2002)

Sylvia Paliege, Neues im österreichen Erbrecht, 32 Zeitschrift für Europarecht, Internationales Privatrecht und Rechtsvergleichung 1991, 169

Walter Pintens, Die Europäisierung des Erbrechts, Zeitschrift für Europäisches Privatrecht 2001, 628

Walter Pintens, Grundgedanken und Perspektiven einer Europäisierung des Familien- und Erbrechts – Teil 1, Zeitschrift für das gesamte Familienrecht 2003, 329

Walter Pintens, Grundgedanken und Perspektiven einer Europäisierung des Familien- und Erbrechts – Teil 2, Zeitschrift für das gesamte Familienrecht 2003, 417

Walter Pintens, 'Need and Opportunity of Convergence in European Succession Laws' in M. Anderson and E. Arroyo I Amayuelas (eds), *The Law of Succession: Testamentary Freedom* (European Law Publishing, 2011), 3

Walter Pintens, 'Tendencies in European Succession Law' in Torstein Frantzen (ed), *Inheritance Law – Challenges and Reform. A Norwegian-German Research Seminar* (Berliner Wissenschafts-Verlag, 2013), 9

Walter Pintens, 'Pflichtteilsrecht in Belgien und in den Niederlanden' in Anne Röthel (ed), *Reformfragen des Pflichtteilsrechts* (Carl Heymanns Verlag, 2007), 215

B.E. Reinhartz, 'Recent Changes in the Law of Succession in the Netherlands: On the Road towards a European Law of Succession?' (May 2007) 11.1 Electronic Journal of Comparative Law, 1

Rummel-ABGB (3rd Edition, MANZ Verlag, Wien 2000)

Ronald J. Scalise Rd., 'Freedom of Testation in United States' in Reinhard Zimmermann (ed), *Freedom of Testation / Testierfreiheit* (Mohr Siebeck, 2012), 143

Ulrich Spellenberg, 'Recent Developments in Succession Law' in Roger Blanpain (ed), *Law in Motion* (Kluwer Law International, Hague 1997), 711

Anton Steiner, Reform des österreichischen Erbrechts und ihre Auswirkungen auf die deutsche kautelarjuristische Praxis, Zeitschrift für Erbrecht und Vermögensnachfolge 2016, 131.

Julius von Staudingers, *Kommentar zum Bürgerlichen Gesetzbuch mit Einführungsgesetz und Nebengesetzen*, Book V, Erbrecht, §§ 2303–2345, Pflichtteil, Erbunwürdigkeit (Sellier – de Gruyter, Berlin 2015)

Paul Terner, 'Perspective of a European Law of Succession' (2007) 2 Maastricht Journal of European and Comparative Law, 147

Sjef van Erp, 'New Developments in Succession Law' (December 2007) 11.3 Electronic Journal of Comparative Law, 1

Sjef van Erp, 'The New Dutch Law of Succession' in Kenneth G C Reid, Marius J de Waal and Reinhard Zimmermann (eds), *Exploring the Law of Succession: Studies National, Historical and Comparative* (Edinburgh University Press, 2007), 193

Antoni Vaquer, 'Freedom of Testation in Spain and Catalonia' in Reinhard Zimmermann (ed), *Freedom of Testation / Testierfreiheit* (Mohr Siebeck, 2012), 85

Antoni Vaquer, 'Wills, Divorce and the Fate of the Dispositions in Favour of the Spouse: A Common Trend in European Laws of Succession' (2003) 6 European Review of Private Law, 782

'Wills, Estates and Succession: A Modern Legal Framework' (2007–2008) 27 Estates, Trusts and Pensions Journal, 5

Helmut Wirner, Erbrechtsänderungsgesetz in Österreich, Mitteilungen des Bayerischen Notarvereins, der Notarkasse und der Landesnotarkammer Bayern 1991, 16

Reinhard Zimmermann, 'The Present State of European Private Law' (2009) 57 (2) American Journal of Comparative Law, 479

Equal v. Fair: Considering Goodwill in the Division of Matrimonial Property

Oleh Prostybozhenko

A. Introduction

Over the course of history the family law regulations have come a long way from allowing one to buy a wife like an object to securing the interests of a 'weaker' spouse. Considering the constant growth of the number of the marital breakdowns and the development of new institutions (e.g., same-sex unions or partnerships) the concept of family law has evolved into a remedial set of regulations aimed at protecting the weaker family member or even at considering marriage as a quasi-legal entity.

Over the past decades there have been significant changes in economic and social relations. Property is no longer the universal measure of wealth. In modern society 'investment in personality' and 'human capital' are becoming increasingly important in legal regulations. However, legislators have been and often still are under the strong Roman law impact regardless of the development in modern law concept of so-called 'unconventional' or 'irregular' civil right objects.

This paper examines a situation where, for instance, a 50-year-old woman, who ran household and cared for children during a marriage, can obtain, after divorce, for few years (often a period for getting education and / or professional skills) some maintenance from her former spouse and the half of the marital property (including liabilities). Divorce usually leaves the supported spouse in a much worse economic position than the educated and employed spouse. It is obvious that the supported spouse does not have equal opportunities compared to her / his former spouse who has pursued a career during the marriage. Furthermore, not all matrimonial assets can be divided due to their nature. Does equality that was struggled for a few centuries always mean fairness?

The aim of the paper is to analyse present regulations of spousal property relationship in European jurisdictions from the historical point of view and to propose their improvement from the perspective of fairness. To achieve this goal, ideas and concepts of marriage and spousal property relations existing in Ancient Rome and their evolution under modern family legislations during the 19th and 20th centuries will be investigated.

B. *Historical overview*

I. Roman Law Background

The law of property under Roman law was very broad and comprised the law of all matters not included in persons or actions. It dealt with the wide divisions or classifications of property. It included personal rights in property or rights arising from obligations. The name given in general to all sorts of property and to property rights was *'res'*. It was a broader term than modern English words 'thing' or 'property'.[1] Roman law distinguished things tangible (*'res corporales'*) and intangible (*'res incorporales'*).[2] Later, in the law of pandects the property comprised active assets (as valuable rights belonging to person) and passive ones (as set of person's obligations).[3]

In family law the Romans distinguished two types of marriage. The first was marriage where the husband had power over his wife (*'matrimonium cum manu'*), and the second was marriage without such power (*'matrimonium sine manu'*).[4] Spousal property relations depended on type of marriage. In the first case the wife's property came into the ownership of her husband, while in another one a husband had no rights at all to the property of his wife, who could acquire property the same way as if unmarried, i.e. in her own name.

---

1 *Burdick*, The Principles of Roman Law and Their Relation to Modern Law, 2007, p. 298–299.

2 *Franciosi*, Corso istituzionale di Diritto Romano, 1997, § 12.

3 *Ulyanishchev*, Basis of Roman Law, chapter 7, available at: http://web-local.rudn.ru/web-local/prep/rj/files.php?f=pf3ad905c46bbc7998501fa839e67 46a44 (visited 26.04.2017).

4 In fact, man's power under a woman (*'manus'*) and marriage were separate institutions in Roman law and appearance of such man's power was not determined only by marriage. However, for this paper it does not matter (see, e.g., *Franciosi*, 1997, §§ 37, 40).

There was, however, another kind of property brought, usually, by the wife to the family. This was the wife's dowry (*'dos'*) which was her contribution to the household expenses. Over the course of Roman law history the dowry was first in the sole ownership of the husband; in the Justinian law it was recognized as the wife's property under her husband's administration.[5] The husband in turn made a marital gift to his wife (*'donatio'*). Similar to the dowry the donation belonged to the wife but the husband had the control of it.[6]

Thus, Roman law did not acknowledge concepts of any spouses' community property and consequently spouse's claim for division of community property. It was open for a spouse to sue another spouse to vindicate property that belonged to him / her.[7]

II. Qualitatively New Changes in the Late 18th – 19th Centuries

Starting in the late 18th century, and throughout the 19th century, rights, as a concept and claim, gained increasing political, social, and philosophical importance in Europe. Change of economic formation and fast economic growth, ebbing of the church's influence on family relationships, development of liberty ideals, women's rights movement and struggle for gender equality, civil law codifications and other social and economic changes during the 19th and 20th centuries led to the number of great changes in legal regulation, both property relations and family intercourse.

During the 19th century the concept of civil turnover's object changed compared to previous periods, but not the Roman law. If before corporeal things had been the main objects of civil rights, then throughout the 19th and 20th centuries intangible 'things' got a new life as the objects of civil law regulation. In contrast with the Roman law, the incorporeal 'things' did not become the ownership objects (that are mainly corporeal things). They are partly subjects of intellectual property rights. Other intangible objects are regulated within the law of obligation, i.e. right of demand (or right of claim) arose from contract or civil delict (tort).

---

5 See more *Franciosi*, 1997, § 43; *Łukasiewicz*, Sytuacja majątkowa małżonków w prawie rzymskim antycznym, (2008) 18 Roczniki Nauk Prawnych, p. 157 (157–171).

6 See *Burdick*, 2007, p. 226–231.

7 See, e.g., *Franciosi*, 1997, § 43; *Berger*, Encyclopedic Dictionary of Roman Law, 2008, p. 766.

By the 19th century only the concept of Roman law doctrine of the wife's subordination to the authority of her husband survived. The Roman marriage *sine manu* was forgotten. Similar to the marriage *cum manu* in Romans, in the United Kingdom any assets made by a woman became the property of her husband. Furthermore, the identity of the wife became legally absorbed into her husband, effectively making them one person under the law. It was the reflection to the doctrine of 'coverture', i.e. spouses were considered one legal entity represented by a husband.[8]

The doctrine of 'marital power' was cultivated in continental Europe. Under this doctrine, a wife was legally a minor under the guardianship of her husband, i.e. a wife did not enjoy the full legal capacity.[9] Unlike the Roman and English law, in civil law countries a husband did not become the owner of his wife's property. The new concept of community of property (later called universal community) as a matrimonial regime was developed. Commonly, all spouses' pre-marital property, including debts, and all the property acquired while married, regardless of title, was consolidated into joint property mass under the husband's management. This matrimonial regime derived from Spanish middle age law[10] and was unified during the 19th century alongside civil law codifications in European countries.[11] At the same time, the Roman law concepts of dowry and marital gift (donation) remained in many legislations (e.g., §§ 1218, 1230, 1232 of Austrian Civil Code) as a guarantee of spousal maintenance.

The women's rights movements of the late 19th century addressed a wide range of issues, including wife's property rights. Consequently, a wife gained some liberty from her husband's authority and limited rights in property relationships, especially rights to work or to have an independent profession and, as a result, to dispose her earnings without her husband's agree-

---

8 See *Ablow*, 'One Flesh', One Person, and the 1870 Married Women's Property Act, in: Felluga (ed), BRANCH: Britain, Representation and Nineteenth-Century History at: http://www.branchcollective.org (visited 22.03.2017); *Combs*, "A Measure of Legal Independence": The 1870 Married Women's Property Act and the Portfolio Allocations of British Wives, (2005) 65 The Journal of Economic History, p. 1028 (1028–1057); *Stone*, The Status of Women in Great Britain, (1972) 20 The American Journal of Comparative Law, p. 592 (592–621).

9 *Goonesekere*, Women's Rights and Children's Rights: the United Nations Conventions as Compatible and Complementary International Treaties, 1992, p. 2.

10 See *Stuntz*, Hers, His, and Theirs: Community Property Law in Spain and Early Texas, 2005.

11 See *Lee*, An Introduction to Roman-Dutch Law, 1946, p. 64–68.

ment, to administer her personal or / and separate property, to inherit property in her own name, to conclude contracts to meet her own needs and day-to-day family needs, as well as to maintain her children herself and, accordingly, to be debtor or defendant in court. A wife's property also became protected from her husband's creditors (see, e.g., the UK Married Women's Property Acts of 1870 and 1882).

Thus, it was not a true fight for equality, but only a fight for freedom from a husband's power. One more achievement from this period is the legally stipulated permission to divorce, although generally only by reason of a spouse's fault. It determined two significant developments: (1) unequal division of matrimonial property in favour of an offended spouse and (2) maintenance of an innocent party by a guilty spouse. Despite the increased legal protection for wives, the doctrines of 'coverture' and 'marital power' still survived. A wife had no right to manage community property or to represent marriage union. A husband was declared head of family and a wife generally must follow him everywhere as well as obey her husband. It is worth noting that at this stage the issue of marital property division was not of primary importance.

III. Family Law Tendencies in the 20th Century

After World War I new changes were inspired by liberal ideals of liberty and the women's liberation movement. This resulted in rapid and radical reform of the family law with the main ideas of equality between the spouses, their independence, and, consequently, the abolition of the husband's guardianship, the principle of separate property, introducing an obligation for maintenance etc.

Due to the influence of the Roman law, legal doctrine and women's rights movement saw the ideal of woman's liberty in a marriage *sine manu* that caused a separate property regime of spouses. However, normative equalization of spouses through the introduction of a separate property system in the Russian Empire and later in the Soviet Union failed to provide the expected results. At that time there were no economic and social conditions which could enable implementation of normative equality in spousal property relations. Formal equalization regarding matrimonial property and mutual independence of spouses in a separate property system put woman into a *de facto* unfair position.[12] Consequently, a new concept of the limited community of property based on the principle of spousal equality and emancipation was introduced in the family codes of 1926 in Soviet Ukraine and Russia.[13] It was the first time a wife obtained equal rights in common property. But the main difference between the Soviet and the European community of property was in the scope of application. The Soviet approach to the community of property as compared to the European one excludes 'premarital' assets as well as property acquired in a marriage by inheritance, donation or gift that are the separate property of each spouse.

The problem of inequality was also, almost at the same time, being resolved in another part of Europe by introducing a deferred community of property which was first developed in the Nordic countries as a result of legal co-operation in 1920s. In matrimonial property relations this reform was supposed to give the wife, who was normally the housekeeper / homemaker, a claim to share the husband's eventual wealth through her right to marital property. Accordingly, the previous regime that was based on the principle of community of property with the husband's guardianship over his wife has been replaced.[14]

Under the influence of the Soviet Union, the Eastern European states (i.e. Poland, Hungary, Czechoslovakia, Yugoslavia, Romania, Bulgaria and Albania) introduced the limited community of property after World War II. Almost all Western European states of the community of property system (i.e. France, Spain, Portugal, Italy, Belgium, Luxembourg and Malta) also adapted the Soviet approach regarding the scope of the community of property. At the same time, matrimonial regimes similar to the deferred community of property, were later introduced in Germany, Switzerland, Greece and Cyprus.

Family law reforms have also focus on the development of a spousal support relationship. New ideas of post-marital support as an allowance based

12 *Antokolskaia*, Harmonisation of Family Law in Europe: A Historical Perspective. A Tale of Two Millennia, 2006, p. 240; *Bradley*, Convergence in Family Law: Mirrors, Transplants and Political Economy, (2001) Oxford University Comparative Law Forum, available at: http://ouclf.iuscomp.org (visited 22.03. 2017).

13 The full title of the code in case of Ukraine is 'Code on Family, Guardianship, Marriage and Acts of Civil Status', in case of Russia – 'Code on Marriage, Family and Guardianship'.

14 *Jäntera-Jareborg*, Marriage Dissolution and Maintenance to a Spouse Following Divorce: Sweden, in: Sibylle/Schwab/Henrich (eds), Scheidung und nachehelicher Unterhalt im europäischen Vergleich, 2003, p. 277 (278–289).

on need has been highlighted. This approach extended in the European states during the whole century. For example, Soviet Russia introduced an ex-spouse's maintenance in case of disability or need in 1918 whereas Switzerland only in 1998. By the same token, the sex of the spouse was deemed irrelevant for the purposes of alimony.

The common goal of the aforementioned reforms of family law was to ensure the economical protection of the weaker spouse, i.e. women, in cases of divorce or termination of marriage. The intention was to equalize the position of women and men in the traditional sense of marriage with a male breadwinner and a female housewife, which was common at that time. A common feature of these reforms is the recognition of the value of indirect contributions with regard to the acquisition and division of marital property. The principle of equal sharing between spouses regardless of the type of contribution is the general rule, not only in contemporary civil law jurisdictions. It also seems to be in use in the present common law jurisdictions.[15] Accordingly, indirect contributions appear to be the essence of the justification.[16]

A clear majority of European states abolished remaining clauses on inequality of spouses until the late 20th century (e.g., Greece in 1983, Switzerland in 1984, France in 1985).

---

15 A wide discretionary power is vested in courts to 'adjust' the property rights of spouses by reference to a requirement for fairness, i.e. the court has authority to redistribute a separate property of each spouse. See more *Svedrup*, Maintenance as a Separate Issue – The Relationship Between Maintenance and Matrimonial Property, in: Boele-Woelki (ed), Common Core and Better Law in European Family Law, 2005, p. 122 (122–126).

16 See *Rešetar*, Matrimonial Property in Europe: A Link between Sociology and Family Law, (2008) 12.3 Electronic Journal of Comparative Law.

C. Current Legal Regulation

I. Notion of Goodwill

Goodwill is a controversial notion in civil law because of its economic essence.[17] Black's Law Dictionary provides the definition as a business's reputation, patronage, and other intangible assets that are considered when appraising the business, especially for purchase; the ability to earn income in excess of the income that would be expected from the business viewed as a mere collection of assets. By the same token, some courts have stated that the difference between goodwill and other elements of going-concern value (i.e. the value of a commercial enterprise's assets or of the enterprise itself as an active business with future earning power) is merely technical and that it is unimportant to separate these intangibles.[18]

Despite goodwill is illiquid according to general rule, it inheres limited transferability. The most typical example of goodwill's transfer is where the principal, franchisor or supplier has access to lists of clients and other similar data either because the commercial agent, franchisee or distributor has provided these lists after the termination of the relationship or because the principal, franchisor or supplier otherwise has access to such data (e.g. because the commercial agent, franchisee or distributor has regularly passed such information on to the principal, franchisor or supplier during the relationship).[19]

An attempt of comprehension of legal regulation related to goodwill has been made in the norm IV.E.-2:305 (Indemnity for goodwill) of the Principles, Definitions and Model Rules of European Private Law, Draft Common Frame of Reference. The general idea supposes entitling a party of a contract to an indemnity from the other party for goodwill if the first party has significantly increased the other party's volume of business and the latter continues to derive substantial benefits from that business. Irrespective of grounds or ways in which the contract ended, the mere fact that the contractual relationship comes to an end may lead to a transfer of goodwill. Goodwill has its own value which must be differentiated from the expectated

17 *Penner*, The Idea of Property in Law, 2000, p. 109–110; *Malaurie/Aynés*, Les biens, 2007, p. 62–67.

18 *Garner* (ed), Black's Law Dictionary, 2009, p. 763–764.

19 *von Bar/Clive/Schulte-Nölke* (eds), Principles, Definitions and Model Rules of European Private Law. Draft Common Frame of Reference (DCFR), 2009, p. 2336.

interest under the contract. Therefore, it should always be refunded irrespective of the way the contractual relationship ended. Indemnity for the clientele does not depend on any sort of fault.

During the late 19th and 20th centuries a new concept of personal (individual, professional) goodwill was developed. It is goodwill attributable to an individual's skills, knowledge, efforts, training, or reputation in making a business successful.[20] Since goodwill related to a legal entity, in principle, can be calculated,[21] there is a difficulty in case of personal goodwill, especially when a person does not possess an enterprise as a separate object of civil transactions. The most complicated issues of personal goodwill are career assets that supposedly confer on a person some positive effect in the future due to his or her education, qualification, and licence for profession, etc.[22] There is the belief that personal goodwill has no value on its own because of its inalienability from a person.[23]

Consequently, goodwill is the intangible asset that has its own economic value and limited transferability. It may be inherent in a legal entity or a natural person involved in an individual professional activity. For the purpose of this paper goodwill means the favour or advantage that a person or a business controlled by a person has acquired especially owing to a number of factors, including education, knowledge, skills, contact network, intellectual property, branding, and good reputation. Depending on circumstances, goodwill may be estimated or not (primary to personal). Finally, only goodwill gained in time of validity of the matrimonial property regime should be taken into consideration.

---

20 *Garner*, 2009, p. 764; *Malaurie/Aynés*, 2007, p. 62–63.

21 There are number of methods to valuate goodwill which depend on such factors as an essence of business, earning history, perspective income, combining with similar business, market value and other. However, uniform approach does not exist. Typically, goodwill's amount appraises as difference between business's value and cost of its other tangible and intangible assets.

22 *Weitzman*, The Divorce Revolution: The Unexpected Social and Economic Consequences for Women and Children in America, 1985, p. 110.

23 *Rosen*, Note: A Critical Analysis of Celebrity Careers as Property upon Dissolution of Marriage, (1993) 61 The George Washington Law Review, p. 522 (545–548); *Wildman*, Casenotes & Comments: Professional Goodwill as Divisible Community Property: How Should Idaho Approach the Issue?, (1994) 30 Idaho Law Review, p. 825 (826–850); *Povarov*, Enterprise as Object of Civil Rights: PhD thesis, 2000, p. 110.

II. Matrimonial Property Relations: Scope and Subjects

Matrimonial property relations comprise spouses' intercourses arising in connection with (1) matrimonial property regime and (2) spousal support (alimony). Matrimonial property regime is a set of rules that regulate property relations between spouses themselves and relate to third parties. Similar to the late Roman law the subjects of the spouses' property regime usually comprise assets (active) and obligations (passive) (see, e.g., Arts. 1401–1428 of French Civil Code).

The modern legislators are strongly influenced by Roman law concepts related to the objects of civil circulation. Therefore, the terms 'property' or 'asset' mean rights in property belonging to persons, rights arising from obligations, i.e. rights to demand, as well as rights in incorporeal values. Only valuable and transferable property is an independent object of civil transactions. Accordingly values which are inalienable from person may not be the objects. For example, similar to Roman law the Civil Code of France discerns corporeal and incorporeal property. As it follows from the implications of the rules of Articles 537, 1607, 1689–1700 of French Civil Code, the only incorporeal property that is alienable by contract or transfer may be the object.[24] It seems a similar approach takes place in Germany.[25]

It should be emphasized that some differences exist between the post-socialist and the Western European approaches to a nature and a scope of the community of property regime. Legislations of the post-socialist states almost always describe matrimonial community of property as joint ownership of spouses. Even the new Czech Civil Code does not diverge (see, e.g., § 712). Consequently, the scope of the community of property regime depends on the objects of ownership right in certain states and may comprise only corporeal things (e.g., Art. 21 of Family Code of Bulgaria[26]) or also

24 *Malaurie/Aynés*, 2007, p. 6–7, 14, 17–18, 56–64; *Terré/Simler*, Droit civil. Les biens, 2006, p. 48–50.

25 *von Enneccerus*, Lehrbuch des Burgerlichen Rechts I, 1931, p. 58–61, § 124; *McGuire*, National Report on the Transfer of Movables in Germany, in: Faber/Lurger (eds), National Reports on the Transfer of Movables in Europe, 2011, p. 1 (10–14).

26 *Mateeva*, Family Law of the Republic of Bulgaria. Extended Lectures on the New Family Code, 2010, p. 117; *Petkova*, Regimes of Property Relations between Spouses according to the Bulgarian Family Law, (2011) 7 Acta Universitatis Danubius. Juridica, p. 100 (103–106).

alienable rights having a monetary value (e.g., Art. 190 of Civil Code of Ukraine). Other assets are usually beyond the scope of matrimonial property. Instead the Western European approach inheres the exclusive rules concerning the matrimonial property relationship, i.e. other mechanisms of property law, such as joint ownership, do not play any role in relations between spouses.[27]

Subject of the ex-spousal maintenance is an obligation of a former spouse to provide support for his or her former spouse in case of insufficient resources to meet his or her needs. It is the main prerequisite in all modern legislations (see, e.g., § 1569 of German Civil Code, Art. 271 of French Civil Code, Art. 75 of Family Code of Ukraine). Marital misconduct also is a matter in the Western European jurisdictions.

There is a difference between German and French approaches to the concept of post-marital maintenance. The German one is based on the principle of marital solidarity lasting even after divorce,[28] while the French approach provides special compensatory allowance that changes a spouses' mutual duty of financial support expired after divorce.[29] Under the German concept ex-spousal support might be determined by caring for a common child, illness, disability, retirement, lack of own earnings etc. As a general rule, in the last case the post-marital maintenance is limited by time to ensure a recipient-spouse an opportunity to obtain or improve education and / or professional skill to meet the needs by himself or herself (see §§ 1573–1575 of German Civil Code). The maintenance is usually paid in fixed periodical payments (see § 1585 of German Civil Code). Instead, in accordance with the French approach primary economic factors are taken into consideration (see Art. 271 of French Civil Code) and the support has to be paid in lump (capital) sum (see Art. 270 of French Civil Code).

Being influenced by Soviet law, the post-socialist approach to ex-spousal alimony supposes depending, on the one hand, on the justified needs of a recipient-spouse and, on the other, the economic and earning ability of a spouse obliged to pay the maintenance (see, e.g., Art. 133 of Polish Family and Guardianship Code, Art. 75 of Family Code of Ukraine). The

27 *Prostybozhenko*, Joint, Solidary and Community Obligations: Approaches to Spouses' Liability for Debts in the European States, in: Vojčik/Filičko/Kolomház (eds), Košické dni súkromného práva I, 2016, p. 237 (239–242).

28 *Martiny/Schwab*, Grounds for Divorce and Maintenance Between Former Spouses. National report: Germany, 2002, p. 23.

29 *Ferrad*, Grounds for Divorce and Maintenance Between Former Spouses. National report: France, 2002, p. 31–33.

amount of maintenance rarely exceeded the minimum living standards and was never intended to ensure the lifestyle which a recipient-spouse had enjoyed before the divorce. At the same time, in the Western European states, maintenance is constructed in order to compensate for, as far as possible, the disparity between the spouses' living conditions resulting from the divorce (see, e.g., Art. 270 of French Civil Code, § 1578 of German Civil Code, Art. 97 of Spanish Civil Code).

D. *How to Consider Goodwill?*

Due to its limited transferability, goodwill is not the separate object of matrimonial property division. It seems that considering goodwill of legal entity, is not complicated in principle. In such case, a business, i.e. company or even enterprise, should be evaluated and then taken into account by a court while distributing marital property. Thus, general rules of certain states are to be applied.

Personal goodwill cannot be divided like other assets. For the purpose of this paper, all matrimonial regimes of European states may be classified in two groups. The first one supposes the division or redistribution of marital property, i.e. means claim *in rem*, after a termination of matrimonial regime (e.g., France, Poland, England), whereas the second one is intended to entitle a spouse to claim for compensation *in personam* (e.g., Germany, Greece). Consideration of personal goodwill is quite possible according to the rules of the second group of matrimonial regimes. For this goal, current legislation is to be amended by a relevant clause on the evaluation of goodwill as a part of marital assets. Even changing the approach of the doctrine and judiciary may be sufficient. It seems that the main obstruction will be connected to the estimation of personal goodwill. It will be possible to do so by applying the approach of 'history income' or 'market value'.

Within the first group of the matrimonial regimes, the above-mentioned approach is inappropriate. In some poor way the legislators reflect elements of goodwill in the maintenance relationship of former spouses. A court usually considers a debtor-spouse's employment ability and property status while awarding alimony in favor of a weaker spouse. However, considering goodwill within the post-marital maintenance relations defeats its purpose because prerequisites for alimony are the needs of an ex-spouse. In principle, maintenance is limited in time and usually expires in case of new marriage of a spouse-recipient. Furthermore, since division of matrimonial property is taken for granted, claim for support is often perceived as assaulting the dignity of a spouse-recipient. The reason is alimony derived from the husband's duty to provide financial support for his wife is therefore a reflection of inequality between spouses, i.e. the alimony is symbolic of a husband's power over his wife. Instead, in case of goodwill, the first role is played by unrealized reasonable expectations of a spouse who supports the family during the other's professional education and career building.

Taking into account that individual goodwill has economic value that is inalienable from a person and cannot be considered in the frame of the post-marital maintenance relationship, a new claim for compensation *in personam* should be elaborated. This legal instrument should be deprived of any ties with alimony regulation and be enshrined within the matrimonial property regime in order to emphasise its essence. French and Spanish legislators were closest to this idea by modelling their system of compensation after divorce and breaking with the idea of spousal duty of financial support after divorce. German legislator was also not far from the idea while establishing the equalisation of the pension aragements between divorced spouse. The aforementioned approaches might be applied to calculate goodwill.

Another less preferable, but quite possible as a transitional remedy, especially in post-socialist states, might be to depart from the rule of spouses' equal shares in community property. In such case, the shares of each spouse will fall within a court's discretion and will depend on certain circumstances. It will be a simplified procedure and it appears that the valuation of goodwill will be determined by a judge in such manner as deemed appropriate.

Finally, the right to claim for goodwill has to be determined by several factors. These include a marriage's duration, a spouses' expenses to make elements of goodwill, the extent to which a spouse has maintained a household and engaged in childcare, received earnings, etc.

E. Conclusions

The positions of each family member and family functions overall have significantly evolved over the past centuries. Completely rightless women have now gained not only full legal capacity, but a place in society. Gender does not matter, men and women have become legally equal and today the marriage union is considered a partnership with shared duties.

The Roman marriage and wife's status *sine manu* that were declared as ideal, have demonstrated their inviability in spousal property relationships since there were no economic and social conditions. It has led to the further development of matrimonial community of property and the invention of new regimes that have been designed to ensure property equalization between spouses. Moreover, new institutions of spousal maintenance have been constituted.

Modern legislation is no longer constructed in light of women's rights protection. It is assumed that gender equality has appeared in the administration and division of matrimonial property as well as in the award of alimony, irrespective of gender. In modern society, 'investment in personality' and 'human capital' might be more valuable than corporeals. However, primary tangible objects and some intangible, but transferable ones are considered during the division of the matrimonial property between spouses. Goodwill is beyond the scope of consideration due to being partially alienable. Considering individual goodwill in the frame of a post-marital maintenance relationships is inappropriate.

Thus, the ruling principle of equality in current family law regulation lies in providing future spouses with the equal possibility to receive an education and make a career, thus allowing the weaker ex-spouse to obtain knowledge and / or professional skills to maintain himself or herself. In practice, reasonable expectations of such weaker spouse to receive advantages from a lucrative career of his or her marriage partner are not taken into consideration.

Further development of family law in the property field has to be aimed at the invention of remedies in favour of a weaker spouse to consider goodwill and other similar values. The ruling principle, therefore, must now be changed. It is time to give the preference for fairness over equality within distribution of spouses' assets. It seems that a new claim for compensation for goodwill has to be provided within the regulation of the matrimonial property regime. Finally, the development of civil law needs to adapt so called 'non-conventional objects' to civil law approaches.

Bibliography

Rachel Ablow, ''One Flesh', One Person, and the 1870 Married Women's Property Act' in Dino Franco Felluga (ed), *BRANCH: Britain, Representation and Nineteenth-Century History*, at: http://www.branchcollective.org/?ps_articles=rachel-ablow-one-flesh-one-person-and-the-1870-married-womens-property-act (visited 22.03.2017)

Masha Antokolskaia, *Harmonisation of Family Law in Europe: A Historical Perspective. A Tale of Two Millennia* (European Family Law Series, Intersentia, Antwerp – Oxford 2006)

Adolf Berger, *Encyclopedic Dictionary of Roman Law* (17th Printing, The Lawbook Exchange, Clark, New Jersey 2008)

David Bradley, 'Convergence in Family Law: Mirrors, Transplants and Political Economy' (2001) Oxford University Comparative Law Forum, at: http://ouclf.iuscomp.org/articles/bradley.shtml (visited 22.03.2017)

William L. Burdick, *The Principles of Roman Law and Their Relation to Modern Law* (3rd Printing, The Lawbook Exchange, Clark, New Jersey 2007)

Mary Beth Combs, '"A Measure of Legal Independence": The 1870 Married Women's Property Act and the Portfolio Allocations of British Wives' (2005) 65 The Journal of Economic History, 1028

Ludwig von Enneccerus, *Lehrbuch des Burgerlichen Rechts I* (Russian translation, printed in Moscow 1950, 13th Edition, Marburg 1931)

Frédérique Ferrad, *Grounds for Divorce and Maintenance Between Former Spouses. National report: France* (2002), at: http://ceflonline.net/wp-content/uploads/ France-Divorce.pdf (visited 30.04.2016)

Gennaro Franciosi, *Corso istituzionale di Diritto Romano* (2nd Edition, G. Giappichelli Editore, Torino 1997)

Bryan A. Garner (ed), *Black's Law Dictionary* (9th Edition, Thomson Reuters, 2009)

Savitri Goonesekere, *Women's Rights and Children's Rights: the United Nations Conventions as Compatible and Complementary International Treaties*, Innocenti Occasional Papers (Florence 1992)

Maarit Jäntera-Jareborg, 'Marriage Dissolution and Maintenance to a Spouse Following Divorce: Sweden' in Sibylle Hofer, Dieter Schwab and Dieter Henrich, *Scheidung und nachehelicher Unterhalt im europäischen Vergleich* (Gieseking Verlag, Bielefeld 2003), 277

Robert W. Lee, An *Introduction to Roman-Dutch Law* (4th Edition, Clarendon Press, Oxford 1946)

Jakub M. Łukasiewicz, 'Sytuacja majątkowa małżonków w prawie rzymskim antycznym' [Property Position of Spouses in Ancient Roman Law] (2008) 18 Roczniki Nauk Prawnych, 157

Philippe Malaurie and Laurent Aynés, *Les biens* (3rd Edition, Defrénois, Paris 2007).

Dieter Martiny and Dieter Schwab, 'Grounds for Divorce and Maintenance Between Former Spouses. National report: Germany' (2002), at: http://ceflonline.net/wp-content/uploads/Germany-Divorce.pdf (visited 30.04.2016)

Ekaterina Mateeva, *Family Law of the Republic of Bulgaria. Extended Lectures on the New Family Code* (2009) (in Bulgarian, VSU "Chernorizets Hrabyr", Sofia 2010)

Mary-Rose McGuire, 'National Report on the Transfer of Movables in Germany' in Wolfgang Faber and Brigitta Lurger (eds), *National Reports on the Transfer of Movables in Europe*, Vol. 3 (Sellier, European Law Publishers, Munich 2011), 1

James Penner, *The Idea of Property in Law* (Oxford University Press, London 2000)

Tsvetalina Petkova, 'Regimes of Property Relations between Spouses according to the Bulgarian Family Law' (2011) 7 Acta Universitatis Danubius. Juridica, 100

Yurii Povarov, *Enterprise as Object of Civil Rights: PhD thesis* (in Russian, Samara State University, Samara 2000)

'Principles, Definitions and Model Rules of European Private Law. Draft Common Frame of Reference (DCFR)' [Comentary. Edited by Christian von Bar, Eric Clive and Hans Schulte-Nölke] (2009), at http://ec.europa.eu/justice/contract/files/european-private-law_en.pdf (visited 25.02.2016)

Oleh Prostybozhenko, 'Joint, Solidary and Community Obligations: Approaches to Spouses' Liability for Debts in the European States' in P. Vojčik, V. Filičko and P. Kolomház (eds), *Košické dni súkromného práva I* (Univerzita Pavla Jozefa Šafárika v Košiciach, Košice 2016), 237

Branka Rešetar, 'Matrimonial Property in Europe: A Link between Sociology and Family Law' (2008) 12.3 Electronic Journal of Comparative Law

Robin P. Rosen, 'Note: A Critical Analysis of Celebrity Careers as Property upon Dissolution of Marriage' (1993) 61 The George Washington Law Review, 522

Olive M. Stone, 'The Status of Women in Great Britain' (1972) 20 The American Journal of Comparative Law, 592

Jean A. Stuntz, *Hers, His, and Theirs: Community Property Law in Spain and Early Texas* (Tech University Press, Texas 2005)

Tone Svedrup, 'Maintenance as a Separate Issue – The Relationship Between Maintenance and Matrimonial Property' in Katharina Boele-Woelki (ed), *Common Core and Better Law in European Family Law* (Intersentia, Antwerp – Oxford 2005), 122

François Terré and Philippe Simler, *Droit civil. Les biens* (7th Edition, Dalloz, Paris 2006)

Viktor Ulyanishchev, *Basis of Roman Law* (in Russian), at: http://web-local.rudn.ru/web-local/prep/rj/files.php?f=pf_3ad905c46bbc7998501fa839e6746a44 (visited 26.04.2017)

Leonore J. Weitzman, *The Divorce Revolution: The Unexpected Social and Economic Consequences for Women and Children in America* (The Free Press, New York 1985)

Erich J. Wildman, 'Casenotes & Comments: Professional Goodwill as Divisible Community Property: How Should Idaho Approach the Issue?' (1994) 30 Idaho Law Review, 825

A Critical Review of Iranian's New Imprisonment Policy Regarding Convicted Debtors

Mehri Barzegar

A. *Introduction*

Convicted debtors are those whose debts have been established by the competent court. The source of the debt might be a civil or criminal complaint (excluding fines and monetary penalties where the state is the real creditor and in which case the following process does not apply), and the most important matter regarding these debts is providing the creditor with an effective process to satisfy his demand. Thus, in these instances there are two significant parties: the creditor, who has completed all of the legal procedures to establish his claim, and the debtor, who should pay what is due. As seems apparent, in cases where the latter party has sufficient assets, the case will be resolved very easily. But in practice most debtors do not seem to have enough assets. Here, the challenging task becomes determining whether they are actually unable to pay the amount due because of inadequate assets (as opposed to merely feigning impoverishment); and relatedly, in the event of a well-grounded claim, the issue is helping the creditor to obtain satisfaction.

Although such tasks may seem unproblematic at first glance, it has always proved a challenge under Iranian law, especially due to low formal information about the real assets that a citizen possesses.

In order to expand the view of this problem, I will briefly explore the historical background of this issue in respect of both its legal and social dimensions. Then I will deal with the new imprisonment policy adopted by the Iranian legislature in 2015. I will address the positive and negative points and possible consequences of this legislation and end by proposing some suggestions.

B. Background

To some, it may seem strange to imprison debtors (until either payment is made or effective arrangements for payment are established or the creditor forgave debts) since jail is mainly a place in which criminals and not debtors are kept. It is therefore helpful to take a look at the historical and legislative context of the matter.

I. Legal Background

Providing suitable means to guarantee the payment of debts has always been a concern of Iranian lawmakers. The first legislation that provided for imprisoning debtors, titled "The Act of Accelerating Trials", was enacted in 1930. Later in 1934 "Insolvency Act" was enacted, providing some procedures allowing debtors who did not own sufficient assets to demonstrate their claim before court. This Act separated ordinary people from businessmen and specified that the process would not be applicable to the latter group. The act did not point out to prison as a resort and most of its articles were applicable until the enactment of "The New Act on Debt Convictions" (2015).

Over the years, different regulations have reflected the challenging paradox of, on one hand, respecting the rights of the prevailing creditor and, on the other, wanting to avoid imprisonment of the debtor.

"The Act on Debt Convictions" of 1972 permitted the imprisonment of condemned debtors with regard to monetary penalties or civil damages ordered as a consequence of committing an offence. In 1973 this Act was revoked by a single-article Act which prohibited all manner of imprisonment as a consequence of debt, except for monetary penalties and in cases where the debtor committed fraud in reporting his assets to the authorities.

Probably due to lack of effectiveness, prison again became the center of attention of the Iranian legislature, and finally, under the "Act on Debt Convictions" (1998),[1] prison was widely accepted for debts derived both from

---

1 It should be observed that there are three acts titled "The Act on Debt Convictions" in the history of Iranian legislation, each one having a different date of enactment. As we will see in the following pages, this article focuses primarily on "The New Act on Debt Convictions" enacted in 2015.

civil and criminal complaints. It will be helpful at this point to briefly review this Act since, as I will discuss later, it played a key role in ensuring the payment of debtors' financial obligations in Iran.

This Act, which included only seven articles, dealt both with the imprisonment of those who were convicted to pay a fine (monetary penalty) and the imprisonment of debtors. Article 2 specifically addressed the latter group and allowed their imprisonment, provided that the court did not find any assets belonging to them and the creditor demanded imprisonment. In terms of what items could be seized and sold in satisfaction of a debt, clear exceptions were established concerning goods which were essential for the debtor's life; additionally, the debtor had the right to file an insolvency action which would be dealt with faster than the usual process (Article 3).

Under Article 4, those who tried to transfer their possessions to others, with the aim of creating a pretense of being impoverished, committed an offence punishable by imprisonment for a period of four to twenty-four months.

This Act, being applicable for more than seventeen years in Iran, had social consequences which will be delved into in the next section.

II. Social Background

As mentioned, the dilemma of insuring the payback of debts has always been a controversial issue in Iran. On the one hand, there are jurists who cite human rights and, specifically, Article 11 of the International Convention on Civil and Political Rights, which states: "No one shall be imprisoned merely on the ground of inability to fulfill a contractual obligation." They point out that Iran joined this Convention in 1975 and, pursuant to Article 9 of Civil Code (1928), regulations which are enacted between Iran and other states under the Constitution are a part of domestic law and therefore must be obeyed as well. There are also theorists and criminologists who are alarmed about the overpopulation of the jails and the negative influences of imprisonment on one's later social life. On the other hand, it seems like there are not enough measures to ensure the payment of debts and that prison, as the last and most effective option, represents an appealing solution.

Practically, it takes a long time before most civil cases will be decided by courts and come into force. A defendant who knows he will be found liable by the court and who has no effective defense will try to defer the action brought against him, hoping that the plaintiff will abandon the process. There are a few (if any) defendant-debtors who willingly submit an asset or pay their debts without compulsion. It should also be considered that there are limited official methods for ascertaining an individual's assets, particularly considering the fact that under "The Act on Debt Convictions" (1998), which was applicable for more than seventeen years in Iran, the court and official authorities had no duty to help the creditor locate assets belonging to the debtor; it is easily understandable that creditors looked upon the sanction of prison as a means of realizing their financial demands. As an attorney who has worked on several cases in Iran, I can assert that such sanction almost always proved to be efficient in ending the dispute, specifically in cases in which the amount at stake was not very high and the debtor had the means of paying it.

However, it is undeniable that such a process sent many people to jail despite not having committed a criminal offence. According to some news broadcasts,[2] 78 per cent of the inmates in Iran prisons are imprisoned because of financial matters. Maybe this high rate and its negative consequences, on both the micro and macro levels, caused the legislature to change its policy in 2015.

C. *The New Act on Debt Convictions (2015)*

After providing a background to explain the legal and social context of the dispute, I will delve into the new Act, which has dramatically altered the imprisonment policy of Iran.

This part will first outline the scheme of the "New Act on Debt Convictions" (2015) as well as its different aspects. It will present the modifications that the Act introduced in comparison with the Act of 1998. Finally, I will evaluate its positive and negative points.

I. Review of the New Act

The new Act contains twenty-nine articles and explicitly repeals the former Act and some other related Acts. It does not prohibit the imprisonment of

2 www.entekhab.ir entekhab broadcasting, published on April 26, 2014 (visited 8.03.2017).

debtors in all cases. Like the former Act, the first tool to ensure payment is the identification of assets followed by their seizure and sale in an auction.

The possibility of imprisonment is contemplated in Article 3, but unlike the former Act, if the debtor, during the thirty days after receiving the court's ruling regarding the debt, submits a list of all his assets and claims to be insolvent, he is not to be taken to jail. Also, if he undertakes this action but does so beyond the expressed deadline, he might not be imprisoned under certain conditions elaborated in clause 1 of Article 3.

The most significant modification lies in Article 7, which deals with the burden of proof.

Before this Act, according to general rules, the burden of proof in insolvency cases was upon the party who claimed it (the debtor). The new Act inverts the burden of proof. Thus, unless the previous situation of the debtor indicates his wealth, the creditor has the burden of disproving his insolvency, and if he fails to do so, the claim of the debtor under oath will prevail. This new article implies that everyone is considered to be insolvent unless the contrary is proved.

Another drastic change is the assistance that public authorities give to the creditor to find assets belonging to the debtor. Inquiries from banks, notaries, municipalities and all related authorities are provided for in the new Act. This means that the court must inquire with related authorities about a debtor's records of possessions, and these authorities also have the duty to respond to such inquiries.

The guarantees of the accuracy of an asset statement is laid out in Article 16, something which did not exist in the former Act, with the debtor being exposed to three to six months of imprisonment as a penalty for a false statement.

Under Article 17, when done with aim of avoiding one's debts, negligent conduct that results in insolvency may result in the debtor being prohibited from leaving Iran, from registering a company or having a position in a company, from receiving loans and monetary facilities from banks and financial institutions, or from owning a checkbook. Such consequences are also novel in the new provision and did not exist previously.

Also, though the prohibition of transferring assets to other people, with the intent of evading payment, was provided for in the former Act, the rules have been slightly tightened in Article 21 of the new Act.

Another assurance which is initiated in the new Act is that the debtor at the request of the creditor, can be prohibited from taking trips abroad (Article 23). The article provides that the court might temporarily permit the debtor to travel abroad in the case of necessary or health-related trips.

The exceptions for seizures in satisfaction of debts[3] are modified pursuant to Article 24 and now include assets like the debtor's telephone and the deposit on a rented domicile that is needed by the debtor, although the excepted assets no longer include the debtor's automobile. The article has explicitly limited the exceptions to the specified assets, and the former rules for determining exceptions of the debts are clearly revoked.

Parallel to the new Islamic penal code (enacted in 2013), which recognized the criminal responsibility of legal persons (Article 143 of the mentioned Act), this Act has stipulated certain regulations about the debts of legal persons such that all of the provisions which are applicable are to be followed. Obviously, imprisonment is not applicable in such cases. Additionally, legal persons cannot claim to be insolvent; rather, they should claim bankruptcy (Article 26).

II. Evaluation of the New Act

An evaluation of the new Act can be divided into assessments of its positive and negative points.

1. Positive Points

Positive changes achieved by the new Act might be listed as follow:

- **Efforts to alleviate the problem of overcrowding in prisons**: Obviously, the main goal of the new Act is to solve this problem by limiting the possibility of imprisonment of debtors, and theoretically, due to drastic changes in this Act, imprisonment will be constrained more than before. However, the extent of success of the new Act is still uncertain,

3 As regarding debts, assets belonging to the debtor which are necessary for his ordinary life cannot be seized or sold by authorities.

and one should wait for the new statistics as the Act has only recently been adopted.

- **Maintenance of debtors apart from criminals in jail:** Since the negative effects of a prison environment on one's behavior are well established in many criminological theories,[4] the new Act has provided for these financial convicts being kept apart from criminals. Also, the preparation of settings and backgrounds of some economic, financial activities of such convicts is provided for (Article 5). Such provisions will not only aid in the debtor's financial life but also help the creditor reach a successful end to his claim.
- **Assistance of the legal authorities in identifying assets:** Unlike the former Act in which the creditor was left alone to allege and identify the assets which belonged to the debtor, in the new Act legal authorities are bound to identify assets via inquiries made to different entities and with all possible legal tools. This means that the court no longer has a passive role in the proceedings. Such active participation of the court, which is justifiable in the case of a creditor's well-grounded claim, will replace the initial measure of prison as a means of ensuring repayment of debts. On the other hand, entities which are addressed in inquiries are obliged to respond to the court (Article 19), which will serve to complete the process and ensure repayment.
- **Orders prohibiting departure from Iran:** As mentioned, this prohibition does not include necessary trips such as those that are health-related (Article 23), but it serves to prevent the flight of a debtor before satisfying his financial obligations. This is a positive change, specifically considering the fact that when a debtor has no registered assets, his travel abroad may make the payment of debts impossible in practice.

2. Negative Points

Although the new Act shows some progress, it fails to provide appropriate regulations in the following regards:

---

4 Just to name a few: Differential Association Theory by Edwin Sutherland; The Prison Community by Donald Clemmer.

- **Reversing the burden of proof:** The most problematic article of the new Act is Article 7, which assumes the insolvency of the debtor unless the contrary is proved. This article will make it more difficult for a creditor to vindicate his rights. After finishing all of the routine and protracted procedures to demonstrate his right, the creditor will now also have the duty to establish the wealth of the defendant. Even though the court will aid him, as mentioned above, this assistance will not be sufficient, as presently there is no complete official record of the assets of citizens in Iran. Many estates are not formally registered in many regions and areas , and informal transactions concerning properties are still very common and entitle the buyer to ownership title without being legally registered. Thus there might be some concerns that a creditor will abandon the whole process if it proves too frustrating. By contrast, the debtor can easily plead insolvency and by taking an oath (or by giving written testimony in the form of two testimonials pursuant to Article 8) his claim will be established.
- **Poor guarantees:** Articles 16, 17 and 21 provide rules on punishment for false declaration of assets, negligence which results in insolvency and the transfer of assets with the intent of evading debt. Notwithstanding these articles, there does not seem to be enough to prevent one from undertaking such conduct, since as mentioned before there are so many informal assets which people may hold, even if not officially registered. Thus, the state will not be able to ascertain the good faith of the debtor in fulfilling his legal duties. Even guarantees that may seem very strict at first glance, like prohibiting departure from Iran, might not always be effective, as unfortunately there are many illegal ways to travel abroad.
- **Recourse to prison:** Although compliance with Articles 16, 17 and 21 is mostly assured by the consequence of imprisonment for non-compliance, a mechanism which is almost always an appealing option, one may logically question the validity of such a guarantee. As mentioned before, the main goal of the new regulation was to avoid imprisonment; nonetheless, the new Act resorts to prison yet again, which is in some ways a return to the starting point.

D. Conclusion

The new "Act on Debt Convictions" (2015) is novel in many ways and will have great influence on current and future cases in the courts. Even though it undertakes some positive initiatives, it seems like it fails to strike a proper balance between the rights of the two parties in some cases and that it neglects the rights of the creditor in cases where a complaint has been legally brought and successfully established.

The following suggestions might be helpful in improving the efficiency of the payment of debts without resorting to imprisonment:

Reforms in some other Acts: regulations on the drafting of unpayable checks, on the financial duties between spouses, and on the family in general are domains which do not seem to be in accordance with the social facts in Iran; moreover, many of the types of cases which used to resort to the Act on Debt Convictions will not be able to do so in the future. Thus, reforming this Act without reevaluating the other related Acts is unfair and will lead to the frustration of one party to the claim.

Better means and contribution: The present means of identifying assets are not precise. Even though Iran's official database system on asset possessions is headed in the right direction, the new Act will not be able to perform in all of its capacities without the establishment of a more exact asset database of citizens.

Mediation: Lastly, some other non-official measures of dispute resolution between debtors and creditors, like mediation, would be greatly helpful and efficient. Although such efforts traditionally play a substantial role in resolving problems Iranian society, it would be advisable that their functions and domains be defined by new Acts so that they regain their popularity officially. Of course, mediation should be an optional tool which has regulated procedures; further, without the agreement of both parties, no claim can be brought to dispute councils.[5]

---

5 It should be observed that the dispute councils have been established in Iran for more than a decade now (established first according to a bylaw in 2008 and then modified as an Act adopted in 2015). Their establishment, role and duties are subject to dispute and require another independent article. Just to mention one key concern briefly, in practice they perform semi-legal tasks and not necessarily mediation.

Bibliography

Leila Asadi, 'Is being a Debtor Criminal? (Aya Bedehkar Mojrem Ast?)' (2002) 26 & 27 Islamic Jurisprudence & Family Law (figh va Hoghooghe Khanevade), 34

Esmaeel Ghandvar Bijarpas, *The Situation of Incarceration in Islamic Jurisprudence and Iranian Criminal Law (Mogheiate Habs dar Figh va HoghogheJjazaye Iran)* (pade Andishe, 2007)

Mojtaba Taghi Zade Daghian, 'Islamic Jurisprudential-Legal Study of the Act on Debt Conviction (Barresi Feghi-Hoghooghi Ghanoone Nahveye Ejraye Mahkoomiathaye Mali)' (2006) 20 Theology and Law Journal (majaleye Elahiat va Hoghogh), 115

Mohammad Saleh Esfandiari, *Sociological Analysis of Prison (Tahlile Jame'e Shenasaneye Zendan)* (Majd, 2014)

Abbasali Mohammadi, The *Disadvantage of Prison (Ziane Zendan)* (Hoghooghi, 2002)

Omid Mohammadi, *Explanation Collection of The Act on Debt Conviction (majmooeye Mohasha az Ghanoone Nahveye Ejraye Mahkoomiathaye Mali)* (Andishe Sabze Novin, 2015)

Heshmatollah Samavati, *Study and Research on Insolvency: Theoretical, Practical and Comparative Considerations (Barresi va Tahghigh Piramoone Esar: Nazari, Karbordi va Tatbighi)* (Kamalan, 2006)

Seyed Ghasem Zamani, 'International Human Rights Regulations and Imprisonment of Financial Convicts in Iran (mavazine Beinalmelali Hoghooghe Bashar va Bazdashte Mahkoonime Mali dar Iran)' (2006) 35 International Legal Journal (majale Hoghooghi Beinalmelali), 71

B. Improvements to the European Law

Multilingualism and the Uniform Interpretation of European Union Law

Katharina Fenkner

A. *Introduction*

> "What then are the principles of interpretation to be applied [by national courts when interpreting European law]? Beyond doubt the English courts must follow the same principles as the European court. Otherwise there would be differences between the countries of the nine. That would never do. All the courts of all nine countries should interpret the Treaty in the same way. They should all apply the same principles."[1]

As early as in 1974, Lord Denning, former English Master of the Rolls, realised that European harmonisation may have affected the methodical approach of national courts to norm interpretation. Whereas each of the nine member states of the European Community at that time had their own traditional methods of interpretation for national laws, it was to be desired that they resorted to a more uniform approach when interpreting European norms.[2] The development of this uniform method for the interpretation of European Union law has been mainly influenced by the Court of Justice of the European Union. While there are certain similarities between this method and those of interpreting national law, they are not fully congruent.[3]

---

1 *H. P. Bulmer Ltd. and another v. J. Bollinger S. A. and others*, Court of Appeal, 22 May 1974, [1974] Ch. 401, p. 425.

2 Ibid., p. 425 ff.

3 *Colneric*, Auslegung des Gemeinschaftsrechts und gemeinschaftsrechtskonforme Auslegung, Zeitschrift für Europäisches Privatrecht (hereinafter ZEuP) 2005, p. 225 (227 ff.).

B. Current Situation

I. Mandatory Comparison of Language Versions

In particular, distinctive features arise due to the multilingualism of European Union law. In this regard, the Court of Justice of the European Union has held:

> "Provisions of EU law must be interpreted and applied uniformly in the light of the versions existing in all EU languages."[4]

This citation and other judgments[5] indicate that the Court of Justice of the European Union holds the opinion that, for interpretative purposes, all language versions of a provision are to be consulted and given a uniform interpretation. The exigence of comparing the different language versions finds its justification in the fact that languages are not totally congruent; they have different structures, concepts and linguistic peculiarities, let alone the different underlying legal ideas.[6] Those differences can only be reconciled if they are made apparent and consciously tackled, which is why a comparison of the different language versions is a useful tool.

According to Art. 55 (1) of the Treaty on European Union as well as Art. 358 of the Treaty on the Functioning of the European Union (hereinafter TFEU), the 24 language versions of the Treaties are equally authentic.[7] Consequently,

---

4 *Criminal proceedings against Lars Ivansson and Others*, 10 July 2014, Case C-307/13, ECLI:EU:C:2014:2058, para. 40.

5 See for example *Wilhelm Mecklenburg v. Kreis Pinneberg – Der Landrat*, 17 June 1998, Case C-321/96E, CLI:EU:C:1998:300, para. 29; or *Firma Söhl & Söhlke v. Hauptzollamt Bremen*, 11 November 1999, Case C-48/98, ECLI:EU: C:1999:548, para. 46.

6 *Stevens*, The Principle of Linguistic Equality in Judicial Proceedings and in the Interpretation of Plurilingual Legal Instruments: The Régime Linguistique in the Court of Justice of the European Communities, (1967) 62 Northwestern University Law Review, p. 701 (715 ff.).

7 Irish has a special status, see Council Regulation (EC) No 920/2005 of 13.06.2005 amending Regulation No 1 of 15.04.1958 determining the language to be used by the European Economic Community and Regulation No 1 of 15.04.1958 determining the language to be used by the European Atomic Energy Community and introducing temporary derogation measures from those Regulations and Council Regulation (EU, Euratom) 2015/2264 of 3.12.2015 extending and phasing out the temporary derogation measures from Regulation No 1

> "[a]ll the language versions must, in principle, be recognised as having the same weight and this cannot vary according to the size of the population of the Member States using the language in question."[8]

Thus, language version comparison becomes crucial. The resulting approach has been described as 'extended grammatical interpretation'.[9] The Court has recognised this requirement in the famous *CILFIT* decision:

> "[I]t must be borne in mind that community legislation is drafted in several languages and that the different language versions are all equally authentic. An interpretation of a provision of community law thus involves a comparison of the different language versions."[10]

In reality, however, it has been reported that language versions other than the French text are only analysed by the Court if there are indications of divergences.[11] The Court of Justice of the European Union has only occasionally conducted a full comparison of language versions. For example, according to *Dederichs*, in 1999 there were only seven decisions referring to a comparison of languages[12] and within these cases, not on all occasions were all languages explicitly cited.

II. Problems De Lege Lata

The problem with the mandatory comparison of language versions is that it involves a strenuous procedure which might have been practical at times when the European community had only a few members and consequently only few official languages, but becomes nearly impossible with a steadily

---

of 15.04.1958 determining the languages to be used by the European Economic Community and Regulation No 1 of 15.04.1958 determining the languages to be used by the European Atomic Energy Community introduced by Regulation (EC) No 920/2005.

8 *The Queen v. Commissioners of Customs and Excise, ex parte EMU Tabac SARL, The Man in Black Ltd, John Cunningham*, 2 April 1998, Case C 296/95, ECLI:EU:C:1998:152, para. 5.

9 *Dederichs*, Die Methodik des Gerichtshofes der Europäischen Gemeinschaften, Europarecht, 2004, p. 345 (353).

10 *Srl CILFIT and Lanificio di Gavardo SpA v. Ministry of Health*, 6 October 1982, Case 283/81, ECLI:EU:C:1982:335, para. 18.

11 *Colneric*, ZEuP 2005, p. 225 (227).

12 *Dederichs*, 2004, p. 345 (352).

increasing number of official languages. The multiplication of authoritative versions renders grammatical interpretation time consuming and demands advanced knowledge of other languages.[13] However, with the current situation of all language versions being equally authentic, analysing only one or comparing just some versions will not suffice in order to ensure a reliable and uniform interpretative result.

Although, for the Court of Justice of the European Union, it might be possible to analyse all 24 language versions of a provision thanks to its vast apparatus of translators, other courts that also have to interpret European provisions such as national courts will encounter difficulties.[14] Of course, national courts have the possibility to refer any interpretative questions to the Court of Justice of the European Union by means of the preliminary reference procedure.[15] This is, however, not practical for all cases, as the Court of Justice of the European Union has limited capacities and cannot decide on all occasions where a comparison of language versions is required (which would comprise – according to its jurisprudence – the totality of legal disputes involving an interpretation of a European legal rule).

Furthermore, the problem of having to compare all language versions not only applies to the national courts, but also to others involved in legal proceedings, particularly to lawyers.[16] Many of them will encounter severe difficulties with having to analyse more than one other language version of a provision and, if the content of European law is only apprehensible when all language versions are contemplated comprehensively,[17] then the interpretation of European law by lawyers is prone to errors and oversights. This can lead to corresponding damage claims and render judicial proceedings more expensive.[18]

---

13 *Weiler*, Grammatikalische Auslegung des vielsprachigen Unionsrechts, ZEuP 2010, p. 861 (862).

14 Ibid., p. 861 (868).

15 *Millett*, Rules of Interpretation of E. E. C. Legislation, (1989) 10 Statute Law Review, p. 163 (177).

16 *Grundmann*, Die Auslegung des Gemeinschaftsrechts durch den Europäischen Gerichtshof: Zugleich eine rechtsvergleichende Studie zur Auslegung im Völkerrecht und im Gemeinschaftsrecht, 1997, p. 235.

17 *Wienand*, Zur Bedeutung der richtlinienkonformen Auslegung für das deutsche Steuerrecht, Betriebs-Berater 1992, p. 969 (974).

18 Ibid.

Additionally, individual citizens will almost certainly not be in a position where they can perform a comparison of all language versions. It is therefore not predictable for a citizen what the Court of Justice of the European Union will decide when interpreting a provision with the help of language version comparison. This is a paradoxical situation as the plurality and equality of language versions is supposed to benefit the European citizens and not interfere with legal certainty which, according to the Court of Justice of the European Union,[19] is an important principle of European Union law. The individual's trust in their own language version is unsettled, as not knowing the content of the other language versions and consequently the possible interpretive result of a court is always a present peril. In reality, no citizen or court can perform a full comparison of language versions, which is why a total equality of language versions cannot be guaranteed[20] and the position of grammatical interpretation is weakened within the methodical framework of statutory construction[21] in the European context. What is meant to increase proximity and benefit the citizens, finally leads to opacity and excess complexity. Thus, it needs to be asked what can be done to remedy this deficiency.

C. *Possible Solutions De Lege Ferenda*

I. Previous Suggestions and Their Deficits

The solution to this problem could involve either putting more weight on other methods of interpretation or renouncing the requirement of an all-comprising comparison of language versions, e.g. by a reduction of the number of versions that are to be compared.[22] The first solution is used by the Court of Justice of the European Union in cases where a clear solution cannot be reached due to conflicting language versions:

---

19 *European Commission v. United Kingdom of Great Britain and Northern Ireland*, 15 July 2010, Case C-582/08, ECLI:EU:C:2010:429, para. 49.

20 *Grundmann*, 1997, p. 234.

21 *Weiler*, ZEuP 2010, p. 861 (869).

22 Ibid., p. 861 (870).

> "Where there is divergence between the various language versions of a Community text, the provision in question must be interpreted by reference to the purpose and general scheme of the rules of which it forms part … ."[23]

The solution for the Court thus seems to consist in dissolving problems resulting from conflicting language versions by devaluing the grammatical element in statutory construction in favour of teleological and systematic interpretation. However, this does not solve the problem of legal certainty that a citizen encounters when trying to rely on the wording of a provision.

Concerning the proposal to reduce the number of required language version comparisons, it is not sensible to only employ such a comparison should one language version raise doubts. The reason for this is that the only language version consulted could be clear in itself, but at the same time the only one deviating from the others.[24] The result of the interpretative process then becomes coincidental according to which language version is the starting point.[25]

Another suggestion entails the quantitative reduction of language versions that are to be compared.[26] For instance, one could concentrate on the original language in which a legal text was framed in.[27] This approach, however, encompasses the problem that it is not always obvious which language version is the original one. Alternatively, it has been proposed by other authors to refer to the working language of the Court, i.e. French, in case of divergences between different language versions.[28] Nevertheless, such approaches are not in conformity with the current legal situation. Future legal rules could, however, either provide for the analysis of language versions from an opposing legal system or a quorum of language versions to be compared; but both suggestions bear the danger of being easily manipulated and may therefore negatively influence legal certainty.[29]

---

23 *Criminal Proceedings against Dirk Endendijk*, 3 April 2008, Case C-187/07, ECLI:EU:C:2008:197, para. 24.

24 *Weiler*, ZEuP 2010, p. 861 (872).

25 The Court of Justice of the European Union will start with the French version of a European law provision since this is the working language of the Court, see *Colneric*, ZEuP 2005, p. 225 (227).

26 *Weiler*, ZEuP 2010, p. 861 (872 ff.).

27 *Grundmann*, 1997, p. 219.

28 See for example *Grundmann/Riesenhuber*, Die Auslegung des Europäischen Privat- und Schuldvertragsrechts, Juristische Schulung 2001, p. 529 (530).

29 *Weiler*, ZEuP 2010, p. 861 (872 ff.).

Deciding according to the majority of language versions or giving language versions weight according to the number of native speakers within the European Union is also not in line with the standards of the Court of Justice of the European Union mentioned above. In this regard it can be said that a common meaning of the majority of language versions can only serve to confirm a meaning found by other interpretative methods.[30]

Similarly, the idea of referring to a common core content of all language versions does not seem sensible. As it was rightly pointed out by *van Calster*, this approach could be *"too sovereignty-friendly"*[31] and consequently lead to member states trying to circumvent or diminish their obligations by looking for deviating language versions.[32]

Likewise, the proposal of not having strict rules but instead deciding according to the idea of judicial interpretation being an *"ars boni et aequi"*[33] does not merit appraisal. It is possible that a flexible method might help in situations where multilingualism leads to problems.[34] Such an approach, however, reduces legal certainty and makes judicial interpretation subject to arbitrariness. The same is true for deciding according to the clearest version or the version in the native language version of a party.[35]

A further proposition, namely to reduce the number of official languages within the European Union,[36] would be a very profound measure. For example, this would prevent citizens from using their native language when writing to European institutions; something that would not be necessary in order to find a solution to the problem of how to consider statutory wording when interpreting a provision.

---

30 *van Calster*, The EU's Tower of Babel – The Interpretation by the European Court of Justice of Equally Authentic Texts Drafted in more than one Official Language, (1997) 17 Yearbook of European Law, p. 363 (380).

31 Ibid., p. 363 (378).

32 Ibid.

33 *Grundmann*, 1997, p. 220.

34 *Riese*, Das Sprachenproblem in der Praxis des Gerichtshofs der Europäischen Gemeinschaften, in: Vom deutschen zum europäischen Recht: Festschrift für Hans Dölle, 1963 (hereinafter: FS Dölle), p. 507 (524).

35 As mentioned in *Stevens*, (1967) 62 Northwestern University Law Review, p. 701 (718).

36 *Weiler*, ZEuR 2010, p. 861 (874).

II. Preferable Solution

Instead, a possible solution seems to be to change the current policy of all language versions being equally authoritative.[37] By only making the English language version authoritative, the problem of having to compare all language versions could be avoided. Citizens, lawyers and national courts would only have to compare the linguistic version of their relevant member state to the English version. This was the case for the Treaty establishing the European Coal and Steel Community with French and led to the situation that confidence in the official translations could not be guaranteed entirely since the French text needed to be consulted in all cases.[38] Nevertheless, the proposed solution would comprise an amelioration of the current situation in which confidence in one's national linguistic version cannot be upheld **and** 23 other versions need to be compared. Furthermore, the method of grammatical interpretation could regain importance, as it would be possible to rely on one decisive wording.[39] This is a solution that is for example currently successfully used for the Council of Europe's European Convention on Human Rights with only English and French being authoritative.[40]

The solution instituting English as the only authoritative language bears the advantage that it is the language which is in total most widely known within the European Union.[41] It is – in contrast to Latin – an active language and has an established canon of European terminology.

The argument that the introduction of only one authoritative language would oppose the idea of equal rights of member states within the European Union and render it difficult for citizens to understand European law could be rebutted by maintaining the current practice of translating all texts into the different languages. It would only be the legal status of language versions that would change. Such a solution has for many years been success-

---

37 Ibid., p. 861 (874).

38 *Riese*, in: FS Dölle, p. 507 (518).

39 *Millett*, (1989) 10 Statute Law Review, p. 163 (164).

40 See postamble of the ECHR: *"Done at Rome this 4th day of November 1950, in English and French, both texts being equally authentic ..."*.

41 *Sturm*, Lingua Latina fundamentum et salus Europae, (2002) 2 European Legal Forum, p. 313 (317).

fully used in public international law.[42] Additionally, the current situation of having to compare all language versions is even less practical for citizens.

III. Remedying Possible Disadvantages

Nevertheless, it may be possible that situations arise in which citizens suffer a disadvantage because they confide in their national linguistic version which differs from the English one. This is the main argument against having only one authoritative language. Thus, if this problem could be remedied, it might be possible to strengthen the argument for introducing the newly proposed language scheme. In order to safeguard citizens against such disadvantages resulting from deviances of meaning due to mistranslations, a claim for compensation could be introduced against the European Union. This would compensate citizens in cases of mistranslations similar to the already existing damage claims in European Union law.

The presently existing claims against member states for not transposing a directive[43] or violating European Union law[44] and the non-contractual liability of the European Union according to Art. 340 (2) TFEU[45] could serve as a model. The conditions of the new damage claim could be as follows:

42 *Kreße*, Mehrsprachigkeit im Recht der Europäischen Union, Zeitschrift für Rechtspolitik 2014, p. 11 (13).

43 *Andrea Francovich and Danila Bonifaci and others v. Italian Republic*, 19 November 1991, Joined cases C 6/90 and C 9/90, ECLI:EU:C:1991:428 and *Gerhard Köbler v. Republik Österreich*, 30 September 2003, Case C-224/01, ECLI:EU:C:2003:513.

44 *Brasserie du Pêcheur SA v. Bundesrepublik Deutschland and The Queen v. Secretary of State for Transport, ex parte: Factortame Ltd and others*, 5 March 1996, Joined cases C-46/93 and C-48/93, ECLI:EU:C:1996:79.

45 For the relevant prerequisites see *Évelye Delauche v. Commission of the European Communities*, 16 December 1987, Case 111/86, ECLI:EU:C:1987:562. These were later repeated continuously, see for example *Arnaldo Lucaccioni v. Commission of the European Communities*, 9 September 1999, Case C-257/98 P, ECLI:EU:C:1999:402.

1. *A sufficiently substantive deviation in meaning between the national linguistic version of the citizen concerned and the authoritative English language version of a European legal provision.*
2. *An actual harm suffered.*
3. *Inevitableness of the damage as the citizen did not and could not reasonably be expected to understand the English version.*
4. *The existence of a causal link between the linguistic discrepancy and the damage suffered.*

The first condition is necessary because it is very difficult to prevent all kinds of deviances of meaning. It lies within the nature of languages that concepts and terms are not fully congruent. As long as the deviation is only small and the citizen is not misled, there is no reason why compensation should be due. Also, it is necessary to restrict the claim to European legal provisions with a certain legal impact such as European regulations in contrast to texts with merely informative character such as information brochures.

This is related to the second condition, namely that the citizen needs to suffer an actual harm. In cases where there is no damage, there is no argument for a possible compensation.

The third condition could be introduced to safeguard against abuse of the compensation claim. If the citizen has consulted and understood the English version, recognised the deviation and nevertheless acted on their national version, they should not be compensated. The same is true for situations where they could reasonably be expected to understand the English version, e.g. where their first language is English or they possess a good command of the English language due to their profession.

Finally, the fourth condition makes sure that there is sufficient causation between the deviation of the language versions and the damage suffered by the citizen. By introducing this requirement, the number of possible claims can be reduced to only those where the damage is really based on the linguistic difference between the texts.

There is, however, no fault element in the conditions for the liability claim. This decision was made as it is not of relevance for the citizen why there is a deviation of the language versions. As the aim of the compensation scheme is to safeguard against possible disadvantages resulting from the fact that only the English version will be authoritative, it is not necessary to ascertain a fault by the translators or the European Union and its member states in checking the final version of the texts. This will be a substantive improvement compared to the current situation where the citizen can be expected to consult all language versions and consequently will not be compensated for any discrepancies.

An argument against the proposed compensation scheme could be that it shifts the interpretative difficulties resulting from a mandatory comparison of 24 languages in judicial processes to another scene, namely the trial on the non-contractual liability. However, this is only partly true. Regarding the compensation, a mere one-to-one comparison has to be conducted (concerning the relevant language version and the English authoritative version). Unproblematic language versions do not need to be taken into account as it is clear that the English version is to prevail.

D. Conclusion

In conclusion, it can be said that the introduction of English as the only authoritative language version of European legal provisions in combination with the proposed compensation scheme would mean a substantive improvement for the citizen compared to the current situation. Citizens would no longer be required to compare all language versions but could focus on their own language version and – where appropriate – the English version. Should they sustain a loss due to discrepancies, they could claim damages. Similarly, the situation for member state courts and the Court of Justice of the European Union as well as for lawyers would be improved. The whole process of interpretation of European Union law would be streamlined and simplified. In cases of doubt, only the English version would have to be consulted. Thus, legal certainty could be improved and the significance of grammatical interpretation augmented.

Yet the question remains whether the European Union or rather its citizens are psychologically ready to give up formal linguistic equality in favour of a more practicable system. However, if they were, the solution of the problems resulting from multilingualism would no longer be left to *"the common will to dispense justice in the European spirit, and the mutual trust"*[46] but could be reduced to less complex measures. This would pave the way for continuing enlargement of the European Union.

---

46 *"[D]er gemeinsame Wille, im europäischen Geist Recht zu sprechen, und das gegenseitige Vertrauen"*; *Riese*, in: FS Dölle, p. 507 (514).

Bibliography

Andrea Francovich and Danila Bonifaci and others v. Italian Republic, 19 November 1991, Joined cases C-6/90 and C-9/90, ECLI:EU:C:1991:428

Arnaldo Lucaccioni v. Commission of the European Communities, 9 September 1999, Case C-257/98 P, ECLI:EU:C:1999:402

Brasserie du Pêcheur SA v. Bundesrepublik Deutschland and The Queen v. Secretary of State for Transport, ex parte: Factortame Ltd and others, 5 March 1996, Joined cases C-46/93 and C-48/93, ECLI:EU:C:1996:79

Geert van Calster, 'The EU's Tower of Babel – The Interpretation by the European Court of Justice of Equally Authentic Texts Drafted in more than one Official Language' (1997) 17 Yearbook of European Law, 363

Ninon Colneric, Auslegung des Gemeinschaftsrechts und gemeinschafts-rechtskonforme Auslegung, Zeitschrift für Europäisches Privatrecht 2005, 225

Criminal Proceedings against Dirk Endendijk, 3 April 2008, Case C-187/07, ECLI:EU:C:2008:197

Criminal proceedings against Lars Ivansson and Others, 10 July 2014, Case C-307/13, ECLI:EU:C:2014:2058

Mariele Dederichs, Die Methodik des Gerichtshofes der Europäischen Gemeinschaften, Europarecht 2004, 345

European Commission v. United Kingdom of Great Britain and Northern Ireland, 15 July 2010, Case C-582/08, ECLI:EU:C:2010:429

Évelye Delauche v. Commission of the European Communities, 16 December 1987, Case 111/86, ECLI:EU:C:1987:562

Firma Söhl & Söhlke v. Hauptzollamt Bremen, 11 November 1999, Case C-48/98, ECLI:EU:C:1999:548

Gerhard Köbler v. Republik Österreich, 30 September 2003, Case C-224/01, ECLI:EU: C:2003:513

Stephan M. Grundmann, *Die Auslegung des Gemeinschaftsrechts durch den Europäischen Gerichtshof: Zugleich eine rechtsvergleichende Studie zur Auslegung im Völkerrecht und im Gemeinschaftsrecht* (Hartung-Gorre, Konstanz 1997)

Stephan Grundmann and Karl Riesenhuber, Die Auslegung des Europäischen Privat- und Schuldvertragsrechts, Juristische Schulung 2001, 529

H. P. Bulmer Ltd. and another v. J. Bollinger S. A. and others, Court of Appeal, 22 May 1974, [1974] Ch. 401

Bernhard Kreße, Mehrsprachigkeit im Recht der Europäischen Union, Zeitschrift für Rechtspolitik 2014, 11

Timothy Millett, 'Rules of Interpretation of E. E. C. Legislation' (1989) 10 Statute Law Review, 163

Srl CILFIT and Lanificio di Gavardo SpA v. Ministry of Health, 6 October 1982, Case 283/81, ECLI:EU:C:1982:335

Lisbeth Stevens, 'The Principle of Linguistic Equality in Judicial Proceedings and in the Interpretation of Plurilingual Legal Instruments: The Régime Linguistique in the Court of Justice of the European Communities' (1967) 62 Northwestern University Law Review, 701

Fritz Sturm, 'Lingua Latina fundamentum et salus Europae' (2002) 2 European Legal Forum, 313

Otto Riese, 'Das Sprachenproblem in der Praxis des Gerichtshofs der Europäischen Gemeinschaften' in Ernst von Caemmerer, Arthur Nickisch und Konrad Zweigert (eds), *Vom deutschen zum europäischen Recht: Festschrift für Hans Dölle*, Vol. 1 (Mohr Siebeck, Tübingen 1963), 507

The Queen v. Commissioners of Customs and Excise, ex parte EMU Tabac SARL, The Man in Black Ltd, John Cunningham, 2 April 1998, Case C-296/95, ECLI:EU:C:1998:152

Frank Weiler, Grammatikalische Auslegung des vielsprachigen Unionsrechts, Zeitschrift für Europäisches Privatrecht 2010, 861

Meilicke Wienand, Zur Bedeutung der richtlinienkonformen Auslegung für das deutsche Steuerrecht, Betriebs-Berater 1992, 969

Wilhelm Mecklenburg v. Kreis Pinneberg – Der Landrat, 17 June 1998, Case C-321/96E, CLI:EU:C:1998:300

Abuse of Rights in EU Law: A General Law Principle Limiting the Exercise of Rights at the EU Level?

Lukas Beck

A. *Freedom of Movement as the Foundation of the Internal Market*

European law comprises two central elements, which serve to create the European Union's (hereinafter EU) legal framework to which the Member States are bound: on the one hand there are fundamental freedoms and on the other, directives and regulations. The application of these legal tools should lead to the improvement of cross-border mobility of all Internal Market actors, which is a goal explicitly acknowledged in the fundamental treaty provision of Art. 3 para. 2 Treaty on European Union (hereinafter TEU):

> "The Union shall offer its citizens an area of freedom, security and justice without internal frontiers, in which the free movement of persons is ensured … ."

In Art. 3 para. 3 it states:

> "The Union shall establish an internal market."

The Internal Market is an evolution of what was earlier known as the common market.[1] The establishment of a common market is not a task to be completed overnight, but rather a permanent and continuous duty of the EU.[2] An explanation as to what exactly should be achieved under the banner of a 'common market' is forwarded by Art. 26 para. 2 Treaty on the Functioning of the European Union (hereinafter TFEU):

> „The internal market shall comprise an area without internal frontiers in which the free movement of goods, persons, services and capital is ensured in accordance with the provisions of the Treaties."

* Special thanks go to my dear colleague Thomas Hardaker, LL. M., for his linguistic support.

1 See *Terhechte*, in: Grabitz/Hilf/Nettesheim (eds), Das Recht der Europäischen Union, 2015, Art. 3 EUV para. 38.

2 Ibid.

The principle aim is to ensure the full, unhindered freedom of movement of goods, persons, services and capital within the EU Internal Market. It follows logically that free movement in this sense encompasses more than a simple freedom to physically transport goods, persons, services and capital. Instead, the common market seeks to ensure rights to the utilization of those objects enjoying fundamental freedom protections. It is here to be acknowledged that it is a fundamental goal of the EU to create a free market in which the economic power of internal actors can be exercised not only in their home countries, but also within the territories of other Member States. The common market should enable this goal.

B. Fundamental Freedoms

According to the requirement to establish an Internal Market contained in Art. 26 para. 2 TFEU, the achievement of the Internal Market has to be considered as a general objective of the EU. A freestanding right of individuals to effect EU action or the omission of EU action in regards to achieving an Internal Market does not exist. Instead, this general objective must be brought to life. The fundamental freedoms provide the impetus in this regard – free movement of goods (Art. 28 et seq. TFEU); free movement of employees (Art. 45 et seq. TFEU); freedom of establishment (Art. 49 et seq. TFEU); freedom of services (Art. 56 et seq. TFEU); freedom of capital (Art. 63 et seq. TFEU).

Even though the wording of these provisions is somewhat unsystematic, it is to acknowledge that interpretation of these freedoms follows a general dogmatic system.[3] The illimitability of the Internal Market is realised within the areas covered by these freedoms. The fundamental freedoms constitute prohibitions of direct and indirect discrimination on grounds of nationality against those wishing to leave their home Member State in favor of a different one. Additionally, these freedoms function as prohibitions upon re-

3 *Ress/Ukrow*, in: Grabitz/Hilf/Nettesheim (eds), Das Recht der Europäischen Union, 2015, Art. 63 para. 29; *Jarass*, Elemente einer Dogmatik der Grundfreiheiten, Zeitschrift Europarecht 1995, p. 202 (202 ff.); *Jarass*, Elemente einer Dogmatik der Grundfreiheiten II, Zeitschrift Europarecht 2000, p. 705 (705 ff.).

strictions in cases involving a cross-border element. In such cases, the nationality of the actor is no longer significant,[4] of central importance is rather the fact that measures equal to a discrimination are also prohibited. Those addressed by the freedoms are the Member States. They are prohibited from undertaking (or maintaining) measures, which are discriminatory or restrictive. The freedoms proscribe unfair disadvantage in two ways: on the one hand, the receiving Member State cannot restrict traffic entering it, while on the other hand the origin Member State cannot restrict traffic leaving it.[5] Where a cross-border element is present, the fundamental freedoms are applicable to both the sending and receiving Member States concerned.

C. Limits to Freedom in the Internal Market

I. Guarantee of Freedoms only "in accordance with the provisions of the Treaties"

A look at the wording of Art. 26 para. 2 TFEU referred to above shows that the provision concludes with the words: "in accordance with the provisions of the Treaties." The Internal Market will only be guaranteed to this extent; this however, can be understood in different ways. The first interpretation proposes that this is a declaration that the EU will not act outside of its competence to guarantee an Internal Market. Such a declaration would be considered a rejection of "competence *ultra vires*" which is self-explanatory: the EU cannot impose an Internal Market upon sovereign territories or nations falling outside of the EU territory, and therefore outside of its authoritative scope. The EU's competencies are objectively and geographically limited: it is impossible for it to remove cross-border boundaries to free movement in territories not falling within its geographical sphere of competence. It is also impossible to create legal obligations where these concern objects falling outside of EU legislative competence.

However, the wording of the article allows an alternative understanding. The sentence proclaiming that freedom of movement within the EU "is en-

4 *Libert/Van Eycken/Bleeckx/Clippele/ Syndicat national des propriétaires et copropriétaires ASBL v. Gouvernement flamand*, 8 May 2013, Joined cases C-197/11 and C-203/11, DNotZ 2013, p. 831 para. 38.

5 Ibid.

sured in accordance with the provisions of the Treaties" can also be understood as "is *[only]* ensured *[as far as it is]* in accordance with the provisions of the Treaties."

This reading of the subsection allows the insertion of a reservation. The freedom of movement is qualified in that it is only guaranteed when it is "in accordance with the provisions of the Treaties." This means that freedom of movement rights based on either, free movement of goods, free movement of persons, the freedom of establishment or service, or freedom of capital cannot be asserted when incompliant with guarantees enshrined in the TEU and TFEU.

Upon closer inspection of the contents of guarantees offered in the Treaties, it is clear that they are explicitly stipulated in treaty articles housing the fundamental freedoms (see above II.), and accordingly that this circular logic does little to help. As fundamental freedoms serve to protect certain behaviors, it follows that other behaviors not falling within the scope of the Treaties remain unprotected. The reservation of Art. 26 para. 2 TFEU would, in this case, be no more than a mere reference to the scope of the fundamental freedoms.

Naturally, such doubling can occur and may be present in the European Treaties on account of the general nature of the articles in comparison to concrete legal norms. In any case, the wording of the article's subsection allows a flexible interpretation. "[I]n accordance with the provisions of the Treaties" covers not only the articles housing fundamental freedoms, but all treaty articles making up the European Treaties. Therefore, such legal requirements not directly related to the Internal Market, but also those having a more general function such as framing EU objectives, may be included. An example of such a general legal requirement may be peace-keeping as laid down in number 12 of the preamble of the TEU. According to these considerations, taking advantage of benefits of the Internal Market is only possible when all requirements of EU law are complied with. Assertions to an Internal Market and the fundamental freedoms are only possible when made within the legal parameters of the European Treaties.

II. Unwritten Principles of European Union Law to Determine, What is "in accordance with the provisions of the Treaties"

The question remains as to how these provisions of European law are to be understood. A consideration of the regulatory system of the Treaties shows that not all questions of European law can be exhaustively answered by reference solely to law defined in the Treaties. Often, the Treaties stipulate only general requirements and unanticipated problems arise first when treaty provisions are applied. If "in accordance with the provisions of the Treaties" is to be interpreted conservatively i.e. limited to its most simple meaning, there is the possibility to exclude those legal requirements of European law, which first become apparent when the Treaties are interpreted. Such a situation cannot however, be intended by the authors of the Treaties, as this would require European law to be viewed as an extremely static system. Legal provisions are however, not to be understood in this regard. They should subscribe an abstract rule capable of being applied to individual cases and should therefore allow for reasonable interpretation.[6] This phenomenon is not limited to European law; all legal systems based upon written abstract provisions must concern themselves with the application of those provisions to factual circumstances at a later date. Upon application of legal provisions a certain element of evaluation occurs which is not explicitly reflected in the wording of the law, or in the case of European law, in the European Treaties. Instead, the evaluation is determined on the basis of all relevant considerations. Important here is the background which frames the origin, evolution and application of the European Treaties.

Every legal system contains, in addition to its statutory provisions, unwritten, ancillary principles of law, which constitute fundamental doctrines used to direct the further construction of law. This is the case because statutory law is always a reflection of the attitudes and convictions of those responsible for enacting the law. It is not simply an issue of the will of the legislator alone, as the legislator is often only the parliament, which drafts the actual provisions and enacts them. More important are the communal principles, which determine the behavioural interaction of its members. These principles construct the factual sphere of action in which legal provisions operate. Therefore, these principles are to be considered when legal provisions are applied.

According to the perspective given here, such fundamental principles also act as limits to the fundamental freedoms expressly referred to in Art. 26 para. 2 TFEU when it is determined within the article that claims

6 See only *Larenz/Canaris*, Methodenlehre der Rechtswissenschaft, 1995, p. 133.

based upon the fundamental freedoms must be "in accordance with the provisions of the Treaties."[7] However, even when this instruction is to be understood in its most basic form, the validity of the general principles to serve as limits to the exercise fundamental freedoms remains at issue. The theory that a legal system limits its own substantive scope through fundamental principles is not dependent upon explicit referral to the principles or upon whether these principles formed the basis of the provisions when enacted. A statutory reservation reflecting the importance of such principles is not necessary.

III. The Unwritten Principle of 'Abusive Use of Rights'

1. The Principle's Existence

European law faces a challenge when its application must be restricted in order to counter abusive action resulting in advantages to the abusing party i.e. when an abusive use of rights is apparent.

In contrast to the handling of abuse under German law (§ 242 German Civil Code, hereinafter BGB), a prohibition of abusive use of rights is not codified in European law as a general legal principle. This does not mean however, that an abusive use of rights is not restricted by European law. This paper proposes a thesis based on the relatively safe assumption that a principle against abuse exists in European law. To bolster this thesis it is necessary to examine the possible sources of such a principle.

2. Provisions in Directives and Regulations

Abuse of rights is explicitly addressed in certain secondary legislation of the EU. For example, Art. 4 para. 3 Regulation 2988/95/EC regulates Euratom[8] under "Administrative measures and penalties" of Title II:

---

7 Similarly: *Kindler*, in: Münchener Kommentar zum Bürgerlichen Gesetzbuch: BGB, 2015, Internationales Handels- und Gesellschaftsrecht, para. 431.

8 Council Regulation (EC, Euratom) No 2988/95 of 18 December 1995 on the protection of the European Communities financial interests.

> "Acts which are established to have as their purpose the obtaining of an advantage contrary to the objectives of the Community law applicable in the case by artificially creating the conditions required for obtaining that advantage shall result, as the case shall be, either in failure to obtain the advantage or in its withdrawal."

In Art. 11 para. 1 lit. a) Directive 90/434/EEC[9] is laid down:

> "A Member State may refuse to apply or withdraw the benefit … where it appears that the merger, division, transfer of assets or exchange of shares … has as its principal objective or as one of its principal objectives tax evasion or tax avoidance; the fact that one of the operations referred to in Article 1 is not carried out for valid commercial reasons … may constitute a presumption that the operation has tax evasion or tax avoidance as its principal objective or as one of its principal objectives."

Art. 7 para. 1 Directive 1999/44/EC[10] on the 'binding nature' of the Directive orders that:

> "Any contractual terms or agreements ... which directly or indirectly waive or restrict the rights resulting from this Directive shall, as provided for by national law, not be binding on the consumer."

This determination was removed by Directive 2011/83/EU.[11] In its place is the succession rule "imperative nature of the Directive" in Art. 25 para. 2:

> "Any contractual terms which directly or indirectly waive or restrict the rights resulting from this Directive shall not be binding on the consumer."

A look at these provisions shows that the European legislator seeks to secure its regulatory framework through various legislative acts. From a methodical perspective however, examination of secondary legislation does not offer a comprehensive solution in the search for the origin of a general principle. This is because the explicit codification of an unwritten general principle of abuse in some legislation and not in others is counterintuitive. Where a particular circumstance is subject to a certain, defined regulatory response, this suggests that a special rule, designed only to have effect in this particular circumstance, is present, rather than a general principle. The

---

9 Council Directive 90/434/EEC of 23 July 1990 on the common system of taxation applicable to mergers, divisions, transfers of assets and exchanges of shares concerning companies of different Member States.

10 Directive 1999/44/EC of the European Parliament and of the Council of 25 May 1999 on certain aspects of the sale of consumer goods and associated guarantees.

11 Directive 2011/83/EU of the European Parliament and of the Council of 25 October 2011 on consumer rights, amending Council Directive 93/13/EEC and Directive 1999/44/EC of the European Parliament and of the Council and repealing Council Directive 85/577/EEC and Directive 97/7/EC of the European Parliament and of the Council.

codification of abuse in various secondary sources of EU legislation therefore does not allow a conclusion to be drawn that a general principle of abuse exists.

In regards to the above listed provisions, it is also apparent that their requirements differ. Whereas in the prohibitory Art. 4 para. 3 Regulation 2988/95/EC, regulating Euratom an 'artificially created' circumstance is required in order to qualify as an abuse of law, the other legislative acts considered above do not apply this requirement. Instead, they necessitate simply that the legal provisions are somehow avoided, whether through an artificial arrangement or not. In conclusion, this is a question of perspective: cases of 'artificially created' circumstances are actually about gaining certain legal standing, in all other cases abuse is about avoiding certain prohibitions.

3. The Reasoning of the ECJ

The European Court of Justice (hereinafter ECJ) has not relied upon such methodical considerations. In its case law, it speaks freely of a "general Community law principle that abuse of rights is prohibited."[12] This principle requires that:

> "Individuals must not improperly or fraudulently take advantage of provisions of Community law. The application of Community legislation cannot be extended to cover abusive practices, that is to say, transactions carried out not in the context of normal commercial operations, but solely for the purpose of wrongfully obtaining advantages provided for by Community law."[13]

The ECJ's derivation of the abuse principle is very interesting on account of its baselessness. It was taken for granted by the court in its consideration of Art. 11 para. 1 lit. a) Directive 90/434/EEC that the provision "reflects [this] general Community law principle." Therewith, the ECJ cannot be accused of departing from methodical consideration but rather of employing a type of manipulation. Intended is not a generalization of the provisions of different directives or their application to each and every circumstance. Instead, the ECJ has determined that even throughout varying legislation,

12 *Kofoed v. Skatteministeriet*, 5 July 2007, Case C-321/05, ECLI:EU:C:2007: 408, para. 38.

13 Ibid.

an express rule to this effect is present. This reasoning is however, not necessary because a general principle of European law is applicable in lieu of express provision.

Although this is a sure basis on which the legal practice can operate, from a dogmatic perspective the question as to the origin of the principle remains unanswered. As the abuse principle is merely referred to in legislative acts of the EU (see above sub III.3.b), its source must be rooted elsewhere.

4. The Origin of the Principle in Harmonisation by Means of Secondary Law

The possibility to view this issue from a different perspective arises when the context of the purpose of EU regulations and directives is considered. Pursuant to Art. 288 para. 2 and 3 TFEU regulations and directives are both binding; they differentiate in terms of their scope.

It is the inherent nature of regulations and directives that they create uniform legal requirements, which are anticipated by, and equally binding throughout, the Member States. Exceptions to this uniformity of obligations are fundamentally not intended. Such a uniform legal requirement is only ensured if arrangements or actions undertaken in order to circumvent regulations, are prohibited.

This safeguard however, has limited effect because the harmonisation intended by the enactment of regulations and directives is restricted to the scope of application of the relevant legislative act. The Member States are under an obligation to regulate circumstances and to guarantee the determined EU legal requirements to the extent intended by the scope of the legislative act. Outside of the scope of regulations and directives, EU harmonisation does not occur. The origin of a general principle therefore cannot be found in European harmonisation.

5. A European Law Principle Deriving from the Common Principles of Member States

There is agreement within European law that legal principles common to all Member States are simultaneously principles of European law.[14] Consideration of the common legal traditions of the Member States is constructive when one considers that the background against which they are created serves to affect and limit their exercise (see above III.2.). Because the EU takes its existence and legitimation from its founding Member States, the background against which EU law is created is in turn influenced by the principles shaping domestic legal systems of the Member States. Therein lays the foundation for an unwritten principle of the abusive use of rights. The root of the principle is not found in the primary or secondary law of the EU, here it is neither explicitly stated nor capable of being extrapolated. The principle originates in the common fundamental legal principles of the Member States and has, from this starting point, been transposed into the conscious of European law.

6. Another Way, When a Directive is Concerned?

A case recently decided by the ECJ concerning German labour law[15] provides an opportunity for directives to follow a different approach in respect to abuse of rights. The case was as follows: the applicant before the ECJ had applied for an employment position, without intending to accept a potential offer of employment. His goal was merely to be classified as a 'candidate' in order that he, upon rejection of the position, could obtain compensation from the potential employer for age discrimination. The German Federal Labour Court submitted to the ECJ to two questions. It asked:

> "1. On a proper interpretation of Art. 3 para.1 lit. a of Directive 2000/78 and Article 14 (1) (a) of Directive 2006/54, does a person who, as is clear from his application,

---

14 See Advocate General, 17 July 1996, Case C-34/95, para. 45; *Lutter*, Zum Umfang der Bindung durch Richtlinien, in: Due/Lutter/Schwarze (eds), Festschrift für Ulrich Everling, 1995, p. 765 (778); *Lutter*, Die Auslegung angeglichenen Rechts, JuristenZeitung 1992, p. 593 (607).

15 *Kratzer v. R+V Allgemeine Versicherung AG*, 28 July 2016, Case C-423/15, NJW 2016, p. 2796.

> is seeking not recruitment and employment but merely the status of applicant in order to bring claims for compensation also qualify as seeking access to employment, to self-employment or to occupation?"

and

> "2. If the answer to the first question is in the affirmative: Can a situation in which the status of applicant was obtained not with a view to recruitment and employment but for the purpose of claiming compensation be considered as an abuse of rights under EU law?"[16]

While the German Federal Labour Court, in respect to the second question, wishes to specifically clarify whether an abuse of rights is present, the first question takes a different approach. In this regard, the Court seeks to establish whether the factual circumstance falls within the scope of the Directive. The end result would be the same regardless of whether the action does not fall within the scope, or where an abuse of rights is present: it remains the same if a right is not granted due to waning requirements, or because it may not be used in individual cases; both circumstances deny the guarantees afforded by the directive.

The ECJ seems to prefer a pragmatic solution: it decided that both questions should be answered together.[17] The court thereby dissolves the problem associated with taking an exact position on a difficult doctrinal question as to when a situation falls within the scope of a directive at all. Despite this, the ECJ does impart its opinion on the aim of the directive,[18] thus indicating a desire to determine the scope in detail. However, it then deals extensively with abuse of rights.[19] From a methodological perspective, this approach only makes sense when the general applicability of the directive is initially affirmed – since a right must first be granted, before it is capable of being abused. It is apparent however, that the ECJ always considers the objective of the relevant European rules in relation to the objective element of an abuse of rights (see below IV.1). The ECJ thus mixes two different principles in the interpretation and application of the law. Dogmatically the

16 Ibid.
17 Ibid.
18 Ibid.
19 Ibid.

interpretation of the meaning and purpose takes priority, as a right must first exist before its abuse can even be considered.[20]

In terms of practical implementation, the difference can be that when interpretation according to the purpose of the provision, the seised court considers only the right on the basis of objective circumstances that the parties have presented. However, where an abuse of rights is concerned the subjective element must also be taken into account (see below IV.1.). But because, in practice, the subjective elements are usually based on objective elements (see below IV.1.), there exists no significant difference. The dispute over the right approach is therefore of (mere) academic interest.

IV. Annex: Whose Opinion Counts in European Union Law?

1. The Member States' Common Sense

As a side note, it has been argued that the European legal system could face a challenge in the identification of such legal principles. Even within the legal system of a single Member State, social requirements and conventions cannot usually, in a clear and definite way, be reduced to a common denominator. The EU consists of 28 Member States, which, more or less, have different social requirements.

It has to be assumed that each of the Member States wished to introduce its own understanding of principles of law as they collectively created primary European law in the form of the European Treaties. This has led to a situation in which a common European legal conception has arisen through means of a composition of European states. When the task at hand is to confirm which unwritten legal principles are introduced by the European Treaties, it must be asked which unwritten legal principles are common to all Member States.

Here the question becomes more complicated. The current versions of the TEU and TFEU were enacted through the Treaty of Lisbon in 2009. In the creation of this treaty however, only the contemporary Member States were involved in its drafting. Cyprus as the 28th Member State first acceded

20 For further reception of this issue see *Larenz*, Methodenlehre der Rechtswissenschaft, 1991, p. 396 and *Honsell*, Rechtsmissbrauch und teleologische Reduktion unter besonderer Beruecksichtigung des schweizerischen Rechts, in: Festschrift für Theodor Mayer-Maly, 1996, p. 368 (368).

to the EU in 2013. In addition, it must be considered that the Treaty of Lisbon preceded other treaties, in which other Member States did not participate.

Originally, the European Economic Community (EEC) consisted of only six countries: Belgium, France, Italy, Luxembourg, the Netherlands and Germany, who agreed to cooperation under the Treaty of Rome. In view of this patchwork of Member States, which socio-legal requirements are significant?

It has to be taken into account that a new version of a treaty, in this case the Treaty of Lisbon, is always built upon the foundation of the former treaty. Into the Treaty of Lisbon flow all values which were fundamental in the previous treaties dating back to the Treaty of Rome. In each new codifycation the values of previously absent, newly acceding Member States are also included. Therefore, the 1993 Treaty of Maastricht contains contributions from states that joined at that time, but did not participate in the founding of the EEC.

The question as to whether the interpretation of European law should also consider the requirements of the acceding Member State despite the lack of a new treaty codification is possibly answered by Art. 49 TEU. This article regulates the accession of Member States to the EU. The accession of a new Member State does not require a re-drafting of the European Treaties. A 'new founding' of the EU to include the new Member State does not take place. In contrast, the acceding Member State must accept the laws of the EU as a constituent obligation of the accession process.[21] The coming into power of the accession agreement stipulates that the acceding Member State is automatically obligated to observe all applicable primary and secondary European law; the so called *acquis communautaire*.[22] The acceding Member State has therefore no opportunity to introduce its own law into the European legal system. On the contrary, the new Member State must adjust its domestic law to comply with all contemporary European law.[23] From the author's perspective this situation must also mean that the new Member State has no opportunity to introduce any unwritten legal principles into the EU system. The accession to an established legal system requires the joining State to submit to the rules of that system. The new Member State enjoys

---

21 Cf. *Republic of Poland v. European Commission*, 2 October 1997, Case C-259/95, ECLI:EU:C:1997:454, para. 17.

22 *Ohler*, in: Grabitz/Hilf/Nettesheim (eds), Das Recht der Europäischen Union, 2015, Art. 49 EUV para. 44.

23 Ibid.

equality with the other Member States; it must however, play by rules upon which it has little influence. Consequently, the Member State does not have the opportunity to introduce its own social requirements. On the contrary, just as with concrete provisions of European law, unwritten legal principles of the established legal order take precedent over those of the acceding Member State.[24]

Specifically, this means that the unwritten legal principles of the EU are to be understood in the context of common action on behalf of the Member States, which have created the European Treaties.[25] Through the Treaties, the Member States have expressed their understanding. For the legal understanding of the Treaty of Lisbon this means consequently that the social requirements of Cyprus cannot be taken into consideration during the search for unwritten legal principles. Politically this situation is unacceptable and non-compliant with the principle of equality of all Member States.

2. A Glance at Brexit

With the announced exit of the UK from the EU (Brexit), the question arises as to how general principles of British law incorporated into EU law, will now be dealt with. Provisions regulating such questions cannot be found in the Treaties. The withdrawal of a Member State is regulated rather sparingly alone in Art. 50 TEU. The withdrawal is accomplished centrally through a withdrawal agreement (Art. 50 para. 2 sent. 2 TEU). Meanwhile, the detailed design is subject to negotiation between the Union and the exiting Member State. Part of the exit negotiations will address whether, and to what extent, EU law shall remain applicable within the legal system of the withdrawing State. It is therefore conceivable that negotiations will focus on the maintenance of desirable legal principles of the withdrawing State within the European legal system. It depends, therefore, on the agreement. If no agreement is reached, one will have to inquire as to the will of the parties. This issue will remain under consideration on a case-by-case

---

24 This is shared by *Meng*, in: von der Groeben/Schwarze/Hatje (eds), Europäisches Unionsrecht, 2015, Art. 49 EUV para. 17 and *Cremer*, in: Calliess/Ruffert (eds), EUV/AEUV, 2011, Art. 49 EUV para. 6.

25 It might confuse that *Alexandros Kefalas*, 12 May 1998, Case C-367/96, ECLI:EU:C:1998:222, para. 29 does not object that the member state applies its own national scale to identify abuse behaviour.

basis. In general, however, the EU will have no interest to maintain the principles of law of a State, which is no longer part of European Union.

D. Case Studies – Making Abusive Use of Fundamental Freedoms

I. The ECJ's Schedule for Identifying Abusive Use of Rights

In its case law, the ECJ has increasingly attempted to establish criteria for the identification of an abusive use of rights. The court considers that as a prerequisite to a finding of abuse there must be objective and subjective elements.[26]

> "With regard to the objective element, it must be apparent from a combination of objective circumstances that, despite formal observance of the conditions laid down by EU rules, the purpose of those rules has not been achieved."[27]

The second prerequisite is represented by a subjective element. This is found in the "intention to obtain an advantage from the Community rules by creating artificially the conditions laid down for obtaining it."[28] Exactly how this subjective element is to be identified is not clear. The ECJ once stated that it "must be apparent from a number of objective factors that the

26 *Torresi v. Consiglio dell'Ordine degli Avvocati di Macerata*, 17 July 2014, Joined cases C-58/13 and C-59/13, NJW 2014, p. 2849; *SICES and others v. Agenzia Dogane Ufficio delle Dogane di Venezia*, 13 March 2014, Case C-155/13, ECLI:EU:C:2014:145, para. 31; similar although less differentiating *O v. B*, 12 March 2014, Case C-456/12 – O, ECLI:EU:C:2014:135, para. 58.

27 *Torresi v. Consiglio dell'Ordine degli Avvocati di Macerata*, 17 July 2014, Joined cases C-58/13 and C-59/13, NJW 2014, p. 2849; *SICES and others v. Agenzia Dogane Ufficio delle Dogane di Venezia*, 13 March 2014, Case C-155/13, ECLI:EU:C:2014:145, para. 32; *Eichsfelder Schlachtbetrieb*, 21 July 2005, Case C-515/03, Slg. 2005, I-7355; *Emsland Staerke*, 14 December 2000, Case C-110/99, Slg. 2000, I-11569.

28 *Torresi v. Consiglio dell'Ordine degli Avvocati di Macerata*, 17 July 2014, Joined cases C-58/13 and C-59/13, NJW 2014, p. 2849; *Eichsfelder Schlachtbetrieb*, 21 July 2005, Case C-515/03, Slg. 2005, I-7355; *Emsland Staerke*, 14 December 2000, Case C-110/99, Slg. 2000, I-11569.

essential aim of the transactions concerned is to obtain an undue advantage."[29] This is the conclusion of a subjective element on hand from objective ones. In other cases, the ECJ has required that the identification of a violation shall be conducted on the basis of "rules of evidence of national law."[30] According to German law at least, the result of both approaches would be the same, as subjective elements of the violation are usually identified on the basis of the objective elements of the violation.

Noteworthy at this juncture is the requirement of the ECJ that the conditions, under which an abusive use of a right is performed, must be created artificially. This approach is found non-uniformly in secondary law of the EU (see above III.3.b). The terminology of the ECJ is correct for present purposes because here a limitation of the guarantee of fundamental freedoms due to the presence of abuse is necessary. Here there exists a case of protection of fundamental freedoms (see above III.3.b). Therefore, it is logically necessary that an arrangement is established which does not reflect the usual arrangement applicable to the exercise of fundamental freedoms. The requirements for their guarantee should firstly be effectuated before simple limitations are applied to them.

II. Centros (ECJ, 9.03.1999 – C-212/97)

A prominent example in European company law is the *Centros* case.[31] The facts of the case are as follows:

Centros Ltd., a private limited company registered on 18.5.1992 in England and Wales requested the Trade and Companies Board of the Danish Department of Trade to register a branch of Centros in Denmark. Centros had a share capital of GBP 100, which had been neither paid up nor made available to the company. The Danish Trade and Companies Board refused the registration on the grounds that Centros was in fact seeking to establish not a branch, but a principal establishment in Denmark by circumventing the Danish national rules requiring contribution of a minimum capital of DKK 200.000.

The ECJ saw no abusive use of the freedom of establishment. It stated:

---

29 *SICES and others v. Agenzia Dogane Ufficio delle Dogane di Venezia*, 13 March 2014, Case C-155/13, ECLI:EU:C:2014:145, para. 33.

30 *Eichsfelder Schlachtbetrieb*, 21 July 2005, Case C-515/03, Slg. 2005, I-7355.

31 *Centros*, 9 March 1999, Case C-212/97, NJW 1999, p. 2027.

> "In the present case, the provisions of national law ... are rules governing the formation of companies ... . The provisions of the Treaty on freedom of establishment are intended specifically to enable companies formed in accordance with the law of a Member State and having their registered office, central administration or principal place of business within the Community to pursue activities in other Member States through an agency, branch or subsidiary. That being so, the fact that a national of a Member State who wishes to set up a company chooses to form it in the Member State whose rules of company law seem to him the least restrictive and to set up branches in other Member States cannot, in itself, constitute an abuse of the right of establishment. The right to form a company in accordance with the law of a Member State and to set up branches in other Member States is inherent in the exercise, in a single market, of the freedom of establishment guaranteed by the Treaty."[32]

In addition

> "... the fact that a company does not conduct any business in the Member State in which it has its registered office and pursues its activities only in the Member State where its branch is established is not sufficient to prove the existence of abuse or fraudulent conduct which would entitle the latter Member State to deny that company the benefit of the provisions of Community law relating to the right of establishment."[33]

III. Cadbury Schweppes (ECJ, 12.09.2006)

Cadbury Schweppes (hereinafter CS), a company resident in the United Kingdom, is the parent company of the Cadbury Schweppes group consisting of companies established in the UK, in EU Member States and in other third countries. The group includes, *inter alia*, two subsidiaries in Ireland, Cadbury Schweppes Treasury Services (hereinafter CSTS) and Cadbury Schweppes Treasury International (hereinafter CSTI), which CS owns indirectly through a chain of subsidiaries at the head of which is Cadbury Schweppes Overseas (hereinafter CSO). CSTS and CSTI, which are established in the International Financial Services Centre Dublin / Ireland (hereinafter IFSC), were subject to a tax rate of 10% at the time of the main proceedings. According to the decision referring the matter to the ECJ, CSTS replaced a similar structure which included a company established in Jersey. It was established for three purposes: firstly, to remedy a tax problem

32 Ibid.
33 Ibid.

encountered by Canadian taxpayers holding CS preference shares; secondly, to avoid the need to obtain consent from the UK authorities for overseas lending transactions; and thirdly, to reduce the withholding tax on dividends paid within the group under the scheme of Council Directive 90/435/EEC of 23 July 1990 on the common system of taxation applicable in the case of parent companies and subsidiaries of different Member States (OJ 1990 L 225, p. 6). According to this decision, those three objectives could have been achieved if CSTS had been incorporated in accordance with UK legislation and if it was established in the UK. CSTI is a subsidiary of CSTS. In the view of the national court, it was incorporated in Ireland in order to avoid the application of certain UK tax provisions on exchange transactions. According to the decision referring the matter, it was common ground that CSTS and CSTI were established in Dublin solely in order that the profits related to the internal financing activities of the Cadbury Schweppes group could benefit from the tax regime of the IFSC. Given the rate of tax applicable to companies established in the IFSC, the profits of CSTS and CSTI were subject to "a lower level of taxation" within the meaning of the legislation on controlled foreign corporations (hereinafter CFCs). The UK tax authorities took the view that, for the 1996 financial year, none of the conditions for exemption from taxation provided for by that legislation applied to those subsidiaries.

By decision of August 18, 2000, the Commissioners of the Inland Revenue therefore claimed, under the CFC legislation, corporation tax from CSO in the sum of UK £8,638,633.54 on the profits made by CSTI in the financial year ending December 28, 1996. The tax notice related only to the profits made by CSTI because, in that financial year, CSTS made a loss. On August, 21 2000, CS and CSO appealed to the Special Commissioners of Income Tax, London against that tax notice. Before that body, they maintained that the legislation on CFCs was contrary to Articles 43 EC, 49 EC and 56 EC.

The national court stated that it was faced with a series of uncertainties as to the application of Community law to the case before it. It asked whether CS was abusing the freedoms introduced by the EC Treaty in establishing and capitalising companies in another Member State solely to take advantage of a tax regime more favourable than that applicable in the UK.

The ECJ answered:

> "[T]he fact that a Community national, whether a natural or a legal person, sought to profit from tax advantages in force in a Member State other than his State of residence cannot in itself deprive him of the right to rely on the provisions of the

Treaty.[34] ... [T]he fact that in this case CS decided to establish CSTS and CSTI in the IFSC for the avowed purpose of benefiting from the favourable tax regime which that establishment enjoys does not in itself constitute abuse. That fact does not therefore preclude reliance by CS on Articles 43 EC and 48 EC."[35]

"On the other hand, a national measure [to prevent abuse] may be justified where it specifically relates to wholly artificial arrangements aimed at circumventing the application of the legislation of the Member State concerned.[36] ... If ... CFC is a fictitious establishment not carrying out any genuine economic activity in the territory of the host Member State, the creation of that CFC must be regarded as having the characteristics of a wholly artificial arrangement."[37]

IV. Conclusion

These two cases illustrate how the ECJ has dealt with abuse within the context of the freedom of establishment. Decisive is not whether a company avoids the provisions of national law, but rather whether a cross-border case (cross-border situations are protected by the freedom of establishment) has been construed in order to ensure that a non-national may rely upon the law of that Member State, despite the absence of an actual cross border circumstance. Such artificial situations are not protected by the freedom of establishment.[38] In order to establish the presence of such a case, the crucial factor to consider is whether the border crossing is also intended to allow the legal subject to undertake an economic activity.

E. Final Conclusion

(1) A guarantee of fundamental freedoms ensured through the European Treaties is only possible in the context of the European Union legal system. These freedoms are therefore guaranteed to the extent that their exercise is not curtailed by fundamental principles of European law.

---

34 *Cadbury Schweppes*, 12 June 2006, Case C-196/04, ECLI:EU:C:2006:544, para. 36.

35 Ibid., para. 38.

36 Ibid., para. 51.

37 Ibid., para. 68.

38 *Teichmann*, Gesellschaftsrecht im System der Europäischen Niederlassungsfreiheit, ZGR 2011, p. 639 (669).

Such principles are however, not always anchored expressly in the European Treaties. There also exist unwritten principles of European law.

(2) One of these unwritten principles is the prohibition of abusive use of rights. This prohibition is expressly contained in some secondary EU legislation, but also finds application outside of the scope of these secondary acts. The principle's origin is found in the common legal traditions of the Member States.

(3) An abusive use of rights is established when a factual circumstance is created that allows rights to be exercised contrary to the purposes the fundamental freedoms intend to protect. The right at issue here involves a cross-border exercise of a specific activity (provision of a service, an establishment, the movement of capital). The factual circumstance is perceived as abusive if it creates the formal appearance of a cross-border activity, without actually involving one, in order to benefit from rights connected merely to the formal aspect of cross-border activity. In such cases, reliance upon the fundamental freedoms is excluded.

Bibliography

Alexandros Kefalas, 12 May 1998, Case C-367/96, ECLI:EU:C:1998:222

Cadbury Schweppes, 12 June 2006, Case C-196/04, ECLI:EU:C:2006:544

Centros, 9 March 1999, Case C-212/97, NJW 1999, 2027

Christian Calliess and Matthias Ruffert, *EUV/AEUV* (4th Edition, 2011)

Eichsfelder Schlachtbetrieb, 21 July 2005, Case C-515/03, Slg. 2005, I-7355

Emsland Staerke, 14 December 2000, Case C-110/99, Slg. 2000, I-11569

Eberhard Grabitz, Meinhard Hilf and Martin Nettesheim (eds), *Das Recht der Europäischen Union* (57th supplement, 2015)

Hans von der Groeben, Jürgen Schwarze and Armin Hatje, *Europäisches Unionsrecht* (7th Edition 2015)

Heinrich Honsell, 'Rechtsmissbrauch und teleologische Reduktion unter besonderer Beruecksichtigung des schweizerischen Rechts' in Margarethe Beck-Mannagetta, Helmut Böhm and Georg Graf (eds), *Der Gerechtigkeitsanspruch des Rechts: Festschrift für Theo Mayer-Maly zum 65. Geburtstag* (Boehlau, Koeln, Wien 1996), 368

Hans D. Jarass, Elemente einer Dogmatik der Grundfreiheiten, Zeitschrift Europarecht 1995, 202

Hans D. Jarass, Elemente einer Dogmatik der Grundfreiheiten II, Zeitschrift Europarecht 2000, 705

Karl Larenz, *Methodenlehre der Rechtswissenschaft* (6th Edition, Springer, Berlin 1991)

Karl Larenz and Claus-Wilhelm Canaris, *Methodenlehre der Rechtswissenschaft* (3rd Edition, Springer, Berlin 1995)

Libert/Van Eycken/Bleeckx/Clippele/ Syndicat national des propriétaires et copropriétaires ASBL v. Gouvernement flamand, 8 May 2013, Joined cases C-197/11 and C-203/11, DNotZ 2013, 831

Marcus Lutter, Die Auslegung angeglichen Rechts, JuristenZeitung 1992, 593

Marcus Lutter, 'Zum Umfang der Bindung durch Richtlinien' in von Ole Due, Marcus Lutter and Jürgen Schwarze (eds), *Festschrift fuer Ulrich Everling* (Nomos, Baden-Baden 1995), 765

Kofoed v. Skatteministeriet, 5 July 2007, Case C-321/05, ECLI:EU:C:2007:408

Kratzer v. R+V Allgemeine Versicherung AG, 28 July 2016, Case C-423/15, NJW 2016, 2796

Münchener Kommentar zum Bürgerlichen Gesetzbuch: BGB (6th Edition, C.H. Beck, München 2013)

O v. B, 12 March 2014, Case C-456/12 – O, ECLI:EU:C:2014:135

Republic of Poland v. European Commission, 2 October 1997, Case C-259/95, ECLI: EU:C:1997:454

SICES and others v. Agenzia Dogane Ufficio delle Dogane di Venezia, 13 March 2014, Case C-155/13, ECLI:EU:C:2014:145

Christoph Teichmann, Gesellschaftsrecht im System der Europaeischen Niederlassungsfreiheit, ZGR 2011, 639

Torresi v. Consiglio dell'Ordine degli Avvocati di Macerata, 17 July 2014, Joined cases C-58/13 and C-59/13, NJW 2014, 2849

In Search of a More Effective Assessment of State Aid Measures in the Aviation Sector

Jadwiga Urban-Kozłowska

A. *Introduction*

It is universally acknowledged that the proper assessment of aid measures plays an important role in ensuring a level playing field for competing companies in all Member States. It also helps to minimize the possible distortions of competition. Article 3 (1) (b) of the Treaty on the Functioning of the European Union (hereinafter TFEU) confers on the European Union exclusive competence when it comes to adopting competition rules necessary for the functioning of the internal market.[1] As a result, the European Commission (hereinafter the Commission) is the only body entitled to authorize the use of public funding.[2]

Within the aviation sector, new guidelines on State aid to airports and airlines[3] (hereinafter the 2014 Aviation Guidelines) were issued by the Commission in 2014. They provide a framework for assessing whether public funds granted to airports and / or airlines that have been classified as State aid may be declared compatible with the internal market on the basis of Article 107 (3) (c) TFEU. It is relevant to note that the 2014 Aviation Guidelines replaced the previously existing Commission guidelines on

* This research was supported by the grant from National Science Centre in Poland awarded on the basis of decision no DEC-2013/11/N/HS5/04234.

1 The fact that the European Union has an exclusive competence in a specific area means that only the European Union may legislate and adopt legally binding acts. As a consequence, the Member States are able to do so themselves only if they have been empowered by the European Union or in case of the implementation of EU acts.

2 For more information about the role of the Commission when it comes to assessing aid measures, see: *Schmauch*, EU Law on State Aid to Airlines: Law, Economics and Policy, 2012, p. 219–222.

3 See: Communication from the Commission – Guidelines on State aid to airports and airlines, OJ C 99, 4.04.2014, p. 3–34.

State aid in the aviation sector, namely the Community guidelines on financing of airports and start-up aid to airlines departing from regional airports (hereinafter the 2005 Aviation Guidelines),[4] as well as the guidelines on the application of Articles 92 and 93 of the EC Treaty and Article 61 of the EEA Agreement to State aids in the aviation sector (hereinafter the 1994 Aviation Guidelines).[5]

The general compatibility criteria are stipulated in point 79 of the 2014 Aviation Guidelines. Pursuant to this provision, a given aid measure may be authorized provided that the following cumulative conditions are satisfied:

- contribution to a well-defined objective of common interest;
- need for State intervention, which means that a State aid measure must be targeted towards a situation where aid can bring about a material improvement that the market cannot deliver itself;
- appropriateness of the aid measure, *i.e.* the aid measure must be an appropriate policy instrument to address the objective of common interest;
- incentive effect, which means that the aid must change the behaviour of the undertakings concerned in such a way that they engage in additional activity which they would not carry out without the aid or they would carry out in a restricted or different manner or location;
- proportionality of the aid, namely the aid amount must be limited to the minimum needed to induce the additional investment or activity in the area concerned;
- avoidance of undue negative effects on competition and trade between Member States;
- transparency of aid, which means that Member States, the Commission, economic operators, and the public, must have easy access to all relevant acts and to pertinent information about the aid awarded thereunder as outlined in section 8.2 of the 2014 Aviation Guidelines.

It is worth emphasizing that these general conditions are common for three types of State aid in the aviation sector, namely: a) investment aid to air-

4 OJ C 312, 9.12.2005, p. 1–14.
5 OJ C 350, 10.12.1994, p. 5–20.

ports; b) operating aid to airports and c) start-up aid to airlines.[6] Their precise meaning may, however, slightly vary and shall be determined with particular reference to provisions dedicated to each category of State aid.

An analysis of the Commission's decision-making process shows that the Commission assesses the conditions of funding in the order in which they are listed in the 2014 Aviation Guidelines.[7] As shall be seen, such an approach does not take due account of the correlations existing between certain requirements. So as to optimize the process, it is the author's contention that the order of the assessment should be modified. The objective of this paper is to propose a modified four-stage assessment, which can be applied to three types of State aid in the aviation sector, *i.e.* a) investment aid to airports; b) operating aid to airports and c) start-up aid to airlines.

According to this approach, the first step should be to examine whether the aid measure at issue contributes to a well-defined objective of common interest. In case of a positive answer, it should be then ascertained whether public funding is indispensable in a given situation. The determination of the best-suited and least distortive aid measure constitutes the third step of the assessment. Finally, it is necessary to make sure that the adverse effects of the aid are sufficiently limited, so that the overall balance of the measure is positive.

This paper is divided into two chapters. The first provides an overview of the most important concepts and main rules concerning State aid in the aviation sector. The second chapter consists of two subchapters, the first describing the material scope of application of the proposed four-stage assessment and the second taking a closer look at the compatibility criteria with a view to explaining the reasoning and the rationale of the new four-stage assessment. The analysis is conducted with reference to the relevant decisions of the Commission.

---

6 See: the 2014 Aviation Guidelines, points 83, 112 and 138.

7 Such an approach is commonly used by the Commission. See, for example: Commission Decision n° SA.43023 on new passenger terminal at Lamezia Terme airport, Brussels, 28.07.2016, C/2016/4807, paras. 43–98; Commission Decision n° SA.40433 on Investment Programme Kärnten Airport, Klagenfurt, Brussels, 6.11.2015, C/2015/7569, paras. 49–96; Commission Decision n° SA.39466 on Start-up aid to airlines operating in the United Kingdom, Brussels, 31.07.2015, C/2015/5254, paras. 47–66; Commission Decision n° SA.18857 on alleged aid to Västerås Airport and Ryanair Ltd, Brussels, 1.10.2014, OJ L 207, paras. 157–176 and 199–215; Commission Decision n° SA.38441 on Isles of Scilly Air links, Brussels, 7.05.2014, C/2014/2626/2, paras. 42–74.

B. *State Aid in the Aviation Sector: the Most Important Concepts and Rules*

Before drawing conclusions and suggesting alternatives, it is important to understand how the current system operates. In this chapter, I will give an overview of the most important concepts and main rules underpinning decisions of State aid to the aviation sector and the institutional procedures that govern these decisions.

I. The Concept of an Undertaking and the Notion of an Economic Activity under EU Competition Law

EU State aid rules are applicable only if public funding is granted to an undertaking. The concept of an undertaking is defined by EU law. It follows on from the Court of Justice case law that it encompasses every entity engaged in an economic activity, regardless of its legal status and the way in which it is financed.[8] As to the notion of economic activity, it means any activity consisting in offering goods and services on a given market.[9]

When it comes to the aviation sector, there is no doubt that airlines are an undertaking within the meaning of EU State aid rules. Whether an airport constitutes an undertaking, however, has been less clear. The 1994 Aviation Guidelines reflected the view that

> "[t]he construction [or] enlargement of infrastructure projects (such as airports, motorways, bridges, etc.) represents a general measure of economic policy which cannot be controlled by the Commission under the Treaty rules on State aids."

---

8 See: *Klaus Höfner and Fritz Elser v. Macrotron GmbH*, 23 April 1991, Case C-41/90, ECR I-1979, para. 21; *Ministero dell'Economia e delle Finanze v. Cassa di Risparmio di Firenze SpA, Fondazione Cassa di Risparmio di San Miniato and Cassa di Risparmio di San Miniato SpA*, 10 June 2006, Case C-222/04, ECR I-289, para. 107; *Federación Española de Empresas de Tecnología Sanitaria (FENIN) v. Commission of the European Communities*, 11 July 2006, Case C-205/03 P, ECR I-6295, para. 25; *Motosykletistiki Omospondia Ellados NPID (MOTOE) v. Elliniko Dimosio*, 1 July 2008, Case C-49/07, ECR I-4863, para. 21.

9 See: *Commission v. Italy*, 16 June 1987, Case 118/85, ECR 2599, para. 7; *Commission v. Italy*, 18 June 1998, Case 35/96, ECR I-3851, para. 36.

The first sign of the gradual change in the perception of this issue was the delivery of the *'Aéroports de Paris'* judgement. In this case EU courts held that the operation of an airport consisting in the provision of airport services to airlines and to various service providers also constitutes an economic activity.[10]

The second major modification in this regard was introduced in the case of Leipzig-Halle airport.[11] In the first judgement given in 2011, the General Court stated that

> "there is no cause to dissociate the activity of building or enlarging infrastructure, ... from the subsequent use to which it is put and that the nature of the development activity must be determined according to whether or not the subsequent use of the infrastructure which has been built amounts to an economic activity."[12]

This new approach was later confirmed by the Court of Justice[13] and incorporated into the 2014 Aviation Guidelines. As a consequence, all public funding spent on the operation and construction of airport infrastructure must be considered as falling within the ambit of EU State aid control, provided that it was granted after the *'Aéroports de Paris'* judgement (12 December 2000).[14]

---

10 See: *Aéroports de Paris v. Commission of the European Communities*, 12 December 2000, Case T-128/98, ECR II-3929, para. 121; *Aéroports de Paris v. Commission of the European Communities*, 24 October 2002, Case C-82/01 P, ECR I-9297, paras. 75–79.

11 For more information about the significance of the judgements in the case of Leipzig-Halle airport see: *Urban-Kozłowska*, Konsekwencje uznania portów lotniczych za przedsiębiorstwa w unijnym prawie pomocy państwa, in: Wójcicka (ed), Europeizacja publicznego prawa gospodarczego i finansowego, 2015, p. 141 (143–148); *Jarecki*, Nowe podejście Komisji Europejskiej do publicznego finansowania budowy infrastruktury transportowej – konsekwencje orzeczenia w sprawie Leipzig-Halle, (2015) 1 internetowy Kwartalnik Antymonopolowy i Regulacyjny, p. 20 (28–29).

12 *Mitteldeutsche Flughafen and Flughafen Leipzig/Halle v. Commission*, 24 March 2011, Joined Cases T-443/08 and T-455/08, ECR II-1311, para. 95. For more information about the so-called 'inseparability criterion' see: *Wilson*, Infrastructure Financing and State Aid Post Leipzig-Halle, (2014) 1 European State Aid Law Quarterly, p. 24 (24–27).

13 See: *Mitteldeutsche Flughafen AG and Flughafen Leipzig-Halle GmbH v. European Commission*, 19 December 2012, Case C-288/11 P, ECLI:EU:C:2012:821, paras. 42–51.

14 See: the 2014 Aviation Guidelines, points 28–29.

The application of EU State aid rules with regard to airport infrastructure has been clarified in the Commission Notice on the notion of State aid in the meaning of Article 107 (1) TFEU.[15] In this document, the Commission differentiates between the use of airport infrastructure for commercial services and those activities that fall under the responsibility of the State in the exercise of its public powers. If an airport infrastructure is intended for the provision of airport services to airlines against payment,[16] which constitute economic activities, the public funding of such infrastructure is subject to EU State aid control. The same rules apply in case of infrastructure constructed to carry out non-aeronautical commercial services to other users.[17] In contrast, public funding of infrastructure projects intended for activities that fall under the responsibility of the State in the exercise of its public powers are not covered by the State aid rules.[18]

II. The Overview of the Rules Governing the Provision of State Aid in the Aviation Sector

If an entity receiving public support is considered to be an undertaking, the provision of such aid is subject to EU State aid rules. According to Article 107 (1) TFEU, a given measure constitutes State aid, provided that four conditions stipulated therein are cumulatively satisfied. State aid is thus any advantage granted by public authorities through state resources on a selective basis to any entity that could potentially distort competition and trade

---

15 See: Commission Notice on the notion of State aid as referred to in Article 107 (1) of the Treaty on the Functioning of the European Union, OJ C 262, 19.07.2016, 1–50.

16 See: the 2014 Aviation Guidelines, point 31.

17 See: ibid., point 33.

18 To illustrate, air traffic control, police, customs, fire-fighting and activities necessary to safeguard civil aviation at an airport against acts of unlawful interference are in principle considered to be of non-economic nature. For more information about the activities that fall under the responsibility of the State in the exercise of its public powers see: *Urban-Kozłowska*, in: Wójcicka, p. 141 (148–150); *Correia*, Les nouvelles lignes directrices de la Commission européenne sur les aides d'État aux aéroports et aux compagnies aériennes, (2014) 3 Zeitschrift fur Luft- und Weltraumrecht, p. 411 (418–421).

in the European Union.[19] The definition of state aid is very broad because 'an advantage' can take many forms, such as grants, loans, guarantees and tax breaks.

In principle, State aid is not allowed in the EU. However, EU legislators did recognize that some types of State aid may be beneficial to the economy and support growth and other policy objectives. That is why the prohibition of State aid stipulated in Article 107 (1) TFUE is not an absolute one. In fact, Article 107 (2) and Article 107 (3) TFUE lay down provisions for specific types of aid that are or may be declared compatible with the internal market.[20]

In regard to aid measures granted to airlines and / or airports, the most important exemption is listed in Article 107 (3) (c) TFUE. According to this provision, the Commission may authorize State aid if it facilitates the development of certain economic activities or of certain economic areas. The use of the word 'may' gives the Commission a wide margin of discretion (the so-called 'discretionary derogation').[21] Furthermore, the wording of Article 107 (3) (c) TFUE is of general nature, which allows for some adjustments to be made so as to better reflect the conditions of a given case. Providing this, flexibility is especially advantageous as this provision may be invoked across all sectors. Notwithstanding this, there is the risk of legal uncertainty. In order to mitigate that threat and bring about greater transparency, the Commission issues a number of guidelines.[22] As indicated earlier, in the context of the aviation sector, it is the 2014 Aviation Guidelines that

---

19 As a result of the limited topic of this paper the conditions set out in Article 107 (1) TFEU will not be addressed in detail. For more information see: *Decocq/ Decocq*, Droit de la concurrence: droit interne et droit de l'Union européenne, 2012, p. 509–536; *Schmauch*, 2012, p. 86–138; *Nicolaides/Kekelekis/Kleis*, State Aid Policy in the European Community, 2008, p. 9–39; *Dudzik*, Pomoc państwa dla przedsiębiorstw publicznych w prawie Wspólnoty Europejskiej. Między neutralnością a zaangażowaniem, 2002, p. 60–131.

20 For more information about the permissible exemptions set out in Article 107 (2) and Article 107 (3) TFUE see: *Schmauch*, 2012, p. 140–176.

21 For more information see: *Aldestam*, EC State aid rules applied to taxes – An analysis of the selectivity criterion, 2005, p. 113–120; *Bacon*, European Community Law of State Aid, 2009, p. 112–114.

22 *Landi*, Exemptions from the General Incompatibility Principle under Article 87 (2) and (3) of the EC Treaty, in: Maria (ed), Competition and State Aid. An Analysis of the EC Practice, 2007, p. 49 (56).

specify the conditions under which aid to airports and / or airlines may be considered compatible with the internal market.

C. *The New Approach of Assessing State Aid to Airports and Airlines*

I. The Material Scope of Application of the Four-Stage Assessment

As has been indicated earlier, the proposed four-stage assessment may be applicable to three types of State aid in the aviation sector, namely: a) investment aid to airports; b) operating aid to airports and c) start-up aid to airlines. To better understand further deliberations, it is useful to present the meaning of these types of State aid.

The 2014 Aviation Guidelines define the notion of investment aid (in French as *'aides à l'investissement'*, in German as *'Investitionsbeihilfe'*) as "aid to finance fixed capital assets, specifically, to cover the capital costs funding gap."[23] To put it simply, it means financial aid provided to airports so as to cover all or part of the costs relating to construction or expansion of the airport infrastructure.[24] Airport infrastructure embraces various kinds of infrastructure and equipment built with a view to providing airport services to airlines as well as service providers.[25] Runways, aprons, taxiways and terminals are typical examples of airport infrastructure that may be supported by public funding. In contrast, the 2014 Aviation Guidelines explicitely exclude the possibility to subsidize the construction of infrastructure or equipment which is primarily necessary for pursuing non-aeronautical activities (e.g. car parks, shops and restaurants). In the same manner, investment aid may not be used to cover ordinary maintenance costs of the airport infrastructure.[26]

---

23 See: the 2014 Aviation Guidelines, point 25 (18).

24 For more information about the notion of investment aid to airports see: *Urban-Kozłowska*, New Rules on Investment Aid to Airports – Do They Clarify It All?, (2016) 2–3 Zbornik Pravnog fakulteta u Zagrebu (hereinafter Zbornik PFZ), p. 289 (290–291).

25 See: the 2014 Aviation Guidelines, point 25 (5).

26 See: ibid., point 25 (15).

As to the issue of operating aid (in French as *'aides au fonctionnement'*, in German as *'Betriebsbeihilfen'*), its aim is to cover all or part of the operating costs of an airport, defined as

> "the underlying costs of the provision of airport services, including categories such as costs of personnel, contracted services, communications, waste, energy, maintenance, rent, administration, etc., but excluding the capital costs, marketing support or any other incentives granted to airlines by the airport, and costs falling within a public policy remit."[27]

In other words, operating aid is intended to cover costs which a company is expected to pay in the normal course of business.[28]

The 2014 Aviation Guidelines do not provide the legal definition of start-up aid to airlines. This type of aid is granted to airlines in order to cover part of airport charges resulting from launching a new route. The objective of this kind of aid is to support new air services by sharing risk during the period of route start-up.

II. The Four-Stage Assessment

With all the above considerations in mind, we shall now take a closer look at the proposed four-stage assessment of aid measures to airports and / or airlines.

1. First Stage – Contribution to a Well-defined Objective of Common Interest

The assessment of an aid measure in the aviation sector shall begin with checking whether it contributes to a well-defined objective of common interest. According to the 2014 Aviation Guidelines this condition is satisfied if the aid measure at issue:

---

27 See: ibid., points 25 (21) and 25 (22).

28 For more information about the notion of operating aid to airports see: *Urban-Kozłowska*, Pomoc operacyjna na rzecz portów lotniczych – kryteria i celowość, in: Dynia/Kuźniar-Kwiatek (eds), Międzynarodowe prawo lotnicze, kosmiczne i technologie, 2016, p. 181 (182–184).

- increases the mobility of European citizens and the connectivity of the regions by establishing access points for intra-Union flights; or
- combats air traffic congestion at major EU hub airports; or
- facilitates regional development.

All those three possible objectives of common interest may be invoked in the case of investment aid[29] and operating aid.[30] In regard to start-up aid, only objectives listed in point a) and c) are applicable.[31] The exclusion of the second objective is quite comprehensible as the launching of new routes will always generate more air traffic at the given airport.

The above-mentioned objectives are diverse in nature. The first and third objective, which are identical for all three types of aid, indicate that State aid granted to airlines and airports may have a positive impact on other EU policies. The second objective focuses on solving one of the crucial problems of the aviation sector, namely excessive congestion at major EU hub airports.[32]

So as to better understand this requirement, let me provide some practical examples. An analysis of the Commission's relevant decisions shows that the investment project at the airport is considered to serve an objective of common interest, in particular, when it improves accessibility of the region concerned,[33] provides employment[34] or stimulates the economic and social development of the region.[35]

It should be pointed out that the duplication of unprofitable airports or the creation of additional unused capacity does not contribute to a well-defined objective of common interest. As a result, every investment project creating new capacity must, in medium terms, meet the forecasted demand

---

29 See: the 2014 Aviation Guidelines, point 84.

30 See: ibid., point 113.

31 See: ibid., point 139.

32 See: European Commission, White Paper – European transport policy for 2010: time to decide, Brussels, 12.09.2001, COM (2001) 370, p. 37; *EURO-CONTROL*, Long-Term Forecast. Flight movements 2010–2030, 2010, p. 9.

33 See: Commission Decision n° SA.18857 on alleged aid to Västerås Airport and Ryanair Ltd, 1.10.2014, OJ L 207, para. 159.

34 See: Commission Decision n° N63/2010 on State guarantee for the construction of Murcia International Airport, Brussels, 10.06.2010, C (2010) 3546, para. 54; Commission Decision n° N 335/2010 on financing the extension of Kassel-Calden airport, Brussels, 20.12.2010, C (2010) 9523, para. 43.

35 See: Commission Decision n° SA.38441 on Isles of Scilly Air links, Brussels, 7.05.2014, C/2014/2626/2, para. 47.

of the airlines, passengers and freight forwarders.[36] Special attention will be paid to those cases of investment aid or operating aid granted to an airport located in the same catchment area[37] as another airport which is not operating at or near full capacity.[38] As to the issue of start-up aid, the Commission will be reluctant to authorize financial assistance for launching a new air route when the connection at issue is already operated by a high-speed rail service or from another airport located in the same catchment area.[39]

This raises an important question: For what reason is this condition to be assessed by the Commission first? This paper contends that the contribution to a well-defined objective of common interest is merely a prerequisite for a proper assessment of aid measures in the aviation sector. Considering the alternative nature of these objectives (meaning it is enough if the aid measure contributes to at least one of them) and the characteristics of the airport sector,[40] it seems that the requirement for the aid measure to contribute to at least one of the objectives of common interest will easily be satisfied.

It is relevant to note that the requirement for an aid measure to contribute to a well-defined objective of common interest is not a new one. Such a condition was already imposed in the 2005 Aviation Guidelines. The major change is that the objectives provided in the 2014 Aviation Guidelines form an exhaustive list while in the 2005 Aviation Guidelines the listing of those objectives was merely illustrative.[41]

---

36 See: the 2014 Aviation Guidelines, point 85.

37 Pursuant to point 25 (12) of the 2014 Aviation Guidelines, the notion of catchment area of an airport means a geographic market boundary that is normally set at around 100 kilometres or around 60 minutes travelling time by car, bus, train or high-speed train.

38 See: the 2014 Aviation Guidelines, points 86, 114–115.

39 See: ibid., point 140.

40 Air transport plays an important role in the integration of the European Union. In case of islands and remote areas, air links often constitute the only or the most efficient way of transportation. Regional airports provide greater accessibility, enhance social cohesion and also boost economic development of the region concerned. Moreover, the air traffic industry is a major employer. The air transport and its infrastructure is, therefore, fundamental to the European economy and society.

41 See: the 2005 Aviation Guidelines, point 61.

2. Second Stage – Is State Intervention Truly Needed?

If it has been decided that the aid measure at issue contributes to a well-defined objective of common interest, it should be then determined whether public funding is indispensable in a given case. Why is it so important to verify that as soon as possible? From the EU law perspective: we must remember that there is a general prohibition of State aid, except for limited justifications listed in paragraph 2 and 3 of Article 107 TFEU. From the perspective of an average person: there is no taxpayers' money that shall be wasted.

It is my contention that there are two conditions listed in the 2014 Aviation Guidelines, namely the necessity of State intervention[42] and the incentive effect[43] that need to be examined together in order to determine if State intervention is indispensible in a given case. The analysis of relevant decisions of the Commission shows that these two requirements are examined by the Commission separately as the second and forth condition respectively. Why should these two requirements be assessed together? The main reason is that they have the same goal, which is to ensure that public funding is required in a given situation.

According to the 2014 Aviation Guidelines, State intervention is necessary when there is a problem which cannot be solved by the market itself, and if the provision of aid will bring about a material improvement in this regard.[44] The possibility to declare State aid compatible with the internal market depends on the size of an airport receiving the assistance or where the new route is about to be launched. The Commission is of the opinion that smaller airports are more in need of investment aid and operating aid. Such an approach is largely true, as it is harder for them to attract private investors.[45] Accordingly, the provision of start-up aid is aimed at compensating for less favourable conditions and bigger risks associated with opening a new route from an unknown and untested airport.

The rules concerning the necessity of State intervention are complex and the annual passenger volume at a given airport is of vital importance. In

---

42 In French as *'nécessité de l'intervention de l'État'*, in German as *'Erforderlichkeit staatlicher Maßnahmen'*.

43 In French as *'effet d'incitation'*, in German as *'Anreizeffekts'*.

44 See: the 2014 Aviation Guidelines, points 87 and 116.

45 See: *Urban-Kozłowska*, (2016) 2–3 Zbornik PFZ, p. 289 (297–298).

principle, investment aid is allowed only for airports with annual traffic of less than 5 million passengers.[46] As regards operating aid, it may be granted only to airports with fewer than 3 million passengers per year.[47] In case of Groningen Airport Eelde, the Commission concluded that there was a need for State intervention. The Commission recognized that Groningen Airport Eelde is a small regional airport with approximately 200 000 passengers per annum, which may not, under present market conditions, be able to fully cover its own operating costs.[48] When it comes to start-up aid, in principal, it will only be considered grantable for routes linking an airport with less than 3 million passengers per annum to another airport within the Common European Aviation Area.[49] However, the 2014 Aviation Guidelines do provide some flexibility in this regard. The most important exception concerns routes linking an airport located in a remote region[50] to another airport (within or outside the Common European Aviation Area). In such a case the start-up aid will be deemed compatible irrespective of the size of the airports concerned.[51]

When it comes to the existence of incentive effect, it means that the provision of public funding changes the situation of the beneficiary. As regards investment aid, it needs to be verified that the investment project would not have been undertaken or would not have been undertaken to the same extent without State aid.[52] If this is confirmed, the Commission will consider that

46 See: the 2014 Aviation Guidelines, point 89.

47 See: the 2014 Aviation Guidelines, points 118–119.

48 See: Commission Decision n° SA.24258 on operating aid in favour of Groningen Airport Eelde NV, Brussels, 9.04.2014, C (2014) 2218, para. 53.

49 Decision 2006/682/EC of the Council and of the Representatives of the Member States meeting within the Council on the signature and provisional application of the Multilateral Agreement between the European Community and its Member States, the Republic of Albania, Bosnia and Herzegovina, the Republic of Bulgaria, the Republic of Croatia, the former Yugoslav Republic of Macedonia, the Republic of Iceland, the Republic of Montenegro, the Kingdom of Norway, Romania, the Republic of Serbia and the United Nations Interim Administration Mission in Kosovo on the Establishment of a European Common Aviation Area (ECAA), OJ L 285, 16.10.2006, 1.

50 Pursuant to point 25 (27) of the 2014 Aviation Guidelines the notion of 'remote regions' encompasses outermost regions, Malta, Cyprus, Ceuta, Mellila, islands which are part of the territory of a Member State, and sparsely populated areas.

51 See: the 2014 Aviation Guidelines, point 143.

52 See: ibid., point 94.

the aid measure has an incentive effect. Operating aid has an incentive effect if it is likely that, in the absence of such aid, the level of economic activity of the airport concerned would be significantly reduced.[53] In the case of start-up aid, it should be proven that without aid the level of economic activity of the airline at the airport concerned would not be expanded.[54] For instance, the new route would not have been launched.

Special attention should be given to point 94 of the 2014 Aviation Guidelines which stipulates that an investment project at an airport may have an incentive effect only if it is not economically attractive in its own right. It seems reasonable to believe that an economically attractive investment project can be pursued without State aid, as it is able to attract private investors willing to finance it. In such a case there is no market failure to be addressed and, therefore, no public funding is necessary. It is also true with regard to a new air route connecting two economically attractive airports which therefore does not need to be financed with public money. The above-mentioned examples imply that every aid deemed necessary must also have an incentive effect.

The findings of the study support the idea that the need for State intervention and the existence of incentive effect should be examined together. It could even be argued that the existence of the incentive effect constitutes a component which verifies whether the provision of State aid is necessary. In essence, only the joint assessment of these two conditions may give an answer to the question whether public funding is truly needed in a given situation.

3. Third Stage – What is the Best-Suited Aid Measure?

Only if it has been verified that the aid measure at issue contributes to at least one of the legitimate objectives set out in the 2014 Aviation Guidelines and is truly needed, the Commission may then move on to the third stage, that is, the determination of the best-suited policy instrument in a given situation. In other words, at this point the Commission needs to assess the appropriateness and the proportionality of the intended aid measure. Since the overriding goal of both these conditions is to choose the best-suited and least distortive policy instrument, it seems reasonable to assess these two

53 See: ibid., point 124.
54 See: ibid., point 148.

conditions together. As one can see, the Commission takes a different approach and examines those criteria separately as the third and fifth condition respectively. In my view, such an approach is inefficient and I therefore propose a different course of action.

Member States must demonstrate that the given aid measure is an appropriate policy instrument to achieve the intended objective or resolve the problems intended to be addressed by the aid.[55] This means that Member States are obliged to consider different viable options and choose the least distortive one that, at the same time, allows them to attain the intended objective.[56] It is therefore advisable to provide State aid in the form of loans, guarantees or repayable advances.[57] As a result, the provision of a direct grant is seen as an instrument of last resort. In the case of start-up aid, it is mandatory to demonstrate that the route receiving public support has prospects of becoming profitable for the airline without public funding after the period of 3 years.[58] In order to ensure coherence in the use of public funds and reduce the administrative burden, Member States are encouraged to design national schemes outlining the main principles concerning public financing in the aviation sector.[59]

When the selected aid measure is appropriate, it is then necessary to assess its proportionality. The aid measure is considered to be proportionate, provided that the same result could not be reached with less aid.[60] In other words, the amount and the intensity of the aid must be limited to the minimum. The 2014 Aviation Guidelines set the maximum permissible aid intensities in relation to each type of State aid.[61]

As the Commission rightly points out the conditions that smaller airports face when developing their services and attracting private financing of their infrastructure investments are often less favourable than those faced by the

55 See: ibid., points 90, 120 and 146.
56 See: Commission Decision n° SA.38441 on Isles of Scilly Air links, Brussels, 7.05.2014, C/2014/2626/2, para. 56.
57 See: the 2014 Aviation Guidelines, point 91.
58 See: ibid., point 147.
59 See: ibid., points 92 and 123.
60 See: Commission Decision n° SA.38441 on Isles of Scilly Air links, Brussels, 7.05.2014, C/2014/2626/2, para. 63.
61 It is relevant to note that the 2005 Airport Guidelines left open the question of permissible aid intensities.

major airports in the European Union. For those reasons, under present market conditions, smaller airports may have difficulties in ensuring the financing of their investments without public funding. Consequently, the need for public funding to finance infrastructure investments will vary according to the size of an airport and will normally be greater for smaller airports. According to the 2014 Aviation Guidelines the permissible aid intensity depends on passenger traffic and ranges from 25% to 75%.[62] In the case of investment aid at Riga airport, the Commission pointed out that the use of competitive tender procedures for the implementation of the investment programme could be a useful tool to minimize the amount of aid.[63]

With regard to operating aid, it may be granted only for a transitional period of 10 years and may cover only up to 50% of the operating losses of an airport.[64] Special provision has been dedicated to operating aid granted to airports with average annual traffic of no more than 700,000 passengers per year.[65] They are allowed to receive State support covering 80% of the initial operating gap for a period of five years.[66] It follows that those airports are not subject to the ten-year transitional period.[67] When it comes to start-up aid, the public funding may cover no more than 50 % of airport charges in respect of a given route for a maximum period of three years.[68]

From the foregoing analysis, it turns out that the appropriateness and the proportionality of an aid measure are two sides of the same coin. Their assessment is equally necessary in order to properly determine the best-suited and least-distortive aid measure. That is why it is proposed that these two requirements should be assessed together.

62 See: the 2014 Aviation Guidelines, point 101.

63 See: Commission Decision n° N41/2010 on State aid related to investments in Riga airport infrastructure, Brussels, 28.04.2010, C (2010) 2539, para. 47.

64 See: the 2014 Aviation Guidelines, points 127–129.

65 See: the 2014 Aviation Guidelines, point 130.

66 For more information about the permissible aid intensities in the case of operating aid see: *Urban-Kozłowska*, in: Dynia/Kuźniar-Kwiatek, p. 181 (182–184).

67 See: *Grespan*, The New European Commission Guidelines for State aid to airports and airlines, (2014) 2 The Aviation and Space Journal, p. 10 (13).

68 See: the 2014 Aviation Guidelines, point 150.

4. Fourth Stage – How to Limit the Negative Effects of the State Intervention?

The classification of relevant public funding as 'State aid' means that the measure at issue generates distortions of competition and affects trade between Member States.[69] The adverse effects of the aid must be sufficiently limited, so that the overall balance of the measure is positive. For this reason, the 2014 Aviation Guidelines require that undue negative effects on competition and trade within the European Union should be avoided.

The 2014 Aviation Guidelines provide several recommendations on how to limit the negative effects on competition and trade. In case of investment aid and operating aid, the beneficiary airport must be open to all potential users and may not be dedicated to one specific user.[70] Moreover, the Commission will carry out a detailed assessment of aid measures granted to airports located in the same catchment area as another airport.[71]

As regards start-up aid, if a connection which will be operated by the new air route is already operated by a high-speed rail service or by another airport in the same catchment area under comparable conditions, it will not be eligible for public funding.[72] Furthermore, the provision of start-up aid cannot be combined with any other type of State aid granted for the operation of a given route.[73]

Making sure that the provision of State aid does not give rise to undue negative effects on competition and trade constitutes an important step in the assessment of aid measures. Nevertheless, this requirement should only be appraised if all the previously mentioned steps have been taken.

D. Conclusions

The aim of this paper was to propose a revised four-stage assessment of State aid in the aviation sector. While assessing aid measures granted to

---

69 For more information about the distortions of competition and the effects of State aid on trade please see: *Bacon*, p. 93–100; *Dony*, Contrôle des aides d'Etat, 2007, p. 71–79; *Ebner/Gambaro*, The Notion of State Aid, in: Maria (ed), Competition and State Aid. An Analysis of the EC Practice, 2007, p. 15 (32–36).

70 See: the 2014 Aviation Guidelines, points 108 and 133.

71 See: ibid., points 106 and 131.

72 See: ibid., point 151.

73 See: ibid., point 153.

airports and airlines, the Commission examines the compatibility conditions in the order in which they are listed in the 2014 Aviation Guidelines. Such an approach is, in the author's view, not the best course of action.

There are two main reasons supporting this opinion. Firstly, the logic behind the order in which the Commission assesses aid measures could be questioned. In contrast, the new four-stage assessment clearly indicates the role of each step. Moreover, every consecutive step results from the previous one. To illustrate, the exemption provided in Article 107 (3) (c) TFEU may only be invoked with a view to facilitating the development of certain economic activities or of certain economic areas. That is why the first step of the new approach involves checking if the aid measure at issue contributes to at least one of the objectives of the common interest. The need for the State intervention is assessed at the second stage. Only if it has been verified that public funding is indispensible in a given situation, it may then be reasonable to ascertain the appropriateness and the proportionality of the intended aid measure. Keeping the above-mentioned considerations in mind, one may wonder why the Commission tends to assess the appropriateness of a given aid measure (third step of the traditional approach) before verifying whether the intended investment is not economically attractive in its own right (forth step of the traditional approach – the existence of incentive effect).[74]

Secondly, the traditional way of assessing the compatibility criteria used by the Commission fails to see the correlations between certain requirements. From the research that has been carried out, it is apparent that only the joint assessment of some of the criteria may give a full picture of the situation at hand. This is especially the case regarding the criteria of necessity of the aid measure and the existence of incentive effect. The same reasoning applies when it comes to appropriateness of the aid measure and its proportionality.

To sum up, it has been the intention of this paper to put forward one particular course of action available to the Commission, namely, a re-examination of the order in which applications are assessed. It is hoped that the central proposal of this article causes debate and re-examination of the existing framework and in doing so, forces changes of the legislation which will provide a more open, transparent and effective process for State aid in the aviation sector.

74 See: ibid., point 94.

Bibliography

Aéroports de Paris v. Commission of the European Communities, 12 December 2000, Case T-128/98, ECR II-3929

Aéroports de Paris v. Commission of the European Communities, 24 October 2002, Case C-82/01 P, ECR I-9297

Mona Aldestam, *EC State aid rules applied to taxes – An analysis of the selectivity criterion* (Iustus Förlag, Uppsala 2005)

Kelyn Bacon, *European Community Law of State Aid* (Oxford University Press, New York 2009)

Commission Decision n° N 41/2010 on State aid related to investments in Riga airport infrastructure, Brussels, 28.04.2010, C (2010) 2539

Commission Decision n° N 63/2010 on State guarantee for the construction of Murcia International Airport, Brussels, 10.06.2010, C (2010) 3546

Commission Decision n° N 335/2010 on financing the extension of Kassel-Calden airport, Brussels, 20.12.2010, C (2010) 9523

Commission Decision n° SA.18857 on alleged aid to Västerås Airport and Ryanair Ltd, Brussels, 1.10.2014, OJ L 207

Commission Decision n° SA.24258 on operating aid in favour of Groningen Airport Eelde NV, Brussels, 09.04.2014, C (2014) 2218

Commission Decision n° SA.38441 on Isles of Scilly Air links, Brussels, 7.5.2014, C/2014/2626/2

Commission Decision n° SA.39466 on Start-up aid to airlines operating in the United Kingdom, Brussels, 31.07.2015, C/2015/5254

Commission Decision n° SA.40433 on Investment Programme Kärnten Airport, Klagenfurt, Brussels, 6.11.2015, C/2015/7569

Commission Decision n° SA.43023 on new passenger terminal at Lamezia Terme airport, Brussels, 28.07.2016, C/2016/4807

Commission v. Italy, 16 June 1987, Case 118/85, ECR 2599

Commission v. Italy, 18 June 1998, Case 35/96, ECR I-3851

Vincent Correia, 'Les nouvelles lignes directrices de la Commission européenne sur les aides d'État aux aéroports et aux compagnies aériennes' (2014) 3 Zeitschrift fur Luft- und Weltraumrecht, 411

André Decocq and Georges Decocq, *Droit de la concurrence: droit interne et droit de l'Union européenne*, Manuel (6th Edtition, LGDJ, Paris 2012)

Marianne Dony, *Contrôle des aides d'Etat* (Editions de l'Université de Bruxelles, Brussels 2007)

Sławomir Dudzik, *Pomoc państwa dla przedsiębiorstw publicznych w prawie Wspólnoty Europejskiej. Między neutralnością a zaangażowaniem* (Kantor Wydawniczy Zakamycze, Zakamycze 2002)

Martino Ebner and Edoardo Gambaro, 'The Notion of State Aid' in A. Santa Maria (ed), *Competition and State Aid. An Analysis of the EC Practice* (Kluwer Law International, The Netherlands 2007), 15

EUROCONTROL, 'Long-Term Forecast. Flight movements 2010–2030' (2010)

Federación Española de Empresas de Tecnología Sanitaria (FENIN) v. Commission of the European Communities, 11 July 2006, Case C-205/03 P, ECR I-6295

Davide Grespan, 'The New European Commission Guidelines for State aid to airports and airlines' (2014) 2 The Aviation and Space Journal, 10

Klaus Höfner and Fritz Elser v. Macrotron GmbH, 23 April 1991, Case C-41/90, ECR I-1979

Stefan Akira Jarecki, 'Nowe podejście Komisji Europejskiej do publicznego finansowania budowy infrastruktury transportowej – konsekwencje orzeczenia w sprawie Leipzig-Halle' (2015) 1 internetowy Kwartalnik Antymonopolowy i Regulacyjny, 20

Niccolò Landi, 'Exemptions from the General Incompatibility Principle under Article 87 (2) and (3) of the EC Treaty' in A. Santa Maria (ed), *Competition and State Aid. An Analysis of the EC Practice* (Kluwer Law International, Netherlands 2007), 49

Ministero dell'Economia e delle Finanze v. Cassa di Risparmio di Firenze SpA, Fondazione Cassa di Risparmio di San Miniato and Cassa di Risparmio di San Miniato SpA, 10 June 2006, Case C-222/04, ECR I-289

Mitteldeutsche Flughafen AG and Flughafen Leipzig-Halle GmbH v. European Commission, 19 December 2012, Case C-288/11 P, ECLI:EU:C:2012:821

Mitteldeutsche Flughafen and Flughafen Leipzig/Halle v. Commission, 24 March 2011, Joined Cases T-443/08 and T-455/08, ECR II-1311

Motosykletistiki Omospondia Ellados NPID (MOTOE) v. Elliniko Dimosio, 01 July 2008, Case C-49/07, ECR I-4863

Phedon Nicolaides, Mihalis Kekelekis and Maria Kleis, *State Aid Policy in the European Community* (2nd Edition, Kluwer Law International, Great Britain 2008)

Magnus Schmauch, *EU Law on State Aid to Airlines – Law, Economics and Policy* (Lexxion Verlagsgesellschaft, Berlin 2012)

Jadwiga Urban-Kozłowska, 'Konsekwencje uznania portów lotniczych za przedsiębiorstwa w unijnym prawie pomocy państwa' in E. Wójcicka (ed), *Europeizacja publicznego prawa gospodarczego i finansowego* (Wydawnictwo im. S. Podobińskiego Akademii im. Jana Długosza w Częstochowie, Częstochowa 2015), 141

Jadwiga Urban-Kozłowska, 'New Rules on Investment Aid to Airports – Do They Clarify It All?' (2016) 2–3 Zbornik Pravnog fakulteta u Zagrebu, 289

Jadwiga Urban-Kozłowska, 'Pomoc operacyjna na rzecz portów lotniczych – kryteria i celowość' in Elżbieta Dynia and Dagmara Kuźniar-Kwiatek (eds), *Międzynarodowe prawo lotnicze, kosmiczne i technologie* (Wydawnictwo Uniwersytetu Rzeszowskiego, Rzeszów 2016), 181

Thomas Wilson, 'Infrastructure Financing and State Aid Post Leipzig-Halle' (2014) 1 European State Aid Law Quarterly, 24

Propositions towards a Potential Revision of Directive 2004/35/EC on Environmental Liability with Regard to the Prevention and Remedying of Environmental Damage (ELD)

Kleoniki Pouikli

A. *Introduction*

The Directive 2004/35/EC on "environmental liability with regard to the prevention and remedying of environmental damage" entered into force on April 30, 2004, with a transposition deadline set for April 2007. The Environmental Liability Directive (hereinafter ELD) aspired to establish an effective model of environmental liability based on the Polluter Pays Principle (hereinafter PPP) that would offer solutions to environmental problems, which are distinguished by the lack of spatial and temporal limits as well as by their dynamic, diffuse and no linear development. The ELD makes Member States responsible for ensuring that significant and measurable damage to water, land, and biodiversity (protected species and habitats) is either prevented by appropriate measures in case of imminent threats, or effectively remedied by restoring the previous condition, if the damage has already been done.

Moreover, the ELD outlines in Annex III the activities for which an operator may be held liable, a set of exemptions as well as certain obligatory and optional defences. The fundamental characteristic of this Directive is the merge away from the traditional civil law liability models and the establishment of a *sui generis* both strict and fault based liability regime that deals straightforward with the pure environmental damage,[1] reinforces the preventive action and emphasizes the need for in natura restoration by providing for a triple system of primary, compensatory and complementary

---

1 *Brans*, Fundamentals of Liability for Environmental Harm under the ELD, in: Bergkamp/Goldsmith (eds), The EU Environmental Liability Directive – A Commentary, 2013, p. 31 (37–38).

remediation.[2] In short, the adoption of an instrument with a general horizontal – and not sectoral – nature like the ELD aimed at the harmonization of the differentiated national environmental liability models by functioning as *a minima* compromise among legal, geographical, economic and ecological diversities.

Though, after eleven years, the ambitious perspectives of this EU initiative have faded away revealing crucial conceptual ambiguities. Given that environmental protection is placed in the area of shared competence between the EU and its Member States, and under the light of the article 193 TFEU which stresses *"that EU rules do not seek to achieve complete harmonization in the environmental field,"*[3] many difficulties stem from the given margin of appraisal, which allows the Member States to adopt stricter measures seeking optimum convergence between the national regulatory systems and EU regulations. This tests sorely the uniform and harmonized application of the ELD and leads to its scant activation (II). As a result, there is inevitably a growing interest in a potential revision of the ELD in order to deal with the existing discrepancies (III).

B. The Main Problems of the Implementation of the Directive

Despite the fact that the ELD aimed to overcome the institutional and regulatory entanglement within a grid pattern of a supranational system of environmental liability, it ended up as a very complicated and uncertain tool due to its weak practical implementation and its inherent ambiguities. Namely, the European Commission identified 16 cases treated under the ELD at the beginning of 2010, and estimated that the total number of these cases across EU at the end of 2012 was 50. Therefore, the national reports submitted in 2013 to the Commission about the experience gained in the application of the Directive confirm emphatically this limited implementa-

---

2 Annex II of the ELD.

3 *Fornasar and Others*, 22 June 2000, Case C-318/98, ECLI:EU:C:2000:337, para. 46; *Dimos Agiou Nikolaou*, 22 April 2010, Case C-82/09, ECLI:EU:C:2010:220, para. 24.

tion. With the exception of Poland, in other European countries the activation of the Directive is particularly limited.[4] Indicatively, in the UK in 2009 four cases have been identified under the regime established by the Directive, in 2010 six cases and in 2011 only three,[5] while in Greece for the period 2009–2012 52 cases were recorded under the transposing system, but only nine of the them were finally closed with the implementation of the relevant measures.[6]

Emerging expressively in the light of the analysis of the national cases is the difficulty to reach the threshold set by the ELD in order for an environmental damage to fall within its scope especially regarding land and water damages. An indicative example comes from the UK and concerns the Rye Harbour spill.[7] In that case of water damage, the relevant Environmental Agency concluded that the requirement under the ELD – that the environmental damage should affect the entire surface water body – was not exceeded. Moreover, the limited application of the ELD can be explained by the interface between its regulations and other EU environmental legislation like the Industrial Emissions Directive and the Water Framework Directive having as a common benchmark the PPP.[8]

Besides, important obstacles regarding the efficient implementation of the ELD are due to the procedural or substantive variations arising from the article 16 (1) of the ELD, which introduces a clause giving the national authorities the discretionary power to maintain or adopt more stringent

4 Available at: http://ec.europa.eu/environment/legal/liability/index.htm (visited 22.03.2017).

5 UK Department for Environment, Food and Rural Affairs, Environmental Liability, 2012, available at: https://www.gov.uk/government/uploads/system /uploads/attachment_data/file/221095/pb13895-indepth-guide-regs09.pdf (visited 22.03.2017).

6 Greek Report on the implementation of Directive 2004/35/EC 'On environmental liability with regard to the prevention and remedy of environmental damage', available at: http://ec.europa.eu/environment/legal/liability/pdf/eld_ms_reports/EL.pdf (visited 22.03.2017).

7 *Environmental Agency*, Review of Incidents at Hazardous Waste Management Facilities, version 2.06.2012, available at: www.environment-agency.gov.uk (visited 22.03.2017).

8 The cases *Van de Walle*, 7 September 2004, Case C-01/03, ECLI:EU:C:2004: 490 and *Commune de Mesquer*, 24 June 2008, Case C-188/07, ECLI:EU:C: 2008:359 present expressly the interplay between the environmental responsibility regime and the legal framework of other specific EU directives.

measures than the ELD's rules. In this vein, differentiations regarding the definition of 'environmental damage' come out in cases where the national transposing legislations incorporated national definitions of the pre-existing environmental liability schemes.[9] With respect to the definition of the 'operator', in the report of the European Commission to the Council and Parliament in 2010 it is stated that the extent of the aforementioned term was "broadened to all but one country, while some of them adopted a particularly broad scope of it."[10]

In addition to this, variations have been noticed regarding the determination of additional responsible parties.[11] Limitations to that possibility of the article 16 (1) was laid down by the CJEU in the case Raffinerie Mediteranee (ERG)[12] and restated in the recent Fipa Group case,[13] where it was elucidated – complying with the PPP – that the operator remains the only primarily liable person, despite the addition of other potential liable parties. Moreover, by their national transposition choices, some Member States have extended the scope of strict liability of the Directive beyond the occupational activities listed in Annex III by adding new activities to that list. This was the case of France, where in the light of the *Coussouls de Crau* case – regarding an oil leak in a nature reserve – they added to the aforementioned Annex III the activities of oil transportation by pipeline.[14]

Furthermore, such an expansion can also be attained either by imposing strict liability for biodiversity damage on non-Annex III activities according to the article 2 (3) (c) like in Greece, or by establishing a general provision

---

9 *BIO Intelligence Service and Stevens & Bolton LLP*, Implementation, challenges and obstacles of the Environmental Liability Directive (ELD), Final Report for the European Commission–DG Environment (2013), p. 38 (40).

10 That applied to Estonia, Finland, Hungary, Lithuania and Poland.

11 Indicatively, according to the Hungarian transposing legislation, a joint and several liability is applied to the owner and possessor user of the real property on which environmental damage or a risk of environmental damage occurs until and unless evidence is provided to the contrary.

12 *ERG and Others*, 9 March 2010, Case C-378/08, ECLI:EU:C:2010:126, paras. 65–66.

13 *Fipa Group and Others*, 4 March 2015, Case C-534/13, ECLI:EU:C:2015:140, paras. 48–53.

14 *Cohignac*, Responsabilité environnementale: La pollution de la Crau estelle concerne par la loi?, 2009, available at: http://www.developpementdurable.com/environnement/2009/08/A2645/responsabilite-environnementale-la-pollution-de-la-crau-est-elle-concernee-par-la-loi.html (visited 22.03.2017).

of strict liability regardless of the type of activity from which the damage originates, as in Denmark and Finland. Finally, similar discrepancies may appear due to the discretionary power that the European legislator has attributed via article 8 (4) (a) and (b) to Member States regarding the 'permit' and the 'State-of-the-art' defences conciliating the provisions of White Paper which did not envisage these exceptions at all and those of the Draft Directive which treated the above cases as exemptions from liability.[15]

C. Suggestions for a Revision of the Directive

As has been emphasized above, the ELD is a complex but potentially powerful liability system. That being said, it is necessary to discuss the potential revision of it, in order to improve some of its problematic points. By way of illustration, it is essential to broaden its scope, since the Directive damages to air, flora and fauna that are not protected by the Birds or Habitats Directives, to cultural buildings and ancient monuments as well as to landscapes – although landscapes may be already partially included if they are located in Natura 2000 sites or include waters covered by the Water Framework Directive.[16]

The main objection concerning the air damage is that it cannot be remediated by removing pollutants like the damages in land and water. Despite this difficulty mainly concerning remedial measures, the inclusion of air in the ELD scope can activate measures to prevent harm to natural resources from airborne pollutants. This is not something insignificant, if we consider that 30% of greenhouse gases going to the atmosphere come from agriculture (deforestation / fertilizers). Concerning any extension of the ELD to cultural buildings and ancient monuments, or landscape would, however, need to be very carefully considered due to the difficulties in establishing thresholds for such damage as well as the insurance implications of such an extension.[17]

---

15 *Fehr/Friedric/Scheil*, Liability Directive – a Useful Tool for Nature Protection?, (2007) 2 Journal for European Environmental and Planning Law, p. 111 (111).

16 *BIO Intelligence Service*, ELD Effectiveness: Scope and Exceptions, Final Report for European Commission – DG Environment (2014), p. 83 (84–87).

17 Ibid., p. 83 (86).

Furthermore, it was also suggested – mainly from Spain[18] – that the costs of extinguishing a fire be considered for inclusion, since the cost of these measures would potentially not be covered by the ELD, unless they were carried out in order to prevent an environmental damage falling into the ELD's scope. Finally, other categories such as odour and noise should be considered for inclusion due to their potential impact on human health, although it is not necessarily easy to determine and measure their negative effect on fauna and flora.[19]

Moreover, the implementation of the ELD may be strengthened by the designation of a special authority on a European level which will supervise the application of the regime and coordinate the national competent authorities. This would be necessary especially because the ELD itself does not give convincing answers about the issue of transboundary pollution.[20] By the same token, either the adoption of an international convention on this issue or the designation of such an authority that will monitor throughout EU the prevention and particularly the reparation of already occurred environmental damage is suggested.[21]

Additionally, a central recommendation with regard to the inefficient implementation of the ELD concerns the lack of sanctions as an indispensable complement of its regulations. The provision of a type of 'penalties' is considered to be essential in order to control and monitor the compliance of the operators to the orders of the public authority. Without mandatory sanctions or control mechanisms like in the Regulation 1907/2006 concerning the *Registration, Evaluation, Authorisation and Restriction of Chemicals*, which explicitly mentions that Member States must adopt sanctions which

18 Spanish report: Questionnaire on the experience gained in the application of the Directive pursuant to Article 18 (1) in conjunction with Annex VI of the ELD available at: http://ec.europa.eu/environment/legal/liability/pdf/eld_ms reports /ES.pdf (visited 22.03.2017).

19 *BIO Intelligence Service*, p. 83 (86).

20 Article 15 ELD.

21 Although the development of new environmental protection institutions at the Union level is limited by the Article 13 of the Treaty and by CJEU case law that restricts delegation of power (*Meroni v High Authority*, 13 June 1958, Case C-9/56, ECLI:EU:C:1958:7, para. 133), this has not stopped the creation of a new Directorate-General for Climate Action (on February 2010) and other new EU environmental bodies.

are "effective, proportionate and dissuasive"[22] it is very difficult to ensure the timely and appropriate enforcement of the Directive rules. This is particularly important for the ELD where its predominant innovative and highly technical character combined with the discretion granted to the national authorities lead very often to a variety of difficulties and inconsistencies that could be to some degree controlled with the parallel provision of sanction or compliance measures.

Furthermore, the lack of a mandatory financial security system for environmental damages[23] addresses the issue of establishing a compensation fund as an alternative viable answer to the complicated environmental cases. Despite the strong criticism that has been levelled against this option (mainly in the American law landscape),[24] such a choice may constitute a potential solution, given that under certain conditions both the existing liability regimes and the premature financial security mechanisms do not provide for adequate answers to the extremely complex structure of current environmental phenomena.[25]

Because the function of such a compensation fund may undermine the application of the PPP, it should be underlined that its activation should have a guarantee or complementary character and be strictly limited inasmuch as it is impossible for the liability rules and the financial security mechanisms to apply. In general, it is very crucial to determine tirelessly the criteria for the activation of such a potential compensation fund especially as far as the identification of the included environmental damages, the circle of potential polluters (and of the fund) and the amount of their contribution is concerned.

Additionally, according to article 5 of the Directive

---

22 Preamble of the Council Regulation (EC) No 1907/2006, para. 122.

23 Mandatory financial security mechanisms are present only in a few countries: Bulgaria, Greece, Czech Republic, Hungary, Romania, Portugal, Spain and Slovakia.

24 *Macey/Cannon* (eds), Reclaiming the Land: Rethinking Superfund Institutions, Methods and Practices, 2007; *Gerrard/Gross*, Amending CERCLA: The post-SARA Amendments to the Comprehensive Environmental Response, Compensation and Liability Act, 2007.

25 *Bocken*, Alternative Financial Guarantees under the ELD, (2009) 18 European Energy and Environmental Law Review, p. 146 (146–151); *Demeester*, L' assurance et les techniques alternatives de financement des dommagesenvrironnementaux, in: Viney/Dubuisson (eds), Les responsabilités environnementales dans l'espace européen, 2006, p. 483 (484).

> "where the environmental damage has not yet occurred, but there is an imminent threat of such damage occurring, the operator shall, without delay, take the necessary preventive measures."

A closer reading of this provision reveals that it does not only refer to the situations where any damage has not yet occurred but also to the situation when an event, accident or omission might have happened but the damage is not yet 'significant', as demanded by the Directive's threshold. Consequently, according to this article fall into the scope of 'preventive measures' not only measures taken to prevent the damage from happening but also measures adopted to prevent the biodiversity damage from becoming significant by minimizing its extent.

Last but not least, regarding the practical implementation of the ELD, it could be very useful to establish at EU level registers of damage cases, which will limit the regional dispersion in ELD application and will contribute to the consistent application of the criterion of '*the significant threshold*'. Accordingly, it is essential to promote the development of common EU databases for the collection of data on the quality of environmental sectors.

D. *Conclusions*

In a final word, it is clear that although the ELD constituted indisputably the first positive step towards a uniform regime that deals with pure environmental damage, its discrepancies reveal that it is actually only a delicate transition phase in a long and difficult search for a really efficient environmental liability system in the EU area. Moreover, given that

> "the most tenacious problem in EU Environmental Law is not the absence of adequate laws, but the flawed and belated Member States transposition (of directives) as well as insufficient application and enforcement of those rules,"[26]

it is essential to highlight the significance of elaborating methods that will monitor and report the ELD's effectiveness.

Hence, the Directive must be seen in general as a unique opportunity to build up a reasonable, balanced and predictable liability regime. The majority of the Member States are still developing their approaches to implementing its provisions and meshing its requirements with their existing liability framework. Thus, despite the fact that the Directive does not prescribe that

---

26 *Wennerås*, The enforcement of EC Environmental Law, 2007, p. 1–2.

all Member States create identical regimes, general consistency in approach will be essential in order to strive for certainty and predictability at EU level. There is still much uncertainty surrounding the operation and enforcement of the ELD, particularly in terms of financial penalties for polluters. This is, however, to be expected, given the geographically wide-reaching scope of the Directive and the variety of the existing and emerging national liability rules. Consequently, in order to take proactive and responsible steps to promote a robust and efficient liability regime across Europe, numerous activities have and can continue to be undertaken by the operator community. On this basis, two activities must be strengthened: firstly, the notion of active information sharing by authorities and operators and, secondly, the transparency via public accessible databases on environmental incidents and practices.

Bibliography

BIO Intelligence Service and Stevens & Bolton LLP, 'Implementation, challenges and obstacles of the Environmental Liability Directive (ELD)' Final Report for the European Commission – DG Environment (2013)

BIO Intelligence Service, 'ELD Effectiveness: Scope and Exceptions' Final Report for European Commission – DG Environment (2014)

Hubert Bocken, 'Alternative Financial Guarantees under the ELD' (2009) 18 European Energy and Environmental Law Review, 146

Edward Brans, 'Fundamentals of Liability for Environmental Harm under the ELD' in Lucas Bergkamp and Barbara Goldsmith (eds), *The EU Environmental Liability Directive – A Commentary* (Oxford University Press, 2013), 31

ERG and Others, 9 March 2010, Case C-378/08, ECLI:EU:C:2010:126

Fipa Group and Others, 4 March 2015, Case C-534/13, ECLI:EU:C:2015:140

Yann Cohignac, 'Responsabilité environnementale: La pollution de la Crau est-elle concerne par la loi?' (2009), at: www.developpementdurable.com

Commune de Mesquer, 24 June 2008, Case C-188/07, ECLI:EU:C:2008:359

Marie-Luce Demeester, 'L'assurance et les techniques alternatives de financement des dommages envrironnementaux' in Geneviève Viney and Bernard Dubuisson (eds), *Les responsabilités environnementales dans l'espace européen* (Bruylant/L.G.D.J, 2006), 483

Dimos Agiou Nikolaou, 22 April 2010, Case C-82/09, ECLI:EU:C:2010:220

Environmental Agency, 'Review of Incidents at Hazardous Waste Management Facilities' (2 June 2012), at: www.environment-agency.gov.uk

Karl-Heinz Fehr, Barbara Friedrich and Susanne Scheil, 'Liability Directive – a Useful Tool for Nature Protection?' (2007) 2 Journal for European Environmental and Planning Law, 111

Fornasar and Others, 22 June 2000, C-318/98, ECLI:EU:C:2000:337

Michael B. Gerrard and Joel M. Gross, *Amending CERCLA: The post-SARA Amendments to the Comprehensive Environmental Response, Compensation, and Liability Act* (American Bar Association, 2007)

Gregg Macey and Jonathan Z. Cannon (eds), *Reclaiming the Land: Rethinking Superfund Institutions, Methods and Practices* (Springer, 2007)

Meroni v High Authority, 13 June 1958, Case C-9/56, ECLI:EU:C:1958:7

Van de Walle, 7 September 2004, Case C-01/03, ECLI:EU:C:2004:490

Pål Wennerås, *The enforcement of EC Environmental Law* (Oxford University Press, 2007)

C. Solutions to International Problems

Resolving Jurisdictional Conflicts Between WTO and RTA Dispute Settlement – Possible Roles for Article 31(3)(c) of the VCLT

Son Tan Nguyen

A. *Introduction*

The number of regional trade agreements (hereinafter RTAs) has grown exponentially in the last several decades.[1] They create a wide overlap of substantive rights and obligations with the WTO.[2] Many of them also include legalized dispute settlement mechanisms[3] operating in parallel to the compulsory and exclusive system of dispute settlement under the WTO.[4] Previous studies have found that the parallel of substantive commitments and legalized dispute settlement mechanisms may potentially result in conflicts

1 As of 7.04.2015, 406 RTAs were in force. *WTO*, Regional Trade Agreements Gateway http://www.wto.org/english/tratop_e/region_e/region_e.htm (visited 8.03. 2017).

2 See e.g., *Bercero*, Dispute Settlement in European Union Free Trade Agreements: Lessons Learned?, in: Bartels/Ortino (eds), Regional Trade Agreements and the WTO Legal System, 2006, p. 383 (400–401); *WTO*, World Trade Report 2011. The WTO and Preferential Trade Agreements: From Co-Existence to Coherence, 2011, p. 128–133; *Horn/Mavroidis/Sapir*, Beyond the WTO? An Anatomy of EU and US Preferential Trade Agreements, (2010) 33 (11) The World Economy, p. 1565 (1565–1588).

3 See e.g., *Porges*, Dispute Settlement, in: Chauffour/Maur (eds), Preferential Trade Agreement Policies for Development, 2011, p. 467; *Morgan*, Dispute Settlement under PTAs: Political or Legal?, in: Buckley and others (eds), Challenges to Multilateral Trade: The Impact of Bilateral, Preferential and Regional Agreements, 2008, p. 241 (241–244); *Kwak/Marceau*, Overlaps and Conflicts of Jurisdiction between the World Trade Organization and Regional Trade Agreements, in: Bartels/Ortino (eds), Regional Trade Agreements and the WTO Legal System, 2006, p. 465 (486–524).

4 See, e.g., *Waincymer*, WTO Litigation: Procedural Aspects of Formal Dispute Settlement, 2002, p. 119–208; *Palmeter/Mavroidis*, Dispute Settlement in the World Trade Organization: Practice and Procedure, 2004, p. 17–48.

of jurisdiction, where a single dispute is submitted in parallel or consecutively to both fora.[5] Even though no such cases have materialized, what happened in *Mexico – Taxes on Soft Drinks,*[6] *Argentina – Poultry Anti-Dumping Duties,*[7] *US – Cattle, Swine and Grain,*[8] and *US – Tuna II*[9] suggests that multiple proceedings over the same dispute may possibly occur

5 *Drahos*, Weaving Webs of Influence: The United States, Free Trade Agreements and Dispute Resolution, (2007) 41 (1) Journal of World Trade (hereinafter JWT), p. 191 (198); *Kwak/Marceau*, in: Bartels/Ortino (eds), p. 465; *Shany*, The Competing Jurisdictions of International Courts and Tribunals, 2003, p. 8; *Pauwelyn*, Adding Sweeteners to Softwood Lumber: The WTO-NAFTA "Spaghetti Bowl" is Cooking, (2006) 9 (1) Journal of International Economic Law (hereinafter JIEL), p. 197 (197–206); *Pauwelyn/Salles*, Forum Shopping before International Tribunals: (Real) Concerns, (Im)Possible Solutions, (2009) 44 Chicago Journal of International Law, p. 77 (77–85); *Lowe*, Overlapping Jurisdiction in International Tribunals, (1999) 20 Australian Year Book of International Law, p. 191; *Marceau*, Conflicts of Norms and Conflicts of Jurisdictions: The Relationship between the WTO Agreement and MEAs and other Treaties, (2001) 35 (6) JWT, p. 1081.

6 *Mexico – Tax Measures on Soft Drinks and Other Beverages (Mexico – Taxes on Soft Drinks)*, WTO Panel Report, 7 October 2005, WTO Doc WT/DS308/R; *Mexico – Taxes on Soft Drinks*, WTO Appellate Body Report, 6 March 2006, WTO Doc WT/DS308/AB/R. In this case, for many years the US had been blocking the establishment of a NAFTA panel to examine Mexico' claim under NAFTA concerning the market access of its cane sugar to the US market. In response, Mexico imposed a tax on US's soft drinks and other beverages; and this, in turn, led the US to initiating a WTO dispute to challenge the tax measures.

7 *Argentina – Definitive Anti-Dumping Duties on Poultry from Brazil*, WTO Panel Report, 22 April 2003, WTO Doc WT/DS241/R. In this case, Brazil requested the WTO panel to find Argentina's antidumping measures inconsistent with the WTO Anti-Dumping Agreement. However, prior to this WTO dispute, Brazil had already challenged the measures before a Mercosur tribunal.

8 Request for Consultations from Canada, *United States – Certain Measures Affecting the Import of Cattle, Swine and Grain from Canada*, 29 September 1998, WTO Doc WT/DS144/1. In this instance, Canada filed parallel requests for consultations under both the NAFTA and WTO procedures involving exactly the same US measures and similar WTO and NAFTA provisions. However, neither of these proceedings was escalated to an adjudicative phase.

9 Request for Consultations by Mexico, *United States – Measures Concerning the Importation, Marketing and Sale of Tuna and Tuna Products (US – Tuna II)*, WTO Panel Report, 15 September 2011, WTO Doc WT/DS381/R; R *US – Tuna II*, WTO Appellate Body Report, 16 May 2012, WTO Doc WT/DS381/AB/R. In this case, Mexico initiated a WTO dispute to challenge the

before the WTO and RTA fora.[10] At the WTO, GATT Article XXIV,[11] does not refer to RTA adjudicative mechanisms, nor does the Dispute Settlement Understanding (DSU) regulate relations between the two systems.[12] As a result, there is no WTO mechanism that can effectively prevent parties from submitting a single dispute to more than one forum.

Outside the WTO, there are some norms that may potentially be able to regulate multiple proceedings. These include the choice of forum clauses included in various RTAs, and common jurisdiction-regulating norms such as *res judicata, lis pendens, forum non conveniens*, comity, and abuse of rights.[13] However, it has been well-established that these norms may not be able to be applied in WTO disputes.[14] The main barrier is DSU Article 23 which states clearly that in resolving WTO disputes, Members have to "recourse to, and abide by, the rules and procedures" of the DSU.[15] It is unrealistic to expect that WTO adjudicators who are extremely mindful of their limited mandate would go against this explicit treaty language and apply norms that would override WTO jurisdiction. Inherent powers, though they

---

US measures concerning the importation, marketing and sale of tuna and tuna products. However, the US strongly disagreed with Mexico's decision to bring the dispute to the WTO because in the US's view, the dispute must be adjudicated at NAFTA under NAFTA Article 2005.4. The US then filed a NAFTA dispute concerning Mexico's failure to move the dispute from the WTO to the NAFTA forum.

10 *Mitchell/Voon*, PTAs and Public International Law, in: Lester/Mercurio (eds), Bilateral and Regional Trade Agreements: Commentary and Analysis, 2009, p. 114 (135–138).

11 Marrakesh Agreement Establishing the World Trade Organization, opened for signature 15 April 1994, 1867 UNTS 3 (entered into force 1 January 1995) Annex 1A (General Agreement on Tariffs and Trade 1994) (GATT) Article XXIV.

12 Marrakesh Agreement Establishing the World Trade Organization, opened for signature 15 April 1994, 1867 UNTS 3 (entered into force 1 January 1995) Annex 2 (Understanding on Rules and Procedures Governing the Settlement of Disputes) (DSU).

13 See, e.g., *Shany*, 2003.

14 See, e.g., *Kwak/Marceau*, in: Bartels/Ortino, p. 465; *Nguyen*, The Applicability of RTA Jurisdictional Clauses in WTO Dispute Settlement, (2013) XVI International Trade and Business Law Review, p. 254; *Nguyen*, The Applicability of *Res Judicata* and *Lis Pendens* in World Trade Organization Dispute Settlement, (2013) 25 (2) Beijing Law Review, p. 123; *Nguyen*, The Applicability of Comity and Abuse of Rights in World Trade Organisation Dispute Settlement, (2016) 35 (1) University of Tasmania Law Review, p. 95.

15 DUS, Article 23.

may exist,[16] might not be a sufficiently concrete basis to enable WTO tribunals to proceed so far.[17] Therefore, WTO tribunals will retain jurisdiction, regardless of any non-WTO norm that may point in the opposite direction. Obviously, there may be no legal solution that can satisfactorily establish jurisdictional priority between the WTO and RTA fora.[18] Multiple proceedings might thus be unavoidable.

This chapter suggests that in the absence of effective rules determining jurisdictional priority, principles of treaty interpretation, particularly Article 31(3)(c) of the Vienna Convention on the Law of Treaties (hereinafter VCLT), might provide a practical and useful alternative to minimize negative consequences of multiple proceedings.

B. Article 31(3)(c) Of The VCLT

Article 31(3)(c) requires that in interpreting a treaty, "[t]here shall be taken into account, together with the context ... any relevant rules of international law applicable in the relations between the parties."[19] Given the growing concerns over the fragmentation of international law,[20] scholars and the ILC

---

16 *Mitchell/Heaton*, The Inherent Jurisdiction of WTO Tribunals: Selected Application of Public International Law Required by Judicial Function, (2010) 31 The Michigan Journal of International Law (hereinafter MJIL), p. 559; *Mexico – Taxes on Soft Drinks*, WTO Appellate Body Report, 6 March 2006, WTO Doc WT/DS308/AB/R, para. 45 (stating that WTO tribunals "have certain powers that are inherent in their adjudicative function").

17 *Brown*, A Common Law of International Adjudication, 2007, p. 78 (emphasizing that "international courts cannot simply assert the existence of inherent powers as a type of carte blanche to do whatever they want").

18 *Kwak/Marceau*, in: Bartels/Ortino, p. 465 (484).

19 Vienna Convention on the Law of Treaties, opened for signature 23 May 1969, 1155 UNTS 331 (entered into force 27 January 1980) (hereinafter VCLT) Article 31(3)(c).

20 *ILC*, Report of the Study Group on the Fragmentation of International Law, Finalized by Martti Koskenniemi, 58th sess, UN Doc A/CN.4/L.682 (13 April 2006), paras. 5–26; *Koskenniemi/Leino*, Fragmentation of International Law? Postmodern Anxieties, (2002) 15 (3) Leiden Journal of International Law, p. 553; *Jenks*, Conflict of Law-Making Treaties, (1953) 30 British Yearbook of Internatio (hereinafter BYIL), p. 401; *Vranes*, Trade and the Environment: Fun-

have "(re)discovered the usefulness of ... Article 31(3)(c)."[21] It is now considered as an 'anti-fragmentation tool'[22] to reduce the negative effects of the fragmentation of international law.[23]

According to Article 31(3)(c), there are three requirements for an external rule to be taken into account in treaty interpretation. Particularly, the external rule must be qualified as a 'rule of international law', 'relevant', and 'applicable in the relations between the parties.'[24] The first[25] and the second elements[26] are easily satisfied in the WTO-RTA context. The real hurdle is the term 'parties.' The critical question is whether the relevant rules are required to be applicable between *all of the parties to the principal treaty under interpretation*, or only *between the parties to the dispute*. If the term 'parties' indeed refers to all of the parties to the treaty under interpretation, Article 31(3)(c) is significantly circumscribed. Indeed, while WTO rules can be used in the interpretation of RTA rules since by definition parties to an RTA are generally parties to the WTO, there would be no RTA to which all WTO Members are also parties.

Research has found that neither the ordinary meaning, the context and drafting history, nor the practice of international courts and tribunals can

---

damental Issues in International Law, WTO Law, and Legal Theory, 2009; *Pauwelyn*, Conflict of Norms in Public International Law: How WTO Law Relates to Other Rules of International Law, 2003.

21 *Tzevlekos*, The Use of Article 31(3)(c) of the VCLT in the Case Law of the ECtHR: An Effective Anti-Fragmentation Tool or a Selective Loophole for the Reinforcement of Human Rights Teleology?, (2010) 31 MJIL, p. 621 (629).

22 *Tzevlekos*, (2010) 31 MJIL, p. 621 (629).

23 *Kammerhofer*, Systemic Integration, Legal Theory and the International Law Commission, (2008) 19 Finnish Yearbook of International Law, p. 157 (160).

24 *Simma/Kill*, Harmonizing Investment Protections and International Human Rights: First Steps towards a Methodology, in: International Investment Law for the 21st Century: Essays in Honour of Christoph Schreuer, 2009, p. 678 (695).

25 *McLachlan*, The Principle of Systematic Integration and Article 31(3)(c) of the Vienna Convention, (2005) 54 (2) ICLQ, p. 279 (290); *Simma/Kill*, in: Essays in Honour of Christoph Schreuer, p. 678 (695); *Gardiner*, Treaty Interpretation, 2008, p. 262–263; *ILC*, UN Doc A/CN.4/L.682, para. 460.

26 *French*, Treaty Interpretation and the Incorporation of Extraneous Legal Rules, 2006 55 (2) ICLQ, p. 281 (304–305); *Simma/Kill*, in: Essays in Honour of Christoph Schreuer, p. 678 (695–697); *McGrady*, Fragmentation of International Law or "Systemic Integration" of Treaty Regimes: *EC – Biotech Products* and the Proper Interpretation of Article 31(3)(c) of the Vienna Convention on the Law of Treaty, (2008) 42 (4) JWT, p. 589 (591).

effectively resolve the ambiguity of the term 'parties.'[27] However, the difficulties in the interpretation of Article 31(3)(c) "hardly constitute a drama;" and Article 31(3)(c) should be employed where necessary.[28] The question is how tribunals could overcome the ambiguity. It has been accepted in doctrine that tribunals might use inherent powers to decide whether the term means parties to the treaty under interpretation or parties to the dispute.[29] This is necessary for tribunals to properly discharge their adjudicatory function, and enables them to fulfil a procedural obligation enshrined in Article 31(3)(c), i.e., consideration of relevant rules that may provide 'operational guidance' on the rules under interpretation.[30]

In the WTO-RTA context, there seem to be a number of factors that lend support to a flexible interpretation, rather than a strict one as done in *EC – Biotech Products*, which requires all WTO Members to be the parties to the treaty containing the relevant rules.[31] *First*, the requirement of duality of membership between the WTO and an RTA is 'unrealistic.'[32] Thus, the strict interpretation would completely remove the chance for the use of RTA rules in interpreting WTO rules.[33] It would be better to require only the identity of parties to the dispute because it would "preserve the realistic possibility that Article 31(3)(c) will be used in the reconciliation of obligations under multilateral treaty regimes, " and enable states "to organize their relations at a bilateral level even where the source of those relations is multilateral in character."[34] *Second*, the strict interpretation of the term 'parties' would have a fragmentation effect because it transforms WTO law into

27 *Merkouris*, Article 31(3)(c) of the VCLT and the Principle of Systemic Integration, 2010, p. 15; *McGrady*, (2008) 42 (4) JWT, p. 589 (594–596); *Gardiner*, 2008, p. 263–265.

28 *Van Damme*, Treaty Interpretation by the WTO Appellate Body, 2009, p. 365; *French*, (2006) 55 (2) ICLQ, p. 281 (307).

29 *Fauchald/Nollkaemper* (eds), The Practice of International and National Courts and the (De-)Fragmentation of International Law, 2012, p. 345.

30 *Mitchell/Heaton*, (2010) 31 MJIL, p. 559.

31 *European Communities – Measures Affecting the Approval and Marketing of Biotech Products*, WTO Panel Report, 29 September 2006, WTO Doc WT/DS291/R, WT/DS292/R, WT/DS293/R, para. 7.68.

32 *Young*, The WTO's Use of Relevant Rules of International Law: An Analysis of the *Biotech* Case, (2007) 56 ICLQ, p. 907 (916); *French*, (2006) 55 (2) ICLQ, p. 281 (307).

33 *Young*, (2007) 56 ICLQ, p. 907 (915).

34 *McGrady*, (2008) 42 (4) JWT, p. 589 (613).

an 'island' by limiting the possibility of taking into account other relevant rules of international law.[35]

Obviously, while the use of WTO rules in interpreting RTA rules is uncontroversial, the reverse scenario, i.e. the use of RTA rules in interpreting WTO rules *could, and should*, be possible where necessary. The real question is *how* that could be done.

C. *Integration Of WTO And RTA Norms On The Basis Of Article 31(3)(c)*

I. How WTO and RTA Tribunals Could Take into Account the Equivalent Norms from the Other Regime?

Article 31(3)(c) provides "little guidance," if any, as to "what to do about overlapping obligations."[36] It tells us that 'relevant rules' must be taken into account; but says nothing about how to do so. Broude and Shany suggest that *"all relevant norms should be construed in light of the parallel norms coming from the other branches of law."*[37] This is a useful starting point. Indeed, tribunals can use the equivalent rules to ***clarify*** the meaning of the rules under interpretation. Such a use of extraneous rules has been supported in doctrine. Orakhelashvili considers that relevant rules within the meaning of Article 31(3)(c) can be used for the purpose of "clarification of meaning of the terms employed in the treaty."[38] Similarly, French, Simma, and Tzevlekos have also emphasized that tribunals could utilize extraneous rules to "seek clarification of what a treaty provision actually means,"[39]

---

35 *Young*, (2007) 56 ICLQ, p. 907 (916); *Marceau*, WTO Dispute Settlement and Human Rights, (2002) 13 European Journal of International Law (hereinafter EJIL), p. 753 (781).

36 *McLachlan*, (2005) 54 (2) ICLQ, p. 279 (281).

37 *Broude/Shany*, The International Law and the Policy of Multi-Sourced Equivalent Norms, in: Broude/Shany (eds), Multi-Sourced Equivalent Norms in International Law, 2011, p. 1 (14) (emphasis added).

38 *Orakhelashvili*, The Interpretation of Acts and Rules in Public International Law, 2008, p. 371.

39 *French*, (2006) 55 (2) ICLQ, p. 281 (282).

"provide meaning for a specific treaty term,"[40] or "complement 'incomplete' text."[41] Dorr recently added that "the terms of a treaty can … be interpreted in the light of those of another treaty, especially where the latter deals with a similar object or addresses the same legal situation."[42]

International adjudicative bodies have frequently employed extraneous rules to clarify the meaning of the rules under interpretation. The European Court of Human Rights (ECtHR) offers the most prominent example.[43] In *Selmouni*, the ECtHR referred to the 1984 UN Convention against Torture to clarify the meaning of the term 'torture' used in Article 3 of the European Convention on Human Rights (ECHR).[44] Similarly, in *Golder*,[45] the ECtHR examined whether the right to access to the court which is not expressively mentioned in Article 6 of the ECHR, falls within the scope of protection provided by this provision.[46] In ascertaining the scope of Article 6, the Court had employed various means of interpretation, including relevant rules of international law within the meaning of Article 31(3)(c).[47] The Court explained that

> "[t]he principle whereby a civil claim must be capable of being submitted to a judge ranks as one of the universally 'recognised' fundamental principles of law; the same is true of the principle of international law which forbids the denial of justice. *Article 6 para.1 … must be read in the light of these principles.*"[48]

This reference to relevant rules of international law had enabled the ECtHR to ascertain that "the right of access [to the court] constitutes an element which is inherent in the right stated by Article 6."[49] Similarly, in *Soering*,[50] even though the ECtHR did not rely explicitly on Article 31(3)(c), it referred to relevant rules of international law to decide whether the extradition

---

40 *Simma/Kill*, in: Essays in Honour of Christoph Schreuer, p. 678 (703–704).
41 *Tzevlekos*, (2010) 31 MJIL, p. 621 (648).
42 *Dorr*, General Rule of Interpretation, in: Dorr/Schmalenbach (eds), Vienna Convention on the Law of Treaties: A Commentary, 2012, p. 521 (562).
43 For a discussion on these cases, see *Tzevlekos*, (2010) 31 MJIL, p. 621 (371–372).
44 *Selmouni v. France*, 28 July 1999, Case 25803/94, 29 EHRR 403, para. 97.
45 *Golder v. United Kingdom*, 21 February 1975, Case 4451/70, 1 EHRR 524.
46 Ibid., para. 29.
47 Ibid., paras. 30–35.
48 Ibid., para. 35 (emphasis added).
49 Ibid., para. 36.
50 *Soering v. United Kingdom*, 7 July 1989, Case 14038/88, 11 EHRR 439.

of a person to a state where he risked to be exposed to the death penalty fell into the scope of Article 3 of the ECHR.[51] The Court emphasized that the absolute prohibition on torture enshrined in Article 3 of the ECHR can also be "found in similar terms in other international instruments."[52] The court observed that the inclusion in other international instruments of the right not to be extradited to a state where a person might be tortured does not "mean that an *essentially similar obligation* is not already inherent in the general terms of Article 3."[53] In the same manner, in *Rantsev*,[54] the Court, after explicitly invoking Article 31(3)(c), referred to a UN Protocol and the Anti-Trafficking Convention, to establish that trafficking in persons falls within the scope of Art. 4 ECHR.[55] Similar use of extraneous rules could also be found in the jurisprudence of the Inter-American Court of Human Rights.[56]

Evidently, there has been a growing acceptance that extraneous rules could be utilized to clarify the meaning of the rules under interpretation. The same technique might also be employed by WTO and RTA tribunals to interpret equivalent norms in multiple proceedings. Particularly, the well-developed body of WTO norms supported by a rich array of case law, and the widespread incorporation of WTO rules into RTA texts, either by reference[57] or paraphrasing,[58] suggest that recourse to the equivalent WTO rules might be a particularly fruitful technique for RTA tribunals to clarify the

---

51 Ibid., para. 87.

52 Ibid., para. 88.

53 Ibid., para. 88 (emphasis added).

54 *Rantsev v. Cyprus and Russia*, 7 January 2010, Case 25965/04, 51 EHRR 1.

55 Ibid., paras. 274–277.

56 See *Lixinski*, Treaty Interpretation by the Inter-American Court of Human Rights: Expansionism at the Service of the Unity of International Law, (2010) 21 (3) EJIL, p. 585.

57 For example, Article 13 of the Japan – Singapore FTA and Article 301.1 of NAFTA incorporate by reference to GATT Article III:2.

58 For example, Article 13.1 of Decision No 2/2000, the EU – Mexico FTA, reproduces GATT Article III:2. See Economic Partnership, Political Coordination and Cooperation Agreement between the European Community and the United Mexican States, signed 8 December 1997, [2000] L276 Official Journal of the European Union 45 (entered into force 1 July 2000 (goods), 1 October 2000 (services)) (EU – Mexico FTA), Decision No 2/2000 of the EC – Mexico Joint Council (2000) L157 Official Journal of the European Union 10 (EU – Mexico FTA, Decision No 2/2000) Article 13.1.

meaning of certain RTA rules. Indeed, in interpreting RTA provisions that incorporate WTO provisions by reference,[59] recourse to the relevant WTO provisions may be vital because some concepts and terms may not be expressly specified in RTAs, but defined in the equivalent WTO provisions. In this case, regional tribunals may refer to the relevant WTO provisions in order to clarify the meaning of the incorporative RTA provisions. In the same vein, the use of WTO provisions as an interpretative aid may also be useful where RTAs incorporate WTO provisions by paraphrasing. For example, Article 13 of Decision No 2/2000, the EU – Mexico FTA, uses similar treaty language to reproduce GATT Article III:2.[60] In this situation, the similarity in wording and substantive obligations suggests that WTO provisions may assist by guiding RTA tribunals to the ordinary meaning of the incorporative RTA provisions.

Even where it is unclear whether the terminological similarity is a product of an incorporation of WTO provisions in RTAs, it might still be relevant to refer to WTO rules to 'flesh out'[61] the meaning and constituents of an RTA rule. Certainly, regardless of whether RTA parties intend to replicate WTO law, their knowledge about WTO law may play a role in the drafting of RTA law.[62]

In general, it might be suggested that in multiple proceedings where WTO and RTA tribunals have to adjudicate on equivalent rules, they may refer to the similar rules of the other regime to clarify the meaning of the rules under interpretation on the basis of Article 31(3)(c). Given the well-established body of WTO norms, and the widespread incorporation of WTO norms in RTAs, it seems particularly useful for RTA tribunals to seek interpretative guidance from the equivalent WTO norms.

---

59 E.g., Japan – Singapore FTA, Article 13; NAFTA Article 301.1.

60 GATT Article III:2; Article 13 of Decision No 2/2000, the EU – Mexico FTA.

61 *Marceau* and others, The WTO's Influence on Other Dispute Settlement Mechanisms: A Lighthouse in the Storm of Fragmentation, (2013) 47 (3) JWT, p. 481 (513).

62 *McLachlan*, (2005) 54 (2) ICLQ, p. 279 (283).

II. Interpretative Weight of Extraneous Equivalent Norms

The key issue in invoking relevant rules of international law is the interpretative weight that tribunals should give to extraneous equivalent rules. It seems plausible to suggest that identical or similar provisions in different treaties may generally have the same meaning unless a different meaning can be gathered from the circumstances.[63] There is a widely accepted presumption against conflicts in international law[64] and, "it cannot be lightly presumed that a State would conclude a bilateral treaty that ... would place the State in breach of obligations owed to multiple other States."[65]

Thus, when states include similar provisions in different treaties, it might be a strong indication that they intend to confirm existing rules. *Absent any clear intention to deviate from the existing law* which may manifest in the terms, context, object, purpose, subsequent agreements and practice, preparatory work, and the circumstances of conclusion of a treaty,[66] it might be reasonable to suggest that similar provisions should be interpreted to bear the same meaning. The ICSID Arbitral Tribunal in *Enron v. Argentina*[67] stated clearly that

> "the interpretation of a bilateral treaty between two parties in connection with the text of another treaty between different parties will normally be the same, unless the parties express a different intention."[68]

63 *Schreuer*, Diversity and Harmonization of Treaty Interpretation in Investment Arbitration, in: Fitzmaurice and others (eds), Treaty Interpretation and the Vienna Convention on the Law of Treaties: 30 Years on, 2010, p. 129 (136).

64 *Dorr*, in: *Dorr/Schmalenbach*, p. 521 (561); *Jenks*, (1953) 30 BYIL, p. 401 (427–429); *ILC*, UN Doc A/CN.4/L.682, paras. 37–43; *Pauwelyn*, 2003, p. 240–244; *Simma/Kill*, in: Essays in Honour of Christoph Schreuer, p. 678 (686–691); *Oppenheim*, International Law: A Treatise. Vol. 1 – Peace, 1948, p. 858–859.

65 *Simma/Kill*, in: Essays in Honour of Christoph Schreuer, p. 678 (706).

66 See, e.g., *Dorr/Schmalenbach* (eds), Vienna Convention on the Law of Treaties: A Commentary, 2012, p. 521–604; *Van Damme*, 2009; *Gardiner*, 2008; *Orakhelashvili*, 2008.

67 *Enron Corporation and Ponderosa Assets, L.P. v. Argentina (Jurisdiction)*, ICSID Arbitral Tribunal, 14 January 2004, Case ARB/01/3.

68 Ibid., para. 47.

The International Court in IMCO also followed the same approach.[69] Clearly, at the simplest level, it might be presumed that similarly worded provisions would have the same normative content. However, *"[t]aken out of its specific context a seemingly similar provision can assume an entirely different meaning."*[70] This point is widely supported in doctrine. Damme and Gardiner suggest that "[a]ll interpretation is contextual"[71] and the ordinary meaning is "immediately and intimately linked with context and then to be taken in conjunction with all other relevant elements of the Vienna rules."[72] Thus, difference in context "explains *why different courts and tribunals can interpret identical or similar treaty language differently*."[73] Similarly, objects and purposes may also have an impact on the interpretative outcome. Slotboom, by carefully comparing provisions dealing with discriminatory internal taxes in EC and WTO law, proved that interpretative outcomes of similarly worded obligations may be different as a result of differences in objectives and purposes of the two agreements.[74] The ITLOS tribunal famously captured that

> "the application of international law rules on interpretation of treaties to identical or similar provisions of different treaties may not yield the same results, having regard to, inter alia, differences in the respective contexts, objects and purposes, subsequent practice of parties and travaux préparatoires."[75]

It is also to this effect, in interpreting national treatment clauses such as NAFTA Article 1102 or similar provisions in BITs, tribunals have refused to simply adopt the practice of GATT / WTO.[76] In *Methanex v. United States*, even though the Tribunal recognized that the language of

---

69 *Orakhelashvili*, 2008, p. 372; *Constitution of the Maritime Safety Committee of the Inter-Governmental Maritime Consultative Organization*, ICJ, 8 June 1960, (1960) ICJ Rep, p. 150 (170).

70 *Schreuer*, in: Fitzmaurice and others, p. 129 (136) (emphasis added).

71 *Van Damme*, 2009, p. 213.

72 *Gardiner*, 2008, p. 162.

73 *Van Damme*, 2009, p. 213 (emphasis added).

74 *Slotboom*, Do Different Treaty Purposes Matter for Treaty Interpretation?: The Elimination of Discriminatory Internal Taxes in EC and WTO Law, (2001) 4 (3) JIEL, p. 557. See also *Qureshi*, Interpreting WTO Agreements: Problems and Perspectives, 2006, p. 121.

75 *Ireland v. United Kingdom (The MOX Plant case)*, PCA, 24 June 2003, Order No 3, 42 ILM 1187, para. 51 (emphasis added).

76 *Schreuer*, in: Fitzmaurice and others, p. 129 (136).

NAFTA Article 1102 and that of GATT Article III:4 may be similar, it stated clearly that "the term is not to be examined in isolation or in abstracto, but in the context of the treaty and in the light of its object and purpose."[77]

Obviously, in absence of clear intention, similarly worded provisions should be interpreted similarly. The assumption appears reasonable because it reflects the task of interpretation as an integrated process whose outcome is jointly defined by various factors described in Articles 31 and 32 of the VCLT. Moreover, the assumption can also balance between the need for *unity* and the need for *reasonable differences*. A different interpretation of similar norms may still be correct if it is backed by concrete reasons.[78]

In the WTO-RTA context, the similarity between WTO and RTA provisions are *not accidental*, but results from the fact that RTAs incorporate WTO obligations into their texts. It means that WTO-like provisions in RTAs generally originate in the relevant WTO provisions. Therefore, RTA rules should *generally* be interpreted in conformity with WTO rules, not the other way around. In national law, there is a presumption that if the legislature intended to make domestic law conform to the treaty, "the court should ... read an incorporative statute to conform to the borrowed treaty text unless it finds compelling evidence that Congress intended a different result."[79]

The same intention to uphold existing WTO obligations also appears to exist where RTA parties incorporate WTO rules into RTAs. This is apparently clear where RTAs contain explicit provisions to this effect.[80] In the

---

77 *Methanex Corp. v. United States (Final Award of the Tribunal on Jurisdiction and Merits)*, Ad Hoc Tribunal (UNCITRAL), 19 August 2005, (2005) 44 ILM 1345, para. 16, citing *Ireland v. United Kingdom (The MOX Plant case)*, PCA, 24 June 2003, Order No 3, 42 ILM 1187, para. 51.

78 *Alexy*, The Reasonableness of Law, in: Bongiovanni and others (eds), Reasonableness and Law, 2009, p. 5 (12–13); *Artosi*, Reasonableness Common Sense and Science, in: Bongiovanni and others (eds), Reasonableness and Law, 2009, p. 69 (70).

79 *Coyl*, Incorporative Statutes and the Borrowed Treaty Rule, (2010) 50 Virginia Journal of International Law (hereinafter VJIL), p. 655 (691). See also, *Nollkaemper*, National Courts and the International Rule of Law, 2011, p. 149.

80 See, e.g., NAFTA, Article 903 (stating clearly that "the Parties affirm with respect to each other their existing rights and obligations relating to standards-related measures under the GATT Agreement on Technical Barriers to Trade"); Article 20.1 of Decision No 2/2000; Article 2, the EU – Mexico FTA, EU – Chile FTA, Annex IV.

absence of such provisions,[81] the intention can still be assumed because the knowledge about WTO law would be undoubtedly the basis for the creation of the equivalent norms in RTAs. If RTA parties wish to create different commitments, they would simply use different treaty language rather than incorporate WTO provisions into RTA texts. Therefore, unless the opposite is stated, it seems consistent with the intention of RTA parties to read the incorporative RTA rules in conformity to the equivalent WTO rules.[82]

The interpretation of RTA rules in conformity with the equivalent WTO rules could also be based on the persuasiveness of the latter.[83] The WTO generally consists of well-developed rules which have also been intensively clarified by a rich body of case law. Thus, RTA tribunals in interpreting incorporative RTA rules may feel compelled by the persuasiveness of the equivalent WTO norms.

The interpretation of incorporative RTA rules in a consistent manner with the equivalent WTO rules would have a significant impact on coherence of international trade law. It might help to eliminate situations in which similar or identical rules are interpreted differently without any concrete reasons. This role of consistent interpretation was already discussed in doctrine. Cho wrote in his 2006 article that

> "[r]egional trade tribunals can also help avoid fragmentation of global trade by interpreting RTA provisions coherently with the WTO rules. By doing so, regional trade tribunals operate in the same normative force field as the WTO tribunal because both tribunals use the common grammar and syntax of free trade."[84]

Consistent interpretation by RTA tribunals might also be a potential channel by which RTA rules can, in the long run, exert effect on WTO law. Certainly, if there is a process of customarization of WTO law,[85] the widespread consistent interpretation performed by various RTA tribunals would speed up this process since it is evidence of the confirmation and reception

81 NAFTA, Article 903; EU – Mexico FTA, Decision No 2/2000, Article 20.1; US – Australia FTA, Article 1.1.2.

82 *Coyl*, (2010) 50 VJIL, p. 655 (691).

83 See *Nollkaemper*, 2011, p. 155–157.

84 *Cho*, Defragmenting World Trade, (2006) 27 Northwestern Journal of International Law & Business, p. 39 (86–88) (emphasis added).

85 *Hsu*, Applicability of WTO Law in Regional Trade Agreements: Identifying the Links, in: Bartels/Ortino (eds), Regional Trade Agreement and the WTO Legal System, 2006, p. 525 (531–535).

of WTO law by various tribunals.[86] Moreover, consistent interpretation by RTA tribunals would contribute to an emergence of a common law of international trade.[87] Such a normative unity would in turn promote jurisdictional coherence because whichever the forum in which a dispute is decided, it would be resolved based on an integrated body of norms, lowering the chance for inconsistencies to arise.

As a basic principle, RTA tribunals should interpret incorporative RTA rules to bear the same meaning with that of the relevant WTO rules. However, if there is compelling evidence, the presumption may be rebutted. The evidence could be found in the contexts, or objectives and purposes. If the divergent interpretation can be justified on such bases, it can be seen as *reasonable*.[88] It is also equally important that where there is no concrete reason to depart from the equivalent WTO norms, a divergent interpretation may be regarded as creating *unreasonable inconsistency*. The role of Article 31(3)(c) is to specifically target this particular kind of inconsistency, rather than all differences.

Consistent interpretation by RTA tribunals is thus different from a "blind or slavish reference" to WTO rules.[89] An interpretation in accordance with Article 31(3)(c) does not mean that the whole interpretation process under Articles 31 and 32 VCLT should be abandoned.[90] In contrast, an RTA tribunal would have to interpret RTA rules in accordance with these interpretation rules and might therefore, in light of that RTA's text, context, object and purpose, come to an interpretation that differs from the relevant WTO rules.[91] The latest development in WTO jurisprudence strongly confirms

---

86 See *Brownlie*, Principles of Public International Law, 2003, p. 6 (finding that international judicial decisions could be seen as a source of *state practice*). See also *Mitchell/Voon*, in: Lester/Mercurio, p. 114 (120–124) (arguing that "the development of PTA rules and PTA jurisprudence could affect the content or status of the customary rule").

87 See *Weiler*, The EU, the WTO and the NAFTA: Towards a Common Law of International Trade?, 2000; *Cho*, Breaking the Barrier between Regionalism and Multilateralism: A New Perspective on Trade Regionalism, (2001) 42 (2) Harvard International Law Journal, p. 419 (452–465).

88 See generally *Bongiovanni* and others (eds), Reasonableness and Law, 2009.

89 *Hsu*, in: Bartels/Ortino, p. 525 (541).

90 Articles 31 and 32 VCLT do not *exhaustively* codify all interpretation means. See *Waincymer*, 2002, p. 373–528; *Van Damme*, 2009; *Gardiner*, 2008, p. 262–263.

91 *Hsu*, in: Bartels/Ortino, p. 525 (541).

this point. In *US – AD/CVD on Products from China*, the panel pointed out that

> "the various citations to the Draft Articles have been as conceptual guidance only to supplement or confirm, but not to replace, the analyses based on the ordinary meaning, context and object and purpose of the relevant covered Agreements."[92]

McLachlan is thus correct to remind that "Article 31(3)(c) is only part of a larger interpretation process."[93]

In general, the proper role for Article 31(3)(c) might be to eliminate unreasonably inconsistent interpretations between WTO and RTA tribunals. Article 31(3)(c) should be granted neither a lesser nor a greater role.

D. Conclusions

Currently, there seem to be no international legal rules that can satisfactorily eliminate the risks of multiple proceedings over essentially the same disputes before the WTO and RTA fora. In this context, Article 31(3)(c) might provide a useful alternative. It is not magic tool, but it can to some extent minimize the risks of inconsistent interpretations and rulings over similar or identical rules. Indeed, in multiple proceedings before the two fora, both WTO and RTA rules might be qualified as "relevant rules of international law applicable in the relations between the parties" within the meaning of Article 31(3)(c) VCLT. Accordingly, RTA rules could be taken into account in interpreting WTO rules; and vice versa. As far as the equivalent WTO and RTA norms are concerned, RTA tribunals should take into account the equivalent WTO rules to clarify the meaning of the rules under interpretation. In doing so, RTA tribunals should generally read the incorporative RTA rules in conformity with the relevant WTO rules on which these RTA rules are based. However, if there is compelling evidence emerging from the full interpretative process, a divergent interpretation can still be reasonable. This consistent interpretation principle could help to avoid situations in which similar or identical rules between the multilateral and

---

92 *United States – Definitive Anti-Dumping and Countervailing Duties on Certain Products from China*, WTO Panel Report, 22 October 2010, WTO Doc WT/DS379/R, para. 8.87. See also *Yearwood*, Interaction between World Trade Organisation (WTO) Law and External International Law: The Constrained Openness of WTO Law (A Prologue to a Theory), 2012, p. 208.

93 *McLachlan*, (2005) 54 (2) ICLQ, p. 279 (311).

regional trade regimes are interpreted differently without any justifiable reasons for doing so.

Bibliography

Robert Alexy, 'The Reasonableness of Law' in Giorgio Bongiovanni and others (eds), *Reasonableness and Law* (Springer, London 2009), 5

Argentina – Definitive Anti-Dumping Duties on Poultry from Brazil, WTO Panel Report, 22 April 2003, WTO Doc WT/DS241/R

Alberto Artosi, 'Reasonableness Common Sense and Science' in Giorgio Bongiovanni and others (eds), *Reasonableness and Law* (Springer, London 2009), 69

Ignacio Garcia Bercero, 'Dispute Settlement in European Union Free Trade Agreements: Lessons Learned?' in Lorand Bartels and Federico Ortino (eds), *Regional Trade Agreements and the WTO Legal System* (Oxford University Press, New York 2006), 383

Tomer Broude and Yuval Shany, 'The International Law and the Policy of Multi-Sourced Equivalent Norms' in Tomer Broude and Yuval Shany (eds), *Multi-Sourced Equivalent Norms in International Law* (Hart Publishing, Oxford 2011), 1

Chester Brown, *A Common Law of International Adjudication* (Oxford University Press, New York 2007)

Ian Brownlie, *Principles of Public International Law* (6th Edition, Oxford University Press, Oxford 2003)

Sungjoon Cho, 'Breaking the Barrier between Regionalism and Multilateralism: A New Perspective on Trade Regionalism' (2001) 42 (2) Harvard International Law Journal, 419

Sungjoon Cho, 'Defragmenting World Trade' (2006) 27 Northwestern Journal of International Law & Business, 39

Constitution of the Maritime Safety Committee of the Inter-Governmental Maritime Consultative Organization, ICJ, 8 June 1960, (1960) ICJ Rep 150

John F. Coyl, 'Incorporative Statutes and the Borrowed Treaty Rule' (2010) 50 Virginia Journal of International Law, 655

Oliver Dorr, 'General Rule of Interpretation' in Oliver Dorr and Kirsten Schmalenbach (eds), *Vienna Convention on the Law of Treaties: A Commentary* (Springer, Heidelberg 2012), 521

Oliver Dorr and Kirsten Schmalenbach (eds) *Vienna Convention on the Law of Treaties: A Commentary* (Springer-Verlag, Berlin, Heidelberg 2012)

Peter Drahos, 'Weaving Webs of Influence: The United States, Free Trade Agreements and Dispute Resolution' (2007) 41 (1) Journal of World Trade, 191

Enron Corporation and Ponderosa Assets, L.P. v. Argentina (Jurisdiction), ICSID Arbitral Tribunal, 14 January 2004, Case ARB/01/3

European Communities – Measures Affecting the Approval and Marketing of Biotech Products, WTO Panel Report, 29 September 2006, WTO Doc WT/DS291/R, WT/DS292/R, WT/DS293/R

Ole Kristian Fauchald and Andre Nollkaemper (eds), *The Practice of International and National Courts and the (De-)Fragmentation of International Law* (Hart Publishing, Oxford and Portland, Oregon 2012)

Duncan French, 'Treaty Interpretation and the Incorporation of Extraneous Legal Rules' (2006) 55 (2) International & Comparative Law Quarterly, 281

Golder v. United Kingdom, 21 February 1975, Case 4451/70, 1 EHRR 524

Henrik Horn, Petros C. Mavroidis and André Sapir, 'Beyond the WTO? An Anatomy of EU and US Preferential Trade Agreements' (2010) 33 (11) The World Economy, 1565

Locknie Hsu, 'Applicability of WTO Law in Regional Trade Agreements: Identifying the Links' in Lorand Bartels and Federico Ortino (eds), *Regional Trade Agreement and the WTO Legal System* (2006), 525

ILC, *Report of the Study Group on the Fragmentation of International Law,* finalized by Martti Koskenniemi (13 April 2006), UN Doc A/CN.4/L.682

Ireland v. United Kingdom (The MOX Plant case), PCA, 24 June 2003, Order No 3, 42 ILM 1187

Wilfred C. Jenks, 'Conflict of Law-Making Treaties' (1953) 30 British Yearbook of Internatio, 401

Jorg Kammerhofer, 'Systemic Integration, Legal Theory and the International Law Commission' (2008) 19 Finnish Yearbook of International Law, 157

Martti Koskenniemi and Päivi Leino, 'Fragmentation of International Law? Postmodern Anxieties' (2002) 15 (3) Leiden Journal of International Law, 553

Kyung Kwak and Gabrielle Marceau, 'Overlaps and Conflicts of Jurisdiction between the World Trade Organization and Regional Trade Agreements' in Lorand Bartels and Federico Ortino (eds), *Regional Trade Agreement and the WTO Legal System* (2006), 465

Lucas Lixinski, 'Treaty Interpretation by the Inter-American Court of Human Rights: Expansionism at the Service of the Unity of International Law' (2010) 21 (3) European Journal of International Law, 585

Vaughan Lowe, 'Overlapping Jurisdiction in International Tribunals' (1999) 20 Australian Year Book of International Law, 191

Gabrielle Marceau, 'Conflicts of Norms and Conflicts of Jurisdictions: The Relationship between the WTO Agreement and MEAs and other Treaties' (2001) 35 (6) Journal of World Trade, 1081

Gabrielle Marceau, 'WTO Dispute Settlement and Human Rights' (2002) 13 European Journal of International Law, 753

Gabrielle Marceau and others, 'The WTO's Influence on Other Dispute Settlement Mechanisms: A Lighthouse in the Storm of Fragmentation' (2013) 47 (3) Journal of World Trade, 481

Benn McGrady, 'Fragmentation of International Law or "Systemic Integration" of Treaty Regimes: *EC – Biotech Products* and the Proper Interpretation of Article 31(3)(c) of the Vienna Convention on the Law of Treaty' (2008) 42 (4) Journal of World Trade, 589

Campbell McLachlan, 'The Principle of Systematic Integration and Article 31(3)(c) of the Vienna Convention' (2005) 54 (2) International & Comparative Law Quarterly, 279

Panagiotis Merkouris, *Article 31(3)(c) of the VCLT and the Principle of Systemic Integration* (PhD Thesis, Queen Mary University of London School of Law, 2010)

Methanex Corp. v. United States (Final Award of the Tribunal on Jurisdiction and Merits), Ad Hoc Tribunal (UNCITRAL), 19 August 2005, (2005) 44 ILM 1345

Mexico – Tax Measures on Soft Drinks and Other Beverages (*Mexico – Taxes on Soft Drinks*), WTO Panel Report, 7 October 2005, WTO Doc WT/DS308/R

Mexico – Taxes on Soft Drinks, WTO Appellate Body Report, 6 March 2006, WTO Doc WT/DS308/AB/R

Andrew D. Mitchell and David Heaton, 'The Inherent Jurisdiction of WTO Tribunals: Selected Application of Public International Law Required by Judicial Function' (2010) 31 The Michigan Journal of International Law, 559

Andrew D. Mitchell and Tania Voon, 'PTAs and Public International Law' in Simon Lester and Bryan Mercurio (eds), *Bilateral and Regional Trade Agreements: Commentary and Analysis* (Cambridge University Press, UK 2009), 11

David Morgan, 'Dispute Settlement under PTAs: Political or Legal?' in Ross P. Buckley and others (eds), *Challenges to Multilateral Trade: The Impact of Bilateral, Preferential and Regional Agreements* (Kluwer Law International, Netherlands 2008), 241

Son Tan Nguyen, 'The Applicability of Comity and Abuse of Rights in World Trade Organisation Dispute Settlement' (2016) 35 (1) University of Tasmania Law Review, 95

Son Tan Nguyen, 'The Applicability of *Res Judicata* and *Lis Pendens* in World Trade Organization Dispute Settlement' (2013) 25 (2) Beijing Law Review, 123

Son Tan Nguyen, 'The Applicability of RTA Jurisdictional Clauses in WTO Dispute Settlement' (2013) XVI International Trade and Business Law Review, 254

Andre Nollkaemper, *National Courts and the International Rule of Law* (Oxford University Press, Oxford 2011)

L. Oppenheim, *International Law: A Treatise. Vol. 1 – Peace* (7th Edition, Longmans Green & Company, London 1948)

Alexander Orakhelashvili, *The Interpretation of Acts and Rules in Public International Law* (Oxford University Press, New York 2008)

Federico Ortino (ed), *Regional Trade Agreements and the WTO Legal System* (Oxford University Press, New York 2006)

David Palmeter and Petros C. Mavroidis, *Dispute Settlement in the World Trade Organization: Practice and Procedure* (Cambridge University Press, UK 2004)

Joost Pauwelyn, 'Adding Sweeteners to Softwood Lumber: The WTO-NAFTA "Spaghetti Bowl" is Cooking' (2006) 9 (1) Journal of International Economic Law, 197

Joost Pauwelyn, *Conflict of Norms in Public International Law: How WTO Law Relates to Other Rules of International Law* (Cambridge University Press, UK 2003)

Joost Pauwelyn and Luiz Eduardo Salles, 'Forum Shopping before International Tribunals: (Real) Concerns, (Im)Possible Solutions' (2009) 44 Chicago Journal of International Law, 77

Amelia Porges, 'Dispute Settlement' in Jean-Pierre Chauffour and Jean-Christophe Maur (eds), *Preferential Trade Agreement Policies for Development* (World Bank, Washington 2011), 467

Asif H. Qureshi, *Interpreting WTO Agreements: Problems and Perspectives* (Cambridge University Press, New York 2006)

Rantsev v. Cyprus and Russia, 7 January 2010, Case 25965/04, 51 EHRR 1

Christoph Schreuer, 'Diversity and Harmonization of Treaty Interpretation in Investment Arbitration' in Malgosia Fitzmaurice and others (eds), *Treaty Interpretation and the Vienna Convention on the Law of Treaties: 30 Years on* (Martinus Nijhoff Publishers, Leiden, Boston 2010), 129

Selmouni v. France, 28 July 1999, Case 25803/94, 29 EHRR 403

Yuval Shany, *The Competing Jurisdictions of International Courts and Tribunals* (Oxford University Press, Oxford 2003)

Bruno Simma and Theodore Kill, 'Harmonizing Investment Protections and International Human Rights: First Steps towards a Methodology' in Christina Binder and others (eds), *International Investment Law for the 21st Century: Essays in Honour of Christoph Schreuer* (Oxford University Press, New York 2009), 678

Marco M. Slotboom, 'Do Different Treaty Purposes Matter for Treaty Interpretation?: The Elimination of Discriminatory Internal Taxes in EC and WTO Law' (2001) 4 (3) Journal of International Economic Law, 557

Soering v. United Kingdom, 7 July 1989, Case 14038/88, 11 EHRR 439

Vassilis P. Tzevlekos, 'The Use of Article 31(3)(c) of the VCLT in the Case Law of the ECtHR: An Effective Anti-Fragmentation Tool or a Selective Loophole for the Reinforcement of Human Rights Teleology?' (2010) 31 The Michigan Journal of International Law, 621

United States – Certain Measures Affecting the Import of Cattle, Swine and Grain from Canada, 29 September 1998, WTO Doc WT/DS144/1

United States – Definitive Anti-Dumping and Countervailing Duties on Certain Products from China, WTO Panel Report, 22 October 2010, WTO Doc WT/DS379/R

United States – Measures Concerning the Importation, Marketing and Sale of Tuna and Tuna Products (US – Tuna II), WTO Panel Report, 15 September 2011, WTO Doc WT/DS381/R

US – Tuna II, WTO Appellate Body Report, 16 May 2012, WTO Doc WT/DS381/AB/R

Isabelle Van Damme, *Treaty Interpretation by the WTO Appellate Body* (Oxford University Press, Oxford 2009)

Erich Vranes, *Trade and the Environment: Fundamental Issues in International Law, WTO Law, and Legal Theory* (Oxford University Press, Oxford 2009)

Jeff Waincymer, *WTO Litigation: Procedural Aspects of Formal Dispute Settlement* (Cameron May, London 2002)

J.H.H. Weiler (ed), *The EU, the WTO and the NAFTA: Towards a Common Law of International Trade?* (Oxford University Press, Oxford 2000)

WTO, *World Trade Report 2011. The WTO and Preferential Trade Agreements: From Co-Existence to Coherence* (WTO, Geneva 2011)

Ronnie R. F. Yearwood, *Interaction between World Trade Organisation (WTO) Law and External International Law: The Constrained Openness of WTO Law (A Prologue to a Theory)* (Routledge, London 2012)

Margaret Young, 'The WTO's Use of Relevant Rules of International Law: An Analysis of the *Biotech* Case' (2007) 56 International & Comparative Law Quarterly, 907

Jurisdictional Immunity of International Organizations – Should It Be Restricted?

Ivan Puškár

A. Introduction

> "International organizations belong to all member states and to none."[1]
>
> James Lorimer

In the 20th century, states established an increasing number of international organisations in order to cooperate on issues that extend beyond the ambit of a single state.[2] There are by now many international organisations that deal with a wide range of issues extending from peace and security to intellectual property.

The presence of international organizations raises questions as to their legal position in a host state. In a host country, international organizations, as sovereign states, are basically excluded from the jurisdiction of domestic courts and also from the jurisdiction of other state organs. However, the immunity of international organizations is partly different from the immunity of member states. That is because member states decide whether international organizations enjoy the immunity, what its extent is and what form the organizations' immunity and privileges have.[3] There are numerous ways of anchoring the immunity of international organizations, for example, by international treaty or special clauses in the founding treaty. Nevertheless, consideration should also be given to the immunity being established

1 James Lorimer discussing the organizational independence of international organizations. *Tesfagabir*, The State of Functional Immunity of International Organizations and Their Officials and Why It Should be Streamlined, (2011) 10 10 Chinese Journal of International Law (hereinafter Chinese JIL), p. 97 (109).

2 *Brownlie*, Principles of Public International Law, 2003, p. 647.

3 *Reinisch*, Immunity of International Organisations and Alternative Remedies against the United Nations, 2006.

through domestic law. For example, the Charter of the United Nations requires member states to confer to the UN such immunities and privileges as may be necessary for the exercise of its functions and the fulfilment of its purposes.[4]

The immunity of states before the domestic courts of other states results from the principle of sovereign equality of states. This immunity follows from the nature of a state, which is a sovereign subject of international law. States have a territory and population against which they exercise jurisdiction through their institutions. The situation for international organizations is considerably different as they lack territory, population and a compact legal order. An aggrieved subject thus has only a limited possibility to defend his / her rights, whereas in the case of a foreign state he / she has the possibility to make a claim to the domestic court of this state.

Thus, international organizations enjoy certain privileges and immunities in order to be able to function without any unnecessary intervention by their member states and to have ensured their international status. However, what appears to be a restrictive concept of immunity in practice turns out to be a fairly broad and almost unlimited immunity from the jurisdiction of national courts. We can therefore formulate two questions, which form the essence of this article: Does the jurisdictional immunity of international organizations limit the individual´s right of access to a court, and should this jurisdictional immunity be restricted?

B. Right of Access to a Court

Although a large amount of human rights documents do not explicitly contain the right of access to a court, from the interpretation of these texts we can conclude that they guarantee the right to a fair trial. For example, the Universal Declaration of Human Rights, the International Covenant on Civil and Political Rights and most importantly the European Convention on Human Rights (ECHR) from 1950[5] implicitly contain this right. In this context it may be pointed out that the draft of Article 10 of the Universal

4 Article 105 of the Charter of the United Nations.

5 Article 10 of the Universal Declaration of Human Rights, Article 14 (1) of the International Covenant on Civil and Political Rights and Article 6 (1) of the European Convention on Human Rights.

Declaration of Human Rights originally laid down the right of everyone to have access to an independent and impartial tribunal.[6]

Human rights documents also clearly establish the right to a fair trial, as an individual´s right entitles him / her to have a fair third-party adjudication of their claims against anyone else, regardless of whether the opponent might be another private party, a foreign state or an international organization.[7] In the last case, there may be a conflict between everyone's fundamental right of access to a court and the jurisdictional immunity of international organizations (the latter of which, as mentioned above, is discussed and decided on by domestic and international courts). Therefore, if an action against an international organization for human rights abuses is brought before a national court and is subsequently rejected because of jurisdictional immunity of the international organization, the state violates the applicant's right of access to a court.

C. *Reasons for granting immunity to international organizations*

For reviewing the conflict of an individual´s right of access to a court and jurisdictional immunity, it is necessary to analyse the reasons for granting jurisdictional immunity to international organizations. The need to ensure organizational independence is one of the reasons why international organizations seek immunity. Independence is considered to be a condition and necessity for an international organization to function properly. According to proponents of organizational immunity, organizational independence may be safeguarded if an organization carries out the common interest of its member states. In order to keep this balance, international organizations need to be free from any form of influence; being subject to domestic courts may vitiate this balance. As mentioned above, international organizations therefore need immunity for their activities. Immunity thus allows organizations to operate with ease in difficult environments.

Jurisdictional immunity is also justified on the grounds of pride and prestige. Absence of any immunity may evocate a large amount of baseless claims and this may undermine the status of international organizations.

---

6 Draft International Declaration on Human Rights.

7 *Reinisch/Weber*, In the Shadow of Waite and Kennedy. The Jurisdictional Immunity of International Organisations, The Individual's Right of Access to the Courts and Administrative Tribunals as Alternative Means of Dispute Settlement, (2004) 1 IOLR, p. 59 (67).

As another argument for granting immunity, we can add that domestic courts may not be neutral in cases that involve international organizations. The concern is that courts may consider an organization as a foreign element whose interests should be secondary to local ones.

It is an indisputable fact that international organizations are justified in claiming restrictive immunity for functional purposes. Nevertheless, it is difficult to see this fact in the prevailing practice, where international organizations often tend to claim absolute immunity. The lack of consensus on the definition and scope of functional immunity further complicates the problem.

D. *Current practise (theoretical and practical problems of functional immunity)*

In order to avoid the potential denial of justice or to mitigate the negative effects of jurisdictional immunity, two options come into consideration. An international organization may waive immunity and thus be under the jurisdiction of a domestic court or can agree to alternative dispute resolution (ADR). These might involve recourse to an internal organ of the organization or recourse to an external entity, such as an arbitral tribunal.[8] Indeed, some multilateral treaties include provisions to ensure that the immunity of international organization does not lead to a denial of justice. Although the decision on waiver of immunity remains at specific organization and is not subject to review by national courts, this form of restriction of jurisdictional immunity also supports the idea that potential applicants should have the right to access certain types of judicial or alternative dispute resolution. Therefore, the availability of ADR is very important in the case of international organizations. Because, as mentioned earlier, while states may be sued before their national courts, the same possibility does not exist for international organizations. It is also important to keep in mind that international organizations rarely waive their immunity.[9] In numerous decisions,

8 *Gaillard/Pingel-Lenuzza*, International Organisations and Immunity from Jurisdiction. To Restrict or to Bypass, (2002) 51 International & Comparative Law Quarterly (hereinafter ICLQ), p. 1 (11).

9 *Reinisch*, The Immunity of International Organizations and the Jurisdiction of their Administrative Tribunals, (2008) 7 Chinese JIL, p. 285 (285–306).

domestic courts assess the availability of ADR in deciding to grant or refuse jurisdictional immunity. This approach has great importance because it is intended to ensure access to court and also to maintain the independence of the international organization. A large number of authors mention that the granting of jurisdictional immunity may lead to a denial of justice in the absence of any ADR.[10]

Based on the results from the case-law of national courts, when there are alternative means of dispute resolution for injured parties, courts have been more inclined to grant jurisdictional immunity. On the contrary, if the availability of any ADR has not been shown, national courts usually refuse to grant immunity. For example, in the well known judgment of *Waite and Kennedy*[11] the European Court of Human Rights (hereinafter ECtHR) acknowledged that the jurisdictional immunity of international organizations was an essential way to ensure the proper functioning of these organizations without unilateral interference by individual governments. The Court also decided that a material factor in determining whether granting jurisdictional immunity is acceptable or not is if the applicants had had a 'reasonable alternative means' to protect their rights under the ECHR. Although the ECtHR did not specify how this term can be understood and did not make the availability of these instruments a strict prerequisite for the granting of immunity, this 'conditionality' has had a great influence on the subsequent decisions of national courts throughout Europe. The possibility of ADR was also important in the Belgian case *Energies nouvelles et environnement v. Agence spatiale européenne,*[12] in which the Court held that ADR must be available for applicants in order to award the European Space Agency jurisdictional immunity. Since such a legal remedy was available, and thus the test of reasonable alternative means was met, the Belgian court dismissed the action.

10 *Reinisch/Weber*, (2004) 1 IOLR, p. 59 (72).

11 *Waite and Kennedy v. Germany*, European Court of Human Rights, 18 February 1999, Application No 26083/94.

12 *Energies nouvelles et environnement v. Agence spatiale européenne*, Brussels Court of First Instance (1st chamber), 1 December 2005, No 6216, 171, ILDC 1229 (BE 2005).

An example where a national court dismissed an action against an international organization due to a lack of jurisdiction resulting from the existence of immunities is the case of *Mothers of Srebrenica.*[13] 'Mothers of Srebrenica' is an activist and lobbying group representing the interests of the survivors of the victims of genocide which took place in 1995 in the Bosnian Srebrenica. This group claimed that the Netherlands and the UN were responsible for the failure to avoid the genocide. The action was filed at the District Court of The Hague, which dismissed it for lack of jurisdiction. Subsequently, the dispute was heard by the The Hague Court of Appeals, which upheld the decision of the court of first instance. Originally it was a dispute between an association and the UN, but later on the side of defendant acceded to proceedings Netherlands and presented a proposal which said that in terms of absolute immunity enjoyed by the United Nations, the court has no jurisdiction to hear the case. The District Court of The Hague therefore held that in the present case, because of the absolute immunity of the UN before a national authority, it had no jurisdiction to decide the case and no right of exemption from such immunity follows from binding standards of international law.

It is also important to mention the example of Italian courts, which also considered actions related to the immunity of international organizations. Despite the general line to grant international organizations full immunity or, more precisely, to reject cases due to the lack of jurisdiction, the arguments put forward by the Italian courts in the 1980s were different. They acted against the immunity of international organization – in particular against the Food and Agricultural Organization (FAO). This was made possible mainly due to the fact that until 1985, Italy had not acceded to the Convention on the Privileges and Immunities of the United Nations. Despite the fact that that these questions have become faint since 1985, we may still find some examples of decisions which illustrate the approach of national courts to claims against international organizations. Although in *Giovanni Poru v. FAO*, the Roman court of first instance dismissed the plaintiff´s action for lack of jurisdiction, the court also expressed the legal opinion that the international organization does not have jurisdictional immunity from national courts in relations of private law in which the organization acts in

---

13 *Mothers of Srebrenica v. The State of the Netherlands and United Nations*, Appeal Court in The Hague, 30 May 2010, No 200.022.151/01.

the same position as individuals. In the case *INPDAI v. FAO*,[14] the defendant rented a building owned by the plaintiff in Rome. INPDAI argued that the FAO should pay a higher rent. The FAO objected to the jurisdiction of the Court based on, *inter alia*, the fact that it had immunity from legal action. The Court rejected the objection on the grounds that the organization could not claim immunity in private contracts such as the one at stake.

Since the judgment *Ashingdane v. the United Kingdom* (1985),[15] the ECtHR has used the so-called Ashingdane test pursuant to which the right of access to court can be limited only under three conditions: 1. Immunity must serve a legitimate purpose, 2. The used means must be proportionate to this purpose, and 3. The very essence of law must not be weakened. Related to the third criterion it is appropriate to add that jurisdictional immunity actually eliminates the right of access to the court, and therefore it is not satisfactory to use this criterion, since immunity by definition influences the substance of this right. It should also be noted that the provisions of the relevant human rights documents providing the right of access to a court do not contain any restrictive wording which implies restrictions applicable to certain categories of persons. This broad text of provisions does not propose any exceptions because of jurisdictional immunity. Despite this, in a large number of its judgments the ECtHR expressly stated that the right of access to a court guaranteed by the European Convention is not absolute and acknowledged its implicit restriction. The jurisdictional immunity of international organizations could be one of those limitations.

However, there also appears to be a lack of common understanding of the terms of this functional immunity, which is noticeable in case law and in the jurisprudence. Muller writes that international organizations are entitled to immunities to the extent that they are required for the effective fulfilment of their tasks,[16] and Singer argues that an organization is entitled to

---

14 *Istituto Nazionale di Previdenza Per l Dirigent Di AziEnde INDUSTRIALI (INPDAI) v. FAO*, Supreme Court of Cassation, 18 October 1982, UNJYB (1982).

15 *Ashingdane v. the United Kingdom*, European Court of Human Rights, 28 May 1985, Application no 8225/78.

16 *Muller*, International Organizations and Their Host States, 1995, p. 151. In *Tesfagabir*, (2011) 10 Chinese JIL, p. 97 (114).

no more privileges and immunities than it strictly needs.[17] On the other side, Bekker prefers immunity which is proportional to the purpose of the organization and envisages an immunity pyramid where the UN sits at the top.[18] Privileges and immunities granted to the UN can therefore be used as the maximum standard for determining whether a certain organization has a similar need of protection. The other extreme would be an organization which performs purely commercial functions. This type of organization has probably no justified need for any privileges and immunities at all, provided that the exclusion from some privileges and immunities does not prevent the organization from effectively exercising its functions. Bekker thus provides the highest and lowest level of functional immunity. His proposal may potentially lead to the creation of a class of immunities. What appears to us as one of the possible solutions for the future.

E. *Possible future?*

There are several proposals as to how jurisdictional immunity could be restricted.[19] One solution may be the creation of a class of immunities inspired by the Bekker´s concept. The first class may constitute a set of claims that arise from activities that are not related to the ordinary activity of an organization. It may include contractual or non-contractual claims or any other claims which do not have a link to the main objective of the organization. The second class may include claims that arise incidentally from ordinary activities of international organization. This situation may occur either unintentionally or by negligence during the performance of the ordinary activity. These cases could include, for example, those that emanate from peacekeeping operations of the UN and those that result from environmental or social impacts of projects financed and managed by operational organizations. The third class of cases may include actions that typically fall within the ordinary activity of an organization. While organizations should

17 *Singer*, Jurisdictional Immunity of International Organizations: Human Rights and Functional Necessity Concerns, (1995–1996) 53 Virginia Journal of International Law, p. 68 (68). In *Tesfagabir*, (2011) 10 Chinese JIL, p. 97 (114).

18 *Bekker*, The Legal Position of Intergovernmental Organizations: A Functional Necessity Analysis of Their Legal Status and Immunities, 1994, p. 123.

19 *Tesfagabir*, (2011) 10 Chinese JIL, p. 97 (127).

not claim immunity in the first two classes, they should enjoy immunity in the third class, but if the activity or the act of claiming immunity itself conflicts with higher norms of international law, then it should not be immune to the extent of the contradiction. A good example in current practice is the France–INTERPOL agreement, which provides immunity to INTERPOL except in private interactions, mainly consisting of contracts and motor vehicle accidents.[20]

F. Conclusion

There are several problems in the prevailing practice of jurisdictional immunity. International organizations often enjoy functional immunity to irrational limits. This can potentially lead to tension with other norms of international law (especially those related to human rights and particularly the right of access to a court). The increasing role of international organizations urges to revisit jurisprudence related to jurisdictional immunity. International organizations are no longer those from the past; their interaction with other subjects of international law is too large to ignore. In the same vein, we need to see arguments focused on restricting jurisdictional immunity from the perspective of general trends of sovereign immunity. A restrictive concept of immunity may induce international organizations to act more carefully in international environments.

Bibliography

Ashingdane v. the United Kingdom, European Court of Human Rights, 28 May 1985, Application no 8225/78

Peter H. F. Bekker, *The Legal Position of Intergovernmental Organizations: A Functional Necessity Analysis of Their Legal Status and Immunities* (M. Nijhoff, Dordrecht 1994)

Ian Brownlie, *Principles of Public International Law* (6th Edition, Oxford University Press, Oxford 2003)

Energies nouvelles et environnement v. Agence spatiale européenne, Brussels Court of First Instance (1st chamber), 1 December 2005, No 6216, 171, ILDC 1229 (BE 2005)

---

20 Agreement between the INTERPOL and the Government of the French Republic regarding INTERPOL's Headquarters in France, 3.11.1982, GA Res AGN/51/RES/1.

Rosa Freedman, 'UN Immunity or Impunity? A Human Rights Based Challenge' (2014) 25 The European Journal of International Law, 239

Emmanuel Gaillard and Isabelle Pingel-Lenuzza, 'International Organisations and Immunity from Jurisdiction. To Restrict or to Bypass' (2002) 51 The International and Comparative Law Quarterly, 1

Thomas Henquet, 'International Organisations in the Netherlands: Immunity from Jurisdiction of the Dutch Courts' (2010) LVII Netherlands International Law Review, 267

Istituto Nazionale di Previdenza Per l Dirigent Di Azi Ende INDUSTRIALI (INPDAI) v. FAO, Supreme Court of Cassation, 18 October 1982, UNJYB (1982)

Mothers of Srebrenica v. The State of the Netherlands and United Nations, Appeal Court in The Hague, 30 May 2010, No 200.022.151/01

Sam Muller, *International Organizations and Their Host States* (Martinus Nijhoff Publishers, The Hague 1995)

August Reinisch, 'Immunity of International Organisations and Alternative Remedies against the United Nations' (2006), http://ilmc.univie.ac.at/uploads/media/Neumann__Immunity_of_IOs_and_alternative_remedies_against_the_United_Nations.pdf

August Reinisch, *International Organizations before National Courts* (Cambridge University Press, New York 2000)

August Reinisch, 'The Immunity of International Organizations and the Jurisdiction of their Administrative Tribunals' (2008) 7 Chinese Journal of International Law, 285

August Reinisch and Andreas Ulf Weber, 'In the Shadow of Waite and Kennedy. The Jurisdictional Immunity of International Organisations, The Individual's Right of Access to the Courts and Administrative Tribunals as Alternative Means of Dispute Settlement' (2004) 1 International Organizations Law Review, 59

Michela Rišová, Jozef Valuch and Radoslav Seman, *Právo medzinárodných organizácií* (C. H. Beck, Prague 2011)

Michael Singer, 'Jurisdictional Immunity of International Organizations: Human Rights and Functional Necessity Concerns' (1995–1996) 53 Virginia Journal of International Law, 68

Kibrom Tesfagabir, 'The State of Functional Immunity of International Organizations and Their Officials and Why It Should be Streamlined' (2011) 10 Chinese Journal of International Law, 97

Gerhard Ullrich, 'Die Immunität internationaler Organisationen von der einzelstaatlichen Gerichtsbarkeit' (2011) 1 Zeitschrift für ausländisches öffentliches Recht und Völkerrecht, 157

Waite and Kennedy v. Germany, European Court of Human Rights, 18 February 1999, Application No 26083/94

The Right of Self-Defence in International Law: Contemporary Developments in the Context of the Fight against Terrorism

Tina Korošec, Maruša T. Veber

A. *Introduction*

The right of self-defence under Article 51 of the United Nations (UN) Charter is one of the exceptions[1] to the general rule on the prohibition of the use of force, often referred to as 'the cornerstone' of contemporary international legal order.[2] The language of Article 51, codifying international law of self-defence, has been interpreted in various ways since its inception. Scholars and the most prominent international institutions, such as the International Court of Justice (ICJ) and the International Law Commission (ILC), have traditionally favoured confining the principle of the prohibition of the use of force and the right of self-defence to inter-state relations. Recent state practice, however, contradicts this position, possibly indicating a modified interpretation of the above-mentioned rules. States commonly justify their forcible measures[3] against non-state actors (mainly terrorist groups) located

---

* The views and opinions expressed in this article are those of the authors and not in any sense those of the European Court of Human Rights.

** This contribution is partly based on the research published in the following article *Tina Korošec and Maruša Tekavčič Veber*, Pravica do samoobrambe zoper nedržavne akterje v luči boja proti terorizmu (Right to Self-Defence against Non-State Actors in the Context of Fight against Terrorism), (2016) Zbornik Znanstvenih Razprav, p. 41.

1 Some authors refer to limitations to the prohibition of the use of force rather than exceptions. See *d'Aspremont*, Mapping the concepts behind the contemporary liberalization of the use of force in international law, (2010) 31.4 University of Pennsylvania Journal of International Law, p. 1089 (1107).

2 *Randzelhofer*, Commentary to Article 2 (4) of the UN Charter, in: Simma/Khan/Paulus (eds), The Charter of the United Nations: A Commentary, 2012, p. 200 (203).

3 Some authors disagree with the view that non-forcible measures can also be taken in the course of self-defence. See e.g. Separate Opinion of Judge Higgins in Legal Consequences of the Construction of a Wall in the Occupied Palestinian Territory, Advisory Opinion, ICJ Reports 2004, p. 136 (215–216), para. 35.

in a foreign state by invoking their inherent right of self-defence enshrined in Article 51 of the UN Charter, implicitly suggesting that self-defence may not be state-exclusive.

The question whether a state attacked by a non-state actor can rely on Article 51 of the UN Charter when using military force extraterritorially, even if the attack cannot be legally attributed to another state, has been widely discussed within the international legal scholarship. The debate has reached unprecedented dimensions in the context of ISIL (hereinafter Islamic State of Iraq and the Levant) terrorist attacks, which triggered forceful reactions of injured (and indirectly injured) states towards other sovereign states where the terrorist groups supposedly responsible for acts were located.

This contribution juxtaposes traditional reading of Article 51 of the UN Charter and its interpretation by the ICJ with contemporary developments in state practice and discusses new trends in this field of international law. The authors focus on the legal interpretation of an 'armed attack' as a precondition for the right of self-defence, in particular the question of the source and the attribution of an attack, as well as the role of the 'unwilling or unable doctrine' in interpreting Article 51. The situation in Syria is discussed as a possible 'game changer' for the legality of the use of force in self-defence against non-state actors located on the territory of another state.

B. Traditional Understanding of the Right of Self-Defence: the Question of Source and Attribution of an Armed Attack

The existence of an inherent right of self-defence in international law is nowadays undisputed.[4] Its customary international law origins can be traced back to the famous *Caroline* incident concerning destruction of a British vessel in American port in 1837 and the subsequent exchange of diplomatic notes. This resulted in the so-called Webster formula which introduced the first criteria for the lawful exercise of self-defence by states in cases of instant, overwhelming danger leaving no choice of means, and no moment for

4 See Legality of the Threat or Use of Nuclear Weapons, Advisory Opinion, ICJ Reports 1996, p. 226 (244, 263), paras. 38, 96.

deliberation.[5] However, it was not until the endorsement of the prohibition of the use of force in the Covenant of the League of Nations,[6] the General Treaty for Renunciation of War as an Instrument of National Policy (Briand-Kellogg Pact)[7] and the UN Charter[8] that this right gained its true value and importance. In particular, self-defence represents one of the exceptions to the prohibition of the use of force and the only legal justification for the unilateral use of force in contemporary international law.[9]

The right of individual and collective[10] self-defence is codified in Article 51 of the UN Charter as:

> "(an) inherent right of individual or collective self-defence if an armed attack occurs against a Member of the United Nations, until the Security Council has taken measures necessary to maintain international peace and security."

It is therefore governed by two sources of international law which continue to coexist even though they do not exactly overlap: customary international law and treaty law.[11] The relationship between them and the content of the right of self-defence in both sources is at the very least controversial.[12] However, due to space constraints the authors will not further elaborate on these controversies. The right of self-defence was also included in Article 21 of the Articles on Responsibility of States for Internationally Wrongful

---

5 *Shewmaker/Stevens/McGurn*, The Papers of Daniel Webster, Diplomatic Papers, Vol. 1, 1841–1843, 1983, p. 856–857. See also *Shaw*, International Law, 2014, p. 820.

6 League of Nations, Covenant of the League of Nations, 28 April 1919.

7 General Treaty for the Renunciation of War (Kellogg-Briand Pact), 27 August 1928, Paris.

8 *United Nations*, Charter of the United Nations, 24 October 1945, 1 UNTS XVI. See also *Greenwood*, Self-Defence in Max Planck Encyclopaedia of Public International Law (2011), para. 1.

9 *Randzelhofer/Nolte*, Commentary to Article 51 of the UN Charter, in: Simma/Khan/Nolte/Paulus (eds), The Charter of the United Nations: A Commentary, 2012, p. 1397 (1400).

10 For the purposes of this article the distinction between individual and collective self-defence is not instrumental, authors therefore use a more general term 'self-defence'.

11 Case Concerning Military and Paramilitary Activities in and Against Nicaragua *(Nicaragua v. United States of America)*, Merits, Judgment, ICJ Reports 1986, p. 14 (94), paras. 175–176.

12 *Shaw*, 2014, p. 820.

Acts (ARSIWA)[13] as one of the circumstances precluding wrongfulness if applied in conformity with the UN Charter.

For the right of self-defence to be exercised lawfully, certain criteria need to be fulfilled: state relying on self-defence needs to suffer an armed attack[14] and can only resort to the force which is necessary and proportional to such attack.[15] Procedure-wise Article 51 of the UN Charter stipulates that measures taken in self-defence have to be immediately reported to the UN Security Council (UNSC) and have to cease when the UNSC has accordingly secured international peace and security.[16]

The question of lawful use of force in self-defence in relation to attacks of non-state actors has been at the forefront of the legal discussions in the

---

13 "The wrongfulness of an act of a State is precluded if the act constitutes a lawful measure of self-defence taken in conformity with the Charter of the United Nations." Articles on Responsibility of States for Internationally Wrongful Acts (ARSIWA), Yearbook of the International Law Commission, 2001, Vol. II (Part Two). While Articles were never adopted by states in the form of a treaty, international courts increasingly refer to them in their case-law and have proclaimed some of them as being part of customary international law. The nature and status of these secondary rules is, however, not completely settled in the international legal scholarship. While some argue for their customary nature, others perceive it as a doctrinal product therefore being "nothing legal at all." See *Focarelli*, International Law and Third-Party Countermeasures in the Age of Global Instant Communication, (2016) QIL, p. 17 (19). For an overview of relevant case-law, see Responsibility of States for International Wrongful Acts, UN Doc. ST/LEG/SER B/25 (2012).

14 Notions of anticipatory and pre-emptive self-defence have been also discussed by scholars, see *Shaw*, 2014, p. 824–827.

15 Case Concerning Military and Paramilitary Activities in and Against Nicaragua (*Nicaragua v. United States of America*), Merits, Judgment, ICJ Reports 1986, p. 14 (94), para. 176; Legality of the Threat or Use of Nuclear Weapons, Advisory Opinion, ICJ Reports 1996, p. 226 (245), para. 41; Case Concerning Armed Activities on the Territory of the Congo (*Democratic Republic of the Congo v. Uganda*), Judgment, ICJ Reports 2005, p. 168 (223), para. 147; Institut de Droit International, Resolution 10A, Present Problems of the Use of Armed Force in International Law, Session de Santiago 27.10.2007.

16 This procedural aspect does not form part of customary international law. Case Concerning Military and Paramilitary Activities in and Against Nicaragua (*Nicaragua v. United States of America*), Merits, Judgment, ICJ Reports 1986, p. 14 (105, 121), paras. 200, 235.

last couple of years.[17] As a result of recurrent threats posed by international terrorism, the source of an 'armed attack' triggering the right of self-defence has become the most controversial criterion of lawfulness.

The right of self-defence (as one of the lawful exceptions to the prohibition of the use of force) is intrinsically related to the principle of the prohibition of the use of force as enshrined in Article 2 (4) of the UN Charter. The right of self-defence, however, cannot be activated as a response to any use of force.[18] On the contrary, it is limited to the force amounting to a certain degree of gravity, i.e. armed attack (as opposed to 'mere frontier incident') this being a *conditio sine qua non* for the lawful invocation of self-defence.[19]

While it is generally accepted that the scale and effects requirements of an armed attack may be fulfilled in the case of armed attack of non-state actors, in particular terrorist groups,[20] it is less clear whether such attacks could occur without substantial involvement of another state. To put it differently, the question is whether self-defence is limited to inter-state relations, confining the notion of armed attack to acts attributed to a certain state, or a non-state actor, such as a terrorist organization, could also launch an attack within the meaning of Article 51 of the UN Charter.

The UN Charter does not provide an explicit answer as it does not specify the modalities of an armed attack and leaves this question open to interpretation. Traditionally, the understanding of the right of self-defence has been confined to inter-state relations.[21] This reasoning is based on the already

---

17 *Corten*, The law against war: The prohibition on the use of force in contemporary international law, 2012, Chapter 3; *Gray*, International Law and the Use of Force, 2008, p. 132.

18 When the acts involve a lesser degree of intensity, they may give rise to the use of countermeasures. See Institut de Droit International, Resolution 10A, Present Problems of the Use of Armed Force in International Law (2007), para. 5.

19 See Case Concerning Military and Paramilitary Activities in and Against Nicaragua *(Nicaragua v. United States of America)*, Merits, Judgment, ICJ Reports 1986, p. 14 (103), paras. 194, 195. The question of the threshold of an armed attack raises numerous controversies, especially in light of the discrepancy between the English (armed attack) and French (aggression armée) wording of the UN Charter.

20 See *Couzigou*, The Fight against the 'Islamic State' in Syria and the Right to Self-Defence, at: http://www.e-ir.info/2016/02/05/the-fight-against-the-islamic-state-in-syria-and-the-right-to-self-defence/ (visited 9.03.2017).

21 *Shaw*, 2014, p. 1132; *Gray*, 2008, p. 199.

emphasized link between the right of self-defence and the prohibition of the use of force enshrined in Article 2(4) of the UN Charter, which clearly operates within the framework of inter-state relations. The ICJ[22] and the ILC[23] have both endorsed the view that the right of self-defence is limited to the context of relations between states.

In the *Nicaragua case*, the ICJ importantly established that an armed attack included not only actions by regular armed forces across an international border:

> "but also 'the sending by or on behalf of a State of armed bands, groups, irregulars or mercenaries, which carry out acts of armed force against another State of such gravity as to amount to' (*inter alia*) an actual armed attack conducted by regular forces, 'or its substantial involvement therein'."[24]

According to the Court's reasoning, the use of force in self-defence can therefore be legal not just as a reaction to attacks of regular army forces, but also when a state dispatches irregular forces to carry out attacks using armed force which is grave enough to amount to an armed attack.[25] The ICJ continued by addressing the question of attribution. When considering whether the United Sates (US) could be held responsible for the acts committed by *Contras*, the Court created the controversial 'effective control standard'. According to this standard, a state may be held responsible for acts of non-state actors if it can be proven "that that state had effective control of the military or paramilitary operations in the course of which the alleged violations were committed."[26] The Court concluded that providing

---

22 Case Concerning Military and Paramilitary Activities in and Against Nicaragua *(Nicaragua v. United States of America)*, Merits, Judgment, ICJ Reports 1986, p. 14 (103), para. 195.

23 Articles on Responsibility of States for Internationally Wrongful Acts with Commentaries, Yearbook of the International Law Commission, 2001, Vol. II (Part Two), p. 74, para. 5.

24 Case Concerning Military and Paramilitary Activities in and Against Nicaragua *(Nicaragua v. United States of America)*, Merits, Judgment, ICJ Reports 1986, p. 14 (103), para. 195. The Court derived this conclusion from Article 3 (g) of the Definition of Aggression annexed to General Assembly Resolution 3314 (XXIX) (1974), stating that acts of aggression include "[the] sending by or on behalf of a State of armed bands, groups, irregulars or mercenaries, which carry out acts of armed force against another State of such gravity as to amount to the acts listed above, or its substantial involvement therein."

25 See also *Shaw*, 2014, p. 823.

26 Case Concerning Military and Paramilitary Activities in and Against Nicaragua *(Nicaragua v. United States of America)*, Merits, Judgment, ICJ Reports 1986, p.14 (96), para. 181.

assistance to irregular forces in the form of provision of weapons and other logistical support by states was not sufficient to fulfil the effective control standard and subsequently activate the right of self-defence of the 'victim state'. The standard established by the court was later included in the Article 8 of the ARSIWA:

> "The conduct of a person or group of persons shall be considered an act of a State under international law if the person or group of persons is in fact acting on the instructions of, or under the direction or control of, that State in carrying out the conduct."

According to the ICJ, the source of the attack is therefore essentially related to the rules of attribution whereby only an attack attributed to another state will fulfil the Article 51 of the UN Charter requirements. This state-centred interpretation of armed attack was confirmed in the subsequent decisions of the ICJ in the *Oil Platforms (Islamic Republic of Iran v. United States of America)*, *Legal Consequences of the Construction of a Wall in the Occupied Palestinian Territory* and *Case Concerning Armed Activities on the Territory of the Congo (Democratic Republic of the Congo v. Uganda)* (see below).[27]

C. *9/11 Attacks as a Possible Game Changer: Start of the End for the Attribution of the Attack Rule?*

On September 11, 2001, 19 militants associated with the terrorist group Al Qaeda carried out suicide attacks against targets in the US that resulted in death of nearly 3,000 people.[28] Prior to the 9/11 terrorist attacks, legal doctrine considered attribution of an attack to a state as a prerequisite, *conditio*

---

27 Oil Platforms *(Islamic Republic of Iran v. United States of America)*, Judgment, ICJ Reports 2003, p. 161 (186–187); Legal Consequences of the Construction of a Wall in the Occupied Palestinian Territory, Advisory Opinion, ICJ Reports 2004, p. 136 (194), para 139; Case Concerning Armed Activities on the Territory of the Congo *(Democratic Republic of the Congo v. Uganda)*, Judgment, ICJ Reports 2005, p. 168 (222–223), para 146.

28 *Bergen*, September 11 attacks in Encyclopaedia Britannica, at: https://www.britannica.com/event/September-11-attacks (visited 9.03.2017).

sine qua non,[29] that activates the right of self-defence under Article 51 of the UN Charter.[30] However, following the Operation Enduring Freedom and other reactions of the international community to the 9/11 attacks, a more expansive reading of an 'armed attack' requirement gained an unprecedented support in the context of the right of self-defence against non-state actors. The traditional *ratione personae* requirement of an armed attack, namely the question of relevance of its origin, was put to the test. To deny the state suffering from horrendous terrorist attacks the right to use force in self-defence against those that plotted and carried out the attacks became unreasonable and unfair. At the forefront of this expansive reading of Article 51 of the UN Charter was the US, arguing for the recognition of the crucial role that states hosting the terrorist groups should play in preventing terrorist attacks originating from their territory.

I. Reactions of the International Community

Several commentators have referred to the 9/11 attacks as the groundbreaking point for the interpretation of the right of self-defence. In their opinion, UNSC resolutions 1368 and 1373[31] adopted in the aftermath of the attacks in 2001 and Operation Enduring Freedom expanded the understanding of the right of self-defence in a way that allows extraterritorial use of force against non-state actors.[32]

---

29 Case Concerning Military and Paramilitary Activities in and Against Nicaragua *(Nicaragua v. United States of America)*, Merits, Judgment, ICJ Reports 1986, p. 14 (103), paras. 194, 195.

30 *Ruys/Verhoeven*, Attacks by Private Actors and the Right of Self-Defence, (2005) 10 JCSL, p. 289 (290–291, 312); *Cassese*, Terrorism is Also Disrupting Some Crucial Legal Categories of International Law, (2001) 12 European Journal of International Law (hereinafter EJIL), p. 993 (997); *Gray*, 2008, p. 199.

31 UNSC Resolution 1368 (2001), Threats to international peace and security caused by terrorist acts, UN Doc. S/RES/1368 (2001); UNSC Resolution 1373 (2001), Threats to international peace and security caused by terrorist acts, UN Doc. S/RES/1373 (2001).

32 Even though resolutions did not explicitly qualify the attacks as an armed attack, they both referred to the right of self-defence, which could presuppose that the terrorist attacks were seen as constituting an armed attack. *Dinstein*, War, Aggression and Self-Defence, 2011, p. 207–208.

The UNSC responded to attacks by adopting resolutions under Chapter VII of the UN Charter, but, apart from explicitly referring to the right of self-defence in their preambles, failed to clarify its position. In the operative part of resolutions, international terrorism is referred to as a threat to international peace and security without alluding to an armed attack. Moreover, the use of wording – inherent right to self-defence as recognized by the UN Charter – does not in itself demonstrate any change in traditional understanding of the right of self-defence.[33] The language of the resolutions is therefore too ambiguous to confirm the existence of the right of self-defence against the attacks of non-state actors.[34] Supporters of the expansionist view have argued that the resolution 1368 was adopted only one day after the attacks, when there was not enough reliable information available to link the terrorists to Afghanistan or to any other state. This has been interpreted as a sign of the UNSC's support for the actions of states in self-defence against armed attacks regardless of their origin.[35]

To back their arguments even further, those rooting for the right to use force in self-defence against non-state actors often cite state practice and practice of international organizations that followed the 9/11 attacks. In October 2001, after negotiations between the US and the Taliban (then *de facto* government in Afghanistan) failed, the US and British military forces launched the Operation Enduring Freedom in Afghanistan.[36] In accordance with the procedural requirement of Article 51 of the UN Charter, both states

---

33 After the 9/11 attacks the UNSC in similar cases of terrorist attacks never confirmed the right of an attacked state to self-defence. See e.g. UNSC Resolution 1530 (2004), UN Doc. S/RES/1530 (2004) and UNSC Resolution 1611 (2005), UN Doc. S/RES/1611 (2005), in which the SC condemned terrorist attacks in Madrid and London but only qualified the attacks as a threat to the international peace and security and reaffirmed its fight against all forms of terrorism under the collective security framework.

34 E.g. *Cassese*, (2001) 12 EJIL, p. 993 (996); *Ruys*, 'Armed Attack' and Article 51 of the UN Charter: Evolutions in Customary Law and Practice, 2010, p. 441.

35 *Kajtár*, Self-Defence Against Non-State Actors – Methodological Challenges, (2010) 54 Annales Universitatis Scientiarum Budapestinensis de Rolando Eötvös nominatae, p. 307 (324).

36 *Salazar Torreon*, U.S. Periods of War and Dates of Recent Conflicts, Congressional Research Service Report (27 February 2015); Letter dated 7 October 2001 from the Permanent Representative of the United States of America to the United Nations addressed to the President of the Security Council, UN Doc. S/2001/946 (2001).

wrote to the UNSC, claiming that their use of force had been legally justified by their inherent right of individual and collective self-defence.[37] The operation was an act against another state – Afghanistan – conducted in response to a prior attack of a terrorist group (Al Qaeda). The coalition forces established a link between the Al Qaeda and the Taliban, but this link was far from fulfilling the above-mentioned effective control standard. Regardless of this clear deviation from the traditional reading of Article 51 of the UN Charter, Operation Enduring Freedom received support from other states and international organizations.[38] For the first time in NATO's history Article 5 of the Washington Treaty was invoked,[39] asserting that the terrorist attacks against the US formed an armed attack against a NATO member state that activated the right of individual and collective self-defence.[40] Organization of American States (OAS) similarly concluded that the 9/11 attacks amounted to an armed attack giving the US the right to act in self-defence.[41]

With an almost universal support for the US actions taken under the self-defence framework, the international law of self-defence was seemingly gaining new dimensions different from the traditionally narrow interpretation of Article 51. This was, however, not confirmed in the subsequent practice of the ICJ.

37 Ibid.; Letter from the representative of the United Kingdom of Great Britain and Northern Ireland to the President of the Security Council, UN Doc. S/2001/947 (2001).

38 *Green*, The International Court of Justice and self-defence in international law, 2009, p. 157. Only Iraq expressed doubts about the legality of the military operation. European Union expressed its full support for the actions taken in self-defence in accordance with the UN Charter and the UNSC Resolution 1368 (2001). See Conclusions and plan of action of the Extraordinary European Council meeting, EU Doc. CL01-057EN (21.09.2001).

39 North Atlantic Treaty, 5 April 1949, 34 UNTS 243.

40 *Buckley*, Invoking Article 5, at: http://www.nato.int/docu/review/2006/issue2/english/art2.html (visited 9.03.2017).

41 Terrorist Threat to the Americas, RC.24/RES.1/01, OAS Doc. OEA/Ser.F/II.24/RC.24/RES.1/01 rev. 1 corr. 1, (21.09. 2001), point 1.

II. Views of the International Court of Justice

Even though some movements breaking away from traditional understanding of self-defence could be discerned after the 9/11 attacks, the ICJ in its subsequent case-law, where it had the opportunity to further evolve and clarify the issue, rather held on to its formalistic[42] and conservative views.

When considering whether the construction of a wall by Israel to protect its citizens against terrorist attacks launched from Palestinian territory could be justified as a non-forcible measure taken in self-defence, it concluded in the negative stating that "Article 51 of the Charter…recognizes the existence of an inherent right of self-defence in the case of armed attack by one State against another State."[43] Since Israel did not claim that the attacks against it were originating from another state, Article 51 of the UN Charter was, according to the Court, of no relevance to the case. The ICJ implicitly rejected the existence of the right to use force against the territory of another state in response to acts of non-state actors emanating from the territory of, but not being attributable to, that state. This narrow reasoning was criticised within and outside the Court.[44] In its Separate Opinion Judge Kooijamans commented the 9/11 attacks and subsequent UNSC resolutions 1368 and 1373 as adding a 'completely new element' to the law of self-defence:

> "Resolutions 1368 (2001) and 1373 (2001) recognize the inherent right of individual or collective self-defence without making any reference to an armed attack by a State … This new element is not excluded by the terms of Article 51 since this conditions the exercise of the inherent right of self-defence on a previous armed attack without saying that this armed attack must come from another State even if this has been the generally accepted interpretation for more than 50 years. The Court has regrettably by-passed this new element, the legal implications of which cannot as yet be assessed but which marks undeniably a new approach to the concept of self-defence."

---

42 See *Scobbie*, "Words My Mother Never Taught Me:" In Defense of the International Court, (2005) 99 AJIL, p. 76.

43 Legal Consequences of the Construction of a Wall in the Occupied Palestinian Territory, Advisory Opinion, ICJ Reports 2004, p. 136 (194), para. 139.

44 *Randzelhofer/Nolte*, in: Simma/Khan/Nolte/Paulus, p. 1397 (1416); *d'Aspremont*, (2010) 31.4 University of Pennsylvania Journal of International Law, p. 1089 (1123).

Judge Buergenthal similarly accused the Court of being too formalistic and unwilling to address "the very issues that are at the heart of this case,"[45] whereas judge Higgins expressed reservation towards the Court's view, stating that "[there is, with respect, nothing in the text of Article 51 that *thus* stipulates that self-defence is available only when an armed attack is made by a State."[46]

Notwithstanding the criticism, the Court reaffirmed its position in the *Case Concerning Armed Activities on the Territory of the Congo (Democratic Republic of the Congo v. Uganda)*.[47] Democratic Republic of Congo (DRC) accused Uganda of an armed aggression, which the latter justified with its inherent right of self-defence against attacks coming from the territory of DRC. In its argumentation, Uganda claimed that "armed attacks by armed bands whose existence is tolerated by the territorial sovereign generate legal responsibility and therefore constitute armed attacks for the purpose of Article 51." This was supposedly "a super-added standard of responsibility, according to which, a failure to control the activities of armed bands, creates a susceptibility to action in self-defence by neighbouring States."[48] Uganda thus tried to establish the right of self-defence without the existence of direction and control (effective control standard) by the territorial sovereign from where the attacks were carried out. It referred to the fact that another state was harbouring non-state actors launching the attacks. The Court rejected these arguments and concluded that the fact that the DRC had not taken actions against armed bands on its territory did not mean that their acts could be attributed to the DRC. Since Uganda failed to prove that attacks coming from the territory of DRC were also attributable to the

45 Legal Consequences of the Construction of a Wall in the Occupied Palestinian Territory, Advisory Opinion, ICJ Reports 2004, p. 136 (243), para. 6.

46 Separate Opinion of Judge Higgins in Legal Consequences of the Construction of a Wall in the Occupied Palestinian Territory, Advisory Opinion, ICJ Reports 2004, p. 136 (215), para. 33.

47 Case Concerning Armed Activities on the Territory of the Congo *(Democratic Republic of the Congo v. Uganda)*, Judgment, ICJ Reports 2005, p. 168.

48 Verbatim record, Public sitting held on Monday 18.04.2005 in the Case concerning Armed Activities on the Territory of the Congo (Democratic Republic of the Congo v. Uganda), CR 2005/7, p. 30.

DRC, the legal and factual circumstances for the exercise of self-defence were not present in this case.[49]

Even though the parties to the conflict expressly asked the court to clarify "whether and under what conditions contemporary international law provides for a right of self-defence against large-scale attacks by irregular forces,"[50] the Court clearly avoided addressing the question. It is not a surprise that this approach was once again criticized. Admittedly, the narrow effective control standard from the *Nicaragua case* (1986) was adopted in circumstances not entirely reflecting contemporary challenges related to terrorism. However, the two subsequent cases, where the Court had a chance to take a step further (or away) from its previous views, were adjudicated after the 9/11 terrorist attacks. In 2004 and 2005 the question of interpretation of Article 51 of the UN Charter was already contentious and clarifications were needed. In its Separate Opinions, judges Simma and Kooijmans regretted the reserved approach of the Court, which refrained from "taking a position with regard to the question whether the threshold set out in the *Nicaragua* Judgment is still in conformity with contemporary international law."[51] Simma concluded that decisions of the Court in relation to self-defence and non-state actors

> "are problematic less for the things they say than for the questions they leave open … the Court (therefore) creates the impression that it somehow feels uncomfortable being confronted with certain questions of utmost importance in contemporary international relations."[52]

In conclusion, after the 9/11 attacks and the subsequent military operation in Afghanistan, three different groups of scholarly views on the law of self-

49 Case Concerning Armed Activities on the Territory of the Congo *(Democratic Republic of the Congo v. Uganda)*, Judgment, ICJ Reports 2005, p. 168 (222–223), para. 146.

50 Ibid., para. 147.

51 Separate opinion of Judge Kooijmans, Case Concerning Armed Activities on the Territory of the Congo *(Democratic Republic of the Congo v. Uganda)*, Judgment, ICJ Reports 2005, p. 168 (313), para. 25.

52 Separate opinion of Judge Simma, Case Concerning Armed Activities on the Territory of the Congo *(Democratic Republic of the Congo v. Uganda)*, Judgment, ICJ Reports 2005, p. 168 (336), para. 9. See also Separate opinion of Judge Kooijmans, Case Concerning Armed Activities on the Territory of the Congo *(Democratic Republic of the Congo v. Uganda)*, Judgment, ICJ Reports 2005, p. 168 (313), para. 25.

defence have emerged.[53] One, more traditional group of scholars, remains faithful to the ICJ's reasoning, requiring the attribution of the non-state actor's attack to a state under the effective control standard.[54] The two other groups challenge this traditional understanding. While the second group merely loosened the effective control threshold of the attribution, which remains *conditio sine qua non* for the lawful use of force in self-defence,[55] the third and the most controversial one completely abandoned the attribution requirement and thus acknowledged that a private armed attack itself can trigger the right of self-defence.[56] Some supporters of this view shifted the focus from the attribution criteria and now examine the involvement of

53 See e.g. *White/Henderson*, Research Handbook on International Conflict and Security Law, 2013, p. 157.

54 *Shah*, War on Terrorism: Self Defense, Operation Enduring Freedom, and the Legality of U.S. Drone Attacks in Pakistan, (2010) 9 Washington University Global Studies Law Review, p. 77 (103).

55 See Separate opinion of judge Jennings, Case Concerning Military and Paramilitary Activities in and Against Nicaragua *(Nicaragua v. United States of America)*, Merits, Judgment, ICJ Reports 1986, p. 14 (542–544); Application of the Convention on the Prevention and Punishment of the Crime of Genocide *(Bosnia and Herzegovina v. Serbia and Montenegro)*, Judgment, ICJ Reports 2007, p. 43 (208), para. 401 (implying a possibility of a lower level of attribution standard departing from the general rules of attribution as laid down by the ILC); *Tams*, Light Treatment of a Complex Problem: The Law of Self-Defence in the Wall Case, (2005) 16 EJIL, p. 963 (973); *Ratner*, Jus ad Bellum and Jus in Bello after September 11, (2002) 96 AJIL, p. 905 (905, 910); *Brent*, Responding to Attacks by Non-State Actors: The Attribution Requirement of Self-Defence, (2009) 16 Australian International Law Journal, p. 133 (133–159); *d'Aspremont*, (2010) 31.4 University of Pennsylvania Journal of International Law, p. 1089 (1124).

56 E.g. Separate opinions of the ICJ judges Simma and Kooijmans in the Case Concerning Armed Activities on the Territory of the Congo *(Democratic Republic of the Congo v. Uganda)*, Judgment, ICJ Reports 2005, p. 168; *Franck*, Editorial Comments: Terrorism and the Right of Self-Defence, (2010) 95 AJIL, p. 839 (840); *Murphy*, Terrorism and the Concept of Armed Attack in Article 51 of the UN Charter, (2002) 43 Harvard International Law Journal, p. 41 (50); *Van Steenberghe*, Self-Defence in Response to Attacks by Non-State Actors in the Light of Recent State Practice: A Step Forward?, (2010) 23 Leiden Journal of International Law (hereinafter LJIL), p. 183 (197–199).

state in armed attack through the 'unwilling or unable' doctrine as a part of the necessity requirement for the lawful use of force in self-defence.[57]

III. Post-Operation Enduring Freedom Developments

State practice related to the lawfulness of the use of force in self-defence against non-state actors on the territory of another state remained unsettled in the aftermath of the 9/11 attacks.

Russian attacks against Chechen rebels in response to their prior terrorist attacks in Russia were not widely discussed in the international community. Yet, the US, which a year earlier reacted similarly in the context of Afghanistan, denied the existence of the right of self-defence to Russia on the Georgian territory.[58] Israeli attacks targeting Palestinian terrorists in Syria in 2003 and Hezbollah in Lebanon in 2006 were condemned by a larger group of states that denounced such use of force and found it incompatible with the postulates of international law.[59] These reactions to the Israeli intervention in Lebanon demonstrate the inconsistency of international community when addressing the question of lawfulness of the use of force in self-defence against non-state actors. In particular, most of the states condemned the Israeli use of force for the reasons of disproportionality, while they at least in principle accepted its right to self-defence against Hezbollah's attacks.[60] The proportionality aspect and not the right of self-defence as such was the source of disagreements also in the context of Turkish military operations against the Kurdish Workers' Party (PKK) in Northern Iraq during the 2007 and 2008 incursions.[61] Lastly, the inconsistency of state practice in abandoning the attribution criterion of a terrorist attack to a state in order to trigger the right of self-defence can be demonstrated with the invocation of a self-defence argument in the case of 2008 Colombian air strikes on

57 See below, Chapter D. Some authors understand this as an indirect 'attack' triggering the right of self-defence. *d'Aspremont*, (2010) 31.4 University of Pennsylvania Journal of International Law, p. 1089 (1124).

58 *Reinold*, State Weakness, Irregular Warfare, and the Right to Self-Defense Post-9/11, (2011) 105 AJIL, p. 244 (256).

59 Ibid., 265–268.

60 Ibid.

61 Ibid. 270. Only Iraq unequivocally denounced the attacks.

FARC (Fuerzas Armadas Revolucionarias de Colombia) in Ecuador.[62] OAS that supported the right of self-defence of the US in 2001, this time clearly condemned Colombia and rejected the right of a state to use force against a terrorist organization located on the territory of another state without its consent.[63]

While the use of force in self-defence against non-state actors' attacks remained controversial, an increasing number of think tanks saw another related problem; states that are victims of terrorist attacks do not have effective mechanisms to address terrorist threats originating from a territory of another state to which they cannot be traditionally attributed.[64] Their documents, recognising the right of states to use force in self-defence against armed attacks of non-state actors under certain strict conditions, are, however, not a source of international law; they build their authority on persuasion by argumentation.

Overall, it is difficult to draw definite conclusions on a changed paradigm of international law of self-defence, but the idea of abandoning the attribution requirement to be able to identify a terrorist attack as an armed attack under Article 51 of the UN Charter has been receiving unprecedented support.

---

62 *Deeks*, "Unwilling or Unable": Toward a Normative Framework for Extraterritorial Self-Defense, (2012) 52 Virginia Journal of International Law (hereinafter VJIL), p. 483 (537).

63 OAD, Convocation of the Meeting of Consultation of Ministers of Foreign Affairs, OAS/CP/RES/930 (1632/08).

64 See e.g. *Wilmhurst*, Chatham House Principles of International law on the Use of Force by States in Self-Defence, at: https://www.chathamhouse.org/publi-cations/papers/view/108106 (visited 9.03.2017); *Schrijver/van den Herik*, Leiden Policy Recommendations on Counter-terrorism and International Law, at: http://www.grotiuscentre.org/resources/1/Leiden%20Policy%20Recommenda-tions%201%20April%202010.pdf (visited 9.03.2017); *Bethlehem*, Principles Relevant to the Scope of a State's Right of Self-Defense against an Imminent or Actual Armed Attack by Nonstate Actors, at: http://www.un.org/law/coun-sel/Bethlehem%20-%20Self-Defense%20Article.pdf (visited 9.03.2017).

D. *Unwilling or Unable Host State: Emergence of a New Doctrine?*

In the years following the 9/11 attacks the growing threat of terrorism and the 'stateless' nature of terrorists increasingly drew attention to the ineffectiveness of the international law in dealing with the problem. There is a common denominator of the past cases in which victim states invoked self-defence as the legal basis for their use of force against non-state actors. Although the attacks could not be (traditionally) attributed to the territorial (host) states, the victim states still tried to establish a link between the non-state actor and the host state.[65] Since the rigidity of the effective control test allows for the attribution of non-state actions to states in a very limited number of cases, the link between the host state and non-state actors on its territory started to be interpreted as the inability or unwillingness of the host state to prevent the attacks. A new doctrine concerning terrorist attacks and responses to them independently of the attribution test has emerged, the so-called 'unwilling or unable' doctrine.[66]

In this connection, it is important for the victim state to establish some kind of a link between non-state actors and the host state because the reactions to terrorist attacks are exercised on the territory of a state that traditionally cannot be held legally responsible for terrorist attacks originating from its territory. Even if the use of force in self-defence against terrorist attacks on the territory of another state is directed against the terrorist targets, this inevitably means that force has been used against that state in breach of its sovereignty.[67] The absence of the attribution of the attack requirement therefore brings about tensions between the respect for territorial sovereignty of the host state and the right of self-defence of the attacked state.

---

65 *Van Steenberghe*, (2010) 23 LJIL, p. 183 (207).

66 The term 'unwilling or unable' state is not a novelty in international law, but it is reaching new dimensions in the context of possible justifications of unilateral use of force. See *Starski*, The "Unwilling or Unable State" as a Challenge to International Law, at: http://www.mpil.de//en/pub/research/areas/public-international-law/the-unwilling-or-unable-state.cfm#project (visited 9.03. 2017).

67 E.g. *Williams*, Piercing the Shield of Sovereignty: An Assessment of the Legal Status of the 'Unwilling or Unable' Test, (2013) 36 University of New South Wales Law Journal, p. 619 (625).

The unwilling or unable doctrine has been invoked on several occasions[68] with a view to pragmatically solving these tensions and justifying the *prima facie* violation of another state's sovereignty.[69] When giving the arguments for justification of their use of force in self-defence in Afghanistan, the US established a link between Al Qaeda and the Taliban by referring to the unwillingness of the Taliban to stop illegal activities of terrorist groups originating from their territory.[70] The unwillingness or inability of the host state argument was also invoked in the case of Russia's use of force against Chechen rebels in Georgia in 2002,[71] Israel's 2006 attacks against Hezbollah in Lebanon,[72] Turkish 2008 attacks on PKK in Northern Iraq,[73] the Operation Neptune Spear in which the US killed Osama bin Laden in Pakistan [74] and Kenya's 2011 response to numerous terrorist attacks of Al-Shabaab by military intervention in Somalia.[75] Moreover, this doctrine was implicitly supported in the African Union Non-Aggression and Common defence Pact.[76] The core of the doctrine is the legal justification of the attacked state (or state under the imminent threat of an armed attack) to use force on a territory of a host state without its consent because the latter is unwilling or unable to prevent terrorist attacks emanating from its territory.[77]

---

68 E.g. *Deeks*, (2012) 52 VJIL, p. 483; *Wilmhurst*; *Lubell*, Extraterritorial Use of Force Against Non-State Actors, 2010, p. 42; UN Human Rights Council, Report of the Special Rapporteur on Extrajudicial, Summary or Arbitrary Executions, UN Doc. A/HRC/14/24/Add. 6 (2010), point 35.

69 *Terry*, Germany Joins the Campaign Against Isis in Syria: A Case of Collective Self-Defence or Rather the Unlawful Use of Force?, (2016) 4 RLJ, p. 26 (49).

70 UN Doc. S/2001/946 (2001).

71 Letter dated 11.09.2002 from the Permanent Representative of the Russian Federation to the United Nations addressed to the Secretary General, Annex, UN Doc. S/2002/1012 (2002).

72 UNSC, 5488th meeting Thursday, 13.07.2006, New York, UN Doc. S/PV. 5488 (2006).

73 *Reinold*, (2011) 105 AJIL, p. 244 (188–192).

74 *Deeks*, (2012) 52 VJIL, p. 483 (485).

75 Letter dated 17.10.2011 from the Permanent Representative of Kenya to the United Nations addressed to the President of the Security Council, UN Doc. S/2011/646 (2011).

76 Article 1/c (xi) of the African Union Non-Aggression and Common Defence Pact, Abuja, Nigeria, 2005.

77 *Lubell*, 2010, p. 42.

I. Unwilling or Unable Doctrine as a Part of the Necessity Requirement

The unwillingness or inability of the host state has not emerged as an independent legal basis for the extraterritorial use of force against non-state actors. It is not linked to the attribution requirement, but to the necessity test of when it is lawful to use force in self-defence.[78] In other words, the victim state can employ force in self-defence if it has no other alternative.[79] If the host state takes all reasonable measures to prevent the use of its territory as a shelter for terrorist activities, the use of force by the victim state against the host state will not be necessary.[80] The centre of the attention in the law of self-defence therefore seemingly shifts from the attribution of the attack of a non-state actor, to the question of the ability of the host state to stop an already launched attack or to prevent future attacks.[81] According to the supporters of the doctrine, the legality of the use of force in self-defence depends on the ability of states hosting terrorist groups to fulfil their international obligations in terms of prevention of terrorist attacks.[82]

---

78 Compare with *Van Steenberghe*, (2010) 23 LJIL, p. 183 (194–195); *Van Steenberghe*, From Passive Consent to Self-Defence after the Syrian Protest against the US-led Coalition, EJIL: *Talk!* at: http://www.ejiltalk.org/13758-2/#more-13758 (visited 9.03.2017). Some international lawyers refer to the unwillingness or inability of the host state as an expanded standard of attribution. E.g. *Randzelhofer/Nolte*, in: Simma/Khan/Nolte/Paulus, p. 1397 (1418); *Corten*, The 'Unwilling or Unable' Test: Has it Been, and Could it be, Accepted?, (2016) 29 LJIL, p. 777 (796, 797).

79 *Arimatsu*, The Law of State Responsibility in Relation to Border Crossings: An Ignored Legal Paradigm, (2013) 89 International Law Studies Series, p. 21 (34).

80 E.g. The Use of Force Against Terrorists (2009), p. 1049; *Deeks*, (2012) 52 VJIL, p. 483 (495).

81 Chatham House Principles *(Wilmhurst)*, Leiden Recommendations *(Schrijver/ van den Herik)* and Bethlehem Principles *(Bethlehem)* support the use of unwilling or unable doctrine in exceptional situations.

82 *Van Steenberghe*, EJIL: *Talk!*; *Dinstein*, 2011, p. 226; *Deeks*, (2012) 52 VJIL, p. 483 (495). Corfu Channel *(United Kingdom of Great Britain and Northern Ireland v. Albania)* (Merits), (1949) ICJ Reports 4, p. 2. State has an obligation to disallow the use of its territory for activities that violate the rights of other states. If the states do not demonstrate due diligence in their attempts to prevent terrorist organizations to operate from its territory, they can be held responsible under international law. The "inability" part of the doctrine brings about the possibility of the victim state to use military force against the host state, even if the host state did not violate any international law rule of international law, which is very problematic. E.g. *Ruys/Verhoeven*, (2005) 10 JCSL, p. 289 (312).

The legal value of the 'unwilling or unable' doctrine and its influence on the traditional understanding of the law of self-defence arguably lies in its potential of being an interpretative standard to the use of force in self-defence under Article 51 of the UN Charter. It is submitted that practice related to the doctrine could potentially amount to "subsequent practice in the application of the treaty which establishes the agreement of the parties regarding its interpretation"[83] in accordance with Article 31/3 (b) of the Vienna Convention of the Law of Treaties (hereinafter VCLT).[84] The notion of practice in this respect "comprises any external behaviour of a subject of international law … insofar as it is potentially revealing of what the party accepts as the meaning of a particular treaty provision."[85] Such subsequent practice could contribute to the clarification of the law of self-defence including "narrowing, widening, or otherwise determining the range of possible interpretations."[86]

However, objections of host states (e.g. Georgia, Lebanon and Iraq),[87] and denouncements of such use of extraterritorial force by other directly uninvolved states,[88] as well as generally inconsistent use of the doctrine (e.g. the US denial of such justification of the use of force in the case of

83 Vienna Convention on the Law of Treaties, 23.05.1969, UNTS, Vol. 1155, p. 331, Article 31/3 (b). See also *Dörr/Schmalenbach* (eds), Vienna Convention on the Law of Treaties: A Commentary, 2012, p. 554–560.

84 This also applies to the constituent acts of international organisations. See Subsequent agreements and subsequent practice in relation to the interpretation of treaties, Text of the draft conclusions provisionally adopted by the Drafting Committee on first reading, International Law Commission, A/CN.4/L.874, Draft conclusion 12.

85 *Dörr/Schmalenbach* (eds), 2012, p. 555.

86 Subsequent agreements and subsequent practice in relation to the interpretation of treaties, Text of the draft conclusions provisionally adopted by the Drafting Committee on first reading, International Law Commission, A/CN.4/L.874, Draft conclusion 7.

87 UNSC, 5489th meeting Friday, 14.07.2006, New York, UN Doc. S/PV.5489 (2006).

88 E.g. Non-Aligned Movement, Final Document of the 14th Summit Conference of Heads of State or Government of the Non-Aligned Movement, Havana, Cuba, 11–16.09.2006.

Russia's intervention in Pankisi Gorge),[89] prevent the authors of this contribution from making unequivocal statements on the role of doctrine in the development of the international law of self-defence. In order to fulfil the standard of the subsequent practice, the doctrine would have to be accepted by all the parties to the UN Charter or there would have to be "at least good evidence that the other, inactive parties have endorsed it."[90] In this respect, the intervention of the US-led Coalition against ISIL in Syria without the territorial state's consent has been perceived as a possible clarification moment for the status of the doctrine in international law.[91]

II. Intervention of the Coalition against ISIL in Syria as the Next Turning Point?

The US-led coalition has conducted military operations against ISIL in Iraq and Syria since 2014.[92] The legal basis for the Coalition's intervention in Iraq is an invitation of Iraqi government to the international community to help fighting ISIL on its territory.[93] The majority of international legal scholars agree that the intervention by invitation, if carried out within the framework of the valid invitation, represents an undisputed legal basis for a military intervention in a foreign state.[94] State consent is namely one of

---

89 *US Department of State*, Russian Bombing of Georgia (Press Release, 24 August 2002), at: http://2001-2009.state.gov/p/eur/rls/prsrl/2002/13002.htm (visited 9. 03.2017).

90 *Dörr/Schmalenbach* (eds), 2012, p. 559.

91 Eg. *Henderson*, Editorial Comment: The Use of Force and Islamic State, (2014) 1 Journal on the Use of Force and International Law, p. 209 (221).

92 See e.g. *Mills/Smith/Brooke-Holland*, ISIS/Daesh: the military response in Iraq and Syria, at: http://researchbriefings.parliament.uk/ResearchBriefing/Summary/SN06995 (visited 9.03.2017).

93 Letter dated 25.06.2014 from the Permanent Representative of Iraq to the United Nations addressed to the Secretary-General, UN Doc. S/2014/440 (2014); Letter dated 20.09.2014 from the Permanent Representative of Iraq to the United Nations addressed to the President of the Security Council, UN Doc. S/2014/691 (2014).

94 *Shaw*, 2014, p. 835; *Crawford*, State Responsibility: The General Part, 2013; *Corten*.

the circumstances precluding responsibility of states for internationally wrongful acts.[95]

However, legal basis for the coalition strikes in Syria is less straightforward and brings about several legal controversies. In order to eliminate the ongoing ISIL threat to Iraq, the US initiated military actions in Syria (Operation Inherent Resolve) in September 2014.[96] Some other members of the Coalition joined these airstrikes in 2015.[97] Syria did not give its consent to the military intervention [98] nor did the UNSC authorize the use of force under Chapter VII of the UN Charter.[99] To justify their military air strikes on the Syrian territory members of the Coalition in several instances referred to their right of individual or collective self-defence.[100]

---

95 Article 20 ARSIWA.

96 *Mills/Smith/Brooke-Holland.*

97 Ibid.

98 Russia has Syria's consent for its military operations in Syria and is thus an exception.

99 UNSC Resolution 2249 (2015), Threats to international peace and security caused by terrorist acts, UN Doc. S/RES/2249 (2015) does not authorize the use of force.

100 In both cases the focal question of the legality of the use of force in self-defence against a non-state actor on the territory of a state that is not responsible for the armed attack of a terrorist group is the same. Differentiation between individual and collective self-defence is thus not legally relevant for this discussion. Letter dated 24.07.2015 from the Chargé d'affaires a.i. of the Permanent Mission of Turkey to the United Nations addressed to the President of the Security Council, UN Doc. S/2015/563 (2015) and, more recently, Identical letters dated 20 January 2018 from the Chargé d'affaires a.i. of the Permanent Mission of Turkey to the United Nations addressed to the Secretary-General and the President of the Security Council, UN Doc. S/2018/53 (2018); Letter dated 7.09.2015 from the Permanent Representative of the United Kingdom of Great Britain and Northern Ireland to the United Nations addressed to the President of the Security Council, UN Doc. S/2015/688 (2015); Identical letters dated 8.09.2015 from the Permanent Representative of France to the United Nations addressed to the Secretary-General and the President of the Security Council, UN Doc. S/2015/745 (2015); Letter dated 9.09.2015 from the Permanent Representative of Australia to the United Nations addressed to the President of the Security Council UN Doc. S/2015/693 (2015); Letter dated 10.12.2015 from the Chargé d'affaires a.i. of the Permanent Mission of Germany to the United Nations addressed to the President of the Security Council, UN Doc. S/2015/946 (2015); Letter dated 13.10.2016 from the Permanent Representative of Denmark to the United Nations addressed to the President of the Security Council, UN Doc. S/2016/513 (2016); Letter dated 3.06.2016 from the Permanent Representative of Norway

To attribute terrorist attacks for which ISIL claimed responsibility (e.g. terrorist attacks in Iraq, Tunisia, Turkey, Paris, Brussels, etc.) to Syria would mean stretching the attribution rules far beyond the effective control standard. ISIL has been operating from the territory no longer under effective control of the Syrian government.[101] Moreover, Syria is itself in a non-international armed conflict with ISIL. The states involved in air operations in Syria, when outlining their legal arguments for the intervention, thus avoided attributing the acts of the ISIL to Syria and rather tried to justify the legality of use of force in self-defence by bringing into the discussion the unwilling or unable doctrine. According to this doctrine, airstrikes in Syria are justified because Syria is unwilling or unable to prevent attacks of ISIL, which is operating from its territory. The authors of this contribution thus conclude that the states participating in the airstrikes on the Syrian territory accepted the concept of an armed attack regardless of its origin and pragmatically abandoned the attribution requirement without going into theoretical justification for this step.

The US, Canada, Australia and Turkey in their letters to the UNSC justified their attacks against ISIL by referring to the right of self-defence which they understand as the right to act when the government of the state (Syria) where the threat (ISIL) is located is unwilling or unable to prevent the use of its territory for such attacks.[102] The UK in turn did not invoke the unwilling or unable doctrine in its letters to the UNSC but its Prime Minister at the time mentioned the unwillingness or inability of the Assad's regime to adopt necessary measures to prevent further attacks on Iraq, the UK and

---

to the United Nations addressed to the President of the Security Council, UN Doc. S/2016/513 (2016); Letter dated 7.06.2016 from the Permanent Representative of Belgium to the United Nations addressed to the President of the Security Council, UN Doc. S/2016/523 (2016); *Cameron*, Memorandum to the Foreign Affairs Select Committee, at: https://www.parliament.uk/documents/commons-committees/foreign-affairs/PM-Response-to-FAC-Report-Extension-of-Offensive-British-Military-Operations-to-Syria.pdf (visited 9.03. 2017), p. 15.

101 E.g. UN Doc. S/2015/946 (2015).

102 Letter dated 23.09.2014 from the Permanent Representative of the United States of America to the United Nations addressed to the Secretary-General, UN Doc. S/2014/695 (2014); Letter dated 31.3.2015 from the Chargé d'affaires a.i. of the Permanent Mission of Canada to the United Nations addressed to the President of the Security Council, UN Doc. S/2015/221 (2015); UN Doc. S/2015/745 (2015); UN Doc. S/2015/563 (2015).

its allies during discussion on the legality of self-defence in the parliament.[103] Similarly, Germany and Belgium did not refer explicitly to the unwillingness or inability of the Syrian Government, but they emphasized the absence of its effective control over the part of the Syrian territory occupied by ISIL.[104] This at least indicates their application of the doctrine on the grounds of the 'inability' of the host state (Syria) to deal with the threat located on its territory.

III. Legal Challenges with the Use of Unwilling or Unable Doctrine

Despite the fact that the above-mentioned state practice gives the impression of broad support for the unwilling or unable doctrine in the context of Syria, there are strong reasons against this doctrine becoming legally relevant within the existing international law of self-defence. Firstly, several states have been at least initially hesitant to expand their military operations from Iraq to Syria in the absence of its consent, despite their knowledge of ISIL's strong presence on Syrian territory.[105] The Netherlands, for example, in 2014 stated that there was no legal basis under international law for its military operations in Syria.[106] Canada, on the contrary, ceased its operation in Syria in February 2016[107] because of a murky legal basis for its intervention without Syria's consent.[108]

Moreover, there are just a few members of the Coalition against ISIL that have been engaged in operations in Syria [109] and of those involved several have not reported the use of force in self-defence to the UNSC as required

103 *Cameron*, p. 16.

104 UN Doc. S/2015/946 (2015); UN Doc. S/2016/523 (2016).

105 *Arimatsu/Schmitt*, Attacking Islamic State and the Khorasan Group: Surveying the International Law Landscape, 2014, 53 Columbia Journal of Transnational Law Bulletin, p. 1 (4).

106 *Rapaport*, Dutch Parliament Commits Soldiers, F-16s to Fight Isis in Iraq, at: http://www.nltimes.nl/2014/09/24/parliament-commits-troops-isis-fight/ (visited 9.03.2017).

107 *Mills/Smith/Brooke-Holland.*

108 *Lesperance*, Canada's Military Operations against Isis in Iraq and Syria and the Law of Armed Conflict, (2015) 10 CIL, p. 51 (61).

109 For the list of states see *Mills/Smith/Brooke-Holland.* See also *Corten*, (2016) 29 LJIL, p. 777 (780–785).

under Article 51 of the UN Charter.[110] This omission can be seen as a sign of uncertainty of the legal grounds for their use of force in self-defence in Syria.

In addition, host states, supported by few other states, persistently reject the arguments underlying this doctrine and consider the use of force on their territory under the disguise of counter-terrorism as an act of aggression and violation of their territorial sovereignty.[111] In its letters to the UNSC, Syria pointed out that any presence of a foreign state on the Syrian territory without its consent under the disguise of fight against terrorism would be considered a violation of Syrian sovereignty.[112] In the context of Turkish incursions in Syria, Russia was pushing for the adoption of a UNSC resolution that would demand respect of Syrian sovereignty and its territorial independence.[113] When Turkey entered Northern Iraq in 2015 without its prior consent to fight the terrorist threat, Iraq immediately denounced Turkish military incursions as a flagrant violation of international law and an act of aggression.[114]

Broadening of the interpretation of Article 51 of the UN Charter was also rejected by the non-aligned movement and by some scholars, the most notable initiative being a "Plea against the abusive invocation of self-defence as a response to terrorism," dismissing the possibility of the use of force in

---

110 Ibid.

111 See e.g. Lebanon in UN Doc. S/PV.5489 (2006).

112 Identical letters dated 17.09.2015 from the Permanent Representative of the Syrian Arab Republic to the United Nations addressed to the Secretary-General and the President of the Security Council, UN Doc. S/2015/719 (2015).

113 *Tasnim News Agency*, US, France Oppose UN Resolution to Respect Syrian Sovereignty, at: http://www.tasnimnews.com/en/news/2016/02/20/1005892/us-france-oppose-un-resolution-to-respect-syrian-sovereignty (visited 9.03.2017). For the position of other States, see *Corten*, (2016) 29 LJIL, p. 777 (788–789).

114 Identical letters dated 17.10.2016 from the Permanent Representative of Iraq to the United Nations addressed to the Secretary-General and the President of the Security Council, UN Doc. S/2016/870 (2016); Note verbal dated 16.09.2015 from the Permanent Mission of Iraq to the United Nations addressed to the Secretary-General, UN Doc. S/2015/723 (2015); Letter dated 11.12.2015 from the Permanent Representative of Iraq to the United Nations addressed to the President of the Security Council, UN Doc. S/2015/963 (2015); League of Arab States, Resolution No 7987, 24.12.2015 7987, in which the Council of the League considered the incursion to be a violation of the sovereignty of Iraq and a threat to Arab national security.

cases where state is "unable to put an end to terrorist activities on its territory."[115]

One can conclude that the unwillingness or inability standard, even in the context of Syria, remains normatively too vague to be adopted as an interpretative standard of the notion of self-defence. There are no generally accepted conditions set out to declare which states are unwilling or unable, which means that discretion of attacked states to identify those conditions is dangerously wide (and thus prone to abuse).[116] Furthermore, states rarely discuss the grounds for identifying another state as unwilling or unable, but rather argue that this is something self-evident that does not warrant additional explanation.[117]

E. Concluding Remarks

The use of force in self-defence against non-state actors remains controversial. There is a clear discrepancy between the traditional views of the ICJ and ILC, confining the law of self-defence to inter-state relations, and more progressive views, arguing for the unwilling or unable doctrine. When relying on the law of self-defence in the context of attacks of non-state actors in the past, countries justified their actions by attributing acts of non-state actors to host states. However, in recent years, there has been a shift from the attribution to the question of necessity. States no longer try to establish the effective control in each individual case, but rather claim that the use of force in self-defence is necessary due to the unwillingness or inability of host states to prevent terrorist attacks originating from their territory.

115 *Corten*, Plea against the abusive invocation of self-defence as a response to terrorism, EJIL: *Talk!* at: http://www.ejiltalk.org/a-plea-against-the-abusive-invocation-of-self-defence-as-a-response-to-terrorism/ (visited 9.03.2017). See also *Corten*, (2016) 29 LJIL, p. 777.

116 Some scholars attempt to identify fundamental principles and parameters of the use of the test, but the discussion has not left academic circles. E.g. *Deeks*, (2012) 52 VJIL, p. 483.

117 States did not offer extensive arguments in the case of Syria. Compare with *Gorman/Barnes*, Spy, Military Ties Aided bin Laden Raid, at: http://online.wsj.com/article/SB10001424052748704083904576334160172068344.html (visited 9.03.2017).

There is an undeniable trend, especially in the context of Syria, favouring the application of the unwilling or unable doctrine. It is therefore not excluded that the doctrine may once change the interpretation of Article 51 of the UN Charter.[118]

However, the substance of the unwilling or unable doctrine is still undefined and leaves a variety of international legal questions opened to discussion. A complete abandonment of the attribution standard in this doctrine calls for a vigilant approach when considering appropriateness of these developments. Loosening the conditions for the unilateral use of force on the territory of another (host) state may call into question the very cornerstone of the modern international community, the principle on the prohibition of the use of force in inter-state relations.[119] If the unwilling or unable doctrine ever became the interpretative standard of Article 51 of the UN Charter, the unilateral use of force on the territory of another state under the counter-terrorism argument would become possible in numerous cases, which could lead to escalation of wars, consequently endangering international peace and security. Finally, the authors want to draw attention to the fact that problems concerning non-state actors illuminated in this contribution are not confined to the law of self-defence. They rather point to a worrisome reality which reflects the general inability and failure of international law to properly address and recognise the status of non-state actors.

Bibliography

Application of the Convention on the Prevention and Punishment of the Crime of Genocide *(Bosnia and Herzegovina v. Serbia and Montenegro),* Judgment, ICJ Reports 2007, 43

Louise Arimatsu, 'The Law of State Responsibility in Relation to Border Crossings: An Ignored Legal Paradigm' (2013) 89 International Law Studies Series, 21

Louise Arimatsu and Michael N. Schmitt, 'Attacking Islamic State and the Khorasan Group: Surveying the International Law Landscape' (2014) 53 Columbia Journal of Transnational Law Bulletin, 1

118 Vienna Convention on the Law of Treaties, 23.05.1969, UNTS, Vol. 1155, p. 331, Article 31/3 (b).

119 For more on the recent state practice undermining the prohibition of the use of force by expanding the notion of self-defence see: *d'Aspremont*, (2010) 31.4 University of Pennsylvania Journal of International Law, p. 1089 (1116).

Peter L. Bergen, 'September 11 attacks' in *Encylopaedia Britannica*, at: https://www.britannica. com/ event/September-11-attacks (visited 10.09.2016)

Daniel Bethlehem, 'Principles Relevant to the Scope of a State's Right of Self-Defense against an Imminent or Actual Armed Attack by Nonstate Actors', at: http://www.un.org/law/counsel/Bethlehem%20-%20Self-Defense%20Article.pdf (visited 3.04.2016)

Michael Brent, 'Responding to Attacks by Non-State Actors: The Attribution Requirement of Self-Defence' (2009) 16 Australian International Law Journal, 133

Edgar Buckley, 'Invoking Article 5', at: http://www.nato.int/docu/review/2006/issue2/english/art2.html (visited 9.03.2017)

David Cameron, 'Memorandum to the Foreign Affairs Select Committee', at: https://www.parliament.uk/documents/commons-committees/foreign-affairs/PM-Response-to-FAC-Report-Extension-of-Offensive-British-Military-Operations-to-Syria.pdf (visited 3.07.2016)

Case Concerning Armed Activities on the Territory of the Congo *(Democratic Republic of the Congo v. Uganda)*, Judgment, ICJ Reports 2005, 168

Case Concerning Military and Paramilitary Activities in and Against Nicaragua *(Nicaragua v. United States of America)*, Merits, Judgment, ICJ Reports 1986, 14

Antonio Cassese, 'Terrorism is Also Disrupting Some Crucial Legal Categories of International Law' (2001) 12 European Journal of International Law, 993

Olivier Corten, 'Plea against the abusive invocation of self-defence as a response to terrorism' EJIL: Talk! (14 July 2006), at: http://www.ejiltalk.org/a-plea-against-the-abusive-invocation-of-self-defence-as-a-response-to-terrorism/ (visited 7.04.2017)

Olivier Corten, *The law against war: The prohibition on the use of force in contemporary international law* (Hart Publishing, Oxford 2012)

Olivier Corten, 'The 'Unwilling or Unable' Test: Has it Been, and Could it be, Accepted?' (2016) 29 Leiden Journal of International Law, 777

Irene Couzigou, 'The Fight against the 'Islamic State' in Syria and the Right to Self-Defence', at: http://www.e-ir.info/2016/02/05/the-fight-against-the-islamic-state-in-syria-and-the-right-to-self-defence/ (visited 3.05.2016)

James Crawford, *State Responsibility: The General Part* (Cambridge University Press, Cambridge 2013)

Jean d'Aspremont, 'Mapping the concepts behind the contemporary liberalization of the use of force in international law' (2010) 31.4 University of Pennsylvania Journal of International Law, 1089

Ashley S. Deeks, '"Unwilling or Unable": Toward a Normative Framework for Extraterritorial Self-Defense' (2012) 52 Virginia Journal of International Law, 483

Yoram Dinstein, *War, Aggression and Self-Defence* (5th Edition, Cambridge University Press, Cambridge 2011)

Oliver Dörr and Kirsten Schmalenbach (eds), *Vienna Convention on the Law of Treaties: A Commentary* (Springer, 2012)

Carlo Focarelli, 'International Law and Third-Party Countermeasures in the Age of Global Instant Communication' (2016) Questions of International Law, 17

Thomas M. Franck, 'Editorial Comments: Terrorism and the Right of Self-Defence' (2010) 95 American Journal of International Law, 839

Siobhan Gorman and Julian E. Barnes, 'Spy, Military Ties Aided bin Laden Raid', at: http://online.wsj.com./article/SB10001424052748704083904576334160172068344.html (visited 2.05.2016)

Christine D. Gray, *International Law and the Use of Force* (Oxford University Press on Demand, Oxford 2008)

James Green, *The International Court of Justice and self-defence in international law* (Bloomsbury Publishing, Oxford 2009)

Christopher Greenwood, 'Self-Defence' in Max Planck Encyclopaedia of Public International Law (2011)

Christian Henderson, 'Editorial Comment: The Use of Force and Islamic State' (2014) 1 Journal on the Use of Force and International Law, 209

Gábor Kajtár, 'Self-Defence Against Non-State Actors – Methodological Challenges' (2010) 54 Annales Universitatis Scientiarum Budapestinensis de Rolando Eötvös nominatae, 307

Tina Korošec and Maruša Tekavčič Veber, 'Pravica do samoobrambe zoper nedržavne akterje v luči boja proti terorizmu' (Right to Self-Defence against Non-State Actors in the Context of Fight against Terrorism) (2016) Zbornik Znanstvenih Razprav, 41

Legal Consequences of the Construction of a Wall in the Occupied Palestinian Territory, Advisory Opinion, ICJ Reports 2004, 136

Legality of the Threat or Use of Nuclear Weapons, Advisory Opinion, ICJ Reports 1996, 226

Robert J. Lesperance, 'Canada's Military Operations against Isis in Iraq and Syria and the Law of Armed Conflict' (2015) 10 Canadian International Lawyer, 51

Noam Lubell, *Extraterritorial Use of Force Against Non-State Actors* (Oxford University Press, New York 2010)

Claire Mills, Ben Smith and Louisa Brooke-Holland, 'ISIS/Daesh: the military response in Iraq and Syria', at: http://researchbriefings.parliament.uk/Research-Briefing/Summary/SN06995 (visited 15.05.2016)

Sean D. Murphy, 'Terrorism and the Concept of Armed Attack in Article 51 of the UN Charter' (2002) 43 Harvard International Law Journal, 41

Oil Platforms (*Islamic Republic of Iran v. United States of America*), Judgment, ICJ Reports 2003, 161

Dörr Randzelhofer and Georg Nolte, 'Commentary to Article 51 of the UN Charter' in Bruno Simma, Daniel-Erasmus Khan, Georg Nolte and Andreas Paulus (eds), *The Charter of the United Nations: A Commentary* (3rd Edition, Oxford University Press, Oxford 2012), 1397

Dörr Randzelhofer, 'Commentary to Article 2 (4) of the UN Charter' in Bruno Simma, Daniel-Erasmus Khan, Georg Nolte and Andreas Paulus (eds), *The Charter of the*

United Nations: A Commentary (3rd Edition, Oxford University Press, Oxford 2012), 200

Emma Rapaport, 'Dutch Parliament Commits Soldiers, F-16s to Fight Isis in Iraq', at: http://www.nltimes.nl/2014/09/24/parliament-commits-troops-isis-fight/ (visited 15. 05.2016)

Steven R. Ratner, 'Jus ad Bellum and Jus in Bello after September 11' (2002) 96 American Journal of International Law, 905

Theresa Reinold, 'State Weakness, Irregular Warfare, and the Right to Self-Defense Post-9/11' (2011) 105 American Journal of International Law, 244

Tom Ruys, *'Armed Attack' and Article 51 of the UN Charter: Evolutions in Customary Law and Practice* (Cambridge University Press, Cambridge 2010)

Tom Ruys and Sten Verhoeven, 'Attacks by Private Actors and the Right of Self-Defence' (2005) 10 Journal of Conflict & Security Law, 289

Nico Schrijver and Larissa van den Herik, 'Leiden Policy Recommendations on Counter-terrorism and International Law', at: http://www.grotiuscentre.org/resources/1/Leiden%20Policy%20Recommendations%201%20April%202010.pdf (visited 2.04. 2016)

Ian Scobbie, '"Words My Mother Never Taught Me:" In Defense of the International Court' (2005) 99 The American Journal of International Law, 76

Sikander Ahmed Shah, 'War on Terrorism: Self Defense, Operation Enduring Freedom, and the Legality of U.S. Drone Attacks in Pakistan' (2010) 9 Washington University Global Studies Law Review, 77

Malcolm N. Shaw, *International Law* (7th Edition, Cambridge University Press, Cambridge 2014)

Kenneth Shewmaker, Kenneth R. Stevens and Anita McGurn, *The Papers of Daniel Webster*, Diplomatic Papers, Vol. 1, 1841–1843 (1983)

Paulina Starski, 'The "Unwilling or Unable State" as a Challenge to International Law', at: http://www.mpil.de//en/pub/research/areas/public-international-law/the-unwilling-or-unable-state.cfm#project (visited 4.07.2016)

Christian J. Tams, 'Light Treatment of a Complex Problem: The Law of Self-Defence in the Wall Case' (2005) 16 European Journal of International Law, 963

Tasnim News Agency: US, France Oppose UN Resolution to Respect Syrian Sovereignty, at: http://www.tasnimnews.com/en/news/2016/02/20/1005892/us-france-oppose-un-resolution-to-respect-syrian-sovereignty (visited 3.05.2016)

Patrick Terry, 'Germany Joins the Campaign Against Isis in Syria: A Case of Collective Self-Defence or Rather the Unlawful Use of Force?' (2016) 4 Russian Law Journal, 26

Barbara Salazar Torreon, 'U.S. Periods of War and Dates of Recent Conflicts' Congressional Research Service Report (27 February 2015)

Kimberley N. Trapp, 'The Use of Force against Terrorists: A Reply to Christian J. Tams' (2009) 20 European Journal of International Law, 1049

US Department of State: Russian Bombing of Georgia (Press Release, 24 August 2002), at: http://2001-2009.state.gov/p/eur/rls/prsrl/2002/13002.htm (visited 3.04. 2016)

Raphaël Van Steenberghe, 'Self-Defence in Response to Attacks by Non-State Actors in the Light of Recent State Practice: A Step Forward?' (2010) 23 Leiden Journal of International Law, 183

Nigel D. White and Christian Henderson, *Research Handbook on International Conflict and Security Law* (Edward Elgar Publishing, Glos 2013)

Gareth D. Williams, 'Piercing the Shield of Sovereignty: An Assessment of the Legal Status of the 'Unwilling or Unable' Test' (2013) 36 University of New South Wales Law Journal, 619

Elizabeh Wilmhurst, 'Chatham House Principles of International law on the Use of Force by States in Self-Defence', at: https://www.chathamhouse.org/publications/papers/view/108106 (visited 3.04.2016)

Responsibility Not to Veto

Marina Žagar

A. *The Responsibility to Protect*

The Responsibility to Protect (R2P) as an emerging norm emphasizes that states must protect their populations from mass atrocity crimes – genocide, crimes against humanity, war crimes and ethnic cleansing.

Since 1945 the international community's promise of 'never again' has been constantly broken around the world. In response to the crimes in the 1990s in Rwanda, Somalia and the former Yugoslavia the world sought to find an appropriate response to the occurrence of mass atrocities. Over the past decade R2P has been developed as a means to prevent, to react and to rebuild after the mass atrocities. At the 2005 World Summit the members of the United Nations unanimously endorsed the concept of R2P and upheld the following commitments:

> "138. Each individual State has the responsibility to protect its populations from genocide, war crimes, ethnic cleansing and crimes against humanity. This responsibility entails the prevention of such crimes, including their incitement, through appropriate and necessary means. We accept that responsibility and will act in accordance with it. The international community should, as appropriate, encourage and help States to exercise this responsibility and support the United Nations in establishing an early warning capability.
>
> 139. The international community, through the United Nations, also has the responsibility to use appropriate diplomatic, humanitarian and other peaceful means, in accordance with Chapters VI and VIII of the Charter of the United Nations, to help protect populations from genocide, war crimes, ethnic cleansing and crimes against humanity. In this context, we are prepared to take collective action, in a timely and decisive manner, through the Security Council, in accordance with the Charter, including Chapter VII, on a case-by-case basis and in cooperation with relevant regional organizations as appropriate, should peaceful means be inadequate and national authorities are manifestly failing to protect their populations from genocide, war crimes, ethnic cleansing and crimes against humanity. We stress the need for the General Assembly to continue consideration of the responsibility to protect populations from genocide, war crimes, ethnic cleansing and crimes against humanity and its implications, bearing in mind the principles of the Charter and international law. We also intend to commit ourselves, as necessary and appropriate, to helping States build capacity to protect their populations from genocide, war crimes, ethnic

cleansing and crimes against humanity and to assisting those which are under stress before crises and conflicts break out.

140. We fully support the mission of the Special Adviser of the Secretary General on the Prevention of Genocide."[1]

In 2009, Ban Ki-moon identified that the R2P is resting on three pillars:[2]

"1. A state has the responsibility to protect its population from genocide, war crimes, crimes against humanity and ethnic cleansing.

2. The international community has the responsibility to assist the state to fulfill its primary responsibility.

3. If the state manifestly fails to protect its citizens from the four mass atrocities, mentioned above and peaceful measures have failed, the international community has the responsibility to intervene through coercive measures such as economic sanctions. Military intervention is considered the last resort."[3]

Prevention is an essential part of R2P and falls under pillars one and two. The ICISS Report[4] divides the Responsibility to Protect into three sub-responsibilities: the responsibility to prevent, to react, and to rebuild. The responsibility to prevent consists of measures aimed at avoiding massive human rights violations in the first place. It emphasizes the importance of early warning mechanisms and root-cause conflict prevention as well as diplomatic, economic, and military instruments to confine a conflict before it escalates. The responsibility to rebuild[5] comprises responsibilities which arise

---

1 *United Nations General Assembly*, 2005 World Summit Outcome (20 September 2005), UN Doc A/60/1, p. 31–32.

2 *Ki-moon*, Implementing the Responsibility to Protect: Report of the Secretary-General (12 January 2009), UN Doc A/63/677.

3 *International Coalition for the Responsibility to Protect*, Key developments on the Responsibility to Protect at the United Nations from 2005–2017, at: http://www.responsibilitytoprotect.org/index.php/about-rtop/the-un-and-rtop (visited: 30.09.2016).

4 International Commission on Intervention and State Sovereignty (ICISS), The Responsibility to Protect (2001), at: http://www.iciss.ca/pdf/Commission-Report.pdf.

5 The responsibility to rebuild has been accompanied by renewed interest in questions of justice after war (the so-called jus post bellum) and was institutionalized by the World Summit through the creation of the UN's Peace-building Commission (PBC). The PBC has a key role in sustaining the attention of the international community on the importance of recovery and capacity-building efforts as a means of preventing conflict reoccurrence. Also, while the PBC assists countries emerging from conflict (not necessarily limited to instances of the four

after a conflict, particularly after a military intervention has been conducted and aims to support the sustainable development of a stable and safe society. The responsibility to react constitutes the normative core of R2P. It applies when massive human rights violations occur in a state that is either unable or unwilling to protect its citizens. In this case, coercive measures short of military action should be taken including diplomatic, economic or military sanctions such as arms embargoes or financial restrictions.[6]

B. Mandate of the UNSC

The United Nation's Security Council (hereinafter UNSC) is the UN's primary and most powerful organ for carrying out the UN's central mission of keeping peace in the world. Article 24 of the UN Charter grants the Council "primary responsibility for the maintenance of international peace and security," and under Article 25 of the Charter, "Members of the United Nations agree to accept and carry out the decisions of the Security Council." The UNSC is charged with both settling disputes peacefully if possible using the powers granted in Chapter VI of the Charter, and with meeting threats to peace by concerted action under Chapter VII. Of particular relevance to the Council's role in international justice is Article 41. Once the UNSC has determined under Chapter VII Article 39 that a threat to peace exists, Article 41 empowers the Council to:

> "decide what measures not involving the use of armed force are to be employed to give effect to its decisions, and it may call upon the Members of the United Nations to apply such measures. These may include complete or partial interruption of economic relations and of rail, sea, air, postal, telegraphic, radio, and other means of communication, and the severance of diplomatic relations."

R2P crimes) the first two PBC cases were Burundi and Sierra Leone. The results were: International Commission of Inquiry for Burundi's final report, which said that genocide was committed against the state's Tutsi population in October 1993, and The Special Court for Sierra Leone – internationalized criminal court. In: *Bellamy*, Conflict Prevention and the Responsibility to Protect. Global Governance: A Review of Multilateralism and International Organizations, 2008, p. 135.

6 *Payandeh*, With Great Power Comes Great Responsibility? The Concept of the Responsibility To Protect Within the Process of International Lawmaking, (2010) 35 The Yale Journal of International Law, p. 468 (481).

Maintaining peace and security is the Council's primary, but not only, power. In addition, the Council is responsible for "promoting and encouraging respect for human rights and for fundamental freedoms for all."[7]

Yet, the Council is a decidedly political body as, its members are not chosen for their wisdom, virtue, or independence, but because they, particularly its five permanent members (P5), have the political, economic and military strength to keep the peace, especially when they act together in the cooperative manner envisioned by the Charter.

Even though the UNSC bears primary responsibility for the maintenance and restoration of international peace and security, mass atrocity crimes have been occurring. The international community has often continued to do little or nothing about them. One barrier to needed action is particularly the UNSC system. Many have accused this UN's body and its working methods, set up in the aftermath of World War II, of being out-dated, unrepresentative, and unreflective of the modern international system. According to the UN Charter, votes on non-procedural matters within the Organization require a consensus by all P5 of the Security Council. Given this veto power, much discussion has evolved on whether or not the permanent members have any responsibility to refrain from using their veto in mass atrocity situations.[8]

The crisis in Syria, which caused hundreds of thousands of dead and several million refugees and internally displaced, is a reminder of what can and does happen to populations when the veto is used or threatened. Indeed, we are seeing a civil war that, since the start of 2011, has caused a humanitarian disaster of a scale great enough to invoke this legal status. Why has the R2P

7 *Moss*, The UN Security Council and the International Criminal Court Towards a More Principled Relationship, Friedrich-Ebert-Stiftung, Global Policy and Development, 2012, p. 2.

8 The rationale for the P5 veto power was to ensure that the UN Security Council did not suffer the same fate as its predecessor the League of Nations. In essence, the veto power was granted to the P5 as reassurance that their interests would not be ignored and in the hope that it would ensure their participation in the new organization. However, after the UN was established there were regular calls to reform the veto power, the most common grounds being that the veto violated the principle of sovereign equality, that it would be used as a tool of great power domination, and that it would effectively exempt the P5 from being governed by the Council. In: *Blätter*, The Responsibility Not To Veto: A Way Forward, at: http://responsibilitytoprotect.org/Responsibility_not_to_Veto_White_Paper_Final_ 7_14__2_.pdf (visited: 01.07.2018).

not been implemented in Syria while it has in the Libya? Russia and China, permanent members of the Council, prevented it by using their right of veto, ignoring the fact that the conditions required for the application of the R2P were present in Syria.[9]

Of course, UNSC vetoes on the Syrian crisis cannot be entirely blamed for crimes which are committed there. Nevertheless, the international community would be closer to a political solution to the crisis if Russia and China did not veto four resolutions on Syria, drafts which ranged from condemning human rights violations to threatening sanctions to renewing the deployment of ceasefire monitors.[10]

P5 have specific geopolitical interests and ideologies. When some members see a need for intervention, P5 are likely to have interests at stake or disagree about the need – and exercise their veto.[11]

So what are China and Russia's specific interests? A closer look at their statements on the vetoed draft resolutions reveals that a real intention of casting their vetoes was and has been to avoid, at all costs, what Russia called a 'regime change' by UN intervention in Syria.[12]

China and Russia have justified their joint vetoes, by arguing that, among other things, the draft resolutions would not be in line with the basic UN principles of state sovereignty, territorial integrity, peaceful settlement of disputes and non-intervention in other states. China and Russia have strictly

---

9 *Cesáreo*, The responsibility to protect and the right of veto in the Security Council: some recent examples, (2014) 3 Journal of the Spanish Institute of Strategic Studies, p. 1 (9).

10 *Patnode*, UN Security Council: The responsibility not to veto, at: https://cic-cglobaljustice.wordpress.com/2015/09/30/united-nations-how-the-regulation-of-use-of-the-veto-can-contribute-to-justice/ (visited: 30.09.2016).

11 *Levine*, Some Concerns About 'The Responsibility Not to Veto', (2011) Global Responsibility to Protect, p. 324.

12 Additional reason why the two veto-wielders have greatly been concerned about regime change is that a collapse of the Syrian government might become 'another Libya' which would set dangerous precedents for UN intervention in their own internal matters, such as e.g. Chechnya for Russia and Tibet, Xinjiang, and Taiwan for China. In: *Seoka*, The Implications and Limitations of the Veto Power in the United Nations: A Critical Analysis of the Use of Veto by China and Russia in the Case of Syria, at: http://acuns.org/wp-content/uploads/2015/06/Nao-Seoka.pdf (visited: 30.09.2016), p. 5.

adhered to the traditional notion of 'sovereignty as a right' rather than 'sovereignty as a responsibility.'[13]

However, their concerns over regime change have not been convincing to the other UNSC members, as the primary purpose of the vetoed draft resolutions was not to overthrow the Assad regime by military intervention, but to disable its ability to keep harming its own civilians by economic sanctions in order to fulfill the mandate of human protection. Given these reasons, China and Russia have failed to bear their special responsibilities as the P5 to contribute to the maintenance of international peace and security. Significantly, the China-Russia joint veto has brought the UNSC's paralysis over the Syrian crisis, and its inability to timely respond to the deteriorating humanitarian situation has damaged the credibility and authority of the Council itself. It has been stated that, even if those vetoes were not illegal, they should be regarded as 'illegitimate' under the UN Charter.[14]

C. *UNSC's Permanent Members and the Obligation to Act*

The R2P concept suggests that the Security Council has an increasingly solidifying legal obligation to act in the face of large scale atrocity crimes.[15] While R2P has not yet formed into a fully hard-law obligation,[16] it has been recognized by the Security Council in numerous resolutions.[17]

Various states have proposed that one permanent member of the UNSC, acting alone, should not prevent action in the face of mass atrocity through use of its veto power.[18] Since the adoption of R2P, permanent members of

---

13 Ibid., p. 6.

14 Ibid., p. 7–8.

15 *Trahan*, the Relationship Between the International Criminal Court and the U.N. Security Council: Parameters and Best Practices, (2013) 24 Criminal Law Forum, p. 417 (469).

16 Several things remain problematic about R2P – its legal status, (non)obligatory nature, as well as the differences between R2P some other areas of international law. There are many views that the R2P did not create new law and many legal commentators agree that R2P is not yet an international legal norm because it lacks clarity and has not been appropriately legislated.

17 See more in: *Peters*, The Security Council's Responsibility to Protect, (2011) International Organizations Law Review, p. 8 (13–15).

18 *Trahan*, (2013) 24 Criminal Law Forum, p. 417 (428).

the UNSC have used their veto nine times in situations where atrocities either occurred or were at risk of occurring. So far, veto was used on resolutions on Syria, Palestine, Myanmar and Bosnia and Herzegovina. Should the P5 agree not to use their veto power to block action in response to genocide and mass atrocities which would otherwise pass by a majority? The concept of the 'Responsibility Not to Veto' (hereinafter RN2V) has been proposed as an element for strengthening the R2P. The use of the veto has also negative implications on justice and accountability process. For example, one vetoed resolution on Syria would have ended the long run of impunity by referring the situation to the International Criminal Court (hereinafter ICC). Adopting an agreement which removes the use of the veto in cases of mass atrocity crimes would be one step to implementing the R2P.[19]

D. Two parallel initiatives: The ACT Code of Conduct and the France / Mexico initiative

Two initiatives have been developed as a response to the irresponsible use of the veto in mass atrocity situations: the France / Mexico initiative on veto restraint and the ACT Code of Conduct.

I. France / Mexico Initiative

Veto restraint in R2P situations was first suggested by French Foreign Minister in 2001. Later on, at the 2013 General Assembly informal dialogue on R2P, the issue of the veto was again raised, this time in specific reference to the ongoing crisis in Syria, which at the time was approaching the beginning of its fourth year of conflict. Nine member states called for a 'voluntary restraint' of the veto in R2P situations like Syria. In October 2013, French Foreign Minister pushed the conversation a step farther by offering his ideas on a new voting procedure – a 'code of conduct' centered on the notion that whenever and wherever human rights abuses on the ground

19 *Patnode.*

amounted to mass atrocities, the P5 of the UNSC should voluntarily agree to not invoke their veto power.[20]

In 2015, France in conjunction with Mexico launched a "Political Declaration on suspension of veto powers in cases of mass atrocity," open to all member States to support. The Political Declaration focused only on the P5 of the UNSC and called for voluntary restraint of use of veto in cases of mass atrocity.[21]

France's proposal is significant as it suggests self-limitation regarding the use of the right of veto from the side of the permanent members of the Security Council. It should be highlighted that the French proposal recommends an 'informal' reform of the right of veto, whereby its adoption by the permanent members of the Council would not demand formal amendment of the Charter.[22] French proposal also stipulated a safeguard clause (and potential Achilles Heel): P5 members can still use a veto when they perceive a 'vital national interest' at stake. Though, 'vital national Interest' should not be a limiting criterion in a code of conduct. Mass atrocity crimes – genocide, crimes against humanity, ethnic cleansing and war crimes – always represent a grave violation of international law. As such, they pose an intrinsic threat to international peace and security. Committing these crimes (or protecting a state or non-state actor that is committing them) can never be excused, exempted or misrepresented as being a matter of 'vital national interest.'[23]

---

20 *International Coalition for the Responsibility to Protect.*

21 *Global Centre for the Responsibility to Protect, UN Security Council Code of Conduct*, at: http://www.globalr2p.org/our_work/un_security_council_code_of conduct (visited 30.09.2016).

22 Formal expanding or otherwise changing the UNSC's structure would require an amendment of the Charter and, therefore, the positive votes of two-thirds of the UNGA – including agreement by each of the P5 – and subsequent ratification by their respective national legislature. Amendments to the UN Charter are made by a procedure set out in Chapter XVIII of the UN Charter (Art. 108–109).

23 *Adams*, The responsibility not to veto, at: http://www.globalr2p.org/media/files/2015-january-adams-veto-restraint-remarks.pdf (visited: 30.09.2016).

II. ACT Code of Conduct

In 2013 the Accountability, Coherence and Transparency (hereinafter ACT) Group was launched, expanding upon the world of the failed 'Small Five (hereinafter S5) initiative'[24], which aimed to improve the transparency of the UNSC, suggesting that States should explain why the veto has been employed in each situation. ACT Group was made up of 21 countries (mostly small and middle powers), focusing on a wide variety of issues related to improving the working methods of the Security Council. Subsequently, the ACT group of States proposed a "Code of Conduct regarding Security Council action against genocide, crimes against humanity and war crimes" in July 2015. The Code of Conduct calls upon all members of the UNSC – elected and permanent – to not vote against any credible draft resolution intended to prevent or halt mass atrocities.[25]

E. The UNSC and its P5 as Bearers of the Responsibility to Protect

It was the UNSC which the ICISS Report experts referred to when using the term 'responsibility' rather than 'obligation'. The intention was to connect the new concept to article 24 of the UN Charter, which relates to the UNSC's "primary responsibility for the maintenance of international peace and security."[26] If R2P is observed as a legal principle, then the UNSC's duty to take action in a R2P situation is not only a moral duty, but a legal

24 In 2012, the 'Small 5 (S5) initiative', led by Costa Rica, Jordan, Liechtenstein, Singapore and Switzerland, advanced a resolution in the General Assembly on improving the transparency of the Security Council, suggesting that P5 states should explain why the veto has been employed or considered in each situation, including a reference to the voluntary restraint of the veto in cases of mass atrocities. This draft resolution was later retracted by the S5 due to pressure from the P5 on the resolution's supporters. In: *United Nations Association – UK*, UN Security Council and the responsibility to protect: Voluntary restraint of the veto in situations of mass atrocity, at: https://www.una.org.uk/ sites/default/files/Veto%20R2P%20code%20of%20conduct%20briefing%20October %202015%20update_0.pdf (visited: 30.09.2016).

25 *Global Centre for the Responsibility to Protect, UN Security Council Code of Conduct*, at: http://www.globalr2p.org/our_work/un_security_council_code_of_conduct (visited 30.09.2016).

26 *Peters*, (2011) International Organizations Law Review, p. 8 (13).

one. The presumption of the UNSC's legal obligation to act is that it is not a political organ operating in a law-free zone, but is exposed to legal limits.[27]

More specifically, the UNSC's actions were subject to legal limits when the International Court of Justice (ICJ) issued the advisory opinion on the admission of new members to the UN in 1948. The Court stated with regard to the UNSC that

> "[t]he political character of an organ cannot release it from the observance of the treaty provisions established by the Charter when they constitute limitations on its powers or criteria for its judgment."[28]

As the UN enjoys international legal personality, it is itself bound by general customary international law and by treaty obligations. Even the most powerful organ of the organization – the UNSC cannot be less subjected to legal obligations than the organization itself, although technically only the organization itself (being the international legal person) is the duty-bearer. Leastwise, the UNSC is bound by the 'Purposes and Principles' of the Charter (Art. 24 (2) of the UN Charter), which include customary human rights law and the right to self-determination (cf. Art. 1 (2) and (3) UN of the Charter).[29] These rights are even more typically at risk in a R2P situation.

In the *Wall Opinion*, the ICJ raised an obligation on the United Nations to react to serious breaches of international law. The Court stated

> "that the United Nations, and especially the General Assembly and the UNSC, should consider what further action is required to bring to an end the illegal situation."[30]

It would be connectable with that opinion to postulate an obligation on the United Nations to react in situations where R2P crimes are occurring.[31]

Further analysis also has to focus on the UNSC's permanent members as they have increased responsibility. The P5 are in legally different position

---

27 Ibid., p. 8 (16).

28 Conditions of Admission of a State to Membership in the United Nations (Article 4 of the Charter), 28 May 1948, Advisory Opinion, International Court of Justice, ICJ Reports 1948.

29 *Peters*, (2011) International Organizations Law Review, p. 8 (17).

30 Legal Consequences of the Construction of a Wall in the Occupied Palestinian Territory, 9 July 2004, Advisory Opinion, International Court of Justice, ICJ Reports 2004, para. 160.

31 *Peters*, (2011) International Organizations Law Review, p. 8 (19).

comparing to the non-permanent ones, because they can obstruct decisions through exercising their veto power. The P5's privilege within the UNSC, the veto power, is thus in effect pointing at special responsibility. It is therefore claimed that the legal obligation to protect populations from R2P crimes particularly falls on the permanent members of the UNSC.[32]

Already the ICISS had suggested that when action is needed to stop or avert a significant humanitarian crisis, and when a permanent member of the UNSC does not claim its vital interests to be involved, it should not use the veto to obstruct the passage of what would otherwise be a majority resolution.[33]

Secretary-General invoked the P5's special responsibility in his 2009 Report on the Implementation of R2P:

> "Within the Security Council, the five permanent members bear particular responsibility because of the privileges of tenure and the veto power they have been granted under the Charter. I would urge them to refrain from employing or threatening to employ the veto in situations of manifest failure to meet obligations relating to the responsibility to protect, as defined in paragraph 138 of the Summit Outcome document, and to reach a mutual understanding to that effect."[34]

F. Conclusion

As noted, UNSC is charged with maintaining international peace and security under the UN Charter and it has legal obligation to act in the face of large scale atrocity crimes.[35] The idea that the international community has R2P is clearly based on the assumption that some form of collective agency exists, which possesses the capacity and willingness to fulfill this responsibility.[36] The inaction and ineffectiveness of the UNSC in dealing with populations at risk of mass atrocities in the past raise doubt about the extent to which it, as the authorized body of choice, can represent the international

---

32 Ibid., p. 8 (25–26).

33 International Commission on Intervention and State Sovereignty (ICISS), para. 6.21.

34 Secretary-General, Implementing the Responsibility to Protect (12 January 2009) UN Doc A/63/677, para. 61.

35 *Trahan*, (2013) 24 Criminal Law Forum, p. 417 (432).

36 *Nasu*, The UN Security Council's Responsibility and the 'Responsibility to Protect' (2011) 15 Max Planck Yearbook of United Nations Law, p. 377 (382).

community and implement R2P.[37] The view has been expressed, even early in UN history, that the UNSC would be failing to fulfill its responsibility if it did not take particular action when it was supposed to or expected to do so. The underlying issue surrounding the legal nature of the UNSC's responsibility lies in the criticism of 'double standards' without principled justification for its collective action. Its failure to act consistently has been criticized as being motivated by the self-interest of permanent members rather than the collective interests of UN Member States,[38] e.g. UNSC invoking R2P by quickly passing resolution on Libya, and failing to do so with Syria for several times.

It is discussed that even if the permanent members support the French / Mexican initiative or the ACT Code of Conduct, neither is legally binding. Still, even though it is not fully realistic to make P5 impossible to use their veto, UNSC veto restraint in mass atrocity situations is a practical solution and a way to reaffirm the principles of the UN Charter and R2P. The P5 have special responsibilities – collectively – to act in order to prevent or react on mass atrocities, and individually – not to block potential rescue / humanitarian protection missions undertaken by other actors.[39] It should be noted therefore, that the P5 need to bear 'veto as a responsibility', rather than 'veto as a right'. Moreover, the P5's special responsibilities have been emphasized since 1945, and in fact, the P5 themselves pledged that they would use their vetoes in moderation.[40] Responsibility Not to Veto proposal is positive initiative worthy of praise. Its simplicity, by not forcing a formal amendment to the Charter represents innovative and potentially achievable approach.

Bibliography

Simon Adams, 'The responsibility not to veto', at: http://www.globalr2p.org/media/files/2015-january-adams-veto-restraint-remarks. pdf (visited: 30.09.2016)

Alex J. Bellamy, 'Conflict Prevention and the Responsibility to Protect' (2008) 14 Global Governance: A Review of Multilateralism and International Organizations, 135

37 Ibid., p. 377 (384).
38 Ibid., p. 377 (392).
39 See also: *Blätter*.
40 Seoka, p. 2–5.

Ariela Blätter, 'The Responsibility Not To Veto: A Way Forward', at: http://responsibilitytoprotect.org/Responsibility_not_to_Veto_White_Paper_Final_7_14__2_.pdf (visited: 01.07.2018)

Cesáreo Gutiérrez Espada, 'The responsibility to protect and the right of veto in the Security Council: some recent examples' (2014) 3 Journal of the Spanish Institute of Strategic Studies, 1

'Conditions of Admission of a State to Membership in the United Nations (Article 4 of the Charter)' Advisory Opinion, International Court of Justice, 28 May 1948, ICJ Reports 1948

Global Centre for the Responsibility to Protect, UN Security Council Code of Conduct, at: http://www.globalr2p.org/our_work/un_security_council_code_of_conduct (visited 30.09.2016)

International Coalition for the Responsibility to Protect, 'Key developments on the Responsibility to Protect at the United Nations from 2005-2017', at: http://www.responsibilitytoprotect.org/index.php/about-rtop/the-un-and-rtop (visited: 30.09.2016)

International Commission on Intervention and State Sovereignty (ICISS), 'The Responsibility to Protect' (2001), at: http://www.iciss.ca/pdf/Commission-Report.pdf (visited: 30.09.2016)

Ban Ki-moon, 'Implementing the Responsibility to Protect: Report of the Secretary-General' (12 January 2009) UN Doc A/63/677

Daniel H. Levine, 'Some Concerns About 'The Responsibility Not to Veto'' (2011) 3 Global Responsibility to Protect, 323

Lawrence Moss, 'The UN Security Council and the International Criminal Court Towards a More Principled Relationship' Friedrich-Ebert-Stiftung, Global Policy and Development (2012)

'Legal Consequences of the Construction of a Wall in the Occupied Palestinian Territory' Advisory Opinion, International Court of Justice, 9 July 2004, ICJ Reports 2004

Hitoshi Nasu, 'The UN Security Council's Responsibility and the 'Responsibility to Protect'' (2011) 15 Max Planck Yearbook of United Nations Law, 377

Angela Patnode, 'UN Security Council: The responsibility not to veto', at: https://ciccglobaljustice.wordpress.com/2015/09/30/united-nations-how-the-regulation-of-use-of-the-veto-can-contribute-to-justice/ (visited: 30.09.2016)

Mehrdad Payandeh, 'With Great Power Comes Great Responsibility? The Concept of the Responsibility To Protect Within the Process of International Lawmaking' (2010) 35 The Yale Journal of International Law, 468

Anne Peters, 'The Security Council's Responsibility to Protect' (2011) International Organizations Law Review, 8

Secretary-General, 'Implementing the Responsibility to Protect' (12 January 2009) UN Doc A/63/677

Nao Seoka, 'The Implications and Limitations of the Veto Power in the United Nations: A Critical Analysis of the Use of Veto by China and Russia in the Case of Syria', at: http://acuns.org/wp-content/uploads/2015/06/Nao-Seoka.pdf (visited: 30.09.2016)

Jennifer Trahan, 'The Relationship Between the International Criminal Court and the U.N. Security Council: Parameters and Best Practices' (2013) 24 Criminal Law Forum, 417

United Nations Association – UK, 'UN Security Council and the responsibility to protect: Voluntary restraint of the veto in situations of mass atrocity', at: https://www.una.org.uk/sites/default/files/Veto%20R2P%20code%20of%20conduct%20briefing%20October%202015%20update_0.pdf (visited: 30.09.2016)

United Nations General Assembly, '2005 World Summit Outcome' (20 September 2005) UN Doc A/60/1

Solutions to the Problem of Climate Change Refugees

Udayan Sanyal

A. *Introduction*

The status of refugees all over the world is quite precarious in many ways. They are treated as unwelcome aliens in most countries. However, the case of climate change refugees is even worse. They are not entitled to formal refugee status, a status which would allow them to successfully apply for life saving refuge and relief. Thus, they are forced to run around the world to save their lives.

Unlike victims of political upheaval, who are protected by international law and can obtain financial and medical aid, food and shelter through governments and international organizations, it is unclear what Conventions and policies protect people displaced by extreme weather events.[1] Even the United Nations has no official status for those who are environmental refugees. Since those affected are termed 'environmental migrants', the legal status of those who should be deemed 'refugees' is undermined to the extent that there is no official obligation to give them asylum. Accordingly, the experts from the United Nations University's Institute for Environment and Human Security (UNU-EHS) has stressed that there is an urgent need to define a new category of refugees.[2]

---

1 *Norwegian Refugee Council/Internal Displacement Monitoring Centre (NRC/IDMC)*, The Nansen Conference: Climate Change and Displacement in the 21st Century, 2011, http://www.refworld.org/docid/521485ef4.html (visited 25.08.2018).

2 *Mante/Kolstrup*, Environmental Refugees – How Climate Change Affects People's Lives, (2014), at: https://en.reset.org/knowledge/environmental-refugees-%E2%80%93-how-climate-change-affects-peoples-lives (visited 25. 08.2018).

B. Climate Change Refugees

> "By 2050, hundreds of millions more people may become permanently displaced due to rising sea levels, floods, droughts, famine and hurricanes. The melting or collapse of ice sheets alone threatens the homes of 1 in every 20 people. Increased desertification and the alteration of ecosystems, by endangering community's livelihoods, are also likely to trigger large population displacements."[3]
>
> – Deputy High Commissioner for Human Rights (February, 2008)[4]

Global warming is leading to environmental disasters such as floods, draughts and desertification. Today, almost two billon inhabitants of the world depend on fragile ecosystems like arid and semi-arid areas, with 90% of these people being from developing countries. Thus, the steady progression of global warming is causing increased competition among people for limited resources, leading to migration and even conflicts. Former United Nations Secretary General Ban Ki-moon, for instance, blames the ethnic and religious violence in Darfur on global warming: "The Darfur conflict began as an ecological crisis, arising at least in part from climate change."[5]

Myers, who predicted that there were 25 million environmental refugees on earth in the mid-1990's, stated in 2005 that the impact of global warming could potentially displace 200 million people by 2050.[6] According to the Red Cross, "climate change disasters are currently a bigger cause of population displacement than war and persecution."[7] The United Nations High

---

3 *Kang*, Office of High Commissioner for Human Rights, Climate Change, Migration and Human Rights, (Geneva 19 February 2008), at: https://www.iom.int/jahia/webdav/shared/shared/mainsite/events/docs/hsn/hsnaddress_kang.pdf, p. 3–4 (visited 25.08.2018).

4 *Docherty/Giannini*, Confronting A Rising Tide: A Proposal For A Convention On Climate Change Refugees, (2009) 33 Harvard Environmental Law Review (hereinafter Har. Env. L. Rev.), p. 349 (352).

5 *Ki-moon*, A Climate Culprit in Darfur, 2007, at: http://www.washingtonpost.com/wp-dyn/content/article/2007/06/15/AR2007061501857.html (visited 25.08.2018).

6 *Brown*, Climate change and forced migration: Observations, projections and implications, UNDP Human Development Report 2007–2008, at: https://www.iisd.org/pdf/2008/climate_forced_migration.pdf (visited 25.08.2018).

7 *Perez*, Climate Refugees – The Human Toll of Global Warming (2006), at: https://www.americanprogress.org/issues/green/news/2006/12/07/2428/climate-refugees/ (visited 25.08.2018).

Commissioner for Refugees (UNHCR) stated that 36 million people were displaced by natural disasters in 2009, and about 20 million of those were forced to move because of climate-change-related issues. According to other estimates, there could be as many as 150 million by 2050 due to climate change.[8]

As nations point fingers at each other, nothing is being done to help the victims to mitigate or to adapt to the effects of climate change. Three characteristics of climate change make it unlike any other type of environmental disaster that the world has previously faced. Firstly, the withholding of support to climate change victims is often justified by citing the lack of consensus regarding the mere existence and scientific causes of climate change. Secondly, the trans-boundary nature of climate change means that prevention cannot be effective if undertaken by isolated parties or nations. Finally, those countries producing the most harmful greenhouse gasses are usually the least affected by climate change disasters, while those producing the least seem to bear the greater burden of global warming harms. Moreover, the victims of climate change, often small islands or poor nations, are frequently in the worst position to adapt to and mitigate the damages.[9]

The term 'environmental refugee' was first introduced by El-Hinnawi in a 1985 United Nations Environment Programme report and defined as: "those people who have been forced to leave their traditional habitat, temporarily or permanently, because of a marked environmental disruption (natural and / or triggered by people) that jeopardized their existence and / or seriously affected the quality of their life."[10] However, avoiding the term 'refugee', the UNHCR has moved towards a definition of 'environmentally displaced persons' as those: "who are displaced from or who feel obliged to

---

8 *Vidal*, Global warming could create 150 million 'climate refugees' by 2050, (Barcelona 2009), at: http://www.theguardian.com/environment/2009/nov/03/global-warming-climate-refugees (visited 25.08.2018).

9 *Duong*, When Islands Drown: The Plight of "Climate Change Refugees" and Recourse to International Human Rights Law, (2010) 31 UPaJInt'lL, p. 1239 (1243).

10 *Kolmannskog, Norwegian Refugee Council*, Future Floods of Refugees, A comment on climate change, conflict and forced migration, (2008), at: http://www.migrationdrc.org/publications/resource_guides/Migration_and_Climate_Change/Future_floods_of_refugees.pdf (visited 25.08.2018).

leave their usual place of residence, because their lives, livelihoods and welfare have been placed at serious risk as a result of adverse environmental, ecological or climatic processes and events."[11]

The International Organization for Migration (IOM), has chosen to define environmental migrants broadly as:

> "persons or groups of persons who, for reasons of sudden or progressive changes in the environment that adversely affect their lives or living conditions, are obliged to have to leave their habitual homes, or choose to do so, either temporarily or permanently, and who move either within their territory or abroad."[12]

Thus, it can be seen that there are a number of terms and definitions for climate change refugees. They may vary at minute levels on issues such as consideration of internal displacement inside a country and temporary displacement. However, the three definitions given above do highlight a compelling need to leave one's home due to environmental factors. Thus, climate change refugees are the category of refugees who are forced to leave their normal places of residence because of environmental changes adversely affecting their lives and livelihood.

C. Scope of Protection of Climate Change Refugees under Existing Legal Instruments

I. Refugee Convention

The United Nations Convention Relating to the Status of Refugees, 1951 defined a refugee in Article 1 as a person who:

> "… Owing to well-founded fear of being persecuted for reasons of race, religion, nationality, membership of a particular social group or political opinion, is outside the country of his nationality and is unable or, owing to such fear, is unwilling to avail himself of the protection of that country; or who, not having a nationality and

---

11 *Boano/Zetter/Morris, Refugee Studies Centre*, Environmentally displaced people, Understanding the linkages between environmental change, livelihoods and forced migration, (2008), at: http://www.unicef.org/socialpolicy/files/Environmentally_displaces_people.pdf (visited 25.08.2018).

12 *International Organisation for Migration*, Definitional Issues, at: https://www.iom.int/definitional-issues (visited 25.08.2018).

> being outside the country of his former habitual residence as a result of such events, is unable or, owing to such fear, is unwilling to return to it."[13]

There are two core requirements:

1) A well-founded fear of being persecuted;
2) On grounds of race, religion, nationality, membership in a particular social group, or political opinion.[14]

Thus, environmental issues are excluded from the list of permissible reasons for seeking refuge. The definition does not leave open for interpretation the reasons for persecution; instead it includes an exhaustive list of reasons, clearly setting the boundaries of the legal application of the Refugee Convention, an approach that has subsequently been supported by refugee law jurisprudence.[15] Climate change refugees simply are not 'refugees' in the legal sense.

Additionally, the Convention requires persecution by a government actor or a non-state actor which the government is unable to or is unwilling to control. However, proving a state to be a persecutor is difficult as governments are unlikely to actively abandon citizens affected by climate change and are actually likely to make efforts to help them.[16]

Attempts to extend the definition of refugees under the Convention have met with strong resistance, especially based on the possibility of "opening the floodgates to refugees." Also, whereas environmental refugees could still take the help of their national governments, traditional refugees cannot do so. The UNHCR has stated that

> "lumping both groups together under the same heading would further cloud the issues and could undermine efforts to help and protect either group and to address the root causes of either type of displacement."[17]

Another problem is that while the Convention covers only those people who have been forced to migrate beyond borders as refugees, a substantial number of climate change refugees are likely to stay within their national borders. This relates to the concept of internally displaced persons (IDPs).

---

13 Convention Relating to the Status of Refugees, United Nations Treaty Series (U.N.T.S.), Vol. 189, p. 137, Art. 1.

14 *Williams*, Turning the Tide: Recognizing Climate Change Refugees in International Law, (2008) 30 Law and Policy, p. 502 (507).

15 Ibid., p. 502 (508).

16 *Ni*, A Nation Going Under: Legal Protection For "Climate Change Refugees", (2015) 38 Boston College International & Comparative Law Review (hereinafter B. C. Int'l & Comp. L. Rev.), p. 329 (338).

17 *Williams*, (2008) 30 Law and Policy, p. 502 (509).

Thus, it is quite clear that the Refugee Convention, which was enacted almost 65 years ago, is unlikely to be able to deal with the contemporary issue of climate change refugees.

II. United Nations Framework Convention on Climate Change

In 1992, the United Nations (UN) negotiated an international environmental treaty at the United Nations Conference on Environment and Development (UNCED). The resulting United Nations Framework Convention on Climate Change (UNFCCC) provides that

> "developed country Parties ... shall also assist the developing country Parties that are particularly vulnerable to the adverse effects of climate change in meeting costs of adaptation to those adverse effects."[18]

Thus, states are called upon not only to reduce emissions but also to provide financial and technical support to developing nations. As the largest emitters of greenhouse gases, developed states are called upon to take the lead in dealing with the challenges of climate change. However, while over 20 years have passed since the signing of the UNFCCC, there is still no binding agreement for a reduction of greenhouse gases.

Significantly, the 2010 Cancun Adaptation Framework specifically recognized an international obligation to respond to climate-induced migration.[19] Prior to this framework, the UNFCCC had not recognized migration as a rational adaptation strategy.

Also, the Paris Agreement of 2015 under the UNFCCC framework recognizes climate induced migration with two references to the issue. The preamble implores states to "respect, promote and consider" the rights of migrants, among other vulnerable groups, when taking action to address climate change.[20] Additionally, the agreement calls upon the Executive

18 *Ni*, (2015) 38 B. C. Int'l & Comp. L. Rev., p. 329 (338).

19 Ibid.

20 *Igoe*, The gathering storm of climate migration, (2016), at: https://www.devex.com/news/the-gathering-storm-of-climate-migration-87857 (visited 25.08.2018).

Committee of the Warsaw International Mechanism to develop recommendations for integrated approaches to avert, minimize, and address displacement related to the adverse impacts of climate change.[21]

Though the UNFCCC applies directly to climate change, it too has legal limitations in dealing with climate change refugees. As an international environmental law treaty, the UNFCCC primarily concerns state-to-state relations; it does not discuss duties that states have in respect of individuals or communities, such as those laid out in human rights or refugee law.[22] It is also preventive in nature and less focused on the remedial actions that are needed in a refugee context. Finally, although the UNFCCC includes an initiative to help states with adaptation to climate change, that program does not specifically deal with the situation of climate change refugees.[23] Like the refugee regime, the UNFCCC was not designed for, and to date has not adequately dealt with, the problem of climate change refugees.[24]

D. Solutions to the Problem

It can be seen that the Refugee Convention and the UNFCCC alone cannot be used for the effective protection of climate change refugees. Thus, this paper seeks to suggest a multi-faceted approach to solve the present problem. The paper outlines three types of measures:

1) Human rights approach
2) Multilateral regional treaties
3) A new Convention

Through a combination of these measures substantial improvement can be achieved in international law with regards to climate change refugees. These measures may be overlapping.

---

21 21st session of Conference of the Parties, Adoption of The Paris Agreement, Draft decision -/CP.21, UNFCCC, (Paris 2015), at: https://unfccc.int/resource/docs/2015/cop21/eng/l09.pdf (visited 25.08.2018).

22 *Docherty/Giannini*, (2009) 33 Har. Env. L. Rev., p. 349 (358).

23 *Williams*, (2008) 30 Law and Policy, p. 502 (519).

24 *Docherty/Giannini*, (2009) 33 Har. Env. L. Rev., p. 349 (358).

I. Human Rights Approach

The human rights approach to climate change would work because of its emphasis on those legal rights enshrined in widely ratified international human rights documents which have become universal norms of customary international law. Even without the articulation of a specific right to the environment, there are many broad rights recognized in the Universal Declaration of Human Rights (UDHR), the International Covenant on Civil and Political Rights (ICCPR), and the International Covenant on Economic, Social and Cultural Rights (ICESCR) as well as in the Convention against Torture[25] and the Convention on the Rights of the Child (CRC)[26] that are relevant to the situation of people whose way of life comes under threat from climate change. States have a responsibility under these instruments to take action to remedy the direct and indirect threats that climate change poses to these rights.[27] The following rights can be used in accordance with this approach:

1. Right to Life

The right to life is protected in both the UDHR and the ICCPR. Article 3 of the UDHR provides that "everyone has the right to life, liberty and security of person." Article 6 (1) of the ICCPR states that "every human being has the inherent right to life." Climate change seriously affects this fundamental right as diseases and deterioration of health will increase. Additionally, this right would be at risk in the case of drowned islands.

---

25 Convention against Torture and Other Cruel, Inhuman or Degrading Treatment or Punishment, U.N.T.S., Vol. 1465, p. 85.

26 Convention on the Rights of the Child, U.N.T.S., Vol. 1577, p. 1 (3).

27 *Von Doussa/Corkery/Chartres*, Human Rights and Climate Change, (2007) 14 Australian International Law Journal, p. 161 (164).

2. Right to Adequate Food

Article 25 of the UDHR and Article 11 of the ICESCR link the rights to life and health with adequate food.[28] Climate change adversely affects the food production system and an adequate food supply.

3. Right to Water

The right to water is intricately related to the preservation of a number of rights; it underpins the right to health in Article 12 and the right to food in Article 11 of the ICESCR. Also, in 2002 the UN Committee on Economic, Social and Cultural Rights recognized that the right to access water was itself an independent right.[29]

4. Right to Health

Article 25 of the UDHR guarantees that everyone has the

> "right to a standard of living adequate for the health and well-being of himself and of his family, including food, clothing, housing and medical care and necessary social services."

Further, Article 12 of the ICESCR recognizes the human right to health as the "right of everyone to the enjoyment of the highest attainable standard of physical and mental health." Climate change also poses a risk of serious health consequences, such as "premature death, grave illness, and the spread of disease."

---

28 International Covenant on Economic, Social and Cultural Rights, U.N.T.S., Vol. 993, p. 1 (3).

29 *UN Committee on Economic, Social and Cultural Rights (CESCR)*, General Comment No 15: The Right to Water (Arts. 11 and 12 of the Covenant) (20 January 2003), E/C.12/2002/11, at: http://www.refworld.org/docid/4538838d11.html (visited 25.08.2018).

5. Rights of Indigenous People

Under the 2007 Declaration on the Rights of Indigenous People, as well as under other international human rights instruments, indigenous people have the right to engage in and revitalize their cultural practices, customs and institutions.[30] More generally, indigenous populations are disproportionately affected by climate change because it presents a danger to the very survival of their communities.[31] Also, Article 1 of the ICESCR protects the right of self-determination, and Article 15 of the ICESCR and Article 27 of the ICCPR guarantee the right to enjoy one's own culture. Thus, climate change refugees are at a risk of losing their cultural, traditional and social history and way of life. If they are forced to migrate they could lose their right and ability to culturally express themselves as they wish.[32]

The obligation to fulfil means that states must take positive action to facilitate the enjoyment of basic human rights. Thus regardless of the cause, a state has a positive obligation to act because state inaction would aggravate the situation. Essentially, a human-rights-based approach provides a conceptual framework for climate change policies: a framework which is normatively based on international human rights standards and which is practically directed at promoting and protecting human rights.[33]

Thus, though academic in nature, this framework may be successfully used to protect the rights of climate change refugees, especially those whose islands have drowned forever.

II. Multilateral Regional Treaties

This concept seeks to enhance the rights and protection of climate change refugees through a series of multilateral regional agreements, treaties, and

---

30 *United Nations Declaration on the Rights of Indigenous Peoples*, A/RES/61/295, Arts. 5, 9 and 11, at: http://www.refworld.org/docid/471355a 82.html (visited 25.08.2018).

31 *Von Doussa/Corkery/Chartres*, (2007) 14 Australian International Law Journal, p. 161 (167).

32 *Duong*, (2010) 31 University of Pennsylvania Journal of International Law, p. 1239 (1260).

33 Ibid., p. 1239 (1253).

Conventions. Approximately 70 to 80 nation-states have adopted regional or multilateral treaties that expand the definition of 'refugee' beyond the Refugee Convention.[34] The 1969 Organisation of African Unity Convention Governing Specific Aspects of Refugee Problems in Africa includes persons fleeing "events seriously disturbing public order" in its expanded definitions of refugee.[35] The definition of refugee in the 1984 Cartagena Declaration on Refugees, entered in Latin America, includes

> "persons who have fled their country, because their lives, safety, or freedom have been threatened by generalized violence, foreign aggression, internal conflicts, massive violation of human rights or other circumstances seriously disturbing public order."[36]

Also, as has been pointed out earlier, though the internally displaced climate refugees cannot be covered under the Refugee Convention, they can be covered effectively through multilateral regional instruments. IDPs are defined by the UNHCR in paragraph 2 of the Guiding Principles on Internal Displacement as

> "persons or groups of persons who have been forced or obliged to flee or to leave their homes or places of habitual residence, in particular as a result of or in order to avoid the effects of armed conflict, situations of generalised violence, violations of human rights or natural or human-made disasters, and who have not crossed an internationally recognised State border."

While the IDP Guidelines lack the formal legal status enjoyed by the Refugee Convention, their value is perhaps essentially significant as they are incorporated into national IDP policies based upon international principles.[37] This allows states to be flexible in the adoption of their respective IDP policies, while retaining the essence of the framework laid down in the guiding principles. Thus, the ongoing national adoptions of this framework may eventually lead to the development of new rules of customary international law, having universal binding effect.[38] Though a lengthy law-making process, this has the capacity of providing a non-controversial solution to the problems associated with climate change refugees, especially internally

34 *Ni*, (2015) 38 B. C. Int'l & Comp. L. Rev., p. 329 (357).

35 Convention Governing the Specific Aspects of Refugee Problems in Africa, 1001 U.N.T.S. 45.

36 *Ni*, (2015) 38 B. C. Int'l & Comp. L. Rev., p. 329 (357).

37 *Williams*, (2008) 30 Law & Pol'y, p. 502 (511).

38 Ibid., p. 502 (512).

displaced ones. This *bottom-up* approach has the ability of providing better recognition of environmental refugees, considering that 70 to 80 nations have already expanded the traditional refugee definition. However, due to the present absence of any binding force, it would take a lengthy period of time.[39]

In light of these potential problems, an alternative system for addressing the predicament of those displaced by climate change may be better coordinated by way of regional agreement, operating under an international umbrella framework. At present, it appears unlikely that states would agree to a globally binding treaty requiring their voluntarily committing to obligations that may have impact on economic, social, and political policy. However, regional cooperation and bilateral agreement appears to be a model better suited to climate change displacement. This was aptly demonstrated by the regional agreements for both Africa and Central America, in which the traditional definition of refugees was extended beyond the meaning given to it by the Refugee Convention.[40] Even the UNFCCC, under its Article 4, calls upon states to take into account their common but differentiated responsibilities and to take measures to facilitate adequate adaptation to climate change, keeping regional considerations in mind.

It appears that an international framework already exists under which regional initiatives can be developed. Ultimately, in the long term, the conclusion and acceptance of various regional agreements concluded under the international climate change framework would lead to the creation of customary international law.

III. A New Convention

A new Convention for the protection of climate change refugees is the ideal solution to the present problem. While it would be a herculean task, considering that even the UNFCCC has not been able to produce a binding framework for greenhouse gas emissions even after 25 years of negotiations, it likely presents the best possible solution for the time that lies ahead. Thus, a number of writers have put forward hypothetical ideas about a possible solution.

---

39 Ibid.

40 Ibid., p. 502 (518).

Athambawa suggests that in order to implement a treaty, the treaty needs to include the following aspects, namely, a) recognition that climate change refugees are in need of international protection, b) the root causes of environmental problems should be addressed, c) a precise definition of climate change refugees should be included, d) various mechanisms should be included in the treaty in such a way that varying levels of protection, such as short-term protection, instant protection, and long-term protection, could be offered to people depending on the needs of real climate change refugees, and e) focus should be given to prevention of environmental crisis.[41]

Docherty and Giannini suggest that any new definition of climate change refugees should include the following six elements: a) forced migration, b) temporary or permanent relocation, c) movement across national borders, d) disruption consistent with climate change, e) sudden or gradual environmental disruption and f) a 'more likely than not' standard for human contribution to the disruption.[42]

It is significant that as part of a Convention, the definition must be suitable for a binding instrument rather than for a general policy. Thus for an effective climate change refugee instrument, Docherty and Giannini argue for the inclusion of the following nine components, grouped under three broad categories:[43]

1. Guarantees of Assistance for Climate Change Refugees

1) Standards for climate change refugee status determination as discussed in the definition above.
2) Human rights protections: The new instrument should guarantee a range of civil and political rights; economic, social, and cultural rights; and rights related to movement that are particular to the refugee context. In addition, the concept of non-refoulement should also be included.
3) Humanitarian aid.

---

41 *Athambawa*, International Law Reform towards the Flood of Future Climate Change Refugees, (2010–2011) 8 Indonesian Journal of International Law, p. 105 (111).

42 *Docherty/Giannini*, (2009) 33 Har. Env. L. Rev., p. 349 (373–391).

43 Ibid.

2. Shared Responsibility

The proposed Convention should spread responsibility among all states to varying degrees.

1) Host states.
2) Home states.
3) International cooperation and assistance: Since climate change is international in origin, it should have an international solution. Not just the home states or the host states, but also the international community should share the burden as the least affected nations are the worst pollutants.

3. Administration of the Instrument

To help administer this complicated regime, the climate change refugee instrument should establish three organs:

1) Global fund.
2) Coordinating agency.
3) Body of scientific experts.[44]

In addition to these three organs, the author of the present article also suggests a fourth body, i.e. a body composed of *socio-economic and human rights experts and activists*, to aid in the development of long-term and short-term climate change refugee management techniques. Such a body will also help in evaluating the work done by the coordinating agency as well as the nations in handling the climate change refugee crisis.

Thus, these suggestions should be considered while framing a binding Convention on climate change refugees. Though difficult, a Convention probably represents the best possible hope for the victims of climate change.

E. Suggestions

The author seeks to make a few broad suggestions which would contribute greatly in implementing the three above-mentioned approaches:

---

44 Ibid.

1) The members of the international community, particularly the countries most affected by the problem of climate change refugees, like the Pacific Islands, should urge the International Court of Justice to give its opinion on the basic human rights of climate change refugees in accordance with the human rights approach.
2) Such affected countries as well as concerned organizations and individuals should try to convince other countries to broaden the definition of refugees to recognize climate change refugees by the introduction of regional treaties or even new legislation or amendments in domestic law.
3) Additionally, attempts should be made to give recognition to the issue of climate change refugees on important multilateral platforms, particularly under the UNFCCC framework.
4) Also, attempts should be made by countries to propose a broad and acceptable legal framework, like a new Convention for climate change refugees.

F. Conclusion

The increasing prevalence of climate change refugees has led to an immediate need to internationally recognize the problem and work towards its solution. The present article seeks to give a broad framework for solutions of three types. While the three approaches may appear to be different in their paths, they are essentially mutually dependent on each other. Thus, they are complementary to each other. While "Rome wasn't built in a day," it is important to "Get it right today as today won't come again." Implementing the human rights approach and the multilateral treaty approach can be started immediately.

The human rights approach, aimed at making use of various international instruments, such as the UN Charter, the UDHR, the ICCPR, the ICESCR, and the Convention against Torture, would hopefully lead to recognition of the very basic human rights of these refugees. Additionally, the implementation of the multilateral treaty approach has already been undertaken by the African and Latin American countries that have broadened the definition of refugees in regional instruments. Therefore, this method can become an effective *bottom-up* approach, leading to internationally recognized customary law.

It can thus be hoped that once these two approaches create international awareness and consensus on the issue of climate change refugees, a solid foundation for a new Convention will already have been laid. Such a Convention would further aid in effectively mitigating the present condition of climate change refugees by defining the role and responsibilities of the various states as well as by empowering the refugees with various rights. This Convention could also, in turn, force states to adopt better provisions for protection of the human rights of climate change refugees at the domestic as well as the regional and multilateral levels.

All three approaches are interdependent on each other and would only strengthen the implementation of one another. Hence, it is necessary that the international community takes urgent steps towards finding the solution for the present problem of climate change refugees.

Bibliography

Mohamed Mowjoon Athambawa, 'International Law Reform towards the Flood of Future Climate Change Refugees' (2010–2011) 8 Indonesian Journal of International Law, 105

Camillo Boano, Roger Zetter and Tim Morris, Refugee Studies Centre, 'Environmentally displaced people, Understanding the linkages between environmental change, livelihoods and forced migration' (2008), at: http://www.unicef.org/socialpolicy/files/Environmentally_displaces_people.pdf (visited 25.08.2018)

Oli Brown, 'Climate change and forced migration: Observations, projections and implications', UNDP Human Development Report 2007–2008, at: https://www.iisd.org/pdf/2008/climate_forced_migration.pdf (visited 25.08.2018)

Bonnie Docherty and Tyler Giannini, 'Confronting a Rising Tide: A Proposal For A Convention On Climate Change Refugees' (2009) 33 Harvard Environmental Law Review, 349

Tiffany T.V. Duong, 'When Islands Drown: The Plight of "Climate Change Refugees" and Recourse to International Human Rights Law' (2010) 31 University of Pennsylvania Journal of International Law, 1239

Michael Igoe, 'The gathering storm of climate migration' (2016), at: https://www.devex.com/news/the-gathering-storm-of-climate-migration-87857 (visited 25.08.2018)

International Organisation for Migration, 'Definitional Issues', at: https://www.iom.int/definitional-issues (visited 25.08.2018)

Kyung-wha Kang, Office of High Commissioner for Human Rights, 'Climate Change, Migration and Human Rights' (Geneva, 19 February 2008), at: https://www.iom.int/jahia/webdav/shared/shared/mainsite/events/docs/hsn/hsn_address_kang.pdf , p. 3–4 (visited 25.08.2018)

Ban Ki-moon, 'A Climate Culprit In Darfur' (2007), at: http://www.washingtonpost.com/wp-dyn/content/article/2007/06/15/AR2007061501857.html (visited 25.08.2018)

Vikram Odedra Kolmannskog, Norwegian Refugee Council, 'Future Floods of Refugees, A comment on climate change, conflict and forced migration' (2008), at: http://www.migrationdrc.org/publications/resource_guides/Migration_and_Climate_Change/Future_floods_of_refugees.pdf (visited 25.08.2018)

Gabriele Mante and Mattias Kolstrup, 'Environmental Refugees – How Climate Change Affects People's Lives' (2014), at: https://en.reset.org/knowledge/environ-mental-refugees-%E2%80%93-how-climate-change-affects-peoples-lives (visited 25.08.2018)

Xing-Yin Ni, 'A Nation Going Under: Legal Protection For "Climate Change Refugees"' (2015) 38 Boston College International & Comparative Law Review, 329

Norwegian Refugee Council/Internal Displacement Monitoring Centre (NRC/IDMC), 'The Nansen Conference: Climate Change and Displacement in the 21st Century' (2011), at: http://www.refworld.org/docid/521485ef4.html (visited 25.08.2018)

Teresita Perez, 'Climate Refugees – The Human Toll of Global Warming' (2006), at: https://www.americanprogress.org/issues/green/news/2006/12/07/2428/climate-refugees/ (visited 25.08.2018)

UN Committee on Economic, Social and Cultural Rights (CESCR), 'General Comment No 15: The Right to Water (Arts. 11 and 12 of the Covenant)' (20 January 2003), E/C.12/2002/11, at: http://www.refworld.org/docid/4538838d11.html (visited 25.08.2018)

The Hon John Von Doussa, Allison Corkery and Renee Chartres, 'Human Rights and Climate Change' (2007) 14 Australian International Law Journal, 161

John Vidal, 'Global warming could create 150 million 'climate refugees' by 2050' (Barcelona 2009), at: http://www.theguardian.com/environment/2009/nov/03/global-warming-climate-refugees (visited 25.08.2018)

Angela Williams, 'Turning the Tide: Recognizing Climate Change Refugees in International Law' (2008) 30 Law and Policy, 50

The Theory and Principles of Banking Regulation after the Financial Crisis: No (Systemic) Risk, No Fun

Juliane K. Mendelsohn

A. *Introduction*

Systemic risk describes the risk that the failure of one or more financial institutions or a shock in the financial system can lead to widespread losses and consecutive failures that threaten the stability of the entire financial system and the real economy at large.

During the financial crisis of 2008 financial institutions that bore this type of risk quickly became known as institutions that are *too big to fail.*[1] Particularly in Europe, however, it soon became apparent, that systemic risks do not solely stem from the sheer size of financial institutions, but have a stronger correlation to their complexity, their interconnectedness and their significance for the real economy. Banks and financial institutions that received bailouts during the financial crisis were therefore also considered *too interconnected, too systemic, too complex* or even (in the case of the German Landesbanken) *too political* or *too many to fail.*[2] These institutions have since been referred to as Systemically Important Financial Institutions (hereinafter SIFIs).[3] The bankruptcy of Lehman Brothers very much marked the onset of a far-reaching *systemic crisis* that affected US and EU financial markets in their entirety. In Europe, the crisis took on a more drastic dimension when the bailing out of financial institutions pushed some of its member states into a liquidity and solvency crisis. One of the most important goals of the since established Banking Union has been the attempt to break the strong links between member states and their respective banking sectors. Along with setting up a single and unified resolution and recap-

---

1 *Sorkin*, Too Big To Fail: Inside the Battle to Save Wall Street, 2010.

2 *Liikanen*, High-level Expert Group on reforming the structure of the EU banking sector, Final Report (2 October 2012), p. 31.

3 *Lastra*, Systemic Risk, SIFIs and financial stability, (2011) 6 (2) Capital Markets Law Journal, p. 197 (197 ff.).

italisation mechanism, it also contains the so-called single rule book / harmonized banking regulation package (the CRD-IV package, consisting of Regulation 575/2013 (CRR) and Directive 2013/36 (CRD-IV)). Both the Regulation and the Directive contain provisions that attempt to remedy some of the causes of systemic risks, by making sure that banks are better capitalised both in general and in times of crisis.

This paper looks at the causes in terms of both the economic description and legal definition of systemic risks. It analyses the consequences of too big to fail / too systemic to fail and the bailing out of financial institutions have on the banking sector and larger economy, not only as a matter of justice, but also for the future functioning of capital markets as a sustainable competitive environment.

The primary question concerning the current regulation of systemic risk and SIFI's is whether legislators and policy maker have done enough – both in terms of the functionality of the rules and in terms of degree – to avoid the next systemic crisis and the consequences (moral hazards) of 'too big to fail'.

Due to the gravity of systemic risks, their regulation has a principle dimension, that requires the careful balancing of such principles or the public interest in the stability of the financial markets against the functioning of competition within them. By borrowing concepts and definitions from legal theory (the principle theory of Ronald Dworkin and Robert Alexy), this paper attempts to show that the correct balancing of these principles can serve as a blueprint for European as well as national legislators in determining which measures to introduce in order to minimise systemic risks. And, in addition, to identify the degree to which they require enforcement.

B. Some of the Causes of the Financial Crisis

In the decades leading up to the crisis of 2008, the belief in the eternal strength and resilience of the financial sector became an article of faith, justifying ever-greater deregulation.[4] The economic models used at the time

4 *Greenspan*, International Financial Risk Management, Remarks before the Council on Foreign Relations, (Washington D.C. 19 November 2002): "These increasingly complex financial instruments have contributed to the development

grew ever more mathematical mathematical, albeit ignoring the likelihood of irrational shocks. Although many economist warned that low capital requirements and the excessive spreading and diversification of risk had led to an intolerable degree of instability in the financial markets,[5] leading institutions and regulatory authorities ignored the possibility of a crisis and continued to neglect the regulation of systemic risks.

The tale of the demise of Wall Street has often been told:

> "By the end of 2007, most of the subprime lenders had failed or been acquired, including New Century Financial, Ameriquest, and American Home Mortgage. In January 2008, Bank of America announced it would acquire the ailing lender Countrywide. Bear Stearns, laden with risky mortgage assets and dependent on fickle short-term lending, was bought by JP Morgan with government assistance in the spring. Before the summer was over, Fannie Mae and Freddie Mac would be put into conservatorship. Then, in September, Lehman Brothers failed and the remaining investment banks, Merrill Lynch, Goldman Sachs, and Morgan Stanley, struggled as they lost the market's confidence. AIG, with its massive credit default swap portfolio and exposure to the subprime mortgage market, was rescued by the government. ... In October, Wachovia struck a deal to be acquired by Wells Fargo. Citigroup and Bank of America fought to stay afloat. Before (summer) was over, taxpayers had committed trillions of dollars through more than two dozen extraordinary programs to stabilize the financial system and to prop up the nation's largest financial institutions."[6]

Simultaneously, the EU banking sector also grew exponentially, with total assets of financial institutions swelling to three and a half times the EU's GDP.[7] Only in 2008, as the mortgage crisis in the US swiftly became a financial and banking crisis, did we realise to what extent this growth also had a strong correlation to the mortgage and real estate bubble in the US. Bear Stearns' write-offs (of Mortgage Backed Securities) and the Lehmann

---

of a far more flexible, efficient, and hence resilient financial system than the one that existent just a quarter of a century ago."

5 *Rajan*, Has Financial Development Made the World Riskier, National Bureau of Economic Research NBER Working Paper (hereinafter NBER Working Paper) No 11728 (2005).

6 *The Financial Crisis Inquiry Commission*, The Financial Crisis Inquiry Report, Final Report of the National Commission on the Causes of the Financial and Economic Crisis in the United States (January 2011), p. 22 ff.

7 *Liikanen*, Final Report (2 October 2012), p. 11.

Brothers' bankruptcy expanded into a systemic cross-Atlantic crisis,[8] leading to the near-insolvency of many European banks.

Both during and after the crisis, the debate on its causes has been polarising. Whilst economics who are generally in favour of more regulation have focussed on the failures of financial markets, the capture of regulators and their reliance on the internal risk management and risk analysis model of financial institutions,[9] others have placed the blame on public institutions, such as the reactions of regulators, the Federal Reserve and European governments.[10] As the inherent instability of financial markets became ever more apparent, more agreement was found on the regulatory insufficiencies and main causes of the crisis.[11] These include the limited amount of capital held by banks and financial institutions, meaning their indebtedness and over-reliance on foreign capital. The second development has been excessive risk-taking. The years leading up to the crisis, saw an excessive expansion of risk diversification and development of ever more complex financial instruments such as Credit Default Swaps (CDS) and Mortgage Based Securities (MBS), which spread risks throughout the financial sector and allowed for far more risk-intensive trading and speculation.

C. *Defining Systemic Risk*

As the slogan *too big to fail* dominated the financial crisis of 2008, it soon became a term that defined both the dilemma and the powerlessness of states facing possible failures of large financial institution. The bailouts that

---

8 *The Financial Crisis Inquiry Commission.*

9 *Stiglitz*, Free Fall: America, Free Markets, and the Sinking of the World Economy, 2010; *Stiglitz*, The Financial Crisis of 2007/08 and its Macro-Economic Consequences' in: Griffith-Jones/Ocampo/Stiglitz (eds), Time for a Visible Hand: Lessons from the 2008 World Financial Crisis, 2009, p. 19; *Rajan*, NBER Working Paper No 11728; *Rajan*, Fault Lines: How Hidden Fractures Still Threaten the World Economy, 2011; *Krugman*, End This Depression Now!, 2012.

10 *Posner*, A Failure of Capitalism, 2011; *Posner*, Crisis of Capitalist Democracy, 2011; *Reinhart/Rogoff*, The Aftermath of the Financial Crisis, NBER Working Paper 14656, 2009; *Reinhart/Rogoff*, This Time is Different: Eight Centuries of Financial Follies, 2009.

11 *Lastra/Wood*, The Causes of 2007–09: Nature, Causes and Reactions, (2010) 13 (3) Manchester Journal for International Economic Law, p. 531.

followed meant that the most basic rule of free markets, that any company or institution that is not efficient enough must leave the market and make room for new enterprises with a better allocation of risks and costs, does not apply to banks.[12]

The risk of the collapse of the entire financial system, the entire banking sector and possibly the real economy, is called systemic risk in economics. Despite its marginal role in banking regulation before the crisis, several economists consider the prevention of systemic risks the most important rationale for banking regulation.[13] Whilst systemic risks were originally strongly associated with economic shocks (macro or micro shocks), the economic literature has since placed a special focus on the effects of these shocks and the spreading of these risks to other financial institutions and the banking sector at large.

In 2008 Stephen Schwarz synthesised the causes and effects of systemic risks, proposing the following working definition:

> "The risk that an economic shock such as market or institutional failure triggers (through a panic or otherwise) either the failure of a chain of markets or institutions or a chain of significant losses to financial institutions, resulting in increases in the cost of capital or decreases in its availability, often evidenced by substantial financial-market price volatility."[14]

Based on this definition, economists Markus Brunnermeier and Tobias Adrian developed a model for measuring systemic risks (called CoVaR – Covariance at Risk) by considering individual institutions' exposure to cascading losses or contagion in 2011.[15]

The economic definition shows that two different, though causally related, types of factors and causes need to be distinguished when analysing systemic risks. The first is the trigger event: a macro or a micro shock. The second are the structures or circumstances that enable cascading losses and

12 *Posner*, Antitrust Law, 2001, p. 27: "Business failures are an indispensable means of imparting incentives for efficient business behaviour, by placing the costs of mistakes on the firms that make them."

13 *Allen/Gale*, Understanding Financial Crisis, 2007, p. 213: "There is widespread agreement that the most important rationale for banking regulation is the prevention of systemic risk."; *Benston/Kaufman*, The Appropriate Role of Bank Regulation, (1996) 688 The Economic Journal, p. 106; *Goodhart/Hartman*, Financial Regulation, Why, How, and Where Now?, 1998; *Cranston*, Principles of Banking Law, 2002.

14 *Schwarcz*, Systemic Risk, (2008) 97 Georgetown Law Journal, p. 193 (204).

15 *Adrian/Brunnermeier*, CoVaR, (2016) 106 (7) American Economic Review, p. 1705.

contagion: the complexity and interconnectedness of the banking sector, as well as its volatility.

Until November 2011, a legal definition of systemic risks was not agreed upon. The Basel Committee has identified relevant factors in ascertaining whether a financial institution was systemically important: its size, its complexity, its interconnectedness, the lack of readily available substitutes for the financial infrastructure it provides, and its global activity. Art. 3 No 10 of the Directive 2013/36/EU (CRD-IV) now defines systemic risk as *"a risk of disruption in the financial system with the potential to have serious negative consequences for the financial system and the real economy."*

Both the economic and the legal definitions still contain a degree of vagueness and refer to a multitude of plausible causes of systemic risks. Hence they are not 'workable' in the sense that necessary measures cannot be directly derived from them and borrow massively from economic descriptions. Economic definitions on the other hand serve the primary purpose of setting up parameters for the development of models (theory) or the empirical research. The first purpose of a legal definition is to adequately capture the full extent of a real-world fact situation (*Lebenssachverhalt*), whereupon measures or remedies can later be based.

Contrary to the definition, the legal instruments that have been introduced come far closer to the underlying problems. In holding with the distinction between the primary causes (trigger events) and the effects (contagion and cascading losses), new regulatory instruments also either try to prevent shocks and anti-cyclical developments or try to make the banking sector more robust against risks and losses. Art. 458 of Reg. 575/2013 contains the procedure for identifying and combating macro-prudential or systemic risks identified at a member state level. In order to prevent contagion and counteract the interconnectedness of the banking sector, Basel III and Regulation 575/2013 (CRR) now includes capital buffers against systemic risks, a leverage ratio and the introduction of contigent convertible bonds (CoCo Bonds).[16] In addition, the introduction of a separate banking system is widely discussed on an EU level and has partially been introduced in some member states. Whilst all of these measures constitute significant pro-

16 CoCo-Bonds enable the conversion of debt into capital in times of crisis and date back to the 18th Century where the Wall Street speculators Jacob Little and Daniel Crew first introduced them to prevent market cornering. *Markham*, A Financial History of the United States, 2002, p. 161.

gress, one must fear that the ever more detailed and isolated manner of dealing with systemic risks can cause regulators to overlook the sizable threat of systemic risks and ignore larger flaws in the financial architecture and extreme volatility of the banking sector.

D. *Bailouts and Competition in the Banking Sector*

In order to establish the adequate instruments for minimizing systemic risks and the occurrence of a systemic crisis, it is important to analyse the effects of bailouts and systemically important financial institutions on the banking sector at large. Bailing out large and complex financial institution does not only burden the budget of member states and is perceived as an injustice towards the taxpayer (alias *privatize profits whilst nationalizing or socializing debt*[17]), it also has detrimental negative effects on the competitive environment in the banking sector.

Bailouts perpetuate the existence of a competitive environment driven by the incentive to take ever-larger risks and hold ever-decreasing amounts of equity capital. Banks that have received bailouts by member states or prospectively by the European Stability Mechanism (hereinafter ESM), have little incentive to change their risk strategies in future. Rather, the knowledge that banks and financial institutions will be bailed-out in future incentivises them to continue engaging in risky business practices. These so-called *moral hazards* – incentives to take more risks because someone else bears their burden – apply to all institutions that have reason to suspect that they will be bailed out in future. These explicit and implicit guarantees, translate directly into better ratings, lower interest rates and better terms and conditions on the capital markets.[18] Beyond these unfair advantages, the resulting negative incentives affect all institutions that directly or indirectly compete with large and systemic financial institutions. This in turn creates

17 *Chomsky*, Failed States: The Abuse of Power and the Assault on Democracy, 2006.

18 *Warren*, Scaling Back `too big´, Boston Globe, 18 September 2013, at: https://www.bostonglobe.com/opinion/2013/09/18/century-glass-steagall-act-will-disable-too-big-fail-bank-risk/cdR0wqqnDIGBBoYAaFFfbO/story.html (visited 22.06.2018): "One study earlier this year showed that their 'too big to fail' status enables the 10 biggest US banks to receive an annual taxpayer subsidy of $83 billion."; *Baker/McArthur*, The Value of the „Too Big To Fail" Big Bank Subsidy, (2009) Centre for Economic and Policy Research, p. 36.

an overall competitive environment that is solely concerned with profit maximization, thus becoming, very volatile and far from prudent.

E. *Balancing Stability and Competition on a Principled Level*

The introduction of anti-competitive stability mechanisms and guarantee schemes (such as bail-outs) and thereby the creation moral hazards is not novel in banking sector regulation. Both the great depression and the banking crisis of 1929 resulted in the introduction deposit insurance funds. Whilst these are now considered vital for the functioning of the financial sector, they can also act as a type of government-sponsored guarantee scheme. Germany, in particular, also has a long history of extensive guarantee and support schemes for its public banks (the Landesbanken and Sparkassen) known as *Anstaltslast* and *Gewährträgerhaftung*. These schemes expressed the public interests in the stability of the financial sector, until they were found to be in violation of European state aid rules.[19]

In light of this, the relationship between stability and competition has always been contentious and it is not clear to which extent the two can co-exist. If, however, the banking sector is to function according to market based principles, there needs to both a degree of stability as well as the existence of the parameters for competition. It is also clear that all types of guarantees skew market discipline and lead to moral hazards that end up destabilising the banking sector in the long run. Hence, the question of how to balance stability and competition becomes a normative one.

Looking at the question of balancing on a principled level can help in identifying the exact goals and aims that are at stake. Furthermore, it may set a theoretical framework to identify the necessary measures in order to secure both stability and competition – alias the functioning of the market economy – in the financial sector. As mentioned above, ignoring the greater significance of systemic risks or the principles at stake, can quickly lead to the introduction of regulatory measures that are either in their nature or in their degree not adequate remedy fundamental shortcoming and prevent a systemic crisis.

In this context, it seems necessary to distinguish legal terms such as *goals* and *aims* or the *conflict of goals*, because of their specific meaning in EU

19 Draft letter of the Commission to the Federal Republic of Germany, C (2002) 1286 of 27.03.2002.

constitutional law. The goals of the EU that are set out in Art. 3 Treaty on European Union (hereinafter TEU) and their transposition into the horizontal clauses of the treaty. We are therefore compelled to turn to the more abstract notion of 'legal principles'. At most the "highly competitive social market economy" (Art. 3 (3) TEU) can be seen as the overriding goal of balancing stability and competition in the banking sector.

The notion of the principles of law is borrowed from Dworkin's and the German legal theorist Alexy's respective theories of legal principles. Dworkin distinguishes principles from rules, as the two most important types of legal norms. Principles are legal considerations that lack the all-or-nothing applicability of legal rules.[20] Principle statements such as 'no man may profit from his own wrong' cannot always be enforced, but are always valid. According to Robert Alexy principles are statements of law that need to be fulfilled to the highest degree possible at any given point in time. When two or more principles come into conflict, they do not cancel each other out, but require balancing and the optimization of each principle: *"wherever legal principles exist, the duty to optimise their normative impact follows."*[21]

Rules are considered rigid norms that are formulated in manner, which does not allow balancing or optimization, but means that they are either to be applied – or not applied. According to Alexy, if a rule cannot be applied and it is not possible to formulate legal exemption, then it is invalid and needs to be eliminated from the legal system. Upholding legal principles, when two or more come into conflict, is more complex than rules. According to Alexy and many of his critics,[22] this first requires the balancing of the conflicting principles. Here it is important to consider the *importance* of each principle, the *probability* of its realization as well as the *intensity* of the loss for either principle.[23] This is what Alexy calls the *Law of Balancing*:

20 *Dworkin*, Taking Rights Seriously, 1977, p. 24.

21 *Alexy*, Fundamental Right, Balancing, and Rationality, (2003) 16 Ratio Legis, p. 135 (135 ff.).

22 See prominently, *Poscher*, The Principle Theory: How Many Theories and What is Their Merit? In: Klatt (ed), Institutionalizing Reason. Perspectives on the Legal Philosophy of Robert Alexy, 2012, p. 218.

23 *Alexy*, Die Gewichtsformel, in: Jickeli/Kreutz/Reuter (eds), Gedächnisschrift für Jürgen Sonnenschein, 2003, p. 771 (790).

"the greater the degree of non-satisfaction of, or detriment to, one principle, the greater must be the importance of satisfying the other."[24]

In most cases, the second step follows from the fact that the result of this balancing will be the partial or complete prioritisation / precedence of one principle over another, but only for a specific case or in a specific circumstance. Here Alexy proposes defining the exact conditions and requirements that need to be fulfilled, in order to give one principle priority. Hereby

> "the circumstances under which one principle takes precedence over another constitute the conditions of a rule which has the same legal consequences as the principle taking precedence."[25]

The formulation and rule of precedence is the most technical, least contended, but possibly also the most important component of Alexy's original theory. It assumes that as the result of balancing, at least one principle will have to be given a degree of priority / precedence and that the conditions for the prioritisation in each individual case require a formulation as legal conditions or a legal rule.

The problem that *too big to fail* poses to the legal system, as well as to the functioning of financial market can be expressed as a tension between different political and legal norms. All the while the overarching goal of this exercise must be the following:

> "(...) finance needs to go back to being an instrument directed towards improved wealth creation and development. To ensure this, the fear of failure needs to return to the business of banking."[26]

On the one hand, the functioning of markets is predicated on the idea, that if a competitor runs extreme losses, he must be forced to exit the market. On the other, the threat of a systemic crisis, dictates bailing out such institutions in order to avoid greater hardship. Both *too big to fail* and the market exit condition serve as rules. When they come into conflict, only one of them can be enforced.

Behind and beyond these rules lie principles. One of the principles of banking regulation is to secure financial stability. A primary principle of

---

24 *Alexy*, A Theory of Constitutional Rights, 2002, p. 47 (48).

25 Letter from the European Commission to the Federal Republic of Germany available at: http://ec.europa.eu/competition/stateaid/cases/133302/1333021179280_213_2.pdf (visted 9.07.2018).

26 See *Lastra/Wood*, (2010) 13 (3) Manchester Journal for International Economic Law, p. 531 (550).

private law, competition law and a functioning market order is that of liability, or as expressed by Dworkin that "*no man may profit from his own wrong.*"

In a competitive social market economy we therefore find two conflicting principles: stability and competition; each of which are served by two conflicting rules: too big to fail and market exit, which cannot co-exist.

Conflicting Prinicples and Rules:

Principle I: Financial Stability
Rule: Too big to Fail

Principles II: Competition, Market Discipline no Moral Hazards
Rule: Market Exit Rule

Many consider the purpose of post-crisis banking regulation to eradicate the *too big to fail* doctrine and reinstate the rule / condition of possible market exit. In order to enforce the market exit rule, the principles of stability and the fundamental principles of functioning competitive markets – market exit and market discipline alias liability – need to be balanced carefully. As a result of this balancing, the competitive market principle would need to be reinstated or given precedence in a manner that does not require the rescue of banks in order to stabilize the financial sector in future. The result of this balancing would therefore be the prevalence of market discipline and liability and the prevention of systemic risks. In order to achieve this precedence and prevent moral hazards, it is necessary to analyse all legal and real possibilities of minimising a systemic risks, whilst upholding the current functions of the banking sector. It is therefore necessary to analyse the exact causes and effects of systemic risks and to what extent it is possible to remedy them.

F. Securing the Principles that Define Competitive Markets by Eliminating the Causes and Effects of Systemic Risks

I. Macro and Micro Shocks

Macro and micro shocks are the trigger events of systemic risks. A micro shock event is usually limited to the failure or dramatic losses in a single financial institution. In the classic bank-run scenario, the suspicion that a financial institution may be having liquidity or solvency problems can quickly lead to a panic reaction of its depositors that can cause the failure of the institution and spills over onto others. Macro shocks are shocks, cyclical fluctuations or drastic changes in prices that affect the economy at large.[27] During the crisis of 2008, the fact that so many institutions held related and connected financial products, meant that their sudden devaluation led to cascading losses and had an effect on the sector at large.

Art. 458 of Reg. 575/2013 (CRR) now includes an intricate new procedure for detecting and preventing systemic risks. The European Systemic Risk Board, the European Banking Authority, the Commission, the Council, the European Central Bank and the regulatory authorities of the member states have all be given new powers and obligations to detect the possible occurrence of a micro or macro shocks phenomenon and to take action against it, by increasing the required capital that certain banks hold. Whilst these are improvements in terms of legal procedure and possible legal remedies, there remains little certainty amongst scholars about whether it will be easier to detect possible shocks in future. As was the case in the past, the governments and regulatory authorities will always have large incentives not to 'cry wolf' during the onset of crisis or even the detection of irregular bubble-like growth in certain sectors, as this can cause panic reactions or simply stifle growth and cause a decrease in overall welfare. It therefore seems *factually* impossible to prevent the trigger events of systemic risks with any degree of certainty.

II. Exposure, Contagion and Cascading Losses

The only way to minimize the occurrence of systemic risks, is to hamper their effects – the contagious and cascading losses that follow a macro or micro shock. Contagion can be linked to the complexity and interconnectedness of the financial sector. Whilst some channels of contagion or forms of interconnectedness, such as those resulting from money and inter-banking markets, are impossible to abolish or sever, it is by and large possible

27 *Bartholomew/Whalen*, Fundamentals of Systemic Risk, in: Kaufman (ed), Banking, Financial Markets, and Systemic Risk, 1995, p. 3; *Kaufman /Scott*, What is Systemic Risk, and Do Bank Regulators Retard or Contribute To It?, (2003) 7 The Independent Review, p. 371 (376).

either to isolate certain types of risks or to make individual institutions significantly more robust and able to absorb losses.

Interconnectedness exits both objectively and subjectively: through actual trading channels and corporate structures, but also through 'psychological channels'. In the latter case, the failure of one bank can have unforeseen, perhaps even irrational consequences. As described by Lastra: "*The belief in a panic is self-fulfilling. Market sentiment can shift suddenly and quickly. Herd behaviour is a recurring pattern in boom and bust cycles.*"[28]

In both cases, such connectors either need to severed or the banking sector and financial institutions need to become less volatile and more robust. Adequate remedies against contagion therefore include stricter capital requirements or the introduction of a separate banking system or comparable means of risk isolation. Their effectiveness is however largely dependent on the extent and degree to which these instruments are introduced and enforced.

1. Capital Requirements

The attempts to stabilize the banking sectors by means of capital requirements are as old as banking regulation itself. The main impediment to the effective enforcement of this measure has been its constant erosion and the financial institutions strive towards ever further deregulation and lower capital requirements. Foreign capital has become ever cheaper in relation to equity capital and banks have become compelled by the notion that a competitive advantage can be gained from investing rather than depositing their own capital. The reliance on internal risk assessment models in order to ascertain the individual appropriate capital requirements under Basel II were a further symptom of deregulation and capture and have been widely criticised. Whilst capital requirement can guarantee the stability of single institutions, they have seldom been used as macro-prudential measures or as remedies against systemic risks. They protect a bank from their own losses and risks but not from macro-economic shocks or exposure to the failure of another institution. Because capital adequacy can however act as a buffer against any type of risk or losses, Basel III and the Regulation 575/2013 (CRR) have introduced some specific capital requirement measures to protect against systemic risks. These include systemic and anti-

28 *Lastra*, (2011) 6 (2) Capital Markets Law Journal, p. 197 (206).

cyclical capital buffers for times of crisis, contingent convertible bonds ('CoCo Bonds') and a leverage ratio. Due to its simplicity and non-reliance on the prior identification of anti-cyclical or systemic development, the leverage ratio is probably the most promising of these instruments. Particularly the attempt to build a systemic capital buffer during the onset of a crisis can turn into a so-called self-fulfilling prophecy. The leverage or debt-to-equity ratio expresses the relative proportion of equity and debt used to finance a financial institution. It thereby prevents financial institutions from becoming too indebted without having to consider their individual equity and risk positions. A 3%-leverage ratio was introduced in Europe in 2018, as set out in Art. 429 Reg. 575/2913.[29] Many scholars and institutions that have emphasized the important of adequate equity capital and the dangers of high debts in the banking sector in the past, see the leverage ratio as the most important tool for stabilising the financial sector and have proposed leverage ratio of 10 % or even 20– 30 %.[30] Whilst capital requirements could reduce systemic risks and reintroduce the market discipline and give prevalence to the fundamental principles that underscore competitive markets, the degree of their current implementation, is far from sufficient.

2. The Separate Banking System

A separate banking system aims to reduce the complexity of the banking sector and create a firewall between commercial and investment banking – hence also isolating the effects of systemic risks. Commercial banks not only hold deposits that need to be protected by the state to avoid bank runs and the eradication of wealth, but also fulfil the crucial function of financing small and medium sized businesses.

A difficulty for those trying to derive lessons from the causes of the financial crisis is the bitter fact that there *hasn't* been one banking model that has fared better than others. Banks pushed into insolvency include large banks (Bear Stearns), small and medium sized banks (Landesbanken), uni-

29 REG 575/2013, 94.

30 *Admati/Hellwig*, The Bankers' New Clothes, What's Wrong With Banking and What to Do About It, 2014.

versal banks (IKB), pure investment banks (Lehman Brothers) and traditional or depository banks (Northern Rocks).[31] The only commonality that can be pointed to is that all of the banks that failed were not isolated from the risk-taking of the investment banking sector, nor from the detrimental effect of major commercial paper and securities markets closing down[32] – in other words, they were all *too interconnected to fail.* This is the reason why the bankruptcy of a pure investment bank, Lehman Brothers, caused the near-insolvency of so many banks across the board. Isolating these risks into separate entities would not only contain the risks in the investment banking sector, but could, if done rigorously, reduce the interconnectedness and thereby the systemic risks that currently underlie the entire banking sector as a whole.[33]

The most famous separate banking system existed under the so-called Glass-Steagall Act, introduced in the US in 1933. This Act required banks to split-off or shut down investment banking business. This created two types of banking entities: commercial banking and investment banking. After the 2008 crisis, many have called for a return to Glass-Steagall, but have had neither the political capital nor the certainty of purpose required to restructure the entire industry. Consequently proposed legislative solutions have – at best – attempted to bask in a feeling of 'Glass-Steagallness': thus the U.S. Volcker Rule, the UK Vickers Report and the EU Liikanen Report all suggest structural reforms with *elements* of a separate banking system. Crucially, however, none of them fully return to the simplicity and rigor that defined the Glass-Steagall Act.

The Dodd-Frank Act's 298-page Volcker rule prohibits proprietary trading (whereby deposits are used to trade on the bank's own account) for commercial banks as well as certain relationships with hedge funds and private equity funds[34]. The complexity of and the number of exceptions to this rule alone casts doubts on whether it will ever be effectively enforced.

---

31 *Altvater/von Schweinitz*, Trennbankensystem: Grundsatzfragen und alternative Regulierungsansätze, Zeitschrift für Wirtschafts- und Bankrecht (WM) 2012, p. 625 (629).

32 *Liikanen*, Final Report (2 October 2012), p. i.

33 *Lastra*, (2011) 6 (2) Capital Markets Law Journal, p. 197 (201): "It is the understanding of the interconnectedness of the system that needs much greater research and analysis in the aftermath of the financial crisis 2007–2009."

34 12 U.S.C., Chapter 17. § 1851: "The term proprietary trading, when used with respect to a banking entity or nonbank financial company supervised by the

Following the Vickers Report on Banking (September 2011) the UK has introduced a 'ring fencing' rule that forces banks to isolate commercial banking activities that are considered vital to the economy from investment banking activities.[35]

In 2012 a High Level EU Expert Group, the Liikanen Group, was asked to analyse the causes of the banking crisis, the effectiveness of regulatory changes and whether further structural instruments would be needed to make the EU banking sector more competitive, stable and sustainable in future. The Group concluded that

> "it is necessary to require legal separation of certain particularly risky financial activities from deposit taking banks within the banking group. The activities to be separated would include proprietary trading of securities and derivatives, and certain other activities closely linked with securities and derivatives markets. (...) Separation of these activities into separate legal entities is the most direct way of tackling banks' complexity and interconnectedness."[36]

The fact that the Liikanen report aims to keep *"the long-standing universal banking model (...) untouched, since the separated activities would be carried out in the same banking group"* and only apply this rule where *"the activities to be separated amount to a significant share of a bank's business,"*[37] shows that this is a compromise between the universal and the separate banking system.

Following the suggestions of the Liikanen Report, Germany has prohibited certain trading activities (mainly proprietary trading – *Eigenhandel)* for

---

Board, means engaging as a principle for the trading account of the banking entity or nonbank financial company supervised by the Board in any transaction to purchase or sell, or otherwise acquire or dispose of, any security, any derivative, any contract of sale of a commodity for future delivery, an option on any such security, derivative, or contract or any other security of financial instrument that the appropriate Federal banking agencies, the Securities and Exchange Commission, and the Commodity Futures Trading Commission may, by rule as provided in subsection (b) (2) determine."

35 *Independent Commission on Banking, UK*, The Vickers Report (30 December 2013), p. 233.

36 *Liikanen*, Final Report (2 October 2012), p. iii: "This would ensure that trading activities beyond the threshold are carried out on a stand-alone basis and separate from the deposit bank. As a consequence, deposits, and the explicit and implicit guarantee they carry, would no longer directly support risky trading activities."

37 Ibid.

certain types of financial institutions in § 3 KWG (German Banking Act). Where reckless and sometimes fraudulent underwriting activities created an unsustainable credit bubble in the years leading up to 1929, reckless proprietary trading activities did the same in the 2000's, causing some of the more prominent failures of systemic banks in Germany. The Deutsche Industriebank (the IKB, a traditional lender to small and medium size enterprises), one of the first European Banks to go insolvent due to the Crisis, provides a textbook case. By means of proprietary trading, the IKB had built a large portfolio of asset backed commercial paper (ABCP) funds and was highly over-leveraged by 'borrowing short' (borrowing money for a couple of days) and 'lending long' (long term loans to the German industry). When the market for ABCPs closed after Bear Stearns revealed huge losses on 16 July 2007, the IKB was immediately pushed into insolvency.[38] Equally, the German Landesbanken became heavily involved in investment banking and international securities activities over the last two decades. Taking the risks entailed in proprietary trading is particularly pernicious in the case of the partially publically held and run Landesbanken, which fulfil the function of being the central banks to many smaller regional commercial banks, the Sparkassen.[39]

Looking at the failures of the Landesbanken and the IKB, it is easy to limit analysis of the causes of their failure to their proprietary trading activities. However, this ignores the greater conflicts of interest and massive public risk created by the existence of a universal banking system. These institutions had large publicly protected deposits at their disposal: the banks' failure would have caused the insolvency of many households and small and medium sized businesses. In short, they were too interconnected and too political to fail, but were also subject to the incentives and pressures of investing in financial products that promised astronomical profits. Introducing a rule that primarily targets proprietary trading runs the risk of being *ex post facto* legislation that could have shielded us from some of the effect of the last crisis, but will not prevent the next one.

38 *Zingales*, German Banks on Top, 18 July 2013, Project Syndicate.

39 *Liikanen*, Final Report (2 October 2012), p. 64.

G. Conclusion

In order to guarantee a functioning, sustainable, social and 'highly competitive' market economy in the banking sector, both stability and the fundamental conditions of competition need to be guaranteed. This paper analyses the balance that needs to be struck between both principles, in order to avoid a further systemic crisis. The most important function of post-crisis banking regulation is elimination of 'too big to fail' and the moral hazards that follow from bailing out financial institutions. Only the regulation of systemic risks and the prevalence of market discipline can guarantee a functioning banking sector. Systemic risks find their causes in micro and macro shocks as well as the interconnectedness and complexity of the banking sector. Both capital requirements and the isolation of risks (by means of a separate banking systems) could reduce the volatility and interconnectedness of the banking sector, which lead to cascading losses and contagion in times of crisis. In determining the degree and scope of these instruments, an analysis of the interplay of the principles at stake serves as an indicator of their sufficiency and effectiveness. Current legislation (capital requirements and the prohibition or proprietary trading) fails to end *too big to fail* both in terms of rigor and degree.

Bibliography

Anat Admati and Martin Hellwig, *The Bankers' New Clothes, What's Wrong With Banking and What to Do About It* (Princeton University Press, 2014)

Tobias Adrian and Markus Brunnermeier, 'CoVaR' (2016) 106 (7) American Economic Review, 1705

Robert Alexy, *A Theory of Constitutional Rights* (Oxford University Press, 2002)

Robert Alexy, 'Die Gewichtsformel' in Joachim Jickeli, Peter Kreutz and Diete Reuter (eds), *Gedächnisschrift für Jürgen Sonnenschein* (De Gruyter 2003), 771

Robert Alexy, 'Fundamental Rights, Balancing, and Rationality' (2003) 16 Ratio Legis, 135

Franklin Allen and Douglas Gale, *Understanding Financial Crisis* (Oxford University Press, 2007)

Christian Altvater and Oliver von Schweinitz, Trennbankensystem: Grundsatzfragen und alternative Regulierungsansätze, Zeitschrift für Wirtschafts- und Bankrecht (WM) 2012, 625

Dean Baker and Travis McArthur, 'The Value of the „Too Big To Fail" Big Bank Subsidy' (2009) Centre for Economic and Policy Research, 36

Philip Bartholomew and George Whalen, 'Fundamentals of Systemic Risk' in George Kaufman (ed), *Banking, Financial Markets, and Systemic Risk* (1995), 3

George Benston and George Kaufman, 'The Appropriate Role of Bank Regulation' (1996) 688 The Economic Journal, 106

Noam Chomsky, *Failed States: The Abuse of Power and the Assault on Democracy* (Metropolitan Books, 2006)

Ross Cranston, *Principles of Banking Law* (2nd Edition, Oxford University Press, 2002)

Ronald Dworkin, *Taking Rights Seriously* (Harvard University Press, 1977)

The Financial Crisis Inquiry Commission, 'The Financial Crisis Inquiry Report, Final Report of the National Commission on the Causes of the Financial and Economic Crisis in the United States' (January 2011)

Charles Goodhart and Phillip Hartman, *Financial Regulation, Why, How, and Where Now?* (Routledge 1998)

Alan Greenspan, 'International Financial Risk Management, Remarks before the Council on Foreign Relations' (Washington D.C. 19 November 2002)

Independent Commission on Banking, UK, 'The Vickers Report' (30 December 2013)

George Kaufmann and Kenneth Scott, 'What is Systemic Risk, and Do Bank Regulators Retard or Contribute To It?' (2003) 7 The Independent Review, 371

Paul Krugman, *End This Depression Now!* (W.W. Norton, 2012)

Rosa Maria Lastra and Geoffry Wood, 'The Causes of 2007–09: Nature, Causes and Reactions' (2010) 13 (3) Manchester Journal for International Economic Law, 531

Rosa Maria Lastra, 'Systemic Risk, SIFIs and financial stability' (2011) 6 (2) Capital Markets Law Journal, 197

Erkki Liikanen, 'High-level Expert Group on reforming the structure of the EU banking sector' Final Report (2 October 2012)

Jerry Markham, *A Financial History of the United States: From Christopher Columbus to the Robber Baron*, Vol. I (1492–1900) (M. E. Sharpe, 2002)

Ralf Poscher, 'The Principle Theory: How Many Theories and What is Their Merit?' in Klatt (ed), *Institutionalizing Reason. Perspectives on the Legal Philosophy of Robert Alexy* (Oxford University Press 2012), 218

Richard Posner, *Antitrust Law* (2nd Edition, Chicago University Press, 2001)

Richard Posner, *A Failure of Capitalism* (Harvard University Press, 2011)

Richard Posner, *Crisis of Capitalist Democracy* (Harvard University Press, 2011)

Raghuram Rajan, 'Has Financial Development Made the World Riskier' National Bureau of Economic Research Working Paper No 11728 (2005)

Rhaguram Rajan, *Fault Lines: How Hidden Fractures Still Threaten the World Economy* (Princeton University Press, 2011)

Carmen Reinhart and Kenneth Rogoff, 'The Aftermath of the Financial Crisis' National Bureau of Economic Research Working Paper No 14656 (2009)

Carmen Reinhart and Kenneth Rogoff, *This Time is Different: Eight Centuries of Financial Follies* (Princeton University Press, 2009)

Steven Schwarcz, 'Systemic Risk' (2008) 97 Georgetown Law Journal, 193

Andrew Ross Sorkin, Too Big To Fail: Inside the Battle to Save Wall Street (Viking, Penguin Group, 2010)

Joseph Stiglitz, *Free Fall: America, Free Markets, and the Sinking of the World Economy* (W.W. Norton, 2010)

Joseph Stiglitz, 'The Financial Crisis of 2007/08 and its Macro-Economic Consequences' in Stephany Griffith-Jones, José Antonio Ocampo and Joseph E. Stiglitz (eds), *Time for a Visible Hand: Lessons from the 2008 World Financial Crisis* (New York 2009), 19

Elizabeth Warren, 'Scaling Back `too big´' Boston Globe, 18 September 2013, at: https://www.bostonglobe.com/opinion/2013/09/18/century-glass-steagall-act-will-disable-too-big-fail-bank-risk/cdR0wqqnDIGBBoYAaFFfbO/story.html (visited 22.06.2018)

Luigi Zingales, 'German Banks on Top' Project Syndicate, 18 July 2013, at: https://www.project-syndicate.org/commentary/germany-s-taxpayers-finance-german-banks--mistakes-by-luigi-zingales?barrier=accessreg (visited 22.06.2018)

The Contribution of the Element of 'Fellowship' to the Recognition of a Positive Right to Die for People Incapable of Committing Suicide

Eliza Kompatsiari

A. *Introduction*

The idea of a right to die draws its origins from perhaps the greatest existential subject of all times: the relationship between a person and their death and the relationship between the society and the death of one of its members. Law is of course only one of the disciplines that study this subject, and it would not be much of a prediction to assume that interest on the matter will follow humanity to the end of its days.

This paper focuses on the right to die of people incapable of committing suicide. Greek legal theorists, but also legal theorists throughout Europe, support a position that effectively amounts to an oxymoron. Specifically, they reject a legal obligation of people to live while at the same time also rejecting a positive right to die. Instead, they put forward the notion of a freedom of people to choose between life and death, also suggesting that the state should abstain from any intervention on the subject. It could be suggested, however, that this position effectively accepts that people incapable of committing suicide have an obligation to live.

Attempting to overcome this legal gap, the present study discusses the social legitimation of law itself and the element of 'fellowship' among members of a society as inherent to the very concept of society. It is proposed that the aforementioned idea of an assumed 'freedom to die' essentially disregards this element in those cases when the refusal of a positive right to die in fact implies obliging a person to suffer an objectively torturous life.

B. Necessary Definitions

I. The Positive Right to Die

Before referring to the issues that constitute the main challenges this study attemts to tackle, it is necessary to define the notion of a 'positive right to die'.

The term 'right to die' is used to describe a variety of legal concepts that have to do with a person's choice to terminate their life, such as their decision to commit suicide, to refuse or withdraw medical intervention, to receive help in order to commit suicide, and to ask someone to terminate their life.

Some of these conditions are also referred by the term 'euthanasia', which is further divided to different kinds of euthanasia: positive, negative, direct, and indirect.

To avoid the confusion that the term 'euthanasia' sometimes creates,[1] for the purposes of the present contribution the term 'positive right to die' is preferred. It must, however, be underlined that it is used to describe a legal claim against the state in which a person seeks to compel the termination of their life.

Understood as described above, though, this 'positive right to die' follows the regular conceptual division of rights into positive and negative which is drawn on the basis of whether they entail an obligation of action or omission, respectively.

II. Which Society?

A presentation of the approaches that have been supported as regards the nature and function of societies goes beyond the focus and the objectives of

---

1 In particular, the terms 'direct' and 'indirect' are often confused with 'active' and 'passive' euthanasia, respectively. See the correct definitions in *Otlowski*, Voluntary Euthanasia and the Common Law, 1997, p. 428 ff.; *Symeonidou-Kastanidou*, Euthanasia in the domestic legal system of Greece, in: Groenhuijsen/van Laanen (eds), Euthanasia in International and Comparative Perspective, 2006, p. 127 (127 ff.).

the present study. It is, however, essential to briefly describe how the concept of society is understood within this paper.

The study follows an approach[2] to society that rejects the idea that it is just an organized *co-existence* of individual solitary people, who manage to survive by this arrangement. Instead, it acknowledges that, even if we accept that people constitute communities not only due to their social nature but also for reasons of survival, what they eventually form is something much bigger than merely a grouping or the sum of their individual selves: *society*.

It does not follow from this understanding of the concept that the nature of society obliges its members to behave in a certain helpful, fellow, or at least non-hostile manner towards each other; *law* is what plays that role. However, it does mean that by being recognized as a member of a given society, each individual belongs to it as one of its integral constituent elements. As a result, the death of each of those constituent individuals *costs* something to society at large. More about that approach on society will follow in the next sections.

C. *The Problem*

I. Neither a Legal Obligation of People to Live nor a Positive Right to Die: the Freedom to Die

Among the different opinions debated on the subject of the right to die, most theorists, even though beginning from completely different bases, tend towards, on the one hand, the non-recognition of a positive right to die and, on the other hand, the rejection of a legal obligation of people to live.

Some legal theorists, who base their analysis on the freedom of personal development or on the principle of human dignity, reject such an obligation, while others argue that this legal obligation of people to live would be practically doomed as it would be impossible to enforce.[3] As for the positive

---

2 *Manoledakis*, Is there a right to die?, (2004) Poinika Chronika, p. 577 (581–582) (in Greek).

3 However, see the different theory of *Kant* on that subject, as presented in *Ellescheid*, Das Paternalismusproblemim System der Kant'shen Moralphilosophie, in: Fateh-Moghadam/Sellmaier/Vossenkuhl (eds), Grenzen des Paternalismus,

right to die, it is refuted by some primarily on the basis of its existential character, which prevents law from intervening.[4] Others point out that recognizing a positive right to die would be contrary to law's very purpose, which is defined as the promotion of life within what *Manoledakis* calls a 'society of law'.[5]

No matter which opinion one finds more convincing, the abovementioned sub-conclusions on the rejection of both a legal obligation of people to live and a positive right to die converge on the recognition of the *freedom* of each person to die.

II. Legal Gap: People Physically Incapable of Committing Suicide

This middle ground, the freedom to die, may seem to be a balanced solution: why should a man's choice to die involve the participation of the state or, perhaps, of anyone else? This solution, though, leaves a significant legal gap: for people physically incapable of committing suicide, the freedom to die exists in name only. For them, the question has to be a choice between a positive right to die and a legal obligation to live.

The insistence on the freedom to die implies that people incapable of committing suicide are in fact obliged to live. It should also be noted that this does not change depending on the legislation of a country on *assisted suicide*. In particular, even in a system where assisted suicide is not considered criminally punishable or even simply unlawful, people incapable of committing suicide would still be made to live until they found someone who would be willing to help them. Moreover, if they managed to find such a willing individual, they would definitely be unable to legally compel their assistance. Therefore, the omission of the state to grant a positive right to die to people incapable of committing suicide effectively equals to the acceptance of their legal obligation to live.

2009, p. 182 (189 ff.). According to *Kant*, law *could* enforce the prohibition of suicide. However, he argues that the obligation of people to live is not legal, but moral in nature.

4 See, *inter alia*, *Paraskevopoulos*, Thoughts about suicide and law, in: Justice in Particular: Festschrift in Honour of Professor P.J. Koziris, 2007, p. 359 (359 ff.) (in Greek).

5 *Manoledakis*, (2004) Poinika Chronika, p. 577 (582) (in Greek).

D. *The Proposal*

At this point I will try to compose my proposal as regards the highlighted legal problem. The instruments required for this purpose lie beyond the law itself. In order to identify them in their full nature, we need to also look to the normative and societal context of law. We need to examine society itself, as the creator of a particular institutional and legal arrangement, and, further still, society's own inherent constituent elements.

I. 'Fellowship' as an Element Inherent to the Concept of Society

In regards to society's inherent elements, for the purposes of the present contribution we must focus on the element of *'fellowship'*. It is, of course, a fact that competing interests always develop within a society. Nevertheless, the very meaning of society, as it has been mentioned already, requires much more than the simple co-existence of its members. It requires a bond among the members of a society that distinguishes them from those external to it and, of course, from its enemies. This bond is what this paper denotes as 'fellowship'. In other words, despite all the conflicts that are being raised within it, as long as the society still reserves its status as such and does not, for example, become divided, all of its members are at a minimum connected with each other through fundamental bonds that hold it together. These bonds are what this paper considers the bonds that constitute its notion of 'fellowship'.

The term is being used not to refer to some moral obligation among the members of a society to help each other or to behave towards each other as fellows. It merely indicates the bond that somehow *connects* all members of a society together and in the end forms the society, as defined above. The construction of the notion of 'fellowship', central in this paper, derives from the work[6] of the Greek criminal law scholar *Manoledakis*, who has referred to it alongside the idea of *'interdependence'* of the members of a society as the constitutive elements that are inherent to the concept of 'society'. Thus, *Manoledakis* rejects the notion of a society consisting of individuals, who act in a selfish way. Instead, he understands society as based upon the bonds of fellowship and interdependence which connect its members, and it is this notion of society that he places at the heart of his theory.

---

6 *Manoledakis*, (2004) Poinika Chronika, p. 577 (581) (in Greek).

II. Law as a Product of Society

Moving on to the relationship between law and society, it must be pointed out that law requires the existence of a society that made it. Furthermore, society not only preexists but also forms law according to its needs and values. Law is, therefore, an *instrument* that societies use and that by its very nature merely means to serve their needs and standards.

III. The Legal Absurdity of Law Setting Aside the Element of Fellowship

Returning to the main subject of this study, people incapable of committing suicide and their – in name only – freedom to die, it is now time to focus on cases where the obligation of those people to live, as mentioned above, constitutes an obligation to suffer an objectively torturous life. By denying them a positive right to die, we are accepting the possibility that a person incapable of committing suicide, who also happens to suffer from a disease that cannot be treated even with palliative measures, will face the worst torture imaginable.

One could perhaps argue that it is not law but the bad health of a person that causes this torture in the first place. Accordingly, by recognizing a freedom to die, law is supposed to maintain its neutrality as regards the causal link to the individual's suffering; law remains external to the causes of this suffering. However, as it is granted that this freedom to die cannot be exercised by people incapable of committing suicide, in cases where they suffer an objectively torturous life, law's ostensible neutrality turns out to be mere hypocrisy.

It has been argued that in such cases the denial of a positive right to die violates fundamental principles and rights.[7] Yet, these arguments face objections based on the legal absurdity of the invocation of principles and

---

7 In addition to the freedom of personal development and the principle of human dignity, which have already been mentioned above, such a denial could also be regarded as an affront to the principle of equality and, in particular, the prohibition of discrimination on grounds of disability and, also, the spirit of the absolute prohibition of torture. *Inter alia*, cf. *Karavokyris*, About the 'right to die', (2010) Administrative Law Journal, p. 114 (114 ff.) (in Greek); *Katrougalos*, The right

rights in the first place, since their enforcement would effectively nullify them by destroying their holder. Therefore, it is suggested that this line of reasoning would essentially result in the self-nullification of the legal order itself.[8] The invocation, for example, of the freedom of personal development as an argument that supports the positive right to die faces the reasonable objection that the death of this freedom's holder would also necessarily imply the forfeiture of his freedom of personal development.

However, besides the legal debate that is based on the violation of fundamental principles and rights, it must be emphasized that obliging a person physically incapable of committing suicide to suffer a torturous life, even by omitting to confer a positive right to die, is an objectively aggressive and hostile stance against her. It actually implies that this person is treated, for all intents and purposes, as an 'enemy'.[9] In other words, in cases involving suffering due to incapacity, by denying a positive right to die, irrespectively of its consideration as a violation of basic human rights and principles, the status of the person whose positive right to die is being denied ends up being far beyond that of a member of a society whose rights are being violated. Rather, it means that the status of such individuals has been effectively turned into that of an enemy of the society they are supposed to be constitutive members of. Even more, this status is ascribed to such people not by

---

to life and death, 1993, p. 84 (in Greek); *Neumann*, The criminal protection of human dignity in the beginning and at the end of life, in: Manodedakis/Prittwitz (eds), The criminal protection of human dignity, 1997, p. 67 (67 ff.) (in Greek); *Papadopoulou*, Is there a right to die? – A discussion with Professor Ioannis Manoledakis, (2014) Revue Hellénique de Droits de l' Homme (hereinafter RHDH), p. 43 (64 ff.) (in Greek); *Vidalis*, Euthanasia and Constitution, in: Kaiafa-Gbandi/Kounougeri-Manoledaki/Symeonidou-Kastanidou (eds), Publications of Medical Law and Bioethics, Vol. 3: Euthanasia, 2007, p. 133 (133 ff.) (in Greek).

8 *Manoledakis*, (2004) Poinika Chronika, p. 577 (581) (in Greek), who emphatically remarks (p. 584) that, as there is no sense in recognizing a right to revolution, it would correspondingly be an absurdum to recognize a right to die. See, however, *Papadopoulou*, (2014) RHDH, p. 43 (47 ff.) (in Greek).

9 We encounter here a concept of great importance for law, philosophy, and politics: the 'Enemy'. It is worth noting, *inter alia*, the theses of *Spinoza*, that people driven by anger, envy, and hatred become "natural enemies (ex natura hostes)"; of *Hobbes*, that people are in nature equals and become enemies due to this equality among them, when they desire the same things; and also that of *Kropotkin*, that solidarity is the favored weapon in the fight between the different species and the environment.

some individual or any particular group inside a society but by the legal order itself.

On the other hand, however, this status is afforded to these individuals through the omission of law to release them from the obligation of suffering a torturous life, *despite* the fact that people incapable of committing suicide who suffer from painful diseases are *not* considered by society as enemies. This leads us to the legal absurdity of law setting aside the element of fellowship that is inherent to the concept of society.

More precisely, given that law is a product of society, rather than the other way around, law is by nature unable to regulate, even through omission, who will become or remain a member of a society and who should be treated by society as an enemy. Therefore, as long as people incapable of committing suicide, who also suffer from painful diseases, are not considered enemies by society, law cannot but confer upon them a positive right to die.

Detailed conditions that should apply to this positive right to die cannot be set out in the present contribution. It must, however, be noted that this is a right and that its exercise is, upon the holder's serious and persistent demand, expressed in free will.[10]

E. *Back to 'Which society?' – Crucial Notes Concerning the 'Fellowship' Element*

Before closing this contribution, some final thoughts must be added on the meaning of 'society' under this study and on the 'fellowship' element.

---

10 The concept of 'free will' raises, of course, infinite debates not only among legal scholars but also, for example, among neuroscientists, many of whom argue that free will is actually an illusion, a thesis that could prove very dangerous in the area of criminal law. For the legal perspective on that debate, see, *inter alia*, *von Hirsch/Neumann*, 'Indirekter' Paternalismusim Strafrecht – am Beispiel der Tötung auf Verlangen (§ 216 StGB), Goltdammer's Archiv fur Strafrecht 2007, p. 671 (671 ff.). For the perspective of jurisprudence, *inter alia*, see the 'classic' BGH case of 05.07.1983 – 1 StR 168/83, BGHSt 32, 38 ('Sirius Fall'), which challenges the relationship between free will and prevailing ideology, even though in that case it is clear that the victim did not believe in a general next level of existence in Sirius – which would perhaps be similar to paradise for Christians – but was persuaded that exceptionally *she* would experience it after fulfilling the required terms, despite people on Earth thinking of her as dead.

I. Fellowship, Hostility and the In-between Cases in Societies of Modern Times

As has already been analyzed, 'fellowship' stands for the bond that connects all members of a society. It has also been noted that people incapable of committing suicide, who also suffer from painful diseases, are not excluded from society for such reasons. However, they could be considered not to be members of a given society for other reasons, irrelevant to their physical condition. This leads us to a few further questions: Would it then be permissible to just let them suffer? And how do we define society in modern times, where increasingly complex multicultural societies emerge?

The latter question becomes even more topical if one considers Europe's migrant and refugee crisis, which brings together people of different cultures, or even cultures that could, on some level, even be considered as opposed. It is becoming clear that traditional instruments such as common history, language, or religion are insufficient for defining societies of modern times.

However, not being a member of a society is not equal to being an enemy of the society. The proposed initial thesis, that it is legally absurd for law to set aside the element of fellowship that is inherent to the concept of society, could perhaps be followed by a similar proposition against law *deforming* the relationship between a society and a non-member, non-enemy person. As much as law cannot on its own define or destroy the element of 'fellowship' it also cannot, on its own, designate someone as an enemy of a given society or a non-member of it. All these designations, inclusions, and exclusions simply lie beyond the functions of law and are societal in nature rather than strictly legal.

II. The Proposal versus the 'Criminal Law of the Enemy' Theory

This distinction between 'members' and 'enemies' of a society may remind readers of the legal theory of the criminal law of the enemy (*'Feindstraf-*

recht'),[11] making this paper's position appear as the reverse side to that theory. However, it must be underlined that the paper's thesis should under no circumstances be considered a supplement or a confirmation of that theory.

In particular, it must be noted that the paper's proposal adopts a starting point that is in fact opposite to that legal theory. Contrary to it, our preferred theory identifies the members of a society and its enemies not on the basis of regulatory requirements but on the basis of the empirical reality. Furthermore, it recognizes a right, rather than rejecting the existence of one. This study does not contribute to a stable distinction between members of a society (or citizens) and enemies. On the contrary, it uses the distinction between the 'members of a society' and its 'enemies' only to suggest a solution to a completely borderline issue, precluding law from forcing this distinction without authorization based on the empirical reality of a certain society.

III. The Proposal versus Other Theories that Accept the Right to Die

It is quite common that the theories accepting the right to die[12] – no matter which conditions they require – do not start by focusing on the society, as this proposal suggests, but on the *individual* and her freedom to determine the way she wants to live and die. It must also be noted that this approach is consistent with a definitinon of society as an organized co-existence of individual selfish people, who thus manage to survive, a definition which – as is already mentioned above – is not followed in this study.

One further argument that is also often put forward is founded upon the indignity which allegedly characterizes the status of people suffering a torturous life who are incapable of committing suicide. We could completely concur that there is a violation of the principle of human dignity when in such cases the right to die, expressed in free will, is denied. On the other

11 *Jakobs*, Bürgerstrafrecht und Feindstrafrecht, Höchstrichterliche Rechtsprechung zum Strafrecht 2004, p. 88 (88 ff.); *Jakobs*, Kriminalisierung im Vorfeld einer Rechtsgutsverletzung, Zeitschrift fur die Gesamte Strafrechtswissenschaft 1985, p. 751 (751 ff.).

12 For a general overview of the theories on the right to die supported in Germany, see, *inter alia*, *Wessels/Hettinger*, *Straftecht – Besonderer Teil 1. Straftaten gegen Persönlichkeits- und Gemeinschaftswerte*, 2013, § 1 paras. 27 ff.

hand, it must be pointed out that an approach that accepts a lack of dignity in the very status of those people could easily lead to a reduction in the legal value of their life, which would of course be totally unacceptable.[13]

IV. The Right to Die and the Internal Contradictions in Society, Legislation, and Its Implementation

It is mentioned above that a great majority of scholars tend to reject both a positive right to die and an obligation of people to live, and eventually accept the freedom of people to decide on the matter. This freedom, or at least the absence of a legal obligation of people to live, is at some level enshrined in the domestic legislation of western countries[14] as well as in European law.[15] However, it could be argued that in many western countries, the law is not very clear about the position it takes on that subject,[16]

---

13 *Karavokyris*, (2010) Administrative Law Journal, p. 114 (120–121) (in Greek).

14 For a comparative analysis of the national legislation on euthanasia in many countries of Europe, but also of the U.S.A., Japan, Israel, and Iran, see *Groenhuijsen/van Laanen* (eds), Euthanasia in International and Comparative Perspective, 2006.

15 In particular, Articles 5 and 9 of the European Convention on Human Rights and Biomedicine of the Council of Europe. See also, the right to consent, as regulated in the Declaration on the Promotion of Patients' Rights in Europe of World Health Organization.

16 It is very interesting, e.g., to compare the two maps that one finds on Wikipedia showing the countries that allow the death penalty (https://en.wikipedia.org/wiki/Capital_punishment_by_country#/media/File:Capital_punishment_in_the_world.svg (visited 02.05.2017)) and those that allow euthanasia (https://en.wikipedia.org/wiki/Legality_of_euthanasia#/media/File:Legality_of_euthanasia. svg (visited 02.05.2017). In the first map, one can easily identify a country's status as regards the legality of the death penalty and then ascertain various details, e.g. about the last enforcement of that penalty in each country. In the second map the reader would notice that for most of the countries depicted the legal status is unknown, and for those where it is known, this status is subject to the respective definition of 'euthanasia' in each case, and the distinction between active and passive euthanasia. If a researcher subsequently wished to refer to academic sources, she would find that the subject's sensitive character is reflected in the variety of national legislations. See *Groenhuijsen/van Laanen* (eds), 2006.

often resulting in internal inconsistencies and contradictions in the legislation.[17] Furthermore, politically and factually it is rather uncertain whether the legislation of the countries that in any case deny a positive right to die would remain as is or would change if the Netherlands, Belgium, and Luxembourg, the three main European countries that clearly grant such a right today, also decided to reject it.

However, this inconsistency of law happens to reflect, with great success, the internal conflicts inside the society on the topic. The right to die is a taboo subject: On the one hand, we cannot bear knowing that such people exist and suffer inescapable pain. On the other hand, though, to nominate killing seems to break with some of the most basic principles of our societies (even though the death penalty still exists, for instance, in the U.S.A.). Furthermore, the establishment of a positive right to die might also have to confront fundamental religious teachings,[18] which in most cases consider life as a gift from God that people are not authorized to discard and that people's faith should be firm no matter what one might have to endure. Additionally, in order to abolish every possibility of abuse, the establishment of the positive right to die needs to overcome very serious practical problems concerning the procedure that should apply as regards the exercise of this right.

However, it must also be noted that, in practice, people suffering from incurable diseases choose to travel to countries that already embrace the positive right to die and end their lives there. At the same time, in all those cases where no such choice is possible, neither the law's prohibition nor religious concerns or practical problems manage to prevent euthanasia from actually happening[19] in hospitals when it comes to people who cannot bear their loved ones' suffering.

---

17 For example, in the Greek legal system, there is a right to refuse a particular medical treatment when the patient is well informed and expresses this refusal freely, even if this will result in his or her death. However, if the doctor overlooks the patient's will, he or she will not face any criminal or civil liability. See *Symeonidou-Kastanidou*, in: Groenhuijsen/van Laanen, 2006, p. 127 (134 ff.); *Voultsos/Njau/Vlachou*, The issue of euthanasia in Greece from a legal viewpoint, (2010) 17 (3) Journal of Forensic and Legal Medicine (hereinafter JFLM), p. 133 (133 ff.).

18 Cf. *Voultsos/Njau/Vlachou*, (2010) 17 (3) JFLM, p. 133 (133 ff.).

19 *Symeonidou-Kastanidou*, in: Groenhuijsen/van Laanen, 2006, p. 127 (142–143); *Voultsos/Njau/Vlachou*, (2010) 17 (3) JFLM, p. 133 (133 ff.).

F. Conclusion

Abuse is a risk no one would take. This is an inherent danger as regards both the regulated euthanasia and illegal euthanasia that occur despite legal prohibitions. Although the present contribution cannot take this discussion further, it must be noted that the question of granting a positive right to die should be followed by the question of how to eliminate the risks of abuse.

In this context, it is essential to point out that the adoption of a positive right to die demands detailed and discreet regulation, but it also requires highlighting the need of building an adequate infrastructure of palliative care. The need to put our weight behind palliative care is confirmed by recent research[20] asserting that requests for euthanasia in the U.S.A. have decreased overwhelmingly in those states where palliative care units have been built.

However, although our faith in scientific progress must never be abandoned, we should not allow this same faith to hide from us the fact that, unfortunately, today even palliative care cannot be effective in *all* cases of people's suffering.[21] The first thing needed to close this gap is a clear position, first in principle and then in practice.

Bibliography

BGH 05.07.1983 – 1 StR 168/83, BGHSt 32, 38

Günter Ellescheid, 'Das Paternalismusproblem im System der Kant'shen Moralphilosophie' in Bijan Fateh-Moghadam, Stephan Sellmaier and Wilhelm Vossenkuhl (eds), *Grenzen des Paternalismus, Ethik im Diskurs* (W. Kohlhammer, München 2009), 182

Atul Gavande, *Being mortal – Medicine and what matters in the end* (Metropolitan Books, Henry Holt and Company, LCC, New York 2014)

Marc Groenhuijsen and Florisvan Laanen (eds), *Euthanasia in International and Comparative Perspective* (Wolf Legal Publishers, 2006)

Frédéric Guirmand, Etienne Dubois, Lucy Laporte, Jean-François Richard and Danièle Leboul, 'Death wishes and explicit requests for euthanasia in a palliative care hospital: an analysis of patient files' (2014) 13:53 BioMed Central Palliative Care

20 *Gavande*, Being mortal – Medicine and what matters in the end, 2014.

21 *Guirmand/Dubois/Laporte/R*ichard/*Leboul*, Death wishes and explicit requests for euthanasia in a palliative care hospital: an analysis of patient files, (2014) 13:53 BioMed Central Palliative Care.

Andrew von Hirsch and Ulfrid Neumann, ''Indirekter' Paternalismus am Beispiel der Tötung auf Verlangen' (§ 216 StGB) Goltdammer's Archiv fur Strafrecht 2007, 671

Günther Jakobs, Bürgerstrafrecht und Feindstrafrecht, Höchstrichterliche Rechtsprechung zum Strafrecht 2004, 88

Günther Jakobs, Kriminalisierung im Vorfeld einer Rechtsgutsverletzung, Zeitschrift fur die Gesamte Strafrechtswissenschaft 1985, 751

Georgios Karavokyris, 'About the 'right to die'' (2010) Administrative Law Journal, 114 (in Greek)

Georgios Katrougalos, *The right to life and death* (in Greek, 1993)

Ioannis Manoledakis, 'Is there a right to die?' (2004) Poinika Chronika, 577 (in Greek)

Ulfrid Neumann, 'The criminal protection of human dignity in the beginning and at the end of life' in Ioannis Manodedakis and Cornelius Prittwitz (eds), *The criminal protection of human dignity* (1997), 67 (in Greek)

Margaret Otlowski, *Voluntary Euthanasia and the Common Law* (Oxford Clarendon Press, New York 1997)

Lina Papadopoulou, 'Is there a right to die? – A discussion with Professor Ioannis Manoledakis' (2014) Revue Hellénique de Droits de l' Homme, 43 (in Greek)

Nikolaos Paraskevopoulos, 'Thoughts about suicide and law' in *Justice in Particular: Festschrift in Honour of Professor P.J. Kozyris* (in Greek, A. N. Sakkoulas, Athens 2007), 359

Elisavet Symeonidou-Kastanidou, 'Euthanasia in the domestic legal system of Greece' in Marc Groenhuijsen and Floris van Laanen (eds), *Euthanasia in International and Comparative Perspective* (Wolf Legal Publishers, 2006), 127

Takis Vidalis, 'Euthanasia and Constitution' in Maria Kaiafa-Gbandi, Eftihia Kounougeri-Manoledaki and Elisavet Symeonidou-Kastanidou (eds), *Publications of Medical Law and Bioethics,* Vol. 3: Euthanasia (2007), 133 (in Greek)

Polichronis Voultsos, Samuel Njau and Maria Vlachou, 'The issue of euthanasia in Greece from a legal viewpoint' (2010) 17 (3) Journal of Forensic and Legal Medicine 2010, 133

Johannes Wesselsand and Michael Hettinger, *Straftecht – Besonderer Teil 1. Straftaten gegen Persönlichkeits- und Gemeinschaftswerte* (37th Edition, C. F. Müller, 2013)

D. Raising the Quality of Law

Principles-Based Regulation and Compliance with Financial Legislation

Olli Salmi

A. *Introduction*

> "Why should not law be equally if not more concerned with the 'puzzled man'... who is willing to do what is required, if only he can be told what it is?"
>
> H.L.A. Hart[1]

The main argument in my article is that legal rules must have such a form, that real life activities can be measured against these rules. In this article, I argue that this is especially the case when it is a question of activities which require continuous compliance with the rules that are supervised and enforced by the public authorities. Firstly, I intend to show that principles-based rules may become too hard to comply with because of the different characteristics of the principles in comparison with the rules. I will argue that the more vague and indeterminate the norms are, the more difficult it is to find out what kind of behavior is or is not compliant with the rules. I also briefly describe why principles-based rules are used in order to highlight the reasons why legislators initially draft such difficult rules.

Secondly, I present the idea of continuous compliance, which I call dynamic compliance. It is important to see how this concept and other kinds of compliance with the rules, which I call static compliance, differ from one another. This categorization helps to demonstrate the need for specific, precise norms in dynamic compliance situations and how a vague and highly generalized formulation of the rules does not always make it possible to comply with the law. This is due to the fact that in the future the open-texture of the rules may result in situations, where it is almost impossible to know whether law is being complied with or not.

Finally, I argue that whichever enforcement regime is chosen where there is public enforcement involved, the enforcement requires weighting or comparison between norms and real life behavior. To reach this situation, the

1 *Hart*, The Concept of Law, 1961, p. 39.

regulators should give their interpretation, or a more precise binding norm, to define the content of the norm; that is, what is the substance of the norm and what kind of behavior does it demand. Only when the exact legislative requirements are known, will it be possible for the regulated entities to adapt their business to the rules and create compliance systems which make it possible to comply with the legal norms.

B. Principles-Based Rules

Principles-based rules are widely used in financial regulation, including one of its special areas, the capital adequacy legislation. This can be seen in legal texts covering both the Banking sector and Insurance sector capital adequacy regimes. Solvency II openly addresses the supervisory and prudential principles[2] and also the Capital Requirements Regulation states in the headings of the paragraphs that there are principles to be followed.[3] By following a principles-based approach the legislators / regulators[4] have created in both regimes sets of complex, long and in many occasions fairly ambiguous legal norms. These, in turn, create difficult problems for subjects, interpreters, and enforcers.

Legal rules, standards, and principles are crafted in different forms and there has been an extensive amount of literature around these. The advantages and disadvantages of each form have been analyzed[5] and so has the optimal precision of the administrative rules.[6] I do not elaborate on the

---

2 According to Parliament and Council Directive 2009/138/EC (Solvency II directive) Art. 30, para. 3 "The supervisory authorities of the home Member State shall determine whether the undertaking is complying with the prudential principles laid down in this Directive." Art. 29 states as a general principle that "Supervision shall be based on a prospective and risk-based approach."

3 In Parliament and Council Regulation (EU) No 575/2013 (CRR) this is stated for example as follows "TITLE II CAPITAL REQUIREMENTS FOR CREDIT RISK CHAPTER 1 General principles."

4 I use terms legislator and regulator in many cases as synonyms meaning official public organs that have power to create legal norms.

5 See for example *Black*, The Rise, Fall and Fate of Principles Based Regulation (2010) 17 Law, Society and Economy Working Paper, p. 1 (2) and articles referred there.

6 *Diver*, The Optimal Precision of Administrative Rules, (1983) 93 The Yale Law Journal (hereinafter Yale L.J.), p. 65.

advantages or disadvantages of the different forms or contemplate the optimal precision, but rather present the fact that dynamic compliance with the rules requires a precise set of rules with which to work.

For present purposes, it is useful to point out the following characteristics which affect how hard or easy it is to apply the rules in practice. Firstly, legal rules can be seen as generalizations. They are usually not made for a specific situation. Instead, they are meant to be applicable in a group of particular situations and thus the rule is meant to cover all of a certain category[7] of situations. These particulars have common characteristics which are seen to cause some phenomena that the legislator wants to prevent. The legislator may also want to make an exception,[8] or give approval or authorization for certain behavior.[9] The rule may be precise, that is the generalization can be made so that the exceptions to the rule do not exist or are rare; in other words, it is fairly easy to say whether the rule applies or not and even how it applies. *Vice versa* rules may also be so open-ended that it is not certain which cases the rule covers and thus exceptions may have to be allowed to avoid unreasonable results.

The scope of the rule[10] may, however, be problematic. On the one hand, the rules may be over-inclusive and they may also apply to cases to which they were not intended to apply when considering the purpose of the rule. On the other hand, they may be under-inclusive, in which case those cases that were supposed to fall within the scope of the rule are omitted. A special case for generalizations is the possibility of future vagueness, which is called the open-texture of the law.[11] This means there is the possibility of a rule becoming under- or over-inclusive because of the uncertainties relating to the future. It may therefore occur that a rule may become under-inclusive in the future when a case is discovered which should have been included in the scope of the rule had it been known when the rule was crafted. On the other hand, there may be totally new information which shows the

---

7 *Schauer*, Playing by the Rules: A Philosophical Examination of Rule-Based Decision Making in Law and in Life, 1991, p. 25.

8 Generally about exceptions, see *Schauer*, Exceptions, (1991) 58 The University of Chicago Law Review (hereinafter U. Chi. L. Rev.), p. 871.

9 *Schauer*, 1991, p. 25–31.

10 With the scope of the rule I mean the particulars i.e. real life cases that the generalization covers.

11 *Schauer*, On the Open Texture of Law, 2011, p. 3.

premises for the rule were insufficient or wrong. It might also be shown that the causes of the phenomena, which were thought to create the evil the legislator wanted to prevent by stipulating the rule, were based on wrong assumptions. New scientific (or other) information may show that the cause of the phenomena was either totally different than expected or that some cause also should have been included in the scope of the rule.[12]

It may be that attempts have been made to prevent these kinds of problems by crafting law in the form of principles. The rules are given in a 'principles like' form, to cover all those possible cases now and in the future, which could cause the 'evil' the legislator wants to prohibit. There are, however, both practical and theoretical problems with using principles to guide decision-making. Principles can be said to have inherently different characteristics than rules when they are applied in legal decision-making. Where rules are said to lead to 'yes' or 'no' answers,[13] stipulating that a certain act ought to be done in certain conditions,[14] principles do not have this character,[15] but are only said to indicate the direction the decision should take if there are problems in applying the rule.[16] Because of their specificity and concrete character, rules stipulate the answer to legal questions and set the legal consequences,[17] whereas legal principles do not express conditions that trigger their application.[18] These theoretical characteristics of the principles make it hard to make decisions in concrete situations.

In addition, there is one more characteristic of principles that may cause the decision-making to be very difficult, especially in situations where decisions on how to apply the rules have to be done on a continuous bases. There is the possibility, as Dworkin states, that principles may be in conflict with each other and that each principle has its own weight, which must be

12 About open-texture see *Schauer*, 1991, p. 34–37 and *Waismann*, Verifiability, (1945) 19 Proceedings of the Aristotelian Society, p. 119.

13 See for example *Dworkin*, The Model of Rules, (1967) 35 U. Chi. L. Rev., p. 14 (25).

14 *Raz*, Legal Principles and the Limits of Law, (1972) 81 The Yale L.J., p. 823 (830).

15 *Dworkin*, (1967) 35 U. Chi. L. Rev., p. 14 (25).

16 Ibid., p. 14 (26).

17 *Tridimas*, The General Principles of EU Law, 2006, p. 2.

18 *Dworkin*, (1967) 35 U. Chi. L. Rev., p. 14 (26).

determined separately in each case.[19] In real life, it is often sufficiently difficult to comply with the rules even though they may provide a yes or no answer. If the decision-making is burdened with the possibly of conflicting principles, the practical decision-making may become excessively challenging, or the way the law is applied may come to resemble a game of chance more than legal decision-making. Legislating by using principles-based rules raises therefore the question of how far the principles-likeness of the rules can go before the legislation becomes too difficult to be complied with in real life situations.

It is said that principles and rules cannot always be identified from their form.[20] This idea seems to apply well when principles-based rules are considered. In fact, it is not easy to say when a rule is principles-based or rules based. It seems to be a question of whether the rule expresses an idea as to what is required or prohibited, in contrast to a clear stipulation of what should or should not take place. The principles-based rules seem to state "what is allowed, in principle," "what is prohibited, in principle" or "what is required, in principle." The difficulty of applying the rule derives from both its linguistic vagueness and from what kind of open-ended expressions the legislator has made when making generalizations. The difference, in this sense, between principles-based rules and clearly defined rules is that at one end of the continuum, strict rules leave very few possibilities or none to interpret how the rule should be applied, and at the opposite end, the principles seem to give a free hand to the interpreter to discover the exact norm as regards how to behave.[21] This idea can also be presented by saying that by crafting a rule in a precise form, the legislator makes the decision as to how the rule should be applied and this is the reverse when the rule is crafted

---

19 Ibid., p. 14 (27).

20 *Raz*, (1972) 81 Yale L.J., p. 823 (836) and *Dworkin*, (1967) 35 U. Chi. L. Rev., p. 14 (28).

21 According to Cunningham "rules and principles are best conceived as residing along a continuum according to a provisions' relative vagueness and posing subtle trade-offs." *Cunningham*, A Prescription to Retire the Rhetoric of "Principles-Based Systems" in Corporate Law, Securities Regulation and Accounting, (2007) 127 Boston College Law School Research Paper, p. 1 (7).

in a principles-based form, where the legislator has left the discretion of how to apply the rule to the subject (regulated), interpreter or enforcer.[22]

Most financial legislation norms are situated somewhere between the extreme ends of the continuum. While a pure example of each of the extreme forms may be very difficult to find, some kind of separation can be characterized between precise rules and principles-based rules. It could be said that with strict rules the penumbra, the shady area where the rules applicability and the way in which they are applied need interpretation, is smaller and with the principles this area is wider.[23]

The question arises why make rules which are so vague that the majority of cases seem to fall into the penumbra of the rule. I present two possible reasons for this,[24] which apply to a rapidly changing and innovative environment such as the financial industry. Firstly, vague formulation has to do with the uncertainty of its scope. The coverage that the rule is intended to provide is hard to define. It may be recognized by the legislator that the rule may unavoidably have an open texture if it is not crafted vaguely. In this type of situation, the legislator will find it hard to formulate the rule to cover all possible situations, including future developments, and, at the same time, to not cover situations which should be excluded. Thus, the generalization should not be over-inclusive, that is, it should not cover unnecessary real life situations, but still be inclusive enough to make circumventing the rule impossible. The open-texture of the rule makes it possible to invent ways to evade the rule with future innovations or with innovations that exist already when the rule was crafted but was unknown to the legislator. Circumvention of the rule with future innovation occurs by using creative compliance, i.e. by making the originally fully-inclusive rule under-inclusive. The wide penumbra of the principles-based rules can be thought to help, if necessary, to widen the scope of the rule, especially against future innovations, by giving authorities flexibility to intervene in undesired activities if necessary; thus, making creative compliance hard or impossible.[25]

Secondly, the legislator may consciously or sub-consciously think that a more precise norm, if needed, can be crafted in practical, case-by-case

---

22 Schauer makes this distinction referring to differences between rules and standards, see *Schauer*, The Tyranny of Choice and the Rulification of Standards, (2004–2005) 14 J. Contemp. Legal Issues, p. 803 (803–804).

23 *Hart*, 1961, p. 119 and *Endicott*, Vagueness in Law, 2000, p. 8–9.

24 There might be other causes as well, but for the purposes of this article I concentrated on these two.

25 About concepts of under- and over-inclusiveness see *Schauer*, 1991, chapter 2.

situations by subjects, interpreters, or enforcers. Legislators may even think that the actors, who, in practice, apply the law, desire this. However, this idea may be misguided, as legal research suggests that legal actors applying vague or principles-based law, tend to seek for a formulation that is more precise. This phenomena, which Schauer calls "the tyranny of choice," suggests that all legislators accomplish by giving freedom to choose is an excessive workload for the legal actors who, before complying with the law, first have to make an effort to discover what the exact content of the law is, and only after that make the effort to comply with it.[26]

C. Static and Dynamic Compliance with the Rules

The question, which needs to be elaborated further, is the applicability of vague or indeterminate rules in situations where decisions about behavior need to be made beforehand and where the future behavior may or may not, or does not even potentially cause negative effects. In current financial legislation, the actors, who are usually companies, need to generate ways to comply with the demands expressed in the legislation. The problem is, however, that these demands are sometimes presented so vaguely that it cannot be said whether the law applies to a certain situation or not, or so indeterminately that it cannot be said for certainty what it is that the law requires to be done.[27]

The situations in which the rules are applied or meant to be applied vary. First of all, rules may be intended to prevent certain kinds of behavior in advance, or to stipulate certain consequence after a certain action has been done. As an example, some activities may require advance permission or the fulfilling of certain other requirements before they can be performed. Secondly, the situation in which the rule is interpreted may differ, this may occur before the activity is done or after it has been completed. Examples of these are situations where something is prohibited and it must be decided whether the rule will be broken or not, and situations when something has already been done and it must then be decided what kind of legal consequences will follow.

26 *Schauer*, (2004–2005) 14 J. Contemp. Legal Issues, p. 803 (803–814).
27 About definition and difference of concepts vagueness and indeterminacy see *Endicott*, 2000, p. 9.

These two situations somewhat overlap. Prevented behavior may be assessed before or after a certain action has been done and consequences can be estimated before or after an action. In essence, I call 'dynamic compliance' the situation in which actions are required to be evaluated against the rules before they are done and it is not known exactly what is going to happen, and 'static compliance' which is the situation where rules are interpreted and measured against actions after those actions have been done or it is known exactly what will happen. Both of these situations occur in the financial industry; an example of static compliance is the preparing and auditing of companies' financial statements. An example of dynamic compliance are those regulations requiring risk controlling concerning risks which relate to future financial products or contracts that have not yet been invented or entered into, which may or may not create risks that are possible to realize.

Characteristically, static compliance situations are those where there is knowledge, or the possibility of gaining knowledge, concerning the substance of the real life activity that has or will take place. The action will happen (or at least is supposed to happen) in a planned way, or alternatively the action has already taken place. For example, when there is a business transaction and one wishes to know the tax consequences, it might be possible to ask this in advance from the tax authorities. A precise plan is presented and the tax authority makes a legal assessment of the tax consequences of that action, that is, interprets tax rules and what the tax consequences in this particular situation are. Then, the actor proceeds with the case and complies with the specific rule (ruling / interpretation) made by the authority, or does things differently and risks another kind of interpretation. Another case of static compliance is the preparation and audit of financial statements. When financial statements are prepared and audited, every single transaction affecting the statement has already occurred (in certainty or with some uncertainty); as a rule, future events do not have to be taken into account.[28] Auditing, which assures the compliance with accounting rules, is thus also backward looking, comparing past events to financial information compiled and again those to financial reporting rules.

---

28 A considerable exception to this is the accounting impairment of financial assets in IFRS 9 which requires expected losses to be taken into account contrary to its predecessor IAS 39 which required that only those credit losses which were certain in a sense that there was objective evidence of their existence were taken

In dynamic compliance, those situations or actions which are governed by the rules have not yet happened. There may even be uncertainty whether they will ever happen or, if they happen, will they cause any negative results. On the other hand, and what is especially interesting, is the question of whether it matters if negative consequences flow from those actions, as long as the rules are complied with. This may seem like a perverse situation. How is it possible that the rules are being complied with if there are negative consequences of those actions? This situation becomes possible when the matter is looked at from the perspective that future events cannot be fully controlled, but that the purpose of the dynamic compliance rules are that the actor prepares for these, especially negative, future events. This is what brings the financial industry especially into the focus of dynamic compliance regulation. In the most basic sense, banks are supposed to prepare for losses that are expected to occur and insurance companies set aside money to compensate for losses that are, statistically speaking, bound to happen. In both cases, negative consequences are expected and also anticipated to happen as a part of the underlying activities.

What is characteristic for dynamic compliance situations is that decisions are directed into the future, to a situation, event or behavior, which is not known at the time of the decision. To be in compliance requires that the risks associated with these unknown situations, events or behavior are prohibited by the regulations. Often, compliance requires considerable imagination and a question must be presented: What could go wrong? Of course, this question requires information from the following question, "what could go wrong to cause *what*?" What is the thing that should be avoided? This is where the form of the legislation intervenes / intercedes. Does the legislation tell the actor what it is that has to be avoided? Does the regulator express his / her expectations so clearly that the actor knows what it is that it should prevent? If not, then the regulated entity does not know what constitutes a situation where it can be stated, that things have gone wrong in a sense meant by the law. It may create a very hard case for the regulated entity to furnish ways that things go wrong and thus to comply with the rule by trying to prevent those from happening.

---

into account. Otherwise it can be stated that accounting rules are still about recording and presenting financial transactions and events which have happened before audited financial statements are published.

D. Enforcement of Dynamic Compliance

It has been established that dynamic compliance is focused on future activities, the substance of which is still unknown. In the law, it is a question of creating compliance systems, i.e. systems that make sure that ongoing activities are in compliance with the rules.[29] There are thus two perquisites that regulated enterprises need to know before rules can be complied with, that is, what is required by the law. Firstly, what is the end-result that needs to be achieved and secondly, what measures are sufficient to make sure that the end-result is achieved. At least one of the perquisites must be given to the regulated actor before he / she can make decisions about the second. It can be argued that the end-results the legislation is trying to achieve can only be achieved if the necessary sufficient actions are defined, or only if the end-results required by the law are known; thus, sufficient actions can be found to assure that the end-results are achieved.

Enforcement of the rules requires that there is something to enforce and that the enforcer knows what he / she has to enforce. This was a necessary precondition in the traditional 'command and control' regime,[30] but it is still a necessary precondition in all of the so-called 'new governance' regimes. It is not argued that the enforcers should necessarily be the ones to advise on or articulate on the content of the rule. However, there can be negotiations between the regulators and those regulated about the meaning of the rule. It seems to bring a necessary flexibility to the markets that regulated actors can make proposals to the regulators. This often seems to be the leading idea of the Principles-Based Regulation (hereinafter PBR) and other new governance regimes.[31]

---

29 About creating compliance systems see *Parker/Gilad*, Internal corporate compliance management systems: structure, culture and agency, in: Parker/Lehmann Nielsen (eds) Explaining compliance: business responses to regulation, 2011, p. 207.

30 Baldwin, Cave and Lodge define command and control regulation as the exercise of influence by imposing standards backed by criminal sanctions. *Baldwin/Cave/Lodge*, Understanding Regulation: Theory, Strategy, and Practice, 2012, p. 106.

31 About negotiantions as an enforcement strategy see for example *Gunningham*, Strategizing compliance and enforcement: responsive regulation and beyond, in: Parker/Lehmann Nielsen (eds), Explaining compliance: business responses to regulation, 2011, p. 199.

What I argue here, however, is that it cannot be left for regulated actors to decide what the content of the law is. In such cases, the result would be that compliance systems should make sure that rules are in compliance with ongoing activities and not the other way around. If the regulated actors decide what the achieved end-results should be and how they are to be achieved, there is little left for the regulator to enforce since it can be argued that if the end-results cannot be achieved with the actions decided by the regulated, the regulated will just makes changes to their end-results, making them fit with the existing actions.[32]

Of course, a counter argument can be given that when regulators accept the end-results or the measures that assure the achievement of those end-results, they cannot be changed afterwards.[33] However, this raises the question of whether it will lead to a situation where the bar is initially set as low as possible by the regulated so that it is easily achievable.[34] Thus, the regulators must give their final word about what measures need to be taken or what the end-results are in a form that is as transparent, accessible, and congruent as possible.[35]

---

32 Of course this could easily violate mutual trust of firms doing their best to comply with the spirit of the rule for there to be close engagement between the regulator and the regulated. Mutual trust is what Black has suggested to be needed as one point for PBR to work. See *Black*, Forms and Paradoxes of Principles Based Regulation, (2008) 13 Law, Society and Economy Working Paper, p. 1 (3–4).

33 Which would be the approach suggested by an enforced self-regulation regime.

34 In legal literature, quite the opposite has been suggested, that vague rules would lead to conservative behavior because of the uncertainty as to what the enforcers will accept. See *Black*, (2008) 13 Law, Society and Economy Working Paper, p. 1 (4) and *Schwarcz*, The Principles Paradox, (2009) 10 European Business Organization Law Review (hereinafter EBOR), p. 175 (175–184). I understand the expression 'conservative' to mean that the regulated chooses that option (among all possible options) to apply the law, which most probably will be interpreted to be in compliance with the law. In this case, the enforcer has wide discretion to give a rulings on the content, whenever ever he feels it necessary. This clearly would lead to a situation where the desired flexibility of the principles-based formulation would be lost and thus at least this potential purpose of the legislation would be undermined. If the discretion of the authority is narrower it gives possibilities for the regulated to undermine the legislation by setting the bar for compliance lower.

35 According to Diver, trade-offs have to be made between the transparency, accessibility, and congruency of the rule and thus it cannot be said that the form

E. Dynamic Compliance with the Rules

Enforcement of compliance has been the focus of legal discussion for decades. In the early 1980s, Bardach and Kagan conducted wide research on regulation, including different enforcement styles and incorporating multiple views on regulation, enforcement, and the conduct of parties towards the regulation.[36] Ever since, the regulatory debate has been ongoing, producing different kinds of regulatory regimes. These range from the Responsive Regulation of Ayres and Braithwaite[37] to the Smart-Regulation of Gunningham and Sinclair,[38] and from the Principles-Based Regulation of Julia Black[39] to the Meta-Regulation of Christine Parker,[40] The difference compared to traditional command and control regulation is that in these later enforcement regimes the old fashioned investigations, which found infringements with the rules and punished every actor equally, are substituted with more subtle approaches. In these regimes, the regulator tries to take account of differences in the regulated actors when enforcing the rules, or tries to enforce the legislation in co-operation with the regulated enterprises; the regulator can also choose to let the regulated actor do the work by choosing and taking measures which would best serve the achievement of the regulatory goals, or by using a mixture of these methods.[41] What is common

---

must be transparent, accessible, and congruent in absolute terms. See *Diver*, (1983) 93 The Yale Law Journal, p. 65.

36 *Bardach/Kagan*, Going by the Book: The Problem of Regulatory Unreasonableness, 1982.

37 *Ayres/Braithwaite*, Responsive Regulation: Transcending the Deregulation Debate, 1992.

38 *Gunningham/Sinclair*, Designing Smart Regulation (abridged version), available at: https://www.oecd.org/env/outreach/33947759.pdf (visited 23.03.2017).

39 *Black*, (2008) 13 Law, Society and Economy Working Paper.

40 *Parker*, Meta-Regulation: Legal Accountability for Corporate Social Responsibility?, in: McBarnet/Voiculescu/Campbell (eds), The New Corporate Accountability: Corporate Social Responsibility and the Law, 2007, p. 207. These writers are not the only ones who have been writing about these subjects. I have selected them and examples of their written production as good representatives of researchers of these subjects. Another notion is, that these regimes have multiple dimensions and thus cannot be put into a single group for comparison.

41 Black states, concerning meta-regulation, (this technique is also called, in the literature, management based regulation, enforced self-regulation or regulation of the firm's own self-regulation,) that "under this regime regulators do not pre-

to all of these regimes seems to be the assumption that regulation can be enforced, in other words, that enforcement is possible. This assumption, however, requires that compliance with the rules can be measured or assessed some way.

While considering the enforcement of principles-based regulations, my argument is that principles-based rules may not be enforced as such, not without giving a more precise content for the rules. I separate here two ways how the content of the rules may be clarified and how these clarifications can be used to make the rules enforceable. The content can be stated positively or negatively. In the first case, the regulator clearly states what is meant by the regulation by describing, for example, the accepted ways of conduct or measures which are deemed sufficient or stating a clear threshold which cannot be exceeded. The second case, the negative statement, is also a way to give an opinion of the content of the rule. An example of this is the regulator's decision that the manner in which the regulated is trying to achieve the regulatory purposes is not sufficient. Of course, by doing this, the regulator is enforcing the regulation *negatively*, that is, not by stating what *the content of the rule is*, but by saying what *the content of the rule is not*.

What is noted here, is that this kind of negative enforcement may still work in a static compliance situation where, as stated above, it is known what has happened or what will happen. In this kind of situation, the regulated party may still draft a new proposal, obtain external expert opinions, produce their own argumentation and, if necessary, contest the authority's opinion in a court of law. This can be done, since the decision made by the authority can also be reflected in the facts and legal argumentation. However, in a dynamic compliance situation, when it is not known what will happen, there is a need for precise knowledge as to what the law requires for compliance with the legislation, or its enforcement. This means that either the goal of the rule or the exact measures that ought to be taken are known. If both the goals and measures, as presented in the law, are or remain unknown, then at least a positive opinion of the content of the rule

---

scribe how regulatees should comply but require them to develop their own systems for compliance and to demonstrate that compliance to the regulator," *Black*, Paradoxes and Failures: "New Governance" Techniques and the Financial Crisis, (2012) 75 The Modern Language Review, p. 1037 (1045).

must be given for either one and a negative opinion for the other before these can be compared even to a hypothetical set of facts.[42]

Principles-based regulations may work in situations where there is a possibility of a liability claim caused by the failure to reach the goals the principles-based rules have laid down.[43] In these situations, it is always possible for an organization to think more concretely about how such a liability might be realized and to choose actions to avoid the liability.[44] However, it is a completely different matter to try to think how to comply when the negative consequences are not even foreseeable. This may be either because all the possible future events cannot be thought of or because the risks are there as an inherent nature of business and cannot be specified as precise hazards that are easy to prepare for. If the risks are inherent to the business, they cannot be totally or even materially eliminated without making the business itself impossible. As a prime example, I present insurance risks. An insurance company cannot eliminate the risks it is facing since the essence of the business is to carry those risks on behalf of insurance policy holders.

A proposition that precise legal rules should be given by the regulator is not a straight forward and easy answer, since, as it has been argued in legal literature, precise and specific rules provide actors with options to circumvent the legislation with creative compliance.[45] What can be said is that more clear instructions are needed for each specific situation so as to know what is meant by the rules, to know which ought to be followed, and to

---

42 It would be fairly fruitless to enforce, for example, a principles-based rule stating "The undertaking must take sufficient measures to assure that customers receive enough information." What is the decision and on what grounds? Either one of the prerequisites 'sufficient measures' or 'enough information' should be defined more precisely and the other negatively before any enforcement measures can be taken.

43 Schwarcz argues that the possibility of liability might make the regulated parties choose more conservative interpretations of the rules to avoid liability. See *Schwarcz*, (2009) 10 EBOR, p. 175.

44 The concept of avoiding the liability refers to window-dressing where the compliance systems are only made for cosmetic reasons on purpose to show supervisory authorities or courts that the rules are being followed. About this kind of behavior see *Krawiec*, Cosmetic compliance and the failure of negotiated governance, (2003) 81 Washington University Law Quarterly, p. 487 (487–544).

45 Creative compliance where the rules underlying purpose are evaded can also be called 'literal compliance with laws technical letter.' See *Cunningham*, (2007) 127 Boston College Law School Research Paper, p. 1 (11).

know whether the rules are applicable to the situation at all. It is a matter of debate whether these kinds of instructions or guidance constitute a formal legal norm or not. It is suggested in enforcement literature that the regulator and the regulated could solve the situation through negotiations.[46] In my view, the content of legal rules cannot be a part of negotiations which only leaves the concrete facts open, not if we consider legal rules as being general and thus applicable same way in every situation with the same characteristics. However, it must be noted that when the rule is vague and its vagueness is due to the fact that the 'triggering events' are not known, the regulator would, in practice, have to negotiate about the rule itself. When an authority gives its opinion on some legal matter, it should naturally be understood from instruction or guidance that the opinion is binding; otherwise this would result in no better situation than in the beginning.

F. Conclusion

As a conclusion, it can be argued that especially in the case of principles-based rules, in particular situations, it remains fairly unclear whether the rule has been followed or not. This may happen when it is not known what the rule means as regards the given facts for that particular situation. Will the facts of the case trigger the application of the rule or not? Even more difficult is the situation in which these vague rules are required to be obeyed before the possible rule-triggering event has occurred or is exactly known. If the non-compliance with the rules comes as a surprise to the regulated entity, there might be questions raised about the arbitrary nature of the regulation. This may occur when the regulated entity believes that it has completed the required actions to comply with the rule. One example of this would be a situation where it is afterwards stated that there is a duty to apply a certain rule to a certain activity that was believed to be exempted from the scope of the rule. A second example is a situation where the regulator demands the regulated to apply a rule in certain way that was not stipulated

46 See *Gunningham*, in: Parker/Lehmann Nielsen, p. 199.

beforehand.[47] These situations may create legal disputes or overall uncertainty about whether other rules have been (sufficiently) complied with or not. To avoid these situations and to create legal certainty it would thus require that the regulator provides the final word on the precise content of the rule. This is a necessary condition without which especially dynamic compliance with the rules or the enforcement of the rules may not be possible.[48]

Bibliography

Ian Ayres and John Braithwaite, *Responsive Regulation: Transcending the Deregulation Debate* (Oxford University Press, New York 1992)

Robert Baldwin, Martin Cave and Martin Lodge, *Understanding Regulation: Theory, Strategy, and Practice* (2nd Edition, Oxford University Press, New York 2012)

Eugene Bardach and Robert A. Kagan, *Going by the Book: The Problem of Regulatory Unreasonableness* (Temple Universsity Press, Philadelphia 1982)

Julia Black 'Forms and Paradoxes of Principles Based Regulation' (2008) 13 Law, Society and Economy Working Paper, 1

Julia Black, 'Paradoxes and Failures: "New Governance" Techniques and the Financial Crisis' (2012) 75 The Modern Language Review, 1037

Julia Black, 'The Rise, Fall and Fate of Principles Based Regulation' (2010) 17 Law, Society and Economy Working Paper, 1

Lawrence A. Cunningham, 'A Prescription to Retire the Rhetoric of "Principles-Based Systems" in Corporate Law, Securities Regulation and Accounting' (2007) 127 Boston College Law School Research Paper, 1

Colin S. Diver, 'The Optimal Precision of Administrative Rules' (1983) 93 The Yale Law Journal, 65

Ronald Dworkin, 'The Model of Rules' (1967) 35 The University of Chicago Law Review, 14

Timothy A. O. Endicott, *Vagueness in Law* (Oxford University Press, New York 2000)

Neil Gunningham, 'Strategizing compliance and enforcement: responsive regulation and beyond' in Christine Parker and Vibeke Lehmann Nielsen (eds), *Explaining compliance: business responses to regulation* (Edward Elgar Publishing, Northampton 2011), 199

47 In these situations the rule does not state what is required to be done to be in compliance. The measures taken may or may not be in compliance with the rule. There simply is no way of knowing.

48 The question of how to communicate more precise content for the rule, and the problems this might entail, is left for further research.

Neil Gunningham and Sinclair Darren, 'Designing Smart Regulation' (abridged version), at: https://www.oecd.org/env/outreach/33947759.pdf (visited 5.02.2016)

H. L. A. Hart, *The Concept of Law* (1st Edition, Clarendon Press, Oxford 1961)

Kimberly D. Krawiec, 'Cosmetic compliance and the failure of negotiated governance' (2003) 81 Washington University Law Quarterly, 487

Christine Parker, 'Meta-Regulation: Legal Accountability for Corporate Social Responsibility?' in Doreen McBarnet, Aurora Voiculescu and Tom Campbell (eds), *The New Corporate Accountability: Corporate Social Responsibility and the Law* (Cambridge University Press, Cambridge 2007), 207

Christine Parker and Sharon Gilad, 'Internal corporate compliance management systems: structure, culture and agency' in Christine Parker and Vibeke Lehmann Nielsen (eds), *Explaining compliance: business responses to regulation* (Edward Elgar Publishing, Northampton 2011), 207

Joseph Raz, 'Legal Principles and the Limits of Law' (1972) 81 The Yale Law Journal, 823

Frederick Schauer, 'Exceptions' (1991) 58 The University of Chicago Law Review, 871

Frederick Schauer, 'On the Open Texture of Law' (SSRN, 2011), at: https://ssrn.com/abstract=1926855 or http://dx.doi.org/10.2139/ssrn.1926855 (visited 11.05.2016)

Frederick Schauer, *Playing by the Rules: A Philosophical Examination of Rule-Based Decision Making in Law and in Life* (Clarendon Press, Oxford 1991)

Frederick Schauer, 'The Tyranny of Choice and the Rulification of Standards' (2004–2005) 14 J. Contemp. Legal Issues, 803

Steven L. Schwarcz, 'The Principles Paradox' (2009) 10 European Business Organization Law Review, 175

Takis Tridimas, The General Principles of EU Law (2nd Edition, Oxford University Press, Oxford, New York 2006)

Friedrich Waismann, 'Verifiability' (1945) 19 Proceedings of the Aristotelian Society, 119

The Principle of Non-Retroactivity and Its Application to Administrative Decisions

Henriette Nilsson Tøssebro

A. *Introduction*

It is not an easy task to describe the phenomenon of 'retroactivity' in law. One specification, which is possibly the most prevalent, is that retroactive laws entail the application of a new law that is adopted, sanctioned and announced *after* a legal position is established or realised in action. This is, for instance, the case when a person is penalised for the infringement of a new criminal provision which did not exist when the action was performed, or when a person according to a new regulation is required to pay back financial support which were lawfully granted prior to the new law. These examples may be considered cases of retroactivity in a strict or narrow sense – cases of so-called 'true' retroactivity.[1] As a general rule, such retroactivity of law is forbidden.[2]

Another account of 'retroactivity', commonly found in legal literature, is when a new law interferes with the *future exercise* of an established legal position. This may, for instance, be the case when a new law lessens or abolishes a right to social benefits, or sets new or more stringent criteria for the conduct of trade. These examples may be regarded in the broad sense of

---

1 See the Norwegian Supreme Court cases available at: www.lovdata.no using the reference numbers Rt-1996-1415; Rt-1996-1440; Rt-2007-1281; Rt-2007-1306; Rt-2010-143. A synonym of 'true' retroactivity is *ex post*-regulation, see *Smith*, Konstitusjonelt demokrati, 2015, p. 492. Another synonym is 'direct' retroactive effect.

2 See parts B and C below. This rule follow explicit from the Constitution of Norway § 97. See also the Supreme Court cases HR-2016-389-A (para. 76), Rt-2013-1345 (para. 84) and Rt-2010-143 (para. 153).

retroactivity – cases of so-called 'false' retroactivity.[3] Such retroactivity of law is generally permitted.[4]

If the principle of non-retroactivity is said to cover both cases of 'true' and 'false' retroactivity, we can see that the principle covers any changes of a normative character that have an effect on the past in addition to the future. There is, however, such striking differences between the two types of retroactivity, which allows them to be treated as two different rules. These rules will be further investigated in what follows.

Through an examination of different legal and structural arguments, I will propose a new view to perceive the principle of retroactivity. It will be suggested in this article that the principle, at least in a Norwegian legal context, has a different content and scope of application than generally supposed. The main findings of this article may be summarised as follows:

i) The two component types of retroactivity, 'true' and 'false' retroactivity, invoke a different assessment and have a disparate threshold for application. Also, different exceptions apply. Altogether, this gives reason to treat 'true' and 'false' retroactivity as two different rules under the retroactivity principle. The substantial characteristics of these rules will be examined in parts B and C.

ii) There is a significant difference between the underlying rationale for 'true' and 'false' retroactivity. While a *prohibition* against giving laws 'true' retroactive effect is founded upon fundamental notions of availability and predictability of law, a *permission* to give 'false' retroactive law is based on the constitutional powers and chief function of making new law. I will elaborate this further in part D.

iii) There is, possibly, a misconstrued link between the two types of retroactivity and the particular features of each legal case. In part E, I will argue that the types of retroactivity must be treated as virtually independent from the particular features of the case; whether the subject-matter is an accomplished action or an established right.

---

3 This may also be called "indirect retroactive effect". This terminology is employd in the EU Court case *Westzucker GmbH v. Einfuhr- und Vorratsstelle für Zucker*, 4 July 1973, Case C-1/73, ECR 1973-00723 (on p. 727).

4 In Norwegian law, this follows from the Supreme Court decision in Rt-1922-624 where it was held that the state authorities have the discretion to bring to an end different sorts of business activities. See also Rt-1996-1415, Rt-1910-174 and LB-2000-325. See also *Lie*, Domstolene og Grunnloven, 1923, p. 55.

iv) There is a close relationship between laws of a 'false' retroactive character on the one hand and the right to compensation for state interference on the other. A possible conceptualisation is that 'false' retroactive law is allowed under the retroactivity principle, but the constitutional ban on state interference will provide a legal basis for compensation for such law. This finding will be discussed in part F, in which a selection of constitutional principles will be presented and compared.

v) In the final part, part G, I will reject the perception that the retroactivity ban can only be applicable to statutory rules and regulations. With certain reservations, the retroactivity principle must also apply to individually drafted administrative decisions that are binding and are made in the role of public authority.

Notwithstanding the fact that a principle of retroactivity is enshrined in many national, bilateral and international legal systems, my main focus will be given to Norwegian constitutional law. On the assumption that the retroactivity ban is uniform in character and similar in content, it is nevertheless my aspiration that the Norwegian legal concept may shed light to equivalent principles in other legal systems.

B. The Distinction between 'True' and 'False' Retroactivity

A principle of retroactivity existed as early as in Roman law,[5] and is still persistent in a number of legal systems.[6] Though the principle typically is devised to govern criminal provisions,[7] it is occasionally also implemented

5 *Aschehoug*, Norges nuværede statsforfatning, 1893, p. 83, with reference to L. 1, Cod. 1-17.

6 See, for example, the Brazilian Constitution Section XXXVI Article 5; the United States Constitution Article I, Section 9; and the French Code Civil Article 2.

7 See the Swedish Constitution, the Instrument of Government Chapter 2 Article 10, which prescribes that "[n]o one may be sentenced to a penalty or penal sanction for an act which was not subject to a penal sanction at the time it was committed" (my translation). See also the Canadian Charter of Rights and Freedoms Section 11 (g); the French Penal Code Article 112-1; the German Grundgesetz-für die Bundesrepublik Deutschland Article 103; the Italian Constitution Article 25. In Norwegian law, it is commonly assumed that the retroactivity ban has its main application in criminal cases, see e.g. Rt-2006-293 (para. 61) and Rt-2010-1445 (paras. 87 and 96).

to cover legal provisions in general. One example is provided in § 97 of the Norwegian Constitution, which stipulates that "no statutory law may be given retroactive effect."

In one of the draft versions of the Norwegian Constitution, it was explicitly asserted that "no one shall be held guilty of a criminal offence *which was not published when the action was committed*" (my emphasis).[8] In a comment on the adopted provision, a Norwegian professor in law, Aschehoug, clarified that the provision was violated if the new law "came into force from a date and time preceding the law's preparation."[9] One may consequently assume that the Constitutional provision was originally directed towards statutory law of a 'true' retroactive character.

However, subsequent to the adoption of the Constitution, the provision was further advanced by Castberg, a Norwegian legal scholar of the 20th century. In a book on retroactivity from 1920, he claimed that the ban implied a twofold protection: i) New laws must not attach new burdens to older actions or omissions, and ii) New laws must not interfere with the citizens' individually-vested rights.[10] This distinction, which arguably

---

8 See *Lie*, 1923, p. 56 referring to the Adler-Falsen's draft of the Constitution. It is worth noting that in some statutory regulations this notion is made more explicit: the Norwegian Criminal Code § 3 prescribes that the "penal provisions that are *effective at the time of the committed crime* shall be applied" (my translation and emphasis).

9 *Aschehoug*, 1893, p. 87. This narrow interpretation of the provision can also be found in recent case law. In the dissenting opinion of the Supreme Court judge Skoghøy in Rt-2010-1445, it was expressed that "it must be regarded as a violation of § 97 of the Constitution to impose more severe punishment than the law prescribes at the time of the crime." With reference to cases Rt-2002-889 (p. 890) and Rt-2004-306 (para. 23), the judge continued: "It must be considered as established law that § 97 does not impede the application of statutory law which is enacted *after* the act was committed insofar as this law is not stricter," see para. 140 (my translation and emphasis).

10 *Castberg*, Grunnlovens forbud mot å gi lover tilbakevirkende kraft, 1920, p. 51. This distinction was followed by Morgenstierne who interpreted the retroactivity ban in § 97 of the Constitution in a way that prohibits the law-giving authorities from intervening in citizens' legal positions so that vested rights were lost or curtailed, see *Morgenstierne*, Lærebok i den norskestatsforfatningsret, 1927, p. 396–397. The same distinction is made in *Fleischer*, Grunnlovens § 97, (1975) Jussens Venner, p. 183 (190 ff.). As identified by Hartley, this position raises a new question: what, exactly, is a «vested right»? See *Hartley*, The foundations of European Union Law, 2014, p. 163. One possible conception is that

amounts to the designated specifications of 'true' and 'false' retroactivity, has later been read implicitly in § 97 of the Norwegian Constitution. Both in court practice and legal theory, the provision is said to cover retroactivity in a 'true' and 'false' sense.[11]

The principle of non-retroactivity has since been extensively debated in legal literature, but the purpose of this article is not to give an in-depth analysis of these theoretical discussions. I will confine my analysis to the general retroactivity ban found in § 97 of the Norwegian Constitution, which has been given much consideration in court practice. Since case law gives a variety of examples on the distinction between 'true' and 'false' retroactivity, this material provides a more complete description of the ban's precise content in practice.

Whether a law is retroative in a 'true' or 'false' sense is dependent on two correlated factors: the time from which the law takes effect in combination with the adoption, sanction and public announcement of the law in order to become binding.[12] If the law is given effect *prior* to the adoption, sanction and public announcement of the law, it is better to consider the law as a case of 'true' retroactivity. If the law is given effect *after* these points

---

an interference to a vested right amounts to an interference equal to expropriation – which is illegal according to § 105 of the Constitution unless damages are given, cfr. part F below.

11 See footnotes 1 to 4.

12 It may be problematized whether the date of Parliament's adoption, the King's sanction or the public announcement of the law should be decisive for whether the issue is one of 'true' rather than 'false' retroactivity. The answer to this question will most certainly vary from one legal system to another, depending on the underlying notions for normativity, such as – but not restricted to – the degree of popular sovereignty, availability and predictability of law.
In Norway, an Act must be adopted by the Parliament, sanctioned by the King and then published in public, see §§ 77 to 78 of the Norwegian Constitution and §§ 1 and 3 of the Norwegian Law Reports Act. In *Smith*, 2015, p. 419, it is argued that the date of public announcement must be decisive even though the notion of predictability is ensured already by the date of the proposition. By the same token, § 39 of the Norwegian Public Administration Act states that an administrative regulation that is not announced at the time it is invoked may only be applied to persons who knew about the regulation.

in time, the issue will normally be considered as a case of 'false' retroactivity. From what date a new law takes legal effect may follow from the statutory instrument itself. [13]

It is important to note that the date of adoption, sanction or public announcement of an Act do not provide an instant answer to the question about when the law takes legal effect; they merely show from what time one can ascertain the principle of legal certainty or the citizens' legitimate expectations. The one and the same new law that are given legal effect from a specific period of time may thus be retroactive both in a 'true' and 'false' sense; governing both subject-matters before and subsequent to the adoption, sanction and public announcement of the law.[14]

One example of 'true' retroactivity is the Supreme Court decision in Rt-2006-293. In this case, a driving school owner had invested in a car to be used in his business. When the car was purchased in 2001, the owner was entitled to tax deduction. However, subsequent legislative changes, effective from 2002, required the owner to return the amount that was received as a tax relief. The Supreme Court found that the new provisions violated the constitutional ban on retroactivity. As the new taxation rules did not exist at the time of investment, the case may be considered an example of 'true' retroactivity.[15]

Another example of the retroactivity principle, now in its 'false' sense, is provided by the Supreme Court decision in Rt-1910-181. In this case, a local city council had decided that wine merchants could not sell wine on weekdays after 17:00. Previously, they were allowed to sell wine until 20:00. The Supreme Court found that the Council's decision involved a substantial interference with the merchant's right to sell wine, and this

---

13 For instance, according to § 26-1 of the Norwegian National Insurance Act, the Act comes into force on the 1st of May 1997. The Act was discussed and passed in the Parliament the 13th and 20th February 1997, and the King's sanction was given on the 28th same month. In cases where the statutory instrument itself does not govern the date when the law takes effect, a general rule may be provided by general legislation. According to § 3 of the Norwegian Law Reports Act, statutory rules will normally take effect one month after the law has been published in the Law Report Book.

14 The 'double' application of law raises difficulties when it comes to ongoing actions. In such cases, the action could be divided into two; the first part of the action as a case of 'true' retroactivity, whereas the second part will be one of 'false' retroactivity. This is, however, not a common perception in legal literature and case law.

15 See para. 49.

interference amounted to a breach of the retroactivity ban. Arguably, this case could be considered as an example of 'false' retroactivity, since the law was made effective for the future exercise of a legal position.

C. Exceptions to the Prohibition and Permission to Give Retroactive Laws

It was shown above that any statutory law that is given effect *prior* to the law's adoption, sanction or public announcement, may be regarded as cases of 'true' retroactivity. Such retroactivity is prohibited by the principle of non-retroactivity, and such law will thus not be given effect to the facts of a specific case.

In case law, an exception has been made to this prohibition by reason of "strong public considerations."[16] Additionally, an exemption is made for minor changes to substantive law.[17] The 'true' retroactive application of new laws is further accepted in cases of calculation of taxes and for procedural rules.[18]

Conversely, the 'false' retroactive application of law is as a main rule permitted. This means, to make clear, that any changes in law that are given effect *after* the adoption, sanction or public announcement of a law are generally applicable to the facts of a specific case.

The permission to give law 'false' retroactive effect is, however, limited by a narrow but important restriction. In a recent case decided by the Supreme Court, 'false' retroactive laws were regarded as inapplicable when such laws were "clearly unreasonable or unfair."[19] In Rt-1996-1415, it was

---

16 Rt-2010-143 (para. 154). See also Rt-2005-855.

17 See Rt-1949-224. In this case, the Supreme Court held that the new legislative rules were not contrary to the retroactivity ban; the rules in question were of a "more remote character".

18 On supplementary taxation, see Rt-1928-452, Rt-1976-1245 and Rt-2006-293. Note that substantive changes to the taxation rules may be contrary to the retroactive ban, see Rt-2005-855. On procedural rules, see Rt-2012-519 (para. 89), Rt-2014-1105 (para. 64) and HR-2016-644-A (para. 28).

19 Rt-2013-1345, Rt-2006-262 and Rt-1996-1440, referring to a verdict in Rt-1996-1415. In Rt-1996-1415, the Supreme Court judge Tjomsland held that it could not be excluded that in 'extreme cases' changes in law could be made which were of such a character that the citizens were protected by the § 97 of

asserted that this standard depends "upon time and changing social conditions."[20] Given the fact that most new laws are made to govern changes in society, the threshold to let the exception apply is high. Hence, in Rt-2007-1281, the 'false' retroactive application of a statutory provision was accepted by the Supreme Court because the provision was based upon a new and clear need to protect the leaseholders.[21]

In summary, there is a striking resemblance between the assessment of both 'true' and 'false' retroactivity. Both rules with their exceptions invite a broad, discretionary judgment by the court. However, their differences are greater than their similarities. This is particularly clear with regard to the threshold for lawful retroactivity, which is set at a different level for each one of the two component types. As I will elaborate in the following part D, this is given the underlying rationale: In cases of 'true' retroactivity, the law is non-existent, while in cases of 'false' retroactivity, the individuals are able to act on a statutory basis that can be known to them.

D. *The Underlying Rationale of 'True' and 'False' Retroactivity*

Law would lose much of its legitimacy if it could be applied prior to the date when it was passed into existence.[22] If binding norms are used as in-

---

the Constitution. It is worth noting that a similar assessment was made on the citizens' right to compensation for state expropriation under § 105 of the Constitution, see Rt-2007-1308 (paras. 61 and 69). See also the Supreme Court decision in Rt-1973-405, where the listing of a salmon river was not regarded as inconsistent with the retroactivity ban, regardless of the fact that it involved substantial interference with the parties' rights.

It should be added that different labels have been used on this exception. In earlier case law, it was said that it was not permissible to give a rule 'false' retroactive effect if the infringed right was of 'significant importance' to the party, see Rt-1890-455. Further, in Rt-1996-1415, the dissenting Supreme Court judge Schei argued that the retroactivity ban only made a restriction on 'false' retroactive law that was "qualified or manifestly unreasonable or unfair."

20 On p. 1436–1437 (my translation). See also Rt-2013-1345, Rt-2006-262 and Rt-1996-1440.

21 Para. 121.

22 See *Lie*, 1923, p. 56, which refers to a draft version of the Norwegian Constitution: "[r]etroactive law (effectum retroactivum) is unfair."

struments to direct individuals' choice of action, it must be a necessary precondition that these norms are available to those they apply to. Obviously, it is difficult to act as required by law if one is deprived of the possibility to know its content.[23] Prior to a law's existence, one might only have a vague expectation or assumption about the lawmaker's own acknowledgment of right and wrong behaviour.[24] By and large, this acknowledgment is already delineated through the existing law. One would therefore expect that any legal changes should take effect from a date subsequent to the date when the laws were made known. This is the underlying rationale for the prohibition to give 'true' retroactive laws.

The argument that it is impossible to act in accordance with non-existent statutory law is, possibly, an argument that is restricted to cases where the legal position is distinct and clear. Conventionally this is, however, the exception rather than the rule. Modern legislation is frequently embossed with vague and ambiguous wording which is less likely to allow for legitimate assumptions about the true content of law. The defining line between retroactive 'true' and 'false' law may therefore be difficult to determine.[25] Accordingly, much law is potentially applicable in a retroactive 'true' sense in addition to being applicable in its 'false' sense.

There is an interesting counter-argument against the notion of availability that runs as follows: In certain legal provisions, it is stated that the rules of law apply regardless of whether it is known to the parties of the case – the principle of *ignorantia juris non excusat.* In Norwegian law, one example is provided in § 26 of the Criminal Code 2005, which stipulates that a person will be held responsible for committing a crime if his unawareness of the law was negligent.[26] It is possible to argue that 'true' retroactive provisions are pushing the principle of *ignorantia juris non excusat* a little further, as 'true' retroactive law is clearly unknown.[27]

---

23 See e.g. *Austin*, Lectures on jurisprudence or the philosophy of positive law, 1911, p. 485. See also LB-2013-81182.

24 *Fuller*, Morality of law, 1965, p. 39 and 103.

25 See Rt-1924-18 on p. 22–23, where it was held that a discretionary tax burden was to be considered as retroactive law. This problem, however, is to some extent remedied by the implied requirement of clarity in law, see Rt-2010-1445 (paras. 84–85).

26 Note also Rt-1937-42, where the Supreme Court held that new statutory regulations, which were not yet published in the Law Report Book, were nevertheless binding on the convicted person. See also Rt-1945-26.

27 *Kelsen*, General theory of law and state, 1945, p. 43–44, 73, 146, 149.

It is, however, worth noting a possible obstacle to this reasoning. The principle of ignorance of law is normally restricted to *negligent* ignorance, and evidently, the citizen is not negligent if the law is non-existent. Thus, it stands to reason that the principle of *ignorantia juris non excusat* simply underlines the point that a legal rule must be available in order to have legal effect.

The underlying rationale is different in cases of 'false' retroactivity. Where such laws are generally permitted, this must be so by reason of Parliament's legislative powers. If there was no opportunity for the lawgiving authorities to make disadvantageous changes in future laws, the retroactivity ban would form an exceptionally strong binding on the legislative authorities. As recognized by Judge Tjomsland in Rt-1996-1415, one can assume that the operative law is subject to changes in the political compositions or new social needs.[28] The mere expectation of a stable and unchanged law is in itself not protected from subsequent legal changes under the principle of non-retroactivity.

However, the mere expectations of the citizens can, as we have seen, bring about a compelling reason for *not* giving statutory law 'false' retroactive effect in certain circumstances.[29] The citizens ought to be positioned to predict their legal status, and this gives the underlying rationale for a narrow exception.[30] As it was observed in the previous section, 'false' retroactive law is permitted, but an exception will apply when such retroactive law is "clearly unreasonable or unfair."

---

28 See p. 1435. See also Rt-2010-143, where the Supreme Court judge Matningsdal held in a dissenting opinion that the Parliament had wide competences to make new tax rules according to § 75a of the Constitution – irrespective of the Constitutional ban on retroactive laws (see para. 198).

29 In a recent case on 'false' retroactivity, the Supreme Court gave much weight to a party's legitimate expectations, see Rt-2013-1345. Note also Rt-1979-1279, where the claimant stored used cars and other scrap on his private property. Subsequent to the enactment of § 16 of the Nature Conservation Act, the claimant was asked by the state authorities to remove the objects. The claimant objected on grounds of the retroactivity ban, but the argument was rejected by the Supreme Court.

30 See *Castberg*, 1920, p. 51. This degree of predictability will necessarily vary depending on the statutory wording. See, for instance, § 18-11 of the National Insurance Act stipulates that the rights conferred by this Act "can be revised, limited or repealed through subsequent statutory laws."

E. On 'True' and 'False' Retroactivity and the Distinction between Actions and Rights

The discussion so far has relied on a distinction between 'true' and 'false' retroactivity, with 'true' retroactivity being prohibited and 'false' retroactivity allowed.[31] Although this appears simple and straightforward, further analysis reveals bigger complexity. This is particularly clear when the subject matter of the case is taken into account.

In certain court cases, the distinction between 'true' and 'false' retroactivity is phrased in the following terms: If the new law is applied to an *accomplished action*, it is regarded as a case of 'true' retroactivity. If the new law interferes with an *established legal position*, it is considered a case of 'false' retroactivity. This description was most recently employed by the Supreme Court in Rt-2013-1345, where 'true' retroactivity was said to cover the situations in which "new burdens were directly put to older *actions which were completed*," while 'false' retroactivity was meant to protect the "existing and future exercise of *legal positions*."[32]

There is undoubtedly a close relationship between the distinction of 'true' and 'false' retroactivity on the one hand and the distinction of actions and legal positions on the other. Among other factors, a person is more likely to be convicted for an accomplished action that infringes a new law, than for the omission of taking full advantage of the opportunity offered by the preceding law. When an individual has carried out an action, he has *ipso facto* infringed a 'true' retroactive provision *if* the retroactive rule is made applicable. This is, with the exception of crimes of omission, not the case if a legal right or duty is *not* brought out in action. Though a legal position may provide a legal ground for action, it also protects the freedom to act without the risk of sanctions. At this point, administrative law converges from criminal law, as the 'true' retroactive provisions in administrative law is normally meant to regulate legal positions, while criminal provisions are normally directed towards actions that violate law. The subject matter of the case may consequently be of guiding character to show the differences between the retroactivity principle in respectively administrative law and criminal law. Despite that, the distinction may be rather misleading if the intention is to demonstrate the principle's general scope of application; as we have seen, the principle will apply to both actions and legal positions.

---

31 See section A.

32 Para. 82 (my emphasis).

Additionally, it is doubtful whether there is a compelling need for more rigid rules to protect actions as opposed to legal positions. In my view, the need for protection seem to be much more dependent on the character of the legal sanction embodied in the new law, and not on whether the subject-matter of a specific case is one of 'actions' rather than 'rights' or 'duties'.

In sum, the distinction between 'actions' and 'legal positions' gives little, if any, indication of the type of retroactivity in question. Instead, this misconstrued relationship undermines the peculiarity between the prohibition to give 'true' retroactive laws and the permission to give 'false' retroactive laws. A retroactivity principle, both in a 'true' and a 'false' sense, must be said to cover all these different cases of normative or factual character: a performed action, an established right or duty, or any other legal position.

F. The Retroactivity Ban and its Correlation with Other Constitutional Principles

The year 2014 was notable in Norwegian legal history. This year the Norwegian Constitution turned 200 years. The anniversary was commemorated by extensive changes to the Constitution itself. A new chapter and nine provisions were introduced, and substantial linguistic modifications were made to the existing sections.[33] In point of fact, so many fundamental changes were made, that it is discussable whether it is still the same legislative instrument.

As it stands today, the Norwegian Constitution provides the individual a wide-ranging 'book of rights' to protect him or her from the state's abuse of authority. This includes constraints on Parliament's law-making power. An important provision in this regard is § 113, which stipulates that any state interference to the detriment of the individual must have a legal basis in statutory law. In legal theory, this provision is recognised as a principle of legality.

From the principle of legality one could assume that any kind of state interference to the detriment of the citizens would be constitutional *if* the

33 The linguistic modifications include the introduction of an additional version of the Constitution in the second official language 'nynorsk'. See Parliament's report (p. 49) available at: https://www.stortinget.no/no/Grunnlovsjubileet/ (visited 23.03.2017).

interference had a statutory basis. This would, however, be a hasty conclusion. Many statutory rules that are of an interfering character have a legal basis as prescribed by § 113 of the Constitution.[34] Yet, they may still be contrary to other constitutional provisions. Given the topic for this article, two provisions in the Norwegian Constitution are of particular interest: § 97 stipulates as mentioned that "no statutory law may be given retroactive effect," while § 105 provides a right to compensation in cases of state interference in terms of expropriation.

There is a close relationship between the retroactivity ban in § 97 and the right to compensation in § 105. First of all, the provisions have an interrelating range of application: a retroactive rule may involve a state interference to the citizens (thereby entitling them to compensation), and vice versa; an interfering rule may have retroactive effect – at least in the 'false' sense of retroactivity. Thus, both of the provisions may be pleaded concurrently before the courts.[35] Moreover, the provisions have the same underlying rationale: both provisions are meant to protect citizens against laws that function to their detriment.[36]

Notwithstanding these similarities, the provisions have different upshots. When a new law is contrary to the retroactivity ban in § 97, the law is not applied in the specific case. The consequence of unconstitutional retroactive laws is, in other words, the non-application of the law to the subject-matter of a case. This is in contrast to the principle found in § 105 of the Constitution which, as an alternative or addition to non-applicability,[37] gives the court discretion to provide for compensation for laws that violate the provision.[38]

It is a general observation that a new law makes changes to established legal positions. Such law is normally given legal effect *subsequent* to the law's adoption, sanction and public announcement. On this basis, most laws are normally cases of 'false' retroactivity. Such retroactivity is, as we have

---

34 One example is provided in chapter 14 of the Criminal Procedure Act which confers a legal basis for the detention of convicted persons.

35 See *Knoph*, Rettslige standarder, 1939, p. 108. According to the legal database *Lovdata*, the retroactivity ban has been subject to the Supreme Court's consideration in 335 cases in the period from 1841 to 2016. In comparison, § 105 of the Constitution was considered in 296 Supreme Court's cases during the same period.

36 See *Odeberg*, Pensjonsdommene, Grunnloven og Høyesterett, (1999) Lov og Rett, p. 78 (88–92). See also the opinion of Tjomsland in Rt-1996-1415.

37 See for example Rt-1931-865.

38 See for example Rt-2004-1985.

seen, accepted by the retroactivity principle. Protection against state interference for such law is therefore better sought on an alternative legal basis to § 97. A possible conceptualisation is, perhaps, to treat a new, infringing law of 'false' retroactive character as potential state interference under § 105 of the Constitution, thereby conferring upon the citizen a specific right to compensation.

G. The Application of the Retroactivity Ban to Administrative Decisions

The retroactivity principle found in § 97 of the Norwegian Constitution governs the retroactivity of legislation – in Norwegian called *'lov'*. Presumably in line with the provision's literal meaning, there is a common assertion that the principle regulates *general* legislative acts as opposed to individual decisions.[39] This includes statutory and administrative regulations, but excludes individually binding decrees such as administrative decisions.[40] Thus, the executive powers are seemingly exempted from the heightened threshold under the retroactivity ban with regard to individual norm-making. But this is only on the face of it.

An issue of retroactivity arises both in a 'true' and 'false' sense in the making of administrative decisions. If a decision takes effect prior to its making, one may assume that it is a case of 'true' retroactivity. Otherwise, the case is better treated as a case of 'false' retroactivity. This gives reason to ask whether administrative decisions can be subject to a similar ban as the one found in § 97 of the Norwegian Constitution.

Curiously, the Norwegian Public Administration Act do not regulate from what time an administrative decision will take effect. But notwithstanding the absence of general regulation on this matter, the rules on the re-making of administrative decisions provide some clarification. In line with the constitutional principle of retroactivity, it is held that administra-

---

39 Rt-2013-1345; SOMB-2001-68; *Smith*, 2015, p. 419; *Høgberg*, Forbud mot tilbakevirkende lover, 2010, p. 153.

40 *Smith*, 2015, p. 419 and *Eckhoff/Smith*, Forvaltningsrett, 2014, p. 304. Following the Norwegian Public Administration Act § 1, an administrative decision is defined as a "decision made under the exercise of public authority that concerns the rights or duties of one or more specific persons" (my translation).

tive reversals may not be given 'true' retroactive effect.[41] 'False' retro-activity, by contrast, is allowed, i.e. an administrative reversal may take effect from the date it was made.[42] This gives a compelling argument for introducing a retroactivity principle to the making of administrative decisions in general. But further arguments may also be advanced in support of this claim.

The principle of *lex superior* implies a hierarchy of norms in which the Constitution is superior all other normative instruments. Since the principle of retroactivity is found in the Constitution, it is given precedence over general statutory law. The courts will review statutory law on these merits. The constitutional principle is therefore primarily directed towards legislative enactments, and is thus a limitation on the legislative powers, i.e. a duty on Parliament.

However, there is, in my view, an underexamined similarity between legislative and executive powers in modern society, and this resemblance calls for the same constraints on the display of powers.[43] Considering the fact that the public administration possesses delegated legislative competences, one could question why the duties on Parliament would not apply to other branches of state authorities. Clearly, it is not an ideal situation if the legislative powers can absolve themselves from responsibility.[44]

This line of reasoning is supported by taking the citizens' perspective into account. For the citizens, the binding force of a legal instrument is likely to be of greater importance than its quality as a general regulation as opposed to an individually drafted decision. General and individual normative instruments have more elements in common than they do not: they are

---

41 See *Woxholth*, Forvaltningsloven med kommentarer, 2011, p. 586, with reference to JDLOV-2008-2952. See further *Eckhoff/Smith*, 2014, p. 308. An important exception to this rule, which also applies to general laws, is when such law is in the citizen's favour, cfr. Public Administration Act § 35.

42 See *Eckhoff/Smith*, 2014, p. 312, where it is held that otherwise it would be simply impossible to take account of the distribution of state funds in the allocation of public privileges.

43 See likewise *Høgberg*, 2010, p. 159.

44 *Høgberg*, 2010, p. 153. There is a tendency in modern legislation to confer the executive powers rights to make exemptions from general law. See, for instance, *lov om aksjeselskaper* av 13.06.1997 nr. 44 § 8-10, *lov om stiftelser* av 15.06. 2001 nr. 59 § 27 and *lov om godkjenning og drift av innretninger til bruk i tivoli og fornøyelsesparker* av 7.06.1991 nr. 24 § 2.

given with the intention of creating legal effects, and their recipients understand them in that way. There is also a striking resemblance with regard to the underlying rationale: the retroactive principle is meant to protect citizens against the misuse of state powers,[45] and this concern is obviously as much apparent for individual decisions as for general laws. What is more, the principle of retroactivity ensures availability and predictability of law, besides safeguarding the citizens legitimate expectations, and these notions are equally evident insofar as administrative decisions are concerned.[46] Altogether, this implies that the same constraints should apply.

For the sake of completeness, there is an argument that may be raised against giving the retroactivity principle an overall range of application. Administrative decisions have certain features in common with court decisions, i.e. that they are binding for one or more specific persons. Still, court decisions are, notably, given retroactive effect in both a 'true' and a 'false' sense.[47] It is therefore not apparent why administrative decisions should be treated as something distinctively different.

This argument may be challenged as there are profound differences between court proceedings and the making of administrative decisions. Most importantly, the courts are expected to apply the law, while the public authorities are given a wide discretion for individual norm-making. Courts will normally view cases *ex post*, while the public administration make decisions that in most cases will have an effect for the future. By comparison, interim legislation are more analogue to administrative decisions than court decisions,[48] and such legislation has been limited by the retroactivity ban in court practice.[49]

Based on the foregoing, a principle of retroactivity, together with its exceptions, should be given a wider range of application so that administrative decisions are also covered. With that said, certain additional restrictions must apply. One evident constraint is that the issue of retroactivity must be viewed closely connected to the merits of the case. Consistent with much

---

45 *Smith*, 2015, p. 418. See also *Høgberg*, 2010, p. 171 for further references.

46 See also *Høgberg*, 2010, p. 155.

47 Ibid., p. 159 and 162 with further references.

48 For one thing, such legislation is also made under executive powers to govern specific cases, see https://snl.no/provisorisk_anordning (visited 8.01.2017).

49 See Rt-1955-439 and Rt-1946-196.

special law,[50] an exception to the prohibition of 'true' retroactive law must apply if the individual is at fault, e.g. if an initial administrative decision is based upon incorrect or misrepresented information provided by him. There is, arguably, no persuasive reason to give the retroactivity principle full force in such cases.

Bibliography

Torkel Halvorsen Aschehoug, *Norges nuværede statsforfatning* (3rd Edition, P.T. Mallings boghandelsforlag, Christiania 1893)

John Austin (revised and edited by Robert Campbell), *Lectures on jurisprudence or the philosophy of positive law* (5th Edition, John Murray, London 1911)

Frede Castberg, *Grunnlovens forbud mot å gi lover tilbakevirkende kraft* (Cappelen, Kristiania 1920)

Torstein Eckhoff and Eivind Smith, *Forvaltningsrett* (10th Edition, Universitetsforlaget, Oslo 2014)

Carl August Fleischer, 'Grunnlovens § 97' (1975) Jussens venner, 183

Lon L. Fuller, *Morality of law* (Yale University Press, New Haven 1965)

Trevor C. Hartley, *The foundations of European Union Law* (8th Edition, Oxford University Press, Oxford 2014)

Benedikte Høgberg, *Forbud mot tilbakevirkende lover* (Universitetsforlaget, Oslo 2010)

Hans Kelsen, *General theory of law and state* (Harvard University Press, Cambridge 1945)

Ragnar Knoph, *Rettslige standarder, særlig Grunnlovens § 97* (Grøndahl, Oslo 1939)

Mikael H. Lie, *Domstolene og Grunnloven* (Norli, Kristiania 1923)

Bredo Morgenstierne, *Lærebok i den norske statsforfatningsret*, Vol. II (O. Christiansen, Oslo 1927)

---

50 See *lov om retten til å delta i fiske og fangst* av 26.03.1999 nr. 15 § 11; *lov om politiet* av 4.08.1995 nr. 53 § 14d; *lov om helsepersonell m.v.* av 2.07.1999 nr. 64 § 57; *lov om skytevåpen og ammunisjon m.v.* av 9.06.1931 nr. 1 § 10; *lov om skifte* av 21.02.1930 § 91e; *lov om mesterbrev i håndverk og annen næring* av 19.06.2015 nr. 65 § 3; *lov om utlendingers adgang til riket og deres opphold her* av 15.05.2008 nr. 35 § 63; *lov om eiendomsmegling* av 29.06.2007 nr. 73 § 8-4; *lov om serveringsvirksomhet* av 13.06.1997 nr. 55 § 19; *lov om anlegg og drift av jernbane; herunder sporvei; tunnelbane og forstadsbane m.m.* av 11.06.1993 nr. 100 § 3g; *lov om revisjon og revisorer* av 15.01.1999 nr. 2 § 9-1; *lov om fritids- og småbåter* av 26.06.1998 nr. 47 § 28b; *lov om yrkestransport med motorvogn og fartøy* av 21.06.2002 nr. 45 § 37f; *lov om veterinærer og annet dyrehelsepersonell* av 15.06.2001 nr. 75 § 35; *lov om apotek* av 2.06.2000 nr. 39 § 2-13; *lov om forebyggende sikkerhetstjeneste* av 20.03.1998 nr. 10 § 24.

Per Odberg, Pensjonsdommene, 'Grunnloven og Høyesterett' (1999) Lov og Rett, 78

Eivind Smith, *Konstitusjonelt demokrati* (3rd Edition, Fagbokforlaget, Bergen 2015)

Westzucker GmbH v. Einfuhr- und Vorratsstelle für Zucker, 4 July 1973, Case C-1/73, ECR 1973-00723

Geir Woxholth, *Forvaltningsloven med kommentarer* (5th Edition, Gyldendal akademisk, Oslo 2011)

On the Nature and Characteristic of Legal Systems as Complex Adaptive Systems

Thossaporn Saensawatt

A. Introduction

One of the cornerstones of human curiosity is to understand how *nature* functions. Along our intellectual journey, it is merely one simple, yet precise question, *how nature works*, that drives our entire – from ancient to modern, from primitive to advanced – human civilization. Nature is beautiful because of its underlying *simplicity*, i.e. because it seems to 'obey' simple laws.[1] On the other hand, it can also be crucial and unpredictable because of its *complexity*. There is a close relation between the simplicities and the complexities of nature. "The central aim of science," stated Cohen and Stewart, "is to render the complexities of the universe transparent, so that we can see through them to the simplicities beneath."[2] This is true not only for the realm of natural science, but also for the realm of social sciences, including our field of study, the *legal science*.

Even though it is undeniable that we all are part of nature (more precise: of the physical reality), we, unlike all other beings, acquired – essentially as a result of natural selection and historical evolution – the exceptional ability to discover and understand the texture of reality. Our love for the truth of nature had resulted in one of the key aspects of human nature: we tend to create things in the same manner and using the same processes, which were used by nature. And by comparing, finding patterns and analogizing the products of both worlds we may be able to find an answer as to how should we work in a new situation never seen before, how can we find

---

* Author is very grateful to Mr. J. Rujirekanusorn for discussion related to the mathematical explication presented in this work, Mr. S. Chowdhury and Ms. A. Roopdee for their supports related to the format of this work, as well as all participants of the conference for their enthusiastic comments and critiques which are highly valuable to this work.

1 *Cohen/Stewart*, The Collapse of Chaos: Discovering Simplicity in a Complex World, 1994, p. 15.

2 Ibid., p. 29.

(not create) a new law scattered throughout our existing, yet imperfect legal systems and social orders.

This essay is accordingly a valiant attempt to explicate the relationship between the artificial and the natural and – simultaneously and to the greatest extent possible – to provide another vital brick of the bridge between both worlds. We will start with the general concept of *complex adaptive system* (B), followed by an analysis of the nature and characteristic of legal systems as complex adaptive system (C).

B. The Science of Complexity and Its Relation to the Complex Adaptive Systems (CAS)

Nature is composed of numerous – infinite, actually – *systems* and *subsystems* working together and forming the physical reality. Even though *not all* of these systems are complex (some of them are merely *complicated*), complex systems seem to dominate the phenomena around us. Among all these complex phenomena, the so-called 'complex adaptive systems', or CAS, are ubiquitous: "Once you learned how to recognize them, in fact, these systems were everywhere."[3] CAS conquer most of our (thus far observable) natural world – from the fundamental microscopic scale such as the inner structure of atoms, cells and neuronal network of brains, immune systems, developing embryos, and ant colonies[4] to the macroscopic world like the formation of galaxies or the entire structure of the universe itself. To summarize, these systems can be succinctly characterized by their inherent abilities (1) to produce complex emergent behaviours out of few simple rules or laws governing the system (the 'complex' element), and (2) to constantly revise and rearrange their inner structure through time (the 'adaptive' element).

Beneath the seemingly chaotic behaviours of these complex systems in the *natural world*, such as the inner structure of atoms, cells and neuronal network of brains, ecologies, ant colonies, and tropical rainforests,[5] lies a set of few 'simple' rules or laws (of nature) governing the whole system:

3 *Waldrop*, Complexity: The Emerging Science at the Edge of Order and Chaos, 1992, p. 145.
4 Ibid., p. 145.
5 *Holland*, Complexity: A Very Short Introduction, 2014, p. 1.

"Complexity at any given level is a consequence of the operation of relatively simple rules one level lower down."[6] An attempt of researchers, scientists, and thinkers from several scientific disciplines to decipher these simple, fundamental rules or laws governing complex systems gave birth to the *sciences of complexity*, which were regarded by some scholars as "the sciences of the twenty-first century."[7] And it is the aim of this work to make an expedition into this area of complexity theory. As illustrated already by the title of this essay, the theory of *complex adaptive systems* and the jurisprudential concept of *legal systems* will serve as the main protagonists for our analysis. Since a detailed and comprehensive explanation about the characteristics and properties of CAS lies outside the scope of this work, we will consider below only some fundamental properties, which are *sine qua non* for all CAS, and some relevant concepts in order to examine and confirm our hypothesis on the nature and characteristic of legal systems as complex adaptive systems.

C. *The Nature and Characteristic of Legal Systems as Complex Adaptive System*

Now we will move from the natural world scenario to our artificial world, the world composed of man-made systems and subsystems. Our main protagonists here will be, on the one hand the common properties of CAS and on the other hand, the artificial-conceptual phenomenon called 'legal system'. It should be noted that, the capacity of human beings to generate artificial complex systems is, according to our opinion, indisputable.[8] In this part we will argue and try to provide evidence that *legal systems* – in the sense of a multilevel-hierarchical organization of national rules of law governed by the state constitution and its general principles – are not only an analogy of the concept of CAS, but also actually *one* of these systems by

6 *Cohen/Stewart*, 1994, p. 219.

7 *Waldrop*, 1992, p. 13.

8 With regard to this idea we agree with *Gell-Mann*, The Quark and the Jaguar: Adventures in the Simple and the Complex, 1994, p. 19–21, that complex adaptive systems "have a general tendency to generate other such systems" and that "new complex adaptive systems [already] arose within human culture: societies, organizations, economics, and the scientific enterprise, to name but a few."

their inherent nature. Our analysis will be interdisciplinary and focus primarily on the relevant scientific theories, especially the complexity theory, and some of the well-accepted theories or ideas in the legal science.

I. Hierarchical Organization as an Inherent Structure of All Developed Legal Systems

The attempts of many researchers to lay the foundation stone of the complexity theory – to search for underlying simplicities, their patterns, and their algorithms governing any given complex phenomenon – have, thus far, provided us with some *characteristic behaviours* that are common to all CAS.[9] These characteristics comprehend also the 'hierarchical organization' of the systems, which is, according to Simon, an inevitable result of their evolution from simple to complex systems.[10]

Here we argue that this *hierarchical structure* is not only one of the properties of the CAS of the natural world, but also verily an intrinsic element of all CAS in our *artificial* world, i.e. our 'complex' cultural and social systems.[11] Even in the realm of natural science, some researchers also enthusiastically support the concept of different, hierarchical levels of organization, which comprises both natural and artificial systems; the concept views, according to Novikoff,

> "the development of matter, from the cosmological changes resulting in the formation of the earth to the social changes in society, as continuous because it is never-ending, and as discontinuous because it passes through a series of different levels of organization–physical, chemical, biological and sociological."[12]

In the realm of legal studies, the idea that any well-designed *legal system* has this hierarchical structure is partially, yet incompletely discussed in some legal theories. In order to successfully complete and provide a reliable and more 'scientific' theory concerning the *true structure* of legal systems and their complex behaviours we need to, at least, find another piece of the mosaic which is until now missing.

---

9 See also *Holland*, 2014, p. 5–6, 24–32.

10 *Simon*, The Sciences of the Artificial, 1992, p. 209: "Among possible complex forms, hierarchies are the ones that have the time to evolve."

11 *Holland*, 2014, p. 1–2.

12 *Novikoff*, The Concept of Integrative Levels and Biology, (1945) 101 Science, p. 209 (209).

The available legal concepts or theories that we lawyers concern ourselves with, e.g. the concept of the hierarchy of laws, are inadequate and insufficient to provide a lucid explanation for the questions such as, *why* all the developed and functional legal systems *always* resulted in this hierarchical structure, which is simultaneously a common fashion of all CAS in the natural world, rather than any other possible structure, and *what* is the link between these two worlds – between the physical-mathematical world of nature and the artificial world of us human beings. The superficial statements like we are part of nature or we are subject to the same physical laws and principles of nature are not enough and, in fact, explain nothing whatsoever. Our observation shows that the answer lies, to a great extent, behind *the accurate and complete description of complex systems*.

Since natural science has already explained that the natural world consists of many levels of hierarchical organization[13] and each level of a hierarchy is governed by its own set of laws or principles,[14] our observation reveals further that, this explanation is certainly true for the structure of our artificial world as well. For instance, let us consider the notion of 'legal system' based on the existing, broadly accepted legal theory, i.e. *the Pure Theory of Law* developed by the great legal theorist and philosopher Kelsen (1881–1973).[15] According to the pure theory of law, a legal norm is valid when – and only when – it has been authorized by another legal norm of a *higher rank*. The reason being, that only norms can 'validate' a source of law, not any other social facts whencesoever.[16] A legal system consisting of several clusters of legal norms in different ranks (of validity or authorization) constitutes therefore and logically a *multilevel-hierarchical organization* of laws.[17] This hierarchy of laws is today one of the basic, yet essential concepts of legal studies in almost every legal system.

---

13 Ibid., p. 209 (209).

14 *Holland*, 2014, p. 4 and 81.

15 See his work in original in *Kelsen*, Reine Rechtslehre, 1983.

16 For an overview of Kelsen's pure theory of law see *Bodenheimer*, Jurisprudence: The Philosophy and Method of the Law (Revised Edition), 1981, p. 100–104; *Dias*, Jurisprudence, 1985, p. 358–374.

17 See also *Kelsen*, Pure Theory of Law, 1967, p. 221–222: "The legal order is not a system of coordinated norms of equal level, but a hierarchy of different levels of legal norms. Its unity is brought about by the connection that results from the fact that the validity of a norm, created according to another norm, rests on that other norm, whose creation in turn, is determined by a third one."

However, it is undeniable that norms and precepts in primitive human societies were initially developed in the domains concerning private relation between members of the society such as the criminal offence and the contractual relation. For instance, it is obvious that private law was highly developed during the reign of the *Roman Empire*, whereas the question as to whether the Romans had a constitution or a developed system of public law – at least in the modern sense – is even now discussible and depends largely on the definition of 'constitution' or 'public law.'[18] According to this empirical view, the origin of law, that is, the notion of *ought*, is highly likely to be the product of a material process evolving upward from individual choices in private relation through precepts and finally to laws;[19] and this more or less *inductive* process does not presuppose any existing, higher norms as a precondition for generating those precepts and laws, let alone the fictional, hypothetical basic norm. In this sense, Kelsen's pure theory of law reversed the chain of causation and contradicted the empirical facts.

Now we know that all developed legal systems have the hierarchical structure with many levels of organization of rules and principles of law working together, but we still have no clue, why each and every system of rules or precepts stipulating the human behaviour will *always and consistently* evolve from simple forms into more complex, 'hierarchical' forms, as if this hierarchical structure reveals the texture of reality. Indeed, not only legal systems, but *all* CAS are organized in a *hierarchical* fashion:[20] It is the structure used by nature to weave her patterns and, simultaneously, the tool used by us human beings to generate complex things. There are no complex things in both worlds – the natural and the human 'artificial' world – that do not have this multilevel-hierarchical structure. In other words, hierarchy, argued Simon, "is one of the central structural schemes that the architect of complexity uses."[21]

---

18 *Wesel*, Geschichte des Rechts: Von den Frühformen bis zur Gegenwart, 2001, Rn. 132; *Jolowicz*, Lectures on Jurisprudence, 1963, p. 320, also noted that the distinction between public and private law is known already to the Greeks and is placed in the forefront both of the *Digest* and *Justinian's Institutes*.

19 *Wilson*, Consilience: The Unity of Knowledge, 1998, p. 274–275.

20 *Holland*, 2014, p. 81.

21 *Simon*, The Architecture of Complexity, (1962) 106 Proceedings of the American Philosophical Society, p. 467 (468).

Notwithstanding the fact that legal systems are hierarchical, we cannot conclude at this stage that they are actually *complex* systems. In the field of complexity theory, the hierarchical organization is closely tied to another characteristic behaviour of CAS, which helps distinguish complex systems from other complicated systems,[22] i.e. the *emergent behaviour*. Unless a legal system exhibits its emergent property, we cannot assuredly regard it as a complex system, for emergence is an essential requirement for calling a system 'complex'.[23] We will consider the concept of emergence again at the end of this chapter, for it requires (at least) another intrinsic property of the system in addition to the hierarchical structure, i.e. the *nonlinearity*.

II. The Concept of Nonlinearity as a Functional Property of Legal Systems

For any system to be able to exhibit an emergent behaviour, such system must contain the characteristic of *nonlinearity* (or *non-additivity*).[24] Nonlinearity is a property where the aggregate behaviour of the whole system (or one level of organization) is not obtained by *summing* the behaviours of the component agents or parts of the system (or the lower level of organization).[25] The difference between linear and nonlinear systems is succinctly summarized by Nicolis as follows:

> "A striking difference between linear and nonlinear laws is whether the property of superposition holds or breaks down. In a linear system the ultimate effect of the combined action of two different causes is merely the superposition of the effects of each cause taken individually. But in a nonlinear system adding two elementary actions to one another can induce dramatic new effects reflecting the onset of cooperativity between the constituent elements. This can give rise to unexpected structures and events whose properties can be quite different from those of the underlying elementary laws, in the form of abrupt transitions, a multiplicity of states, pattern formation, or an irregular markedly unpredictable evolution in space and time referred to as deterministic chaos."[26]

---

22 *Holland*, 2014, p. 4.
23 Ibid., p. 6.
24 *Goldstein*, Emergence as a Construct: History and Issues, (1999) 1 Emergence, p. 49 (55).
25 *Holland*, 2014, p. 25.
26 *Nicolis*, Introduction to Nonlinear Science, 1995, p. 1–2.

The concept of nonlinearity is, similar to the hierarchical organization, closely tied to the concept of *emergence*. All these characteristics – hierarchy, nonlinearity, and emergence – can be roughly described by the famous phrase: "The whole is more than the sum of its parts."[27] Even though many common properties of individual complex systems are *linear* (the whole is *equal* to the sum of the parts), e.g. volume, weight, etc.,[28] most aggregate actions and behaviours of the systems are nevertheless nonlinear. In fact, most of the interesting things in the world function in the nonlinear fashion, including our brains.[29] What about the legal systems? Do they also operate in this *nonlinear* fashion like many other complex systems of the natural world? Our answer is: yes.

Considering the fact that most of the actual legal systems variedly functioning in many states of the world are so diverse and intricate, we are accordingly confronted with the practical problem of indicating and proving the nonlinear behaviours of those real systems, wherefore it is suggested that we perform here a *thought experiment* in order to exhibit the nonlinearity of (hypothetical and simplified) legal systems. The experiment can be called "the tale of three cities": We assume, to begin with, two equivalent systems as our object of study, i.e. city A and city B (= controlled variable). Then we set out some initial conditions that are shrared by both systems for their manufacturing of product *y* (= dependent variable).[30] Then we introduce the independent variables in the form of different 'rules of law' for city A and city B with some additional conditions as follows:

---

27 *Holland*, 2014, p. 4; see also *Lam*, Nonlinear Physics for Beginners, 1998, p. 6–7: "A system is nonlinear if the output from the system is not proportional to the input. ... In fact, almost all known systems in natural or social sciences are nonlinear when the input is large enough. ... Mathematically, the signature of a nonlinear system is the breakdown of the superposition principle which states that the sum of two solutions of the equation(s) describing the system is again a solution. The physical consequence is that in a nonlinear system, the behavior of the whole is more than the sum of its parts."

28 *Holland*, 2014, p. 54.

29 *Waldrop*, 1992, p. 65.

30 The *initial conditions* for both systems are as follows: Each city has 20 workers for manufacturing product *y*. Each worker has an initial capacity to manufacture product *y* at the rate of one product an hour. All workers work eight hours a day. All stipulated laws (= independent variables) in both cities shall be absolutely followed by the workers.

Law of city A	Law of city B
'Killing is prohibited.'	'Stealing is prohibited.'
Additional condition for city A	**Additional condition for city B**
There is a 50 per cent chance for each day for each worker in city A to steal one manufactured product from another worker; each collective act of stealing decreases the capacity of all workers permanently by one product a day starting from the next day of manufacture.[31]	There is a 50 per cent chance for each day for each worker in city B to kill another worker.

Now we can run the experiment, ceteris paribus, from the initial state (t_0) through the first day (t_1) and the second day (t_2) and finally (at this stage) to the third day (t_3) of manufacture and collect our result; we then had the data (aggregate amount of product *y* manufactured in each city) as follows:

	Aggregate product at t_1	Aggregate product at t_2	Aggregate product at t_3
City A	150	280	390
City B	80	120	140

At this stage, we had the data that exhibit an *effectiveness* of the different rules of laws in both cities in relation to the production rate and the aggregate amount of product *y* at any given time (t). Mathematically speaking we can say, in general, that the law of city A is *more* effective than the law of city B because it guarantees a higher rate of production. From the data we can also derive the *mathematical functions* for both cities as follows:

City A: $f(x) = -10x^2 + 160x \mid \text{when } x = 1 \text{ to } 8$
City B: $f(x) = 160 - 160/(2^x)$

However, in order to demonstrate the *nonlinear behaviour* of legal systems we need another stage of experiment. Our main purpose here is to examine whether the property of superposition (or additivity) of the rules of law

31 As a result of which, if an act of stealing occurred for eight days consecutively, the decrease in capacity will reach the point where each worker manufactures 0 product a day.

holds or breaks down in this second stage of experiment. We will then introduce *another* controlled variable into the experiment, i.e. city C. In this city C, we apply *both* the law of city A and the law of city B *simultaneously*, which is equivalent to the superposition of both laws. Then, again, we run the experiment, *ceteris paribus*, and collect the following result:

	Aggregate product at t_1	Aggregate product at t_2	Aggregate product at t_3
City C	160	320	480

In this halcyon city C there is – pursuant to the laws – neither killing nor stealing whatsoever, and all 20 workers can manufacture product y to a greatest extent of their capacity, that is, at the rate of 160 products a day. Consequently, we can derive the following mathematical function for city C:

City C: $f(x) = 160x$

Here comes the conundrum of this thought experiment: we have to prove, now, that the property of superposition of both laws broke down in this experiment, that the function for city C is not obtained by *summing* the function for city A and the function for city B. If the answer is *positive*, then we can conclude that legal systems function in a *nonlinear* fashion rather than in a linear fashion. By adding two rules or principles of law to one another we induce novel properties, behaviours, or effects not attained by the simple summation of the *separated* properties, behaviours, or effects of those laws functioning in distinct, unrelated systems. We can do so by summing the functions of city A and city B, and then divide it by two due to a double of total worker force:

City A + City B: $(-10x^2 + 160x) + (160 - 160/2^x)$
$= -10x^2 + 160\text{x} + 160 - 160/2^x$
(City A + City B)/2: $(-10x^2 + 160\text{x} + 160 - 160/2^x)/2$
$= -5x^2 + 80\text{x} + 80 - 80/2^x$

The result obviously proved that the sum of two functions (divided by two) is *not equal* to the function for city C where both laws are simultaneously and interactively applied as illustrated in Figure 1:

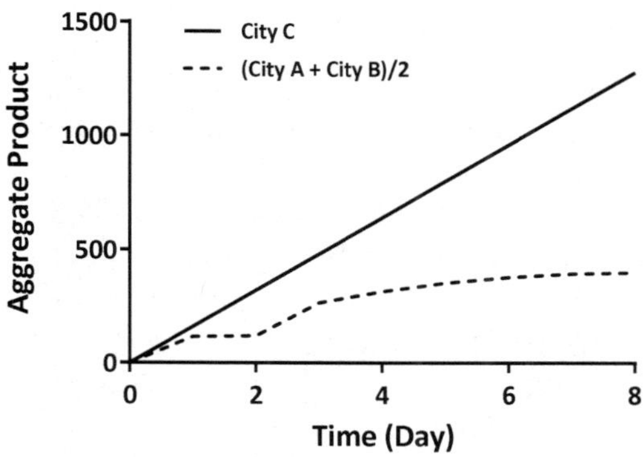

Figure 1: The correlation between the summation of two functions (city A and city B) and the function of city C exhibits the *nonlinear* character of legal rules: the sum of two rules applied separately in different systems is *not equal* to the application of both rules simultaneously and interactively in one single system.

What caused, or what could be the cause of, this nonlinear character of legal rules? Considering our thought experiment, there is one notable *difference* between two scenarios of the experiment, that is, when we applied both rules separately in the first stage and when we applied them simultaneously in the second stage: in the second stage, in city C, both rules – in addition to their own function described above – also *interacted* with each other. This 'interaction' between several rules of law can be our potential candidate for the cause of the nonlinear behaviour of legal systems.[32] In other words, this complex, nonlinear effect "arises when the dependencies among the elements [here: the laws] become important."[33] The concept of nonlinearity of laws also suggests that, if we remove a part or some parts from any functioning legal system or from its subsystem, the consequence will also be nonlinear, that is, it will yield effect not only on the removed part(s), but also on the remaining parts of the system. In this sense, analogously, ten minus one will be *not equal* to nine. And, in the worst-case scenario, it may lead to a collapse of the whole system, providing such removed parts constitute an essential, indispensable part of the system.

32 For instance, by applying the law of city B ("Stealing is prohibited.") to the legal system of city A, the law of city B, in this case, not only prohibits the act of stealing as it did when it was applied separately but also eradicates the conditional possibility that "each collective act of stealing decreases the capacity of all workers permanently by one product a day starting from the next day of manufacture" withal, which will happen only in the scenario where we apply both laws simultaneously and interactively in one single system.

33 *Miller/Page*, Complex Adaptive Systems: An Introduction to Computational Models of Social Life, 2007, p. 9.

III. The Concept of Initial Conditions and Its Relation to the Chaotic Behaviour of Dynamical Legal Systems

In physical science, it is general knowledge that in order to completely specify the evolution of any given system, especially a physical system, two ingredients are required: its *dynamical laws* that can be used to evolve the system from one state to another through time and its *boundary conditions* that fix which state the system is in at some particular moment.[34] In his latest book Wilczek (Nobel Prize in Physics in 2004) said that the description of the world divides into two parts, i.e. *dynamical equations* and *initial conditions*.[35] The concept of initial conditions and its relation to the laws of nature are also concisely, yet precisely explained by Wigner (Nobel Prize in Physics in 1963):

> "The regularities in the phenomena which physical science endeavors to uncover are called the laws of nature. The name is actually very appropriate. Just as legal laws regulate actions and behavior under certain conditions but do not try to regulate all actions and behavior, the laws of physics also determine the behavior of its objects of interest only under certain well defined conditions but leave much freedom otherwise. The elements of the behavior which are not specified by the laws of nature are called initial conditions. These, then, together with the laws of nature, specify the behavior as far as it can be specified at all: if a further specification were possible, this specification would be considered as an added initial condition. As is well known, before the advent of quantum theory it was believed that a complete description of the behavior of an object is possible so that, if classical theory were valid, the initial conditions and the laws of nature together would completely determine the behavior of an object."[36]

In complexity theory, the concept of initial conditions also plays a vital role; the reason being the *chaotic behaviour* of complex systems where small changes in their initial conditions produce large later changes.[37] This so-

---

34 *Carroll*, From Eternity to Here: The Quest for the Ultimate Theory of Time, 2010, p. 345.

35 *Wilczek*, A Beautiful Question: Finding Nature's Deep Design, 2015, p. 115. The boundary conditions that fixed the initial state of a system can also be called *initial conditions*, or, as formulated Richard Feynman (Nobel Prize in Physics in 1965), the "conditions when thing started." See *Feynman/Leighton/Sands*, The Feynman Lectures on Physics, 2010, p. 46–48.

36 *Wigner*, Events, Laws of Nature, and Invariance Principles, (1964) 145 Science, p. 995 (995).

37 *Holland*, 2014, p. 5; see also *Cohen/Stewart*, 1994, p. 189–192.

called *sensitive dependence on initial conditions*, aka the butterfly effect ("If a butterfly flaps its wings in Tokyo, then a month later it may cause a hurricane in Brazil."),[38] is, according to our view, one of the *inherent characteristics* of dynamical legal systems as well. This means that each and every legal system, like other complex systems, not only consists of a set of dynamical laws regulating actions and behaviours of its members but also intrinsically contains – and tries to preserve – the initial conditions which specified the state of that system *when it started.*

With regard to our legal science, what are, then, the initial conditions of a legal system? Our observation reveals that this concept of initial (or boundary) condition is, more or less, totally unrecognized in contemporary legal studies, and we jurists tend to think of a legal system that consists merely of *dynamical laws*, whether legal rules or legal principles.[39] These legal *norms* can be thought of – like the dynamical laws of physics – as a machine that tells us, given what the situation (or the fact) is like right now, what legal consequence it will unfold a moment later, i.e. in terms of *evolution through time*[40] as illustrated in Figure 2:

Figure 2: The character of conventional legal norms (rules, principles, etc.) as *dynamical laws* that tell us what the legal world will evolve into a moment later. (Modified from Carroll, *From Eternity to Here: The Quest for the Ultimate Theory of Time* [2010], 124.)

But initial conditions function in another fashion: they *specify* the initial state of the legal system *from the start.* If we use Figure 2 as our reference,

38 *Cohen/Stewart*, 1994, p. 191; for the sensitive dependence on initial conditions see also *Strogatz*, Nonlinear Dynamics and Chaos, 1994, p. 320–323.

39 For the distinction between legal rules and legal principles see *Dworkin*, The Model of Rules, (1967) 35 The University of Chicago Law Review (hereinafter U. Chi. L. Rev.), p. 14 (14 ff.); *Raz*, Legal Principles and the Limits of Law, (1972) 81 The Yale Law Journal, p. 823 (823 ff.); *Alexy*, Theorie der Grundrechte, 1985, p. 71 ff.

40 See also *Carroll*, 2010, p. 124.

we could say – metaphorically speaking, however – that the *ellipsoidal* shape of the legal world (system) was chosen, from the beginning, by its initial conditions. In order to get a glimpse of the initial conditions of our so familiar legal systems, we need to agree beforehand upon one thing, that there is *no* significant difference – in terms of system analysis – between the laws of nature and the artificial laws of us human beings. The fact that we apply the term 'law' for both sets of phenomena, whether intentionally or unintentionally, means something: they both took the form of *dynamical equation* that takes, at every moment, the current state and evolves it into the next state.[41] The *sine qua non* character of initial conditions, which helps distinguish them from the dynamical laws, is rather their nature like 'an empirical fact'.[42] These conditions are, from the beginning, 'just imposed once and for all'[43] on the system. With regard to the legal systems, the initial conditions of a legal system are those 'fundamental decisions' (*Grundentscheidungen*) of the constituent power (*verfassunggebende Gewalt*; *pouvoir constituant*), which specified the framework of the constitution and, simultaneously, the initial state of the new established legal system. These fundamental decisions, e.g. the decision as to whether the state will be a democratic or a non-democratic one, the decision about the form of the state (single or federal state) and the head of the state (kingdom or republic), and other decisions of the same nature, fixed the initial state and gave the starting point to the legal system rather than prescribing the dynamical evolution of the legal system through time:

Considering some fundamental decisions of the current German constitution, i.e. the Basic Law for the Federal Republic of Germany (*Das*

41 *Carroll*, 2010, p. 345; *Bodenheimer*, 1981, p. 188 has already pointed out this uniformity in the functional pattern, which is particularly noteworthy for our analysis: "For semantic as well as functional reasons, it seems desirable to insist that the element of generality is an important ingredient of the concept of law. First, this approach produces a linguistic uniformity in the use of the term law. In the physical sciences, the word law is reserved for the description of uniform causal patterns or at least statistical regularities in the operations of nature, and it is not applied to unusual events inexplicable in terms of repetitive experience. ... Although this goal of semantic uniformity can seldom be reached in full measure, there appears to exist no convincing reason why the term law should be employed in the social sciences in a sense which differs very materially from its meaning in the natural sciences."

42 *Carroll*, 2010, p. 345.

43 Ibid., p. 345.

Grundgesetz für die Bundesrepublik Deutschland), for instance, Art. 1 I GG which states that human dignity is sacrosanct,[44] or Art. 20 I GG which states that the Federal Republic of Germany is a democratic and social federal state, it is obvious that these provisions of the Basic Law exhibit more an empirical fact about the initial, fixed state of the German legal system and its accordingly established society than a dynamical law or rule. From the theoretical point of view, these normative decisions, unlike other dynamical legal rules, are not subject to any change or revision through time: The father of the Basic Law, and also the Basic Law itself, will, that these fundamental decisions are permanently preserved and that the final state of the legal system will have – as much as possible – the same fundamental characteristics and basic structure as its initial state. In case of the Basic Law, this intention was clearly illustrated by the fact that its founders had introduced Art. 79 III GG, the so-called *Ewigkeitsgarantie* (the eternal guarantee), into the system, which provided them the immunity from possible amendment by the parliament.

It should be noted that, despite their existential *form* as fundamental *decisions* of the constituent power these initial conditions of the legal system are not completely arbitrary. Even the holders of the constituent power are bound to something; it can be morality, the postulate of justice, the idea of natural law, the historical background of the nation, or even human nature itself: "The initial conditions must be the outcome of the dynamic evolution itself."[45] The existence of this material limitation or boundary (*materielle*

44 Most of the translations of the Basic Law have chosen the word 'inviolable' for translating the German word *'unantastbar'* in Art. 1 I GG, which is, according to my opinion, semantically inaccurate. This adjectival word *unantastbar* means literary more than the inviolability; it means rather – in the true sense of the word – the 'untouchability'. Taken into account also the fact that the father of the Basic Law used the term only once for the protection of human dignity in Art. 1 I GG, those translations that did not distinguish the word *unantastbar* form the word *unverletzlich* by grouping them under the same translated word 'inviolable' are incorrect. Here the adjective 'sacrosanct' was chosen based on the special characteristic of the concept of human dignity, its highest position within the constitutional order, and its historical background, to be a proper translation of the word *unantastbar*.

45 *Prigogine/Stengers*, Order Out of Chaos: Man's New Dialogue With Nature, 1984, p. 61.

Grenzen) that bound even the *constituent power* was acknowledged and represented by many scholars in the field of constitutional law.[46]

In each and every complex system, including the legal system, even the *smallest change* in those initial conditions will produce a large uncertainty and unpredictability of the system, and will lead, in the end, to a completely different system, i.e. the *far from initial state* system, due to the amplification of this small difference in initial conditions.[47] In other words, it is a difference in these initial conditions that leads to totally different kinds of dynamics (of a system): steady, periodic or chaotic.[48] Our proposed *hypothesis* here is: if initial conditions of the constitution are changed or modified, that legal system will – in the long run in the case of small modification or soon in the case of a drastic change – inevitably develop into a different system (in comparison with its initial state); the system may also develop into a chaotic state, in which the behaviours of the system are aperiodic and

---

46 *Bachof*, Verfassungswidrige Verfassungsnormen?, 1951, p. 30–31; *Maunz*, Die verfassunggebende Gewalt im Grundgesetz, Die Öffentliche Verwaltung 1953, p. 645 (646); *Götz*, Die Zuständigkeit für normative Entscheidungen über schicksalsbestimmende Fragen in der Bundesrepublik, Neue Juristische Wochenschrift 1958, p. 1021 (1021); *Böckenförde*, Die verfassunggebende Gewalt des Volkes – Ein Grenzbegriff des Verfassungsrechts, 1986, p. 30; *Heller*, Staatslehre, 1983, p. 315; see also BVerfGE 23.10.1951 – 2 BvG 1/51 – (21. Leitsatz): "Sie ist nur gebunden an die jedem geschriebenen Recht vorausliegenden überpositiven Rechtsgrundsätze und – als verfassunggebende Versammlung eines werdenden Gliedes des Bundesstaates – an die Schranken, die die Bundesverfassung für den Inhalt der Landesverfassungen enthält."

47 *Prigogine/Stengers*, 1984, p. 270–272; *Poincaré*, Science and Method, 1914, p. 67–68.

48 *Cohen/Stewart*, 1994, p. 192. This chaotic behaviour was first discovered by *Edward Lorenz* (1917–2008) and published in his 1963 groundbreaking paper (*Lorenz*, Deterministic Nonperiodic Flow, [1963] 20 Journal of the Atmospheric Sciences, p. 130 [130 ff.]). The main message of his discovery is quite simple, yet very profound: A very-long-range weather prediction seems to be impossible; reason being, practically speaking, the inevitable inaccuracy and incompleteness of weather observations and, theoretically speaking, the instability of the system (here: weather) with respect to small modifications, "so that slightly differing initial states can evolve into considerably different states." The same is also true for any long-range anticipation of future state or behaviour of the legal systems, especially those systems that are subjected to the possibility of modifications in their initial conditions.

unpredictable.[49] Unlike the constitutions of many other states, the Basic Law for the Federal Republic of Germany initially contains the provision, i.e. Art. 79 III GG, which prohibits any modification (even though a legal one by means of a constitutional amendment) in the initial state of the Basic Law and of the German legal system, that is to say, the state, framework, and boundaries of the legal system determined by the so-called *'verfassungsrechtlichen Grundentscheidungen'* of the Basic Law.[50]

In conclusion, our analysis of the concept of initial conditions, including an analogy between the workings of nature governed by physical laws and those of our artificial world, strongly suggested that there is much to be gained from this novel idea to divide the description of legal systems into two parts, *laws* and *initial conditions* (or boundary conditions). Even though both of them are necessary for each and every legal system, they are very different things and we are not allowed to treat them equitably. Rather, we have to treat them differently and, logically and naturally, develop their own sets of theories – even though correlatively – separately from each other. Our hypothesis of the sensitive dependence on initial conditions of legal systems suggested further a *conjecture* that a legal system associated with unstable initial state tends to develop into a chaotic state *faster* than a system with more stable initial conditions, provided that both systems are exactly comparable. In the light of our analysis, it is this instability with respect to modifications of the initial state that determines the dynamic of the legal system and the degree of our capacity to forecast the system's future,[51] and, more importantly, exhibits one of the inherent characteristics of legal systems as the (artificial) complex adaptive system.

---

49 See also the definition of chaos in *Strogatz*, 1994, p. 323: "Chaos is aperiodic long-term behavior in a deterministic system that exhibits sensitive dependence on initial conditions."

50 Article 79 paragraph (3) of the Basic Law (translated by author): "An amendment to this Basic Law, by which the structuring of the Federation into states [Länder], the fundamental participation of the states in the legislation, or the principles laid down in Articles 1 and 20 are affected, is inadmissible."

51 For the basis of our analogy see also *Lighthill*, The Recently Recognized Failure of Predictability in Newtonian Dynamics, (1986) 407 Proceedings of the Royal Society of London. Series A, Mathematical and Physical Sciences No 1832, p. 35 (35–50).

IV. The Emergent Behaviour of Legal Systems

As mentioned earlier, *emergence* is the *sine qua non* property of all complex systems. But what is actually the emergence or an emergent phenomenon? The first step, a common starting point, for our understanding of the emergence concept can be, again, the famous phrase *"the whole is more than the sum of its parts."* The second step is where the conflict started, however. Now theorists in complexity and evolutionary theory, where the concept of emergence plays a dominant role, have to consider whether their explanation or interpretation of emergence should focus on *the whole* or on (interactions between) *the parts*.[52] In other words, whether to choose between the *holistic, multileveled selectionist* approach[53] which focuses mainly on the irreducible behaviour of the whole or the *reductionist* approach which finds its interest more in the simple laws governing the constituent parts and their interactions.

Indeed, both approaches are essential for a full understanding of the emergent phenomena.[54] But since our analysis is mainly concerned with the character of legal systems as a complex adaptive 'agent-based' system, we will concentrate primarily on the interactions of their parts, i.e. the *rules of law* functioning in legal systems. As suggested by Holland, the interpretation of emergence should concentrate on "interactions where the aggregate exhibits properties *not* attained by summation,"[55] i.e. the non-additive interactions of the system's building blocks.[56] But the concept of emergence – as *terminus technicus* of our study – comprises more than this non-additive interactions between the parts (nonlinearity); it also refers to, said Goldstein, "the arising of novel and coherent structures, patterns, and properties during the process of self-organization in complex systems."[57] All emergent

---

52 As a matter of fact, we have indeed four ingredients to be considered rather than two, i.e. the whole, the parts, the interactions between the parts, and the interaction between the parts and the whole.

53 For a synthesis between two approaches see *Corning*, The re-emergence of emergence, and the causal role of synergy in emergent evolution, (2012) 185 Synthese, p. 295 (295–317); *Corning*, Holistic Darwinism: Synergy, Cybernetics, and Bioeconomics of Evolution, 2005, p. 132–139.

54 Ibid., p. 138–139.

55 *Holland*, 2014, p. 4.

56 Ibid., p. 49.

57 *Goldstein*, (1999) 1 Emergence, p. 49 (49).

phenomena require not only the interrelationship between the parts but also the *communication* between those parts and the whole. (The word 'communication' being used here illustrates the exchanging of information, i.e. the two-way process, between the parts and the whole.) So the meaning of the term emergence can be considerably reduced to the phenomena where "constituent parts with different properties are modified, re-shaped or transformed by their participation in the whole."[58] In fact, it is this 'communication between things' that generates all complex phenomena in our physical reality. To summarize, *emergence* refers to those phenomena, where – as simply, yet precisely concluded by Anderson (Nobel Prize in Physics in 1977) – "the whole becomes not only more than but very different from the sum of its parts."[59]

According to our observation, *legal systems*, especially a developed one, can also generate emergent phenomena like many other complex systems. One of the emergent behaviours of legal systems is the development of the so-called *legal principles*. However, even though the idea that legal systems consist of not only legal rules but also another type of standard called 'principles' was firmly anchored by many theorists in legal science, including its famous pioneer Dworkin, the origin and true characteristic of this phenomena are somehow nebulous and still remain to be seen; reason being, that most of the theorists concentrated merely on the *difference* between rules and principles, not on their origin or inherent nature, let alone their correlation.[60] In contrast, we will argue in this work that legal principles are in fact *emergent phenomena* generated from the interactions within the well-developed legal systems, where certain sets of legal rules work together, forming clusters of more general-abstract and more complex *principles* which will serve as a building block for hierarchically higher level of organization of the legal system.

In order to thoroughly examine the emergent character of legal principles, however, we need in fact an *empirical study* with scientific data analysis, which lies beyond the scope of this work. What we can do here is to discuss briefly *how* our legal cultures gave birth to the set of standards called legal principles. Let us consider the *Rechtsstaatsprinzip* as our object

58 *Corning*, 2005, p. 132–133.

59 *Anderson*, More Is Different: Broken Symmetry and the Nature of the Hierarchical Structure of Science, (1972) 177 Science, p. 395 (395).

60 See for example *Dworkin*, (1967) 35 U. Chi. L. Rev., p. 14 (25–26).

of analysis: our study of the history of law revealed that, the concept of *Rechtsstaat* – as it is understood in the contemporary sense – did not suddenly emerge from the myriads of disconnected, unorganized legal rules, but rather arose from the gradual *transition* from a set of several *coherently connected individual elements*[61] to the notion of *Rechtsstaatsprinzip* as a *unified emergent whole* with its own independent meaning and function beside and beyond those individual elements.[62] As a result of which, the development of the *Rechtsstaatsprinzip* as a legal principle is *ipso facto* an emergent behaviour of the (German) legal system.[63]

The development of legal principles is merely one example of the emergent phenomena which occurrs during the evolution of our legal systems. In actuality, emergence is not only an essential property of the functional legal systems but also their ultimate goal or final purpose withal. For instance, the two basic concepts of the institute of law, *order* and *justice*,[64] are verily the emergent phenomena. And among all operating legal systems, only the systems that fulfil the requirements for complexity (self-organization, hierarchical structure, non-linearity, emergence, etc.) are the ones that can establish or realize order and justice for the societies.

D. *Recapitulation*

There has been an attempt in the preceding chapter to illustrate that well-developed and functional legal systems are *ipso facto* one of the complex

---

61 For instance, the separation of power (*Gewaltenteilung*), the supremacy of the constitution (*Vorrang der Verfassung*), the legality of the administration (*Gesetzmäßigkeit der Verwaltung*), to name but a few.

62 See also *Stern*, Das Staatsrecht der Bundesrepublik Deutschland, 1984, p. 778.

63 It can be argued further, that emergence is the reason why we can decently derive some *unwritten contents* from legal principles (especially from the constitutional principles) apart from their positive contents explicitly laid down in the constitution, for instance, the derivation of the principle of proportionality (*Grundsatz der Verhältnismäßigkeit*) and the prohibition on retroactivity of laws (*Rückwirkungsverbot*) from the *Rechtsstaatsprinzip*; therefore it is neither a coincidence nor a surprising fact, that the *Rechtsstaatsprinzip* – similar to other constitutional principles like the principle of democracy (*Demokratieprinzip*), the federalism (*Bundesstaatlichkeit*), and the human dignity (*Menschenwürde*) – is regarded by some authors as the "basis for the unwritten constitutional rules of law" (see *Wolff*, Ungeschriebenes Verfassungsrecht unter dem Grundgesetz, 2000, p. 211).

64 *Bodenheimer*, 1981, p. 171, 246 ff.

adaptive systems by their inherent nature and fundamental properties. In other words, we have tried to prove their 'complex' element. However, due to the limited scope of this work we cannot go into detail about their 'adaptive' element, which is of equal importance for our complete understanding of the true architecture of legal phenomena. For any system to be capable of evolving and surviving in the ever-changing conditions and environments of the physical reality, the 'adaptation' is an essential desideratum. In the light of our analysis and observation, adaptive behaviour is one of the intrinsic characteristics of the legal system alongside its complex nature. Since the concepts such as adaptation, nonlinearity, and emergence are hitherto not *de rigueur* in the realm of legal science, we would like to recapitulate here our ideas, the fruits of our expedition into the area of complexity theory:

(1) The intrinsic *character* of legal systems as complex adaptive system (CAS) is exhibited by the essential properties that are shared by all CAS: the sensitive dependence on initial conditions (aka the chaotic behaviour), nonlinearity, a multileveled-hierarchical organization, emergent phenomena, and adaptation. Since legal systems actually are complex adaptive systems, any theoretical tool and formal framework developed in the field of complexity theory[65] is potentially capable of studying the true nature of legal systems, including their multi-dimensional functions and complex behaviours.

(2) Inasmuch as the physical science is composed of two fundamental grand theories (the theory of relativity for explaining the macroscopic and quantum mechanics for explaining the microscopic behaviours of the physical reality), as the economics can be conveniently divided into microeconomics and macroeconomics, we suggest that legal science needs also a new set of theories, a new branch of knowledge indeed, that focuses particularly and principally on the *macroscopic* behaviours, the *interaction* between the components (e.g. rule–rule, rule–principle, and principle–principle), the *nonlinear* and *emergent* phenomena, and the *adaptation* of the legal systems. In order to achieve such theories, we need a set of more scientific and reliable tools beyond

65 These theoretical and formal frameworks can be found in the central schools of research making up the backbone of complexity theory, i.e. the complex adaptive systems theory, the nonlinear dynamical systems theory, the synergetic school, and the far-from-equilibrium thermodynamics. For more detail see *Goldstein*, (1999) 1 Emergence, p. 49 (56–57).

those hermeneutic, metaphysical and philosophical tools we already acquired, e.g. statistical data analysis, analytic mathematical modeling, genetic algorithms, and interdisciplinary research, to name but a few.

Bibliography

Robert Alexy, *Theorie der Grundrechte* (Nomos, Baden-Baden 1985)

Philip W. Anderson, 'More Is Different: Broken Symmetry and the Nature of the Hierarchical Structure of Science' (1972) 177 Science, 395

Otto Bachof, *Verfassungswidrige Verfassungsnormen?* (J. C. B. Mohr, Tübingen 1951)

BVerfGE 23.10.1951 – 2 BvG 1/51

Ernst-Wolfgang Böckenförde, *Die verfassunggebende Gewalt des Volkes – Ein Grenzbegriff des Verfassungsrechts* (Alfred Metzner Verlag, Frankfurt am Main 1986)

Edgar Bodenheimer, *Jurisprudence: The Philosophy and Method of the Law* (2nd Edition, Harvard University Press, 1981)

Sean M. Carroll, *From Eternity to Here: The Quest for the Ultimate Theory of Time* (Dutton, 2010)

Jack Cohen and Ian Stewart, *The Collapse of Chaos: Discovering Simplicity in a Complex World* (Viking Penguin, 1994)

Peter A. Corning, *Holistic Darwinism: Synergy, Cybernetics, and Bioeconomics of Evolution* (University of Chicago Press, 2005)

Peter A. Corning, 'The re-emergence of emergence, and the causal role of synergy in emergent evolution' (2012) 185 Synthese, 295

Reginald Walter Michael Dias, Jurisprudence (5th Edition, Butterworths, London 1985)

Ronald Dworkin, 'The Model of Rules' (1967) 35 The University of Chicago Law Review, 14

Richard P. Feynman, Robert B. Leighton and Matthew Sands, *The Feynman Lectures on Physics,* Vol. I (New Millennium Edition, Basic Books, 2010)

Murray Gell-Mann, *The Quark and the Jaguar: Adventures in the Simple and the Complex* (W. H. Freeman & Co, 1994)

Jeffrey Goldstein, 'Emergence as a Construct: History and Issues' (1999) 1 Emergence, 49

Heinrich Götz, Die Zuständigkeit für normative Entscheidungen über schicksalsbestimmende Fragen in der Bundesrepublik, Neue Juristische Wochenschrift 1958, 1021

Hermann Heller, *Staatslehre* (6th Edition, J. C. B. Mohr, Tübingen 1983)

John H. Holland, *Complexity: A Very Short Introduction* (Oxford University Press, Oxford 2014)

Herbert F. Jolowicz, *Lectures on Jurisprudence* (edited by J. A. Jolowicz, 1963)

Hans Kelsen, *Pure Theory of Law* (translated by Max Knight, University of California Press, Berkeley 1967)

Hans Kelsen, *Reine Rechtslehre* (reprint of 2nd Edition, 1983)

Lui Lam, *Nonlinear Physics for Beginners* (World Scientific Publishing, Singapore 1998)

James Lighthill, 'The Recently Recognized Failure of Predictability in Newtonian Dynamics' (1986) 407 Proceedings of the Royal Society of London, Series A, Mathematical and Physical Sciences No 1832, 35

Edward N. Lorenz, 'Deterministic Nonperiodic Flow' (1963) 20 Journal of the Atmospheric Sciences, 130

Theodor Maunz, Die verfassunggebende Gewalt im Grundgesetz, Die Öffentliche Verwaltung 1953, 645

John H. Miller and Scott E. Page, *Complex Adaptive Systems: An Introduction to Computational Models of Social Life* (Princeton University Press, New Jersey 2007)

Grégoire Nicolis, *Introduction to Nonlinear Science* (Cambridge University Press, Cambridge 1995)

Alex B. Novikoff, 'The Concept of Integrative Levels and Biology' (1945) 101 Science, 209

Henri Poincaré, *Science and Method* (translated by Francis Maitland, Thomas Nelson and Sons, London 1914)

Ilya Prigogine and Isabelle Stengers, *Order Out of Chaos: Man's New Dialogue With Nature* (1984)

Joseph Raz, 'Legal Principles and the Limits of Law' (1972) 81 The Yale Law Journal, 823

Herbert A. Simon, 'The Architecture of Complexity' (1962) 106 Proceedings of the American Philosophical Society, 467

Herbert A. Simon, *The Sciences of the Artificial* (2nd Edition, The MIT Press, Massachusetts 1992)

Klaus Stern, *Das Staatsrecht der Bundesrepublik Deutschland*, Vol. I (2nd Edition, C. H. Beck, München 1984)

Steven H. Strogatz, *Nonlinear Dynamics and Chaos: With Applications to Physics, Biology, Chemistry, and Engineering* (Westview Press, 1994)

M. Mitchell Waldrop, *Complexity: The Emerging Science at the Edge of Order and Chaos* (Simon & Schuster, New York 1992)

Uwe Wesel, *Geschichte des Rechts: Von den Frühformen bis zur Gegenwart* (2nd Edition, 2001)

Eugene P. Wigner, 'Events, Laws of Nature, and Invariance Principles' (1964) 145 Science, 995

Frank Wilczek, *A Beautiful Question: Finding Nature's Deep Design* (Allen Lane, UK 2015)

Edward O. Wilson, Consilience: *The Unity of Knowledge* (Vintage Books, New York 1998)

Thossaporn Saensawatt

Heinrich Amadeus Wolff, *Ungeschriebenes Verfassungsrecht unter dem Grundgesetz* (J. C. B. Mohr, Tübingen 2000)

Contributors

Dr. Mehri Barzegar, PhD (Allame Tabatabai University), Guest Researcher at the Max Planck Institute for Foreign and International Criminal Law

Dr. Lukas Beck, Assessor, Jurist (Univ.), Diplom-Jurist Univ., Europajurist (University of Würzburg), Judge at the Regional Court of Hanau and Lecturer at the Law Faculty of the University of Würzburg

Katharina Fenkner, LL.M. (University of London), MBA (University of Bayreuth), Research and Teaching Assistant as well as PhD Candidate at the Law Faculty of the University of Augsburg

Eliza Kompatsiari, LL.M. in Criminal Law (Aristotle University of Thessaloniki), LL.M. in Public and Administrative Law (Democritus University of Thrace), PhD Candidate in Criminal Law and Graduate Teaching Assistant at the Law Faculty of the Aristotle University of Thessaloniki

Tina Korošec, LL.M. (University of Groningen), Assistant Lawyer at the Registry of the European Court of Human Rights

Markus Kotowski, LL.M. (La Trobe University Melbourne), PhD Candidate at the Law Faculty of the University of Augsburg, Lawyer at DLA Piper UK LLP

Mgr Joanna Kruszyńska-Kola, PhD Candidate at the Law and Administration Faculty of the Adam Mickiewicz University in Poznań

Mgr Agata Krygier, PhD Candidate at the Law Faculty of the University of Augsburg

Dr. Stefan Lorenzmeier, PhD (University of Augsburg), LL.M. in EC Law (Leiden), Academic Councillor (*akademischer Rat*) at the Law Faculty of the University of Augsburg

Lorna MacFarlane, LL.B., LL.M. by Research (The University of Edinburgh), Tutor and PhD Candidate at the University of Edinburgh Law School

Dr. Juliane K. Mendelsohn, PhD (Free University of Berlin), Academic Director of the Master of Business and Regulatory Law at the Free University of Berlin

Dr. Dorota Miler, PhD (University of Passau), LL.M. (McGill University), Research and Teaching Assistant at the Law Faculty of the University of Augsburg

Dr. Son Tan Nguyen, PhD (Monash University), LLM (Melbourne University), Lecturer at the School of Business and Management of RMIT International University Vietnam (Vietnam)

Dr. Kleoniki Pouikli, PhD (Aristotle University of Thessaloniki), Course Director in Environmental Law - ERA Academy of European Law, Trier (Germany), Post Doctoral Researcher in Environmental Law at the National and Kapodistrian University of Athens (Greece)

Dr. Oleh Prostybozhenko, PhD (Kyiv University of Law of the National Academy of Sciences of Ukraine), Lecturer at the Kyiv University of Law of the National Academy of Sciences of Ukraine, Research Fellow at the Academician F. H. Burchak Scientific Research Institute of Private Law and Entrepreneurship of National Academy of Legal Sciences of Ukraine

Mgr. Ivan Puškár, PhD Candidate and External Lecturer at the Law Faculty of the Masaryk University in Brno

Thossaporn Saensawatt, LL.M. (University of Passau), LL.B. (Thammasat University), PhD Candidate at the Law Faculty of the University of Passau

Olli Salmi, LL.M. (Trained on the Bench), M. Sc. (Econ.), PhD Candidate at the Law Faculty of the University of Turku

Udayan Sanyal, B.A. LLB. (Hons.) (Hidayatullah National Law University, Naya Raipur, India), working as Legal Assistant at the Secretariat, Government of Chhattisgarh, India

Henriette Nilsson Tøssebro, Master i rettsvitenskap (University of Oslo), LL.M. (University of Southampton), PhD Candidate in administrative law at the Faculty of Law of the University of Oslo

Mgr Jadwiga Urban-Kozłowska, Master of French law (University of Orléans), PhD Candidate at the Law and Administration Faculty of the Jagiellonian University in Kraków, Attorney-at-law at the Kozlowski Law Firm

Maruša T. Veber, Assistant and PhD Candidate at the Law Faculty of the University of Ljubljana

Marina Žagar, mag. iur., PhD candidate at the Law Faculty of the University of Ljubljana, Legal Practitioner at the The Kosovo Specialist Chambers and Specialist Prosecutor's Office

Index